Andean Archaeology

BLACKWELL STUDIES IN GLOBAL ARCHAEOLOGY

Series Editors: Lynn Meskell and Rosemary A. Joyce

Blackwell Studies in Global Archaeology is a series of contemporary texts, each carefully designed to meet the needs of archaeology instructors and students seeking volumes that treat key regional and thematic areas of archaeological study. Each volume in the series, compiled by its own editor, includes 12–15 newly commissioned articles by top scholars within the volume's thematic, regional, or temporal area of focus.

What sets the *Blackwell Studies in Global Archaeology* apart from other available texts is that their approach is accessible, yet does not sacrifice theoretical sophistication. The series editors are committed to the idea that useable teaching texts need not lack ambition. To the contrary, the *Blackwell Studies in Global Archaeology* aim to immerse readers in fundamental archaeological ideas and concepts, but also to illuminate more advanced concepts, thereby exposing readers to some of the most exciting contemporary developments in the field. Inasmuch, these volumes are designed not only as classic texts, but as guides to the vital and exciting nature of archaeology as a discipline.

Andean Archaeology

Edited by

Helaine Silverman

Blackwell
Publishing

© 2004 by Blackwell Publishing Ltd

BLACKWELL PUBLISHING
350 Main Street, Malden, MA 02148-5020, USA
9600 Garsington Road, Oxford OX4 2DQ, UK
550 Swanston Street, Carlton, Victoria 3053, Australia

The right of Helaine Silverman to be identified as the Author of the Editorial Material in this Work has been asserted in accordance with the UK Copyright, Designs, and Patents Act 1988.

First published 2004 by Blackwell Publishing Ltd

3   2007

Library of Congress Cataloging-in-Publication Data

Andean archaeology / edited by Helaine Silverman.
    p. cm. – (Blackwell studies in global archaeology)
Includes bibliographical references and index.
    ISBN 0-631-23400-4 (alk. paper) – ISBN 0-631-23401-2 (pbk.: alk. paper)
    1. Indians of South America – Andes Region –Antiquities. 2. Indians of South America–Andes Region–History. 3. Indians of South America–Andes Region–Politics and government. 4. Andes Region–Antiquities. 5. Andes Region–History. I. Silverman, Helaine. II. Series.

    F2229.A555   2004
    980`.012–dc22

                                                                      2003017579

ISBN-13: 978-0-631-23400-5 (alk. paper) – ISBN-13: 978-0-631-23401-2 (pbk.: alk. paper)

A catalogue record for this title is available from the British Library.

Set in 10 on 12.5 pt Plantin
by SNP Best-set Typesetter Ltd, Hong Kong
Printed and bound in India
by Replika Press Pvt. Ltd

The publisher's policy is to use permanent paper from mills that operate a sustainable forestry policy, and which has been manufactured from pulp processed using acid-free and elementary chlorine-free practices. Furthermore, the publisher ensures that the text paper and cover board used have met acceptable environmental accreditation standards.

For further information on
Blackwell Publishing, visit our website:
www.blackwellpublishing.com

Contents

Series Editors' Preface

This series was conceived as a collection of books designed to cover central areas of undergraduate archaeological teaching. Each volume in the series, edited by experts in the area, includes newly commissioned articles written by archaeologists actively engaged in research. By commissioning new articles, the series combines one of the best features of readers, the presentation of multiple approaches to archaeology, with the virtues of a text conceived from the beginning as intended for a specific audience. While the model reader for the series is conceived of as an upper-division undergraduate, the inclusion in the volumes of researchers actively engaged in work today will also make these volumes valuable for more advanced researches who want a rapid introduction to contemporary issues in specific sub-fields of global archaeology.

Each volume in the series will include an extensive introduction by the volume editor that will set the scene in terms of thematic or geographic focus. Individual volumes, and the series as a whole, exemplify a wide range of approaches in contemporary archaeology. The volumes uniformly engage with issues of contemporary interest, interweaving social, political, and ethical themes. We contend that it is no longer tenable to teach the archaeology of vast swaths of the globe without acknowledging the political implications of working in foreign countries and the responsibilities archaeologists incur by writing and presenting other people's pasts. The volumes in this series will not sacrifice theoretical sophistication for accessibility. We are committed to the idea that usable teaching texts need not lack ambition.

Blackwell Studies in Global Archaeology aims to immerse readers in fundamental archaeological ideas and concepts, but also to illuminate more advanced concepts, exposing readers to some of the most exciting contemporary developments in the field.

Lynn Meskell and Rosemary A. Joyce

Editor's Preface

The opportunity to create a new survey of Andean archaeology was irresistible when I was contacted by Rosemary Joyce and Lynn Meskell, the editors of Blackwell's new Global Archaeology series. For many years Richard Keatinge's edited volume, *Peruvian Prehistory* (Cambridge University Press, 1988) has been the only comprehensive edited volume available for teaching and it was necessarily out of date almost as soon as it was published because of the fast pace of archaeological research in the late 20th century. Michael Moseley rendered great service to the field with his excellent textbook, *The Incas and their Ancestors* (Thames & Hudson, 1992), in which he masterfully presented the evolution of ancient societies in the Central Andes. The revised edition (2001) of his book is current with the literature through 1998. *Andean Archaeology* updates some of the issues considered by Moseley while adding others.

Moreover, Andean archaeology has become significantly more theoretically engaged than when Keatinge compiled his reader, and, by the nature of his purpose, Moseley could not overly problematize his volume. Therefore, I have conceived of *Andean Archaeology* as a companion volume for Moseley's textbook that places Central Andean prehistory within a larger theoretical framework, while updating aspects of the contributions in Keatinge's edited volume.

Andean Archaeology showcases the field at the start of its second century (using Max Uhle as our baseline). As such this edited volume should stimulate debate and further research while being accessible to archaeologists working elsewhere.

In commissioning the chapter contributions I have been guided by my own sense of the important empirical and theoretical issues in contemporary Andean archaeology as well as by the didactic necessity of presenting case studies for the major time periods and geographical regions of the Central Andes so that the primary function of this book as a companion textbook is served. Nevertheless, because Moseley's textbook is so useful and because professors create their own readers of photocopied material, I am liberated from the need to offer full coverage because this book is intended to be one of several volumes that will be used in a course on Andean archaeology.

Moreover, this volume sits at a discursive crossroads. The concepts of "culture area" and "increasing complexity through time" have long influenced how archaeologists (Andeanists and others) frame their research and interpret their data. But the artificial archaeological borders drawn between Peru/Central Andes, Bolivia/South Andes, and Ecuador/North Andes are not meaningful at all times, and various North Andean societies appear to have been as complex as and more complex than various of the non-state social formations of the Central Andes.

Furthermore, our relative chronologies – whether a so-called period scheme or developmental stage framework – have become unwieldy and obsolete given the massive increase in radiocarbon measurements over the past 30 years (see further discussion in Chapter 1). This volume is not the place to resolve this problem, although it is appropriate to signal it. Unless otherwise indicated, dates provided herein by the various authors are uncorrected. The reader is directed to *Andes: Radiocarbon Database for Bolivia, Ecuador and Peru* by Mariusz S. Ziólkowski, Mieczyslaw F. Pazdur, Andrzej Krzanowski, and Adam Michczyski (Andean Archaeological Mission of the Institute of Archaeology, Warsaw University and Gliwice Radiocarbon Laboratory, 1994) for the more detailed reporting of hundreds of radiocarbon dates – uncalibrated and calibrated – until 1994. In the past decade pressure appears to be mounting for the presentation of all radiocarbon dates in calibrated form (today, "Early Man" studies largely follow this convention), yet until an international commission calibrates all published dates and imposes a scholarly standard of calibration, chaos will still reign in this matter.

As I view the field today, the outstanding issues in Andean archaeology are investigated by two basic research agendas that some scholars are able to successfully blend into an admirably holistic archaeology. One paradigm is processual in nature and focuses on the vital empirical problems of cultural evolution: how did complex societies arise in the Central Andes and what was the nature (the social, economic, political, religious organization) of these civilizations; how hierarchized were the various social formations and how did they vary from one another? The other direction in Andean archaeology privileges contemporary theorizing about agency, practice, spatiality, social identity, ethnogenesis, migration, political legitimation, inequality, ideology, memory, and materiality to name only a few of the frames within which contemporary research is being situated. But – and this is very important – among almost all Andeanists these "postprocessual" concerns are still firmly and literally grounded in fieldwork and do not replace the processualist practice that must remain the heart of an empirically sound archaeology. In Andean archaeology one can still read an article, chapter, or book and finish it with knowledge of where, when, and how the ancient people of the particular society lived and what material culture was produced. The important change in recent Andean archaeology seems to be that increasingly more scholars are showing why our research matters to archaeologists working outside the Andes. The present volume attempts to integrate theoretical and areal domains.

In putting together this volume I have commissioned contributions from leading scholars in the chosen research areas and I have sought to give recently minted but field-seasoned archaeologists a venue for their novel interpretations since they will likely be among the leaders of the field in coming years.

Chapter 1 provides a brief introduction to situate the ancient societies of the Andes in time and space. It furthermore problematizes areal and temporal definition as issues of knowledge production and presents the Andean environment as a stage upon which cultural landscapes were created by the different societies and segments thereof. The introduction also examines the theoretical engagement of Andeanists with the larger field of archaeology, as indicated above.

Chapters 2 and 3 present the early prehistory of the Andean region, from the first settlers in the region through the precocious "birth of civilization" as manifested most especially at the site of Caral in the Supe Valley.

Chapter 4 is significant as the first synthetic update of the great ceremonial center of Chavín de Huántar in more than a decade. The new data and interpretations presented here are revolutionary.

In Chapter 5 the volume shifts gears as some of the well-known regional polities are brought under critical scrutiny through several theoretical lenses. Paracas and Nasca, Lima, and Recuay societies, located in the south coast, central coast, and north highlands, respectively, are paradigmatic examples of how different societies constructed the role of ancestors in the lives and politics of the living during a period of several centuries (Early Intermediate Period) between two eras of differently themed areal integration (the Early Horizon and the Middle Horizon). Chapter 6 considers the role of highly symbolic material culture in the production and reproduction of political inequality, using Moche as the example. Chapter 7 continues this focus on materiality in its specific consideration of the extraordinary importance of textiles in generating and maintaining a social order and political world in the Central Andes. Chapter 8 applies this focus to the Wari state of the south-central highlands in an excellent comparative study for Chapters 6 and 7.

Chapter 9 interrogates the material world of social life and political activity from yet another perspective, the hermeneutics of phenomenological space, this time turning our attention to the capital cities of the Wari Empire and its contemporary competitor in the Lake Titicaca Basin, Tiwanaku. The spatial dimension of Andean life continues to be interrogated in the multiply scaled treatment of domestic life at Tiwanaku offered in Chapter 10.

The volume then turns its attention to the late prehispanic period, examined through several complementary approaches. Chapter 11 presents, compares, and contrasts a range of polities that developed in the time span after the fall of the Wari and before the rise of the Incas.

How the Incas organized themselves into the greatest empire of the New World is a problem that has long fascinated scholars. Increasingly, archaeologists are considering the legacy of Wari statecraft upon which the nascent Inca state may have been able to draw. In this regard Chapter 12 presents a controversial reading of the one of the Spanish chroniclers and compares it to impeccably gathered archaeological data. At issue is how archaeologists know the Inca past, how historical documents are used, and how these prove and challenge current interpretations of the archaeological record. Of particular note is the argument that history is multiply constructed by its authors, contemporary readers, and later audiences.

The volume concludes with Chapter 13, a comparative analysis of the Wari and Inca states as Andean empires, assessing their similarities and differences.

In keeping with this volume's use as a guide or reader, I have formatted the chapters similarly, each with an "introduction" and "conclusions." The exception is Garth Bawden's beautifully written final but prospective section on "The End of the Moche Political System," which needed its own specific heading.

The uniform formatting of this volume is discontinued, however, for the spelling of Quechua words. I decided to respect the orthographical choices of authors within their individual chapters. This is most noticeable in Chapters 12 and 13 with words such as Inca/Inka, Manco Capac/Manqo Qhapac, Huascar/Washkar, etc., respectively. In addition, the names of the periods of the relative chronology are capitalized (Preceramic Period or Preceramic, Initial Period, Early Horizon, Early Intermediate Period, Middle Horizon, Late Intermediate Period, Late Horizon).

I wish to thank the authors for their willingness to contribute to this volume. I hope that students and colleagues alike are stimulated by the many fascinating arguments contained within.

Helaine Silverman

List of Figures and Tables

Figures

Tables

List of Contributors

Garth Bawden is Professor of Anthropology, Director of the Maxwell Museum of Anthropology, and Director of the Maxwell Center for Anthropological Research at the University of New Mexico. He has conducted fieldwork in the Middle East and Andean South America with special focus on coastal Peru. His primary interest is the nature of ideology and its role in the construction of political systems in early civilizations.

Duccio Bonavia is Profesor Extraordinario Investigador at the Universidad Peruana Cayetano Heredia in Lima, Peru. He has worked extensively in Peru on various research topics, including art, early humans, archaeobotany, and zoo-archaeology.

Ran Boytner is a Research Associate at the Cotsen Institute of Archaeology at the University of California, Los Angeles. He conducted fieldwork in Ecuador and Peru, focusing on the social role of textiles in the Andes.

Christina A. Conlee is Assistant Researcher at the Institute for Social, Behavioral, and Economic Research at the University of California, Santa Barbara. Her fieldwork in Nazca, Peru, focuses on issues of collapse, power, and social transformations.

Anita G. Cook is Associate Professor in the Department of Anthropology at the Catholic University of America.

Winifred Creamer is Professor at Northern Illinois University and Executive Director of their Anthropology Museum.

Terence N. D'Altroy is Associate Professor in the Anthropology Department at Columbia University.

Lisa DeLeonardis is Visiting Professor in Ancient American Art at the Johns Hopkins University Department of the History of Art. Her current research involves archaeological investigations of the Paracas and Nasca cultures of the lower Ica Valley, Peru.

Tom D. Dillehay is the T. Marshall Hahn Jr. Professor of Anthropology at the University of Kentucky. Professor Dillehay has carried out numerous archeological and ethnoarchaeological projects in Peru, Chile, and other South American countries and in the United States. His main interests are models of long-term political and economic changes and methodology. He has published numerous books and research articles, and has been a Visiting Professor at several universities around the world.

Jalh Dulanto is Assistant Professor in the Department of Humanities at the Pontificia Universidad Católica del Perú. He has conducted fieldwork in the North Coast and Central Coast of Peru. His main interests include archaeological theory, quantitative data analysis in archaeology, the archaeology of death, and the archaeology of late prehispanic Andean societies.

Jonathan Haas is the MacArthur Curator of Anthropology at the Field Museum and an Adjunct Professor of Anthropology at the University of Illinois at Chicago. The focus of his research is the evolution of political systems with areal interests in Andean South America and the southwestern United States.

Juha Hiltunen is a Docent for Native American Studies in the Department of Art Studies and Anthropology at the University of Oulu in Finland. He has specialized in ethnohistorical research, New World writing systems, and dynastic propaganda and history.

William H. Isbell is Professor of Anthropology at the State University of New York-Binghamton and Permanent Visiting Professor at the Universidad Nacional San Cristóbal de Huamanga, Peru. He directs archaeological research in the Peruvian highlands as well as the Bolivian altiplano and has written extensively on Huari, Tiwanaku, and urban processes in the Central Andean past.

John W. Janusek is Assistant Professor of Anthropology at Vanderbilt University. He has conducted archaeological research in the Bolivian Andes since 1987, developing analyses of social identity and power relations in urban and rural settlements.

Peter Kaulicke is Professor of Archaeology at the Pontificia Universidad Católica del Perú. Professor Kaulicke's primary interests are the origins of complex society, early art and religion, memory, ritual and mortuary practices, and comparative archaeology. He has carried out more than three decades of extensive archaeological research on a wide variety of Preceramic and Ceramic cultures in the highlands and on the coast of Peru. He has published twelve books and contributed more than a hundred journal articles and chapters to edited volumes.

Silvia Rodriguez Kembel is a Visiting Scholar in the University Center for International Studies at the University of Pittsburgh. Her research focuses on monumental architecture of the Andean Formative Period.

George F. Lau is Lecturer at the Sainsbury Research Unit, University of East Anglia, UK. His research centers on Andean archaeology, social systems, and material culture.

Carol J. Mackey is affiliated to California State University at Northridge.

Gordon F. McEwan is Associate Professor of Anthropology at Wagner College in New York City. He has done fieldwork in Cuzco, Peru, for 25 years, investigating the origins of the Inca.

John W. Rick is Associate Professor, Chair of Anthropological Sciences Department, and Director of the Archaeology Center at Stanford University. He specializes in Andean archaeology, particularly of the Preceramic and Formative Periods.

Katharina Schreiber is Professor of Archaeology in the Department of Anthropology at the University of California, Santa Barbara.

Helaine Silverman is Associate Professor in the Department of Anthropology at the University of Illinois, Urbana-Champaign. She conducted archaeological fieldwork on the south coast of Peru for 15 years, investigating the ancient Paracas, Nasca, and Carmen societies. She is currently studying archaeological tourism and issues of identity formation in contemporary Peru.

Charles Stanish is Professor of Anthropology and Director of the Cotsen Institute of Archaeology at University of California, Los Angeles. He specializes in the archaeology of the circum-Titicaca Basin focusing on the evolution of complex political and economic organization.

Alexei Vranich is a Research Associate at the University of Pennsylvania Museum of Archaeology and Anthropology. He has been conducting fieldwork in Bolivia since 1995, primarily at the site of Tiwanaku, where he has been investigating the form and meaning of the monumental architecture.

1
Introduction: Space and Time in the Central Andes

Helaine Silverman

Issues of Space and Spatial Definition

American archaeologists have drawn the spatial boundaries of the Central Andean region in various manners during the course of the 20th century on the basis of environmental considerations, style distribution, technology, perceived level of sociopolitical complexity, and chronological alignments (see, e.g., Bennett 1948a: fig. 2; Burger 1984a; Hocquenghem 1991; Lanning 1967; Steward 1944; Vescelius 1960; Willey 1971: fig. 3.1). This issue of areal delimitation is significant because it implicates patterns of long-distance interaction and the differential deployment of material culture in the creation and diminution of cultural borders over time as well as how scholars conceive of cultural evolution in the Andes. As Crumley and Marquadt (1990:75–76) observe, a "region never has the same meaning, nor does it occupy the same boundaries throughout its history." Moreover, the areal definition of the Central Andes has changed as different theoretical paradigms have entered the literature, such as peer–polity interaction and the core–periphery or world systems model. Lovell (1998:13) correctly argues that the "production of territory is itself embedded in the production and reproduction of knowledge."

Arguably, the greatest change in contemporary perceptions about the purview of Central Andean archaeology is the importance now recognized for the far south coast of modern Peru as a result of two decades of intensive and outstanding fieldwork in Moquegua and surrounding valleys (see Figure 1.1 for a map of the major coastal valleys and principal highland rivers of the Central Andes). Also, continuing fieldwork and pottery analysis on the north coast of Peru – concerning archaeological cultures known as Cupisnique, Tembladera, Salinar, Vicús, Moche, and Chimú – seem to implicate significant interaction with Ecuador such that it would not be incorrect to define a North Andean culture area running from Jequetepeque (coast) and Cajamarca (highland) through the coast and highlands of what today is Ecuador. Especially for those archaeologists working at the edges of the Central

Figure 1.1. Map of the major coastal river valleys and principal highland rivers of the Central Andes

Andes as traditionally defined, it is time to stop talking in terms of contemporary international borders; we need to conceptualize the past across those artificial lines of demarcation. Of course, pragmatically, this is not easily accomplished given that funding and fieldwork permits are country-specific, not to mention the literal minefields still implanted in the previously contested tropical highlands between Peru and Ecuador.

Stanish (2001:56) suggests that we should cease viewing western South America as having a single trajectory of pristine state development and, rather, conceive of three discrete developments: Moche (north coast), Wari (south-central highlands), Tiwanaku (Titicaca Basin). I think that this formulation is correct as well as productive. Building on Stanish's exciting formulation, I would argue that these states are autochthonous variations on ancient Andean themes at the same time that each social formation achieved its own particular configuration in a discrete geo-ecological setting. In interacting with their physical environment human societies projected their culture onto nature (Crumley and Marquadt 1990:73), and vice versa.

Moreover, by removing the Inca blanket from the vast landscape of prior societies and by recognizing independent cases of political evolution in the Central Andes, archaeologists are better able to compare these and other Central Andean societies to each other and to complex societies that existed elsewhere in South America and beyond.

Finally, Stanish's model raises the issue of uneven political development among contiguous peoples as well as between more distant neighbors. This is a topic that some Andeanists have engaged, but it has not been a disciplinary program. Thus, Patterson (1986 inter alia) has written about resistance and domination and core–periphery relations in the Inca Empire, while D'Altroy (1992) has evaluated various models of imperial Inca organization, among which is the core–periphery model which he discusses as a world systems approach. Such perspectives lead us to ask why, for instance, on the north coast, there was a continuous elaboration of a cultural pattern spanning at least three thousand years whereas the Wari Empire was short-lived in a region that earlier and later was never a locus of "civilization." And why did the state not develop in ancient Nasca society despite evidence of contact with the more complex Lima and Moche societies? Or, what was the nature of political development as well as social organization in the small valleys *between* the Lima and Nasca spheres and *between* the Lima and Moche polities? And even earlier, what happened to the Supe Valley after its astounding precocity in the Late Preceramic Period (see Chapter 2, this volume)? What was society like in some of the valleys of the far south coast of Peru whose members were in contact with Nasca people and later with the Wari state? Aside from the empirical interest such "societies in between" hold for culture historical and processual reconstructions, they are theoretically important and remain to be systematically investigated.

Lumbreras (e.g., 1969:12, 1981:42) has argued for decades that spatially the Andean area includes almost all of western South America from near the Caribbean coast of Colombia to the edge of Amazonian jungle and Argentine pampas to the beginning of temperate Chile. His formulation is very much the result of a political vision that sees ancient interactions as a model for progressive social, economic, and political action in the present. This is not to say that Lumbreras does not discriminate within this vast area. He does. His maps and accompanying texts clearly problematize the far north/circum-Caribbean, North Andes, Central Andes, south-central/Titicaca region, South Andes, and far South Andes (Lumbreras 1981), each of which is defined similarly to prevailing views in contemporary American scholarship. The difference is that Lumbreras is much more inclined to engage the ancient past beyond contemporary Peruvian borders when he writes about Andean archaeology. This is evident in his directorship of the *Gaceta Arqueológica Andina* that, from its first issue, has published articles on Colombia, Ecuador, Chile, Bolivia, and Argentina, in addition to the more frequent contributions focused on the Peruvian Andes.

The cultural landscape

At a smaller scale and to better engage in societal reconstruction, explanation, and interpretation archaeologists need to consider the nature and potential effects of ancient eco-cognition and cosmology on human settlement and the cultural landscape. Archaeology, ethnohistory, and ethnography must be used together, in addition to ecological and natural environment studies, in order to study the landscape in a broader and more nuanced manner, recognizing that ancient people culturally constructed and physically modified the given tangible properties of their world in significant ways, the meaning of which must be elucidated if we are to understand the society to which they corresponded.

Landscapes have life cycles, life histories, and evolutionary trajectories. The meanings ascribed to landscapes are today and were in the past contestable. They may rely on memories of collective identification (see Lovell 1998:16). We must recognize the sociohistorical contingency of the landscape through political, legal, and economic structures, and interpret these structures and physical structures (e.g., climate, topography, geology) in aesthetic, symbolic, religious, and ideological terms that recursively determine and are defined by the landscape. The landscape is simultaneously place, process, and time. Change in and on the landscape occurs for physical reasons – for instance the effect of El Niño, which is natural – as well as cultural reasons – for instance the terracing of vast tracts of the Andean highlands – and in combination.

In all human societies people make sense of and impose tangible and ideological cultural order on the varied natural world. Human beings imbue space with meaning, thereby creating places and, ultimately, the landscape. The landscape is not naturally occurring. People cognitively, symbolically, and physically construct the landscape. Andean people created built environments encompassing the non-architectural space as well as buildings per se (see, especially, Chapters 4 and 9, this volume).

Silverman (2002: ch. 1) has argued that ancient Andean people created multiple geographic, hydrological, ecological, cultural, economic, and social landscapes that were operationalized situationally and in overlapping, complementary ways. By "situationally" she means that the physical space and place of human activity were vivified by social relations. Social relations produced the landscape and spatial organization was recursively constructed and subject to constant negotiation. Therefore, we can consider the spatiality of social life (see, especially, Chapter 10, this volume).

Social life is constituted by "spatialized social relations – and narratives about them – which not only lay down ever-new regional geographies . . . but also work to reshape social and cultural identities and how they are represented" (Allen, Massey, and Cochrane 1998:1–2).

Agriculture along the desertic Peruvian coast was dependent on irrigation, and water for irrigation came from the highlands when it rained. Water was not and is not abundant in the Central Andes. It is therefore not surprising that concepts about water were key elements of Andean ideology and ethnogenesis (see Sherbondy 1992:52–53) and that the system of land tenure was interlinked with the political economy and social structure (see Ramírez 1996:42). In order to understand Andean agrarian societies, Ramírez (1996:45) argues that we must seek to establish "how the natives themselves conceived of land and its use. Access to land cannot be rightfully separated from indigenous ideas about their past, their kinship system, and their functioning political economy. In fact, indigenous land tenure patterns were manifestations of these values and beliefs." The reconstruction of late precolumbian agrarian systems is facilitated by ethnohistoric documents (see, e.g., Chapter 11: "The Central Coast Polities," this volume) as well as creative use of ethnography and archaeology, which also can ameliorate the lack of documentation for the earlier precolumbian periods (see, especially, Trawick 2001).

Silverman (2002) has emphasized the difference between the indigenous Andean construction and cognition of the physical world in precolumbian times and a contemporary pragmatic western conceptualization. As revealed in the Huarochirí Manuscript (Salomon and Urioste 1991), in the ceque system of Cuzco (Bauer 1998; Zuidema 1964), in Hernández Príncipe's (1923) discussion of Recuay's mythology, and in numerous other historical and ethnohistorical accounts, the Andean world was animistic: it was populated with supernatural beings, sacralized mountains, lakes, springs, irrigation canals, boulders and caves, numina-lodging objects, and anthropomorphized forces of nature. It was a world of huacas. It was gendered. It was based on social relations. And it was temporalized, with time and space/place being inseparably bound in a concept called pacha (see Salomon 1991:14). The ancient Andean world was integrated by a well-articulated body of philosophical principles and values that were a continuous attempt to maintain balance, harmony, and equilibrium in the material, social, and moral spheres of community life (Urton 1997:211).

The Andean textualization of space created a legible landscape and made social life legible, comprehensible. All domains of ancient societies were represented on the landscape: social, economic, political, religious, and ideological. Meaning and power produced and were produced by the nested landscapes in mutually reinforcing relationships. Through the act of physical construction – volumetric or not – the landscape was made to target an audience: the members of the construction group, others of the same society, others outside the society, both groups, different groups within a society, and so on. The Andean landscape was a macro-scale text that could be read en route by means of many visible markers, as well as by looking up at the sky. The landscape was mnemonic and was surely read by all members of a particular society, though the storyline would have varied somewhat or significantly according to the viewer-participant's social and situational perspective and knowledge. The scale of reference ranged from local to all encompassing. Andean people's territoriality was a "mental map of social groups attached to place – deities and localized ancestors . . . Immense huaca-studded spaces of canyons and high tundra, fields and trails, embodied an Andean world view" (Salomon 1991:23).

What today we see as archaeological sites were places that in their time made visible statements about the current and proper workings of the world. Landmarks on this landscape – whether naturally occurring or built – were repositories of memory and stimuli for action. Landmarks enabled people to navigate their way around a landscape: they foregrounded contextually important information from amid a noisy (occupied, built-up, marked, etc.) background. Different landmarks were salient in accordance with the landscape that was called into action by situation. Landmarks were significant for those who imbued them with meaning and they could be sites of contestation. Though observable by all, landmarks went unnoticed if they were not part of a cultural scenery.

Architecture and built environments implicated social memories of the past and projections/expectations of the status quo into the future. Collective memory, ritual performance, and commemorative ceremonies were interlinked and inscribed on the stage of a cultural landscape and cued by it. For instance, the volume, mass, and rebuilding of so many sites – especially civic-ceremonial – clearly indicates the intent of the makers that they perdure (see discussion in Chapter 4, this volume). Inevitably, however, circumstances evolved so that over time the meanings ascribed to these memory vehicles were negotiated and contested, and they changed. Eventually, memory was replaced by forgetting, by cognitive erasure, and by new narratives built of other texts. These processes produced the palimpsests that archaeologists study as settlement patterns.

Andeanists and Theory

Andeanists have not usually phrased their research in terms of the major theoretical paradigms driving archaeologists in other parts of the world. It has been rare to see terms such as "agency," "practice," "resistance," or "world systems" in the titles and abstracts of articles written by Andeanists until very recently. This is not to say that Andeanists have eschewed theory, only that they have not typically showcased it. Remarkably, an examination of some of the classic cultural history of 40 years ago reveals passages that read like the best of contemporary theory, but these contributions lack or even precede engagement with the larger supra-disciplinary literature. An example is Menzel's (1960) observation that the local population of Ica reacted negatively to the Inca occupation as manifested by the Iqueños' collection and, sometimes, imitation of Epigonal (MH4) and Chulpaca (early LIP = LIP1–5) pottery. This antiquarianism (representing 6 percent of the pottery found in later LIP gravelots) revived stylistic elements of the Wari intruders, a time not in living memory. Immediately upon the end of the Inca domination there was an outright nativistic reaction. The Iqueños reverted "wholesale . . . to the local style which immediately preceded the relatively brief Inca occupation period . . . no vessel found is free from its stylistic effects . . . This revival coincides with an almost complete loss of features of Inca origin" (Menzel 1960:597). In a startlingly modern statement about domination and resistance Menzel argued,

> It was unquestionably a reaction to the Inca occupation based on frustration rather than extreme hardship. The primary point of sensitivity at Ica involved local pride in prestige based on pottery artistry of some two to three hundred years' standing. Ica prestige did not diminish in this respect under the Inca, but it became second to foreign prestige wares, such as Inca and North Coast pottery, and a symbol of Inca domination. It is thus not the loss of prestige but rather the alteration of its symbolic associations and status that caused the reaction at Ica. It is no accident that the nativistic reaction manifested itself so emphatically in pottery, since pottery was a major symbol of local pride and independence in pre-Inca times. (1960:599–600)

This statements fits with the best identity and domination and resistance paradigms of contemporary archaeology.

A small number of Andeanists have deployed contemporary theory directly. For instance, D'Altroy (1992) explicitly rejects the world systems model in favor of one he terms territorial-hegemonic, which he regards as more amenable to a cost-benefit analysis of empire and more sensitive to spatial variation, to the effects and constraints of geography, not just the structural dependency that is implied by core–periphery (and see discussion in Chapter 13, this volume). I think that some of the resistance of Andeanists to world systems theory comes from its very name. Despite disclaimers by Wallerstein and his archaeological followers, the semantics of "world" suggests an analytical scale so large that the specific properties of Andean societies will be eschewed. Certainly, as many scholars have vociferously stated, the application of a model of capitalist systems to the pre-capitalist and non-western world may be inappropriate through its privileging of external over internal dynamics.

Perhaps the fundamental resistance to world systems theory among most Andeanists resides in its premise of trade and large-scale inter-regional economic exchange networks composed of several competing polities. This economic interdependence could be construed as antithetical to the ethnohistorically argued ethos or culture of the ancient Andean world in which markets did not exist and highland communities were so driven to be self-sufficient in desired staple and luxury resources, such as maize and coca leaf, that permanent colonists were transplanted to distant ecological zones in order to produce these goods and send them to the distant motherland (Murra 1972 inter alia). On the other hand, Burger and Matos (2002) recently advocated the relevance of a world systems model of core–periphery relations for ancient Chavín society. And Willey (1991) has contemplated the relevance of the world systems model for all of Peruvian *and* Mesoamerican prehistory, as I explain below.

On the coast of Peru, some 40 river valleys with repetitive ecology are separated from each other by a stretch of desert of varying distance. Each of these valleys has the same set of resources as the next and ("objectively") requires nothing from the highlands. The geographically self-contained nature of the coastal Peruvian valleys is manifested archaeologically by a profusion of pottery styles which tend to occur in a single or a few neighboring valleys, thereby creating the archaeological cultures we equate with ancient social formations. These societies have been considered to be so discrete in the early part of the first millennium A.D. that the period of time in which they flourished is frequently called Regional Florescent or Regional Development Period to emphasize the perceived lack of long-distance contact and interaction among them.

Indeed, since the beginning of the 20th century the prehistory of Peru has been temporalized and interpreted as the story of regional societies whose isolation has been broken only three times, each time by a highland group: first by a religious cult and then, much later, by two successive episodes of conquest-empire. This model of culture history and political development has been considered the dynamic driving the rise of civilization in Peru, as seen most recently in Willey's (1991) article on horizonal integration and regional diversity. Willey (1991:209) recognized significant similarities between his model of cultural evolution and, as he put it, Wallerstein's "more prestigious parallel from world culture history and economics." He said,

> While I realize that the world systems of industrial states do not replicate ancient Mesoamerican or Peruvian horizonal integration systems, both share the potential for growth and complexity that mark the interconnected whole as something greater than the sum of its parts. In a word, very important forces in culture change appear to be generated and realized through integrative networks. (Willey 1991:209)

I find it particularly inspirational that the grand old culture historian could be so intellectually engaged that, independently of the younger archaeologists who are working with the world systems model (see review and summary bibliography in Peregrine and Feinman 1996), he considered the possibilities that Wallerstein's model could hold for archaeology.

By calling attention to the similarities between world systems theory and traditional archaeological interaction spheres Willey (1991) implicitly raised the issue of "packaging." For instance, is world systems theory in archaeology anything more than a face lift for the already extant core–periphery model which is especially obvious in literature published in the late 1980s/early 1990s (e.g., Champion 1989)? Has the world systems perspective served as a better heuristic device than core–periphery orientations for focusing attention more precisely and systematically on fundamental issues of causality and process in interregional interaction? Stein (2002) highlights the various flaws in these and other traditional approaches to the archaeology of interregional interaction. Not the least of these flaws are the passivity attributed to the peripheral societies and the exclusion of important kinds of culture contact situations such as colonization.

I see a healthy call for a more nuanced reading of interregional interaction and the power relations of its implied culture contact from multiple perspectives, what

Stein (2002) calls "multiscalar" (citing Lightfoot, Martinez, and Schiff 1998), and in all of the many forms of interregional interaction that Stein mentions. Certainly current advances in theory and method have moved us light years beyond an interest in classifying culture contact situations (e.g., Lathrap 1956).

Yet another issue arises from the classic construction of archaeological cultures in the Central Andes. I refer to the relationship between style and ethnicity, long considered in archaeology (see summary statements in Conkey and Hastorf 1990; see also Lumbreras 1984) and now updated to consider style as the dynamic practice of material life (Pauketat 2001; Toren 1999 inter alia) with recognition of individual idiosyncrasies (Whitten and Whitten 1988) and with acknowledgment of potentially weak as well as dynamic spatial boundaries when viewed from a larger social scale. Thus, normative stylistic behavior that is traditionally translated by archaeologists into archaeological cultures is replaced by what Pauketat (2001) calls "historical processualism." Pauketat (2001:73) argues that archaeologists should study cultural practices – "what people did and how they negotiated their views of others and of their own pasts – as these were and are the actual processes [generators] of cultural change." Material culture becomes understood as the "embodiment or active representation – intentional or unintentional – of cultural traditions. Material culture . . . is itself causal. Its production – while contingent on histories of actions and representations – is an enactment or an embodiment of people's dispositions – a social negotiation – that brings about changes in meanings, dispositions, identities, and traditions" (Pauketat 2001:88). Acceptance of this theoretical perspective casts the "edges" of great societies or great traditions in a light more nuanced than core–periphery or simply "influence." This is because individual and grouped actors create their bonds of identity and boundaries of exclusion through a range of conscious and unconscious behaviors or practices (see, e.g., Chapter 10, this volume).

Following from this in terms of culture areas, I think we should be interested in the issue of cultural borders in the sense of societies at the "edges of" and "in between" regional and cultural formations, understanding at the same time that every society has another beyond it ("one society's core is another's periphery"). Identities and borders as well as cores and peripheries are socially constructed and are situationally as well as temporally dynamic.

Also, we need to consider the dynamic transformation of the contact zones ("borderlands," "frontiers") over time under a range of situations such as peer polity and non-peer polity interaction and trade, expansive religious movements, state conquest, colonization, and so on, and how intercultural contact is operationalized by human actors through deliberate as well as unstrategized practices and interactions. Moreover, we need to discard the notion of *culture*, or *a culture*, as a discrete, bounded, homogeneous system shared by all members of a society. I am arguing against the essentialist view that assumes cultural fixity and against a firm territorial configuration; indeed, the reality of ecological complementarity in the Andes demonstrates that different societies can occupy the same territory. The archaeological record shows resource sharing by lowland people and highland people pertaining to small-scale societies (e.g., Dillehay 1979); perhaps this can be compared to Stein's (2002) diaspora autonomy in which neither the host community nor intruder is able to exercise full control. This is not the same thing as great polities intruding into the territory of much less powerful ones for the purpose of acquiring resources. Lorandi (1977) has argued that verticality (see Murra 1972 inter alia) is actually a conquest process, not a mere arrangement of economic convenience. This maximal Andean situation is reminiscent of Stein's (2002) trade diaspora and diaspora dominance, although the colonists are not considered to be specialized merchant groups and their economic activity is presumed to be directed only at the home community. Indeed, herein lies the most significant difference, for by merchant I assume Stein to be talking about volitional and group-enhancing colonization whereas in the Andean case the coercion of colonists must be considered. In the Andes I know of no case corresponding to Stein's (2002) diaspora marginality, though the possibly economically motivated Inca expulsion of the Urus into the unoccupied marshes of Lake Titicaca may provide material for consideration.

Colonization is an event and process especially amenable to theorization within practice, agency, and historical processual paradigms. Stein (2002:913) suggests that we consider "a more general model of variable power relations within the interaction networks that link homelands, resident foreigners, and local host communities." In the Central Andes the goal of colonization among highland groups was to achieve vertical control of a maximum number of ecological niches so as to access lands on which desired goods could be produced that were incapable of growing at high altitude. The classic case of Andean colonization (Murra 1972) has been largely ignored or not included by scholars working outside the Central Andes (e.g., Stein 2002), despite its recent theorization (see Goldstein 2000).

Since direct colonization was first recognized, archaeologists have suggested that indirect exchange mechanisms were also operative in the Andes. The term zonal complementarity refers to non-colonization strategies of procurement such as kin- or non-kin-based barter, long-distance exchange, elite alliances, and so forth. Furthermore, whereas direct colonization and zonal complementarity are typically dichotomized, in fact both strategies were deployed by prehispanic populations in order to cope with changing political, economic, and social conditions. Thus, there was flexibility in the Andean approach to procuring resources. Andeanists have struggled to explicitly distinguish these different strategies on the ground.

In the Central Andes archaeological cultures traditionally have been defined on the basis of pottery styles that are then equated with social identity and called societies. In Andeanist research, we typically consider as peripheries those regions without florescent pottery complexes. And it must be admitted that, in general, there is an isomorphism between the lack of a corporate style (see Moseley 2001:78–79) and a lesser level of sociopolitical complexity. But the great regional cultures or societies of ancient Peru cannot be understood as only local-level cultural phenomena, despite the impression of isolation that is conveyed by territorially specific pottery styles and the regional chronologies developed from them. Thus, in my own work treating one such regional social formation called Nasca, I am finding previously ignored evidence of significant but differential contact with non-Nasca groups immediately to the north and south (see Silverman 1997,

2002:176–179; Silverman and Proulx 2002:68–95). In the case of Nasca and its neighbors, there appear to be clines rather than sharp boundaries in terms of the performance and negotiation of identity.

Issues of Time

Cultural landscapes and the societies that created them existed at a particular time and were constantly evolving and changing – systemically and subsystemically – at different rates. Archaeologists are typically able to recognize change in generational or longer blocks of time. But Kubler (1970) has cogently highlighted the existence of centers and peripheries of spatial action and slow and fast temporal boundaries. For instance, in his section of Chapter 11, Charles Stanish indicates that if the Late Intermediate Period is defined as the time after the collapse of Tiwanaku and before the beginning of Inca influence in the south-central Andes then the dates of the LIP vary by as much as two centuries. "This is because the actual emergence of autonomous polities out of the Tiwanaku collapse was an uneven process, beginning as early as A.D. 900 in the Pacific drainages and not starting until A.D. 1000 or 1100 in the Tiwanaku heartland proper." The veracity of Kubler's (1970) observation needs to be acknowledged by Andeanists if we are to find a way out of the now oppressive temporal framework within which we work, whether the cultural developmental stages construct favored by Peruvian archaeologists (e.g., Lumbreras 1969: cuadro cronológico) or the period scheme favored by Americans (J. Rowe 1962; J. Rowe and Menzel 1967: chronological table).

The greatest debate surrounds the "Formative." The Peruvian Formative Period is typically subdivided into early/lower, middle, and late/upper divisions corresponding to the pre-Chavín, Chavín, and immediately post-Chavín eras, respectively (e.g., Lumbreras 1969, 1974a). But Kembel and Rick's new data on Chavín de Huántar throw this scheme into question (see Chapter 4, this volume). Kaulicke (1994a) has proposed a five-part scheme for the Formative in which the Early Initial Period is separated out as the Final Archaic (2000–1500 B.C.) and the Formative epochs are called Early (1500–1000 B.C.), Middle (1000–600 B.C.), Late (600–400 B.C.), Final (400–200 B.C.), and Epiformative (200 B.C.–A.D. 100), each corresponding to particular sites and suites of behavior and/or material culture correlates; but more radiocarbon dates and evidence for cross-dating are needed.

For those archaeologists using the Formative terminology in the cultural developmental or evolutionary sense, the late division is particularly awkward since the regional societies and polities that emerged upon the collapse of the Chavín interaction sphere were organized in a distinctly non-Formative manner that augured the rise of strong regional polities (e.g., Bennett and Bird 1964:102–113; Burger 1988:143; Lumbreras 1974a:81). Lumbreras (1993:64) states that the Chavín horizon is "contemporary with forms that, like Salinar, already correspond to another epoch" – raising significant problems of cross-dating, chronological terminology, and culture process. Kaulicke (1994a:503–576) recognizes this problem and proposes an Epiformative as the bridge between the Formative cultural configurations and florescent regional polities of the Regional Developmental Period/Early Intermediate Period such as Moche and Nasca.

In John Rowe's (1960) period scheme the Initial Period would correlate to the Early Formative, and the Early Horizon to the Middle Formative. The Early Horizon is defined by Rowe as the time between the first appearance of Chavín influence in the Ica Valley and the replacement of resin painted pottery by polychrome slip painted pottery in Ica. Rowe's Early Horizon is especially problematic since it is a millennium-long period that encompasses pre-Horizon Chavín and non-Chavín cultures, the Horizon spread of Chavín art and ideology, and post-Chavín cultural manifestations.

The problem with "the Formative" is well captured by DeBoer (2002:122). He observes that some scholars have suggested that "the Formative is an abstraction of how cultural evolution ought to proceed if it weren't for the contingent forces and fixtures that actually give history its shape." He concludes that "One could not ask for a better diagnosis of how nineteenth-century social metaphysics still impede the development of archaeological theory." Certainly, the new debates surrounding the "maritime foundations of Andean civilization" (see Moseley 1975a) demonstrate how slippery periodification is (see, e.g., Pozorski and Pozorski 1999: 181–182).

There are several solutions to the conundrum of time and cultural process in which Andeanists are currently stuck. The first two solutions respect the history of use for the two national chronological terminologies. The third solution calls for radical change.

A first solution would be most applicable to the North American relative chronology. It would modify Rowe's period framework so as to put the horizon (Willey and Phillips 1958:32–34) back in the horizons (see earlier statement in Silverman 1996a). In terms of the Early Horizon, Burger (1981, 1988) has argued forcefully that Chavín had a Horizon-like pattern of behavior with geographically widespread features existing for a relatively short period of time, i.e., his Janabarriu Phase, which he dated to ca. 400–200 B.C. This Chavín or Early Horizon would be terminologically isolated from the pre-Horizon manifestations of Chavín and its antecedents. Thus, the term Initial Period would be used for all those cultures contemporary with the block of time existing between the first appearance of pottery in the Ica Valley and the appearance of Chavín influence in Ica (as per J. Rowe 1960). The Early Horizon would begin with the introduction of Janabarriu Chavín traits into the pottery of Ica which, according to Burger (1988), correlates with Ocucaje 3. All societies contemporary with Janabarriu's Ica manifestation would be Early Horizon cultures, irrespective of their degree of integration in the Chavín interaction sphere. In Ica, Ocucaje 1 and 2 (see Menzel, Rowe, and Dawson 1964) would be removed from the Ocucaje ceramic sequence for lack of evidence (Burger 1988; Massey 1986). Ocucaje 3 and any other Chavín-influenced stylistic phases of Ica would be placed in the Early Horizon. Any post-Chavín Paracas phases and cultures as may be demonstrated to exist would be shifted into the Early Intermediate Period. In Ica, minimally, the Early Intermediate Period would begin with Ocucaje 8, followed by Ocucaje 9, Ocucaje 10, and then the Nasca phases. Since the Ica Valley is used as the master column, this modified period scheme is advantageous because it clearly marks the Chavín Horizon, recognizes the importance of the Oculate Being in Ica Valley society, and better reconnects the Nasca archaeological culture to its Paracas antecedents. *However*, this first solution is challenged by the recent architectural and radiometric findings of Silvia Kembel and John Rick from Chavín de Huántar itself that are presented in this volume (see Chapter 4).

The issue over the Middle Horizon (i.e., keeping it a horizon) appears more easily resolved within this first solution. The Middle Horizon would begin with the appearance of Wari iconography and pottery in the Ica Valley, as per Rowe, but would close with the fall of the Wari state rather than with the appearance of the Ica style in the Ica Valley. The Middle Horizon, as the period of the Wari state in Ayacucho, would correspond only to Menzel's (1964) epochs 1A, 1B, 2A, and 2B. Menzel's epochs 3 and 4 of the Middle Horizon would become Late Intermediate Period phases because during this time Ica society was no longer affected by the Wari state. But what about the situation of ongoing Wari culture in the Cuzco Valley discussed by Hiltunen and McEwan in this volume (see Chapter 12)?

A second solution would modify the Peruvian terminology (e.g., Lumbreras 1969, 1974a) with the addition of Kaulicke's (1994a) formulation and, arguably, minor adjustments. Thus, prior to the Formative there would be an Archaic Period (see Chapters 2 and 3, this volume; see Kaulicke 1999) and after the Formative Period there would be a pre-Wari Horizon block of time (an "Early Regional Developmental Period") corresponding to the many florescent regional societies, and a post-Wari/Tiwanaku Horizon/pre-Inca Horizon block of time (a "Late Regional Developmental Period") corresponding to the later florescent regional societies. This scheme could function well for archaeologists working in the Andes on societies for which no connection or comparison (stylistic or cultural) can be meaningfully made with the Ica Valley.

A third solution would forsake the period and stage schemes altogether and in their place use either uncorrected radiocarbon dates or calibrated radiocarbon dates for defining centuries of occupation within and between which one could make comparisons. In the preface to this volume I argued for the need for the latter solution. Thus, archaeologists could speak in absolute terms about what was happening in any part of Peru in a particular century B.C. or A.D. Right now there is chaos in the literature, with most scholars using uncorrected dates or both kinds of dates.

Ultimately the decision of where to create a horizontal line break (the temporal factor) in a vertically organized (the spatial factor) chronological chart is arbitrary and homogenizing (see Kubler 1970) as well as political (see Lumbreras 1969, 1981). Therefore, the third solution may well be the best. Let's consider why in more detail by focusing on the construction of chronological charts.

The chronological organization used by most North American archaeologists evolved over the course of the 20th century from an original period scheme (Kroeber 1925:229–232), to cultural evolutionary stages of development (Bennett 1948b), to the standard periodification devised by J. Rowe (1960; J. Rowe and Menzel 1967: chronological table). Rowe used the succession of pottery styles in the Ica Valley as the master column for the Central Andean region to which pottery styles from elsewhere could be cross-dated. Periods were created based on stylistic definitions. Occasionally, "homogenizing" cultural phenomena known as horizons occurred (see critical discussion in Rice 1993). The stage-like quality of Rowe's relative chronology is usually unrecognized.

George Kubler challenged this and other period schemes with a series of devastating criticisms. Kubler (1985:386) argued that style – as a concept – is an imposition of space upon time that denies duration for, indeed, every work of art "is a bundle of components of different ages, intricately related to many other works of art, both old and new, by a network of incoming and outgoing influences." It is the scholar who divides time, either stressing regularity or irregularity of occurrence. Style is the "illusion of a coherent surface" and the "single identity of any agent depends . . . upon the position and motion of the person perceiving his identity . . . singleness ["styleness"] is assured by the shorter durations and by instantaneous exposure to a reliable and constant perceptor" (Kubler 1985:388). Style, says Kubler (1985:389) "is identifiable only among time-bound elements. Yet if the components are in differential change, as they always are, the relation among them is a changing one." Kubler (1985:390) concludes, therefore, that the "idea of style is best adapted to static situations . . . It is an idea unsuited to duration, which is dynamic, because of the changing nature of every class in duration." This argument is critical for assessing the validity of a relative chronology based on style, such as the period scheme used by most North American Andeanists.

Kubler (1970) also explains that periods are not self-evident and that the act of spatializing time harbors many perils. One of these is that "archaeological history is often written as though time turned itself on and off, stopping whenever the archaeologist demands, and beginning again" (Kubler 1970:128). In reality, the lines that demarcate periods vary regionally and in tempo (slow and fast) and both frames (geographical and temporal) are readily reversible.

Luis G. Lumbreras has long argued that temporal divisions should be explicitly socio-economic and conceived as stages similar to V. Gordon Childe's "savagery," "barbarism," and "civilization," but with different names having a comparative value (see, e.g., Lumbreras 1981:24). Like Childe's Marxism, Lumbreras (1969:27) also argues that the change from one stage to another is not abrupt but has its antecedents in the previous configuration, negating those (in today's postmodern archaeology this is reconceived as historical contingency or historical processualism, see, e.g., Pauketat 2001). For Lumbreras, there is a dialectical process of evolution and revolution. Thus, Lumbreras (1972: plate 1) presents Hunters and Gatherers of the Lithic Stage, Village Agriculturalists of the Archaic Stage, Despotic Urban Societies and Theocratic Reigns of the Formative and subsequent Regional Developmental Stage, and Despotic Urban Societies and Militaristic States corresponding to the Wari Empire, followed by the Stage of Regional States, and finally the Inca Empire. Lumbreras (especially 1974b) forcefully argues that the processes of the past are at work in the present and that archaeology must be a social practice, engaged with the problematic real world.

Conclusions

Archaeologists who work in the Central Andes deal with societies that had long evolutionary trajectories of development, accommodation, and innovation within culturally and geographically constrained limits. The practice of everyday life in the Andes was operationalized by and conducted within Andean ideologies, and led to behaviors that are recoverable in the archaeological record.

Time and space are culturally produced and central to social life. Time–space relations are constitutive features of social systems. Time-space expresses the nature of society and its material manifestations. Time-space is always dynamic. People exist within their changing but repetitive daily lives (practice) and the longue durée of institutions. Archaeology is significantly empowered to tackle time-space problems because of the deep temporal and wide spatial perspective it achieves through survey and excavation. Archaeologists also must attend to the actual historical, social, and political contexts of their research.

2

The First Settlers

Tom D. Dillehay, Duccio Bonavia, and Peter Kaulicke

Introduction

The long Preceramic Period, from at least 11,000 to 4,500 years ago, was a time when people equipped with a wide variety of experiences and tools faced the challenges of nature and molded out of a hunter and gatherer lifeway the beginnings of a more complex Andean society. Their achievements include technical and engineering feats that allowed humans to survive and flourish in different environments, economic innovations that reshaped the Andean world, and symbolic accomplishments that still have meaning. The early part of this period was a time of intense creativity and change that set the stage for the initial impulses of civilization in the fourth and third millennia B.C. Although civilization appeared in other areas of South America, current information indicates that sedentism, social differentiation, agriculture, pastoralism, and urbanism were achieved independently in the Central Andes during the Preceramic Period; this was nearly as early as in other regions of the world. Important are the seminal effects that these transformations had on the formation and character of Andean civilization in general.

Recent research on the Preceramic Period has focused upon the earliest dates for human entry into the continent, as well as new approaches to the study of cultural dynamics in forager societies, with particular reference to Lanning's (1967) Preceramic periods IV–V (ca. 6000–2500 B.C.). This is when regional populations employed different combinations of hunter-gatherer, maritime, pastoral, and/or agricultural economies that ultimately allowed a larger, more secured food supply, increased territorialism and a sense of local community, greater social interaction between communities, and more regionally diversified societies. General population growth, increasing numbers of permanent communities, formalized burial ritual, symbolism, and intergroup conflict also accompanied the introduction of these economies. People also began to affect their environment to a greater extent than before. In Preceramic Periods IV–V they burned selected areas, affected the distribution of animal populations, introduced alien species of plants, and irreversibly altered the natural ecosystem of many regions.

In turning briefly to the way archaeologists examine this period, several factors influence our study and interpretation. The relatively young discipline of Andean archaeology, its models and interpretations, is continually rejuvenated and modified by a steady and growing body of new data, the quality and type of data available, and the way we study those data. For instance, our knowledge of Preceramic populations is richer on the desert coast than it is in the highlands and the eastern tropical lowlands (Figure 2.1). This is largely due to better preservation, greater visibility, and to the fact that more work has been carried out on the coast. On the other hand, highland sites generally produce longer occupational sequences, which is important for studying long-term demographic and socio-cultural change. Other than the presence of a few stone tool scatters, nothing substantial is known about the Preceramic Period in the tropical lowlands. Also lacking are detailed palaeoecological studies and radiocarbon dates for local cultural sequences in many areas of the Central Andes. Despite limitations in our database, enough is known to conclude that not all regions experienced the same scales and rates of change; for example, more rapid, innovative change took place on the north and north-central coasts and in certain highland areas of Peru.

Another factor influencing the way we view the past is the topics we choose to study. Archaeologists generally consider changes in technology and subsistence activities to be the primary motivators of early Preceramic social and cultural transformations, perhaps because it is easier to find evidence for toolmaking and food remains in the material record of the past. Of equal, or probably greater importance, however, are the organizational and interactional adaptations of different human populations that accompanied these changes, especially in Periods IV–V. The particular tools or facilities that signify a transformation in Period V, for example, were definitely important at the time, but their role was transitory, because in most cases they were rapidly replaced. Changes in the size and distribution of human populations and the social organization and interaction between them, on the other hand, were so fundamental that their structure often continued throughout subsequent millennia and many of their effects are visible today in indigenous Andean populations.

Another factor is our interpretative stance. Empirical advances are impressive, particularly in the archaeological study of mortuary practices, large-scale edifices, and symbolism. Yet theoretical and comparative work lags behind, limiting the usefulness of much of the archaeological data for social and cultural analysis. When Andeanists employ theory to understand Preceramic society, they traditionally have taken an evolutionary approach, in which economic inequality, wealth, power, and prestige are assumed to have led to increased socio-cultural complexity. This approach has focused much of our work on social inequality and power relations in the archaeological record. As a result, Andeanists have given primary emphasis to monumental architecture, lavish tombs, and art styles. Less attention has been given to less conspicuous archaeological records and to other possible forms of societal development. This does not deny the importance of monuments and

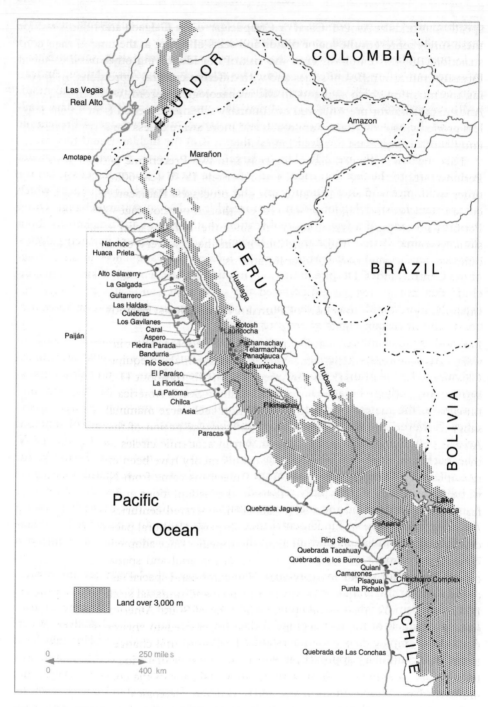

Figure 2.1. Distribution of major Preceramic period sites in the Central Andes

spectacular finds at Aspero, Caral or Chupacigarro, La Galgada and other sites, for these surely represent the major trends and seats of power at the time of their construction. But this emphasis runs the risk of not identifying other possible social forms operating at different scales and with different cultural expressions. By focusing too much on these elements in the archaeological record, we often make the Andean past mirror preconceived evolutionary schemes. Needed is an archaeology less prone to the evolutionary approach and more aware of less conspicuous records and historical processes of social interaction.

This chapter is divided chronologically into two Preceramic periods, Lanning's Periods I–III (ca. 9500–6000 B.C.) and Periods IV–V (ca. 6000–2500 B.C.), in order to discuss general cultural trends and processes. Radiocarbon dates are discussed in uncalibrated radiocarbon years. Although our coverage of the Preceramic Period focuses on research carried out since the 1970s, earlier studies are occasionally mentioned for their contributions in the discovery of sites, chronology-building, and recognition of cultural patterns.

Initial Entry and Dispersion of Human Populations: Periods I–III

For decades, archaeologists thought that the first people to enter into the New World were highly specialized big-game hunters and toolmakers equipped with a fluted Clovis point who arrived in North America from Siberia about 11,500–11,000 years ago and moved very rapidly southward, reaching South America within a few centuries as well as helping to drive to extinction such large mammals as mastodons, saber-toothed tigers, and giant sloths. This popular notion of the peopling of the Americas (Fagan 1987) came to be known in academic circles as the Clovis-first theory. In recent years the deficiencies of this theory have been exposed. It is now recognized that although the first South Americans came from North America by way of land or possibly along the seacoast, their adaptations and experiences were far from being the same ones that had been generated centuries before in North America and had by now become a highly dispersed cultural package that effected certain social transformations and land use strategies once adopted (Dillehay 2000). This package was associated with a series of material and spatial cultural forms: different scales and types of economies, base camps and special task localities, intergroup networks, preferred habitats, and bifacial and unifacial stone tool industries. By the time people first reached the southern tip of South America, they had developed social, behavioral, and cognitive skills that created an environment and experience perhaps more conducive to highly diverse cultural change. These skills and changes are evidenced archaeologically by the presence of a wide variety of regional technologies and economies by 9000 to 8500 B.C. across the continent, especially in areas of the Andean mountains where different ecological zones were closely juxtaposed.

Information about the earliest stages of human occupation in the Central Andes is still scanty, although increasing with new excavations and surveys. New palaeoecological studies also have increased our knowledge of past environments and climates during the Late Pleistocene and Holocene Periods (Clapperton 1993). Some archaeologists postulate that the first humans to arrive in the Central Andes came from the north along the spine of the Andes (Lynch 1983) or along the Pacific coastline (Gruhn 1998), but there is no hard evidence to support either hypothesis. Most likely people entered from various directions at various times (e.g., Bonavia 1991; Dillehay et al. 1992). The earliest firm dates for arrival are between 9000 and 8500 B.C., which is slightly later than other regions of the continent. The warming of the climate and recession of the ice at the end of the Pleistocene Period brought considerable changes, as the extended coastlines of the low-lying desert plains became submerged and likely buried many early littoral sites. Thus, finds are richer in the highland and coastal river valleys. The earliest occupation of coastal Peru is found at Amotape (Richardson 1978) and Paiján sites (Chauchat et al. 1992) on the north coast. These are dated between about 9000 and 8200 B.C. Sites reflecting an early human presence focused primarily on the exploitation of marine resources and dating between 8600 and 7000 B.C. also have been located at the Ring Site (Sandweiss et al. 1989), Quebrada Tacahuay (Keefer et al. 1998), Quebrada Jaguay (Sandweiss et al. 1998), and Quebrada de los Burros (Lavallée et al. 1999) on the south coast and at Quebrada de Las Conchas (Llagostera 1979) and Huentelafquen (Llagostera 1979) on the north coast of Chile. At about 8500 B.C. several caves around 4,000 m in elevation in the central highlands of Peru were occupied, indicating the gradual establishment of rich biotic regimes as the effects of glaciers receded. Among these localities are Lauricocha (Cardich 1964), Guitarrero Cave (Lynch 1980), Pikimachay (MacNeish et al. 1981), Uchkumachay (Kaulicke 1980), Pachamachay (Rick 1980), Panaulauca (Pires-Ferreira, Pires-Ferreira, and Kaulicke 1976), Telarmachay (Lavallée et al. 1995). Farther south in the arid puna of southern Peru and northern Chile are other cave and open-air sites indicative of human occupation between 10,800 and 9,000 years ago (Aldenderfer 1998; Núñez and Santoro 1990).

The sequence of early stone tool industries is not well known. Between 11,000 and 9,000 years ago, Fishtail and Paiján points and unifacial implements were interdigitated on the north coast of Peru but in no clear chronological succession (Briceño 1999). Contemporaneous assemblages in the highlands are generally assigned to the Central Andean Tradition (Moseley 2001), which dates between 11,000 and 10,000 years ago, but characterized by triangular, subtriangular, and willow leaf-shaped points. Curiously, a geographic division occurs in point styles with those in the central and southern highlands of Peru showing stylistic affinities with those in the highlands of Bolivia, Chile, and Argentina where specialized camelid hunting continued until Period VI. In the northern Peruvian Andes and along the coast, there are fewer and different stylistic continuities. Unifacial lithic industries, which are widely distributed along the coast from Ecuador to Chile in parts of the tropical lowlands (Bryan 1986; Dillehay 2000; Lavallée 2000), have received less emphasis from archaeologists. Most likely, all of these industries represent parallel adaptations to different economic opportunities, rather than to a single stone tool culture (although they may trace back their origins to a common early source). Where good preservation occurs, as at Guitarrero Cave (Lynch 1980) in the north highlands of Peru, there was a proliferation of other tool types in Periods I–III, including bone, cordage, hide, shell, and wood, to make other tools and ornaments.

With the exception of the puna in central and southern Peru and in northern Bolivia, Chile, and Argentina, the first Central Andean economies were generally broad-spectrum from the outset. At Pachamachay, Uchkumachay, Panaulauca, and other puna sites, people primarily hunted camelids and secondarily trapped small game, exploited plants around wetlands, and occasionally exploited cervids in lower elevations (Kaulicke and Dillehay 1999). The presence of large quantities of animal bones in these sites indicates that hunting lasted long after other areas had adopted agriculture (Bonavia 1996b). Evidence from lower highland sites suggests seasonal movement at different elevations within circumscribed territories (MacNeish et al. 1981). Some archaeologists postulate that early territorial populations may have existed at sites like Pachamachay and Lauricocha.

Along the coast of Ecuador, Peru, and Chile are found numerous open-air sites dating to Periods I–III that are associated with both bifacial and unifacial stone tool industries used to exploit coastal wetlands and multiple habitats stretching from the coastal plains to the western vegetated slopes of the Andes. The early exploitation of mangrove swamps is evidenced at the Las Vegas site (7800–4000 B.C.) in southern Ecuador and possibly at Amotape sites (ca. 9000–7100 B.C.) in northern Peru, where unifacial lithic industries were likely used to produce wood and bone tools. The inhabitants of Las Vegas exploited a wide range of mangrove and terrestrial resources, including fishes, mollusks, deer, small game, and bottle gourds between 6000 to 5000 B.C. (Stothert 1988). Also found at the site were 192 human skeletons dating primarily between 6000 and 5000 B.C., some of which were associated with ornaments suggestive of early social differences. The separation of cemetery and living spaces and the appearance of burial goods at Las Vegas suggest recognition of the transition from biological death to cultural death and memory of the dead. Other early human skeletal remains are associated with Paiján sites dating around 10,200 years ago (Chauchat et al. 1992).

Perhaps the best-documented early culture in Peru is Paiján dated between 8700 and 5900 B.C. Numerous early Paiján sites are located in or near several highly juxtaposed resource-rich habitats on the Peruvian coastal plains, especially in the north. Chauchat once believed this was a littoral-adapted culture, but recent studies (Dillehay et al. 2003) have shown that the sites range widely in location from the coastal plains to 1,500 m in elevation on the western slopes of the Andes, indicating that Paiján people exploited a diverse range of habitats and plant, animal, and marine resources and were mobile across several spatially proximal and compressed habitats. The Paiján industry also shows a wide variation in the lithic types found at different sites, including stemmed points, various unifaces and limaces, and occasionally grinding stones.

Between 8600 and 8000 B.C., the compression of early Paiján people into several circumscribed habitats from the coast to the western Andean slopes probably led to increased contact and promoted the later development of more complex social relationships. There is growing evidence that late Paiján groups dated between 8000 and 6500 B.C. were decreasing their mobility, aggregating, and establishing more permanent camps at the edge of the hilly ecotone near active springs and within equidistance of the coast and the lomas hillsides (Dillehay et al. 2003). These sites were highly localized, as indicated by the presence of local lithic raw material, large and numerous grinding stones, various floral and faunal food remains, and two to eight permanent stone structures suggestive of circular domestic huts. Excavations in these structures reveal thick habitation floors (5–15 cm) indicative of continuous or permanent occupation. Earlier sites are characterized by large to moderate lithic scatters and thin habitational surfaces (<5 cm) that are more suggestive of short-term occupation. Collectively, these data indicate an early Paiján settlement pattern of larger bands based on movement between the coastal plains and mountain slopes, probably on a seasonal basis, to a later circumscribed pattern of smaller groups in localized and diverse habitats along the ecotone of the coast and foothills. The later, more permanent sites probably provided a stable place for people to prolong social contact and exchange, and enhanced conditions for eventual population growth. During this period, several cultural traits were likely developed: planning and decision-making, risk management, resource-sharing between different groups, and technological innovations.

In summary, Periods I–III laid the social and economic foundations for the significant cultural changes that were to follow in Period IV (6000–4200 B.C.) and particularly Period V (4200–2500 B.C.). Early developments in Periods I–III show cultural diversity at the outset of human entry into the Central Andes and the subsequent establishment of increasingly distinct regional economic combinations. Generally speaking, broad spectrum economies developed in areas characterized by closely spaced mosaics of distinct ecological zones; specialized hunting and gathering occurred in areas where less diversity is found, such as the puna and the littoral zones.

Although the evidence is too scanty to discern the specifics of these developments, three general transitions are discerned. The first transition was a change in adaptive strategies and organizational abilities in Periods I and II. This transition signifies the rapidly increasing ability of people to recognize the environmental potentials that existed in some areas, to communicate these potentials to others and to take advantage of them, and to develop the social organization required to exploit resources in a wider variety of environments. Second, early people probably learned many hunting techniques, and on occasion employed them to bring down large animals. But with the exception of the puna, there is no hard evidence to show that hunting was the mainstay of the earliest known coastal (and even tropical) economies. The social and psychological requirements of hunting probably played an important part in molding group organizational skills. But the same can be said of collecting plants and gathering or fishing marine resources. Most marine resources such as clams, limpets, and seaweed were procured close to the shore, but some fish may have been caught from small watercraft or from the shoreline by using baskets, weirs, fish traps, and nets. Although early water traffic may have involved no more than paddling a crude watercraft along the coast, it required the development of new skills and adventurousness of a kind that might have attracted even more prestige than hunting large animals. But we see these issues as secondary to the real prime mover of greater social complexity, and that is the practice of coordinating the procurement of food and sharing food within an organized, aggregated social group. And third, the current evidence suggests that some Early Preceramic societies were highly territorial and others were not. A number of coastal sites associated with specialized collecting tasks, such as marine resources at Quebrada Tacahuay and the Ring Site, appear to have been occupied intermittently for a long time on the coast. Several early sites in the highlands (Guitarrero) and along the lower western slopes (Paiján) of the Andes suggest seasonal movement between closely juxtaposed high and lower elevations. Regional variation in stone tools and the low to rare frequency of exotic raw materials at many early sites also suggests mobility within confined territories. These sites most likely represent small bands with reduced territories that eventually experienced population growth. Yet common tool types, especially triangular to subtriangular points of the Central Andean Tradition, suggest non-territorial populations maintaining contact among dispersed groups. This suggests that the composition of local groups could have varied seasonally and situationally according to location, task, and food supply.

Domestication: Changing Relations between Humans, Plants, and Animals

Why plant domestication and agriculture began when and where they did is difficult to discern. Perhaps it was a combination of the onset of warmer conditions with the passing of the Pleistocene Period, and the social readiness of a few hunter-gatherer groups that led to their development at different times and in different places (Bonavia 1991, 1997). Although much debate has taken place about the timing, place, and process of domestication, one fact is clear: without hunter-gatherer manipulation of the natural habitats of plants (and animals) civilization would never have developed. Although the details of this process remain unclear, it is generally accepted that people independently domesticated plants in at least seven areas of the world, including the Central Andes (K. Brown 2001). Our understanding of plant domestication is often limited by seeing it as an event rather than a long-term process and by applying generalized ecological and behavioral models to all seven areas in search of universal patterns. Similar cultural, geographical, and ecological conditions were likely shared by all areas, especially the biological understanding and manipulation of plants by hunters and gatherers that eventually led to domestication. But there also must have been major differences in regional processes. In studying this process in the Central Andes, two factors must be realized: the archaeological study of plant remains began late and there has been little subsequent interest among botanists to study them. Although several naturalists were interested in these remains in the 1800s, it was not until Junius Bird excavated Huaca Prieta in the 1940s that they were radiocarbon dated to the second millennium B.C.

In order to understand the domestication process in the Central Andes, we must recognize the unique ecological diversity of the Andes. Of the 103 world life-zones defined by Holdridge (1967), 84 are located in the Andes and 17 of these are ecotone environments (Tosi 1960). Although some Andean cultigens were likely developed in the eastern tropical lowlands, most were probably domesticated in the temperate montane valleys of the Andes, especially in the northern highlands of Peru where a wide variety of closely juxtaposed ecological zones and plant types exist. These conditions are exceptionally ideal for the manipulation of wild plants (Hawkes 1969:26; Vavilov 1926). Further, the exploitation of diverse ecological zones and resources also must have necessitated the development of new economic strategies, social structures, cultural landscapes and domestic spaces, and regional forms of interaction, especially when groups began relying more on domesticated plants and animals.

Although no reliable archaeological evidence exists to support the notion that domestication occurred in elevations around 2,000 m, it is likely that diverse groups of mobile hunters and gatherers selectively exploited plants in montane valleys on both the eastern and western slopes of the Andes. As these groups seasonally moved between different ecological zones, they must have observed a wide variety of plants unique to different elevations (Lynch 1983). Plants probably adapted slowly to different habitats once they were transported by natural forces (e.g., wind and animals; Lynch 1983:125–126), and by humans who must have carried plants into new environments. Introduction to different habitats probably placed new selective and adaptive pressures on plants. Humans may have accelerated this process by selecting certain plants for different economic needs, which may explain the wide variety of crops, such as potatoes and maize, produced in the Andes today.

The best archaeological evidence for the early use of cultigens is on the dry desert coast between 6000 and 4000 B.C., where preservation of organic remains is excellent. Although no secure plant remains have yet been found in early Paiján sites on the north coast, the presence of large grinding stones suggests the use of wild plants and some domesticated plants during Periods I–III (Chauchat et al. 1992:355). Some evidence also suggests that chili peppers, squash, lúcuma, olluco, beans, pacay, and oca may have been domesticated between 8000 and 6000 B.C. (Table 2.1). In the following Periods IV–V, two areas have produced archaeobotanical evidence that suggests plant manipulation in the montane valleys adjacent to the coastal desert. These are the Zaña Valley on the north coast, where a relict tropical montane forest was heavily exploited as far back as 10,500 B.C., and the mouth of Huarmey Valley on the north-central coast. In the Zaña Valley, the late Pircas culture, dated between 5000 and 4000 B.C., yielded wild and possibly cultivated squash, chenopodium, peanut, yucca, and several unidentified wild fruits (Dillehay, Rossen, and Netherly 1997; Rossen, Dillehay, and Ugent 1996). In the Huarmey Valley at Los Gavilanes and other sites dated between 4000 and 1800 B.C., Bonavia (1996a) documented a shift from gatherers to foragers exploiting a wide variety of marine products in addition to gourds, squash, unidentified tubers, and Poaceae. Cotton, avocado, beans, achira, peanuts, pacay and possibly coca appear around 2000 B.C. During the later occupation chirimoya, lima bean, yucca, guayaba, chili peppers, and maize appear (Bonavia 1996a; Bonavia et al. 1993). Around 2100 B.C., the occupants of Los Gavilanes built pit silos to store large quantities of maize,

Table 2.1. List of domesticated plants in the Central Andes by preceramic periods and geographic areas

Period III: 8000–6000 B.C.			
	Coast	Highland	Tropical lowland
Chili pepper (*Capsicum chinense*)	X	X	
Squash (*Cucurbita sp.*)	X	X	X (in Ecuador)
Lúcuma (*Pouteria sp.*)	X		
Olluco (*Ullucus sp.*)	X	X?	
Lima bean (*Phaseolus lunatus*)	X	X?	
Common bean (*Phaseolus vulgaris*)	X	X	
Pacay (*Inga sp.*)	X	X	
Oca (*Oxalis tuberosa*)	X	X	
Lucumo (*Pouteria lucuma*)		X?	

Period IV: 6000–4200 B.C.			
	Coast	Highland	Tropical lowland
Quinua (*Chenopodium sp. Cf. quinua*)	X		
Peanut (*Arachis hypogaea*)	X		
Yucca (*Manihot esculenta*)	X		
Gourd (*Lagenaria siceraria*)	X		
Achira (*Canna sp.*)	X		
Cotton (*Gossypium sp.*)		X	
Squash (*Cucurbita sp.*)	X		X (in Amazonia)
Maize (*Zea sp.*)			X (in Amazonia and Ecuador)

Period V: 4200–2500 B.C.			
	Coast	Highland	Tropical lowland
Squash (*Cucurbita andreana, C. ecuadorensis, C. ficifolia, C. moschata, C. maxima*)	X		
Poacea	X		
Unidentified tubers	X		
Chili pepper (*Capsicum baccatum*)	X		
Cotton (*Gossypium barbadense*)	X		
Pacay (*Inga feuillei*)	X		
Avocado (*Persea americana*)	X		
Lúcumo (*Pouteria lucuma*)	X		
Maize (*Zea mays*)	X	X	
Jack bean (*Canavalia sp.*)			X (in Ecuador)

Period VI: 2500–1800/1500 B.C.			
	Coast	Highland	Tropical lowland
Guayabo (*Psidium guajaba*)	X		
Coca? (*Erythroxilum coca*)	X		
Jíquima (*Pachyrrhizus tuberosus*)	X		
Chirimoya (*Annona cherimolia*)	X		
Jack bean (*Canavalia sp.*)	X		
Potato (*Solanum tuberosum or S. stenotomum*)	X		
Achira (*Canna edulis*)	X		
Chili pepper (*Capsicum chinense*)	X		
Achira (*Canna sp.*)		X	
Quinua (*Chenopodium sp.*)		X	

forming the earliest and most complex food storage system known anywhere at this time. The presence of cultigens at Los Gavilanes and other sites suggests that the domestication process was underway by at least 5,000 years ago (Bonavia et al. 2001). In the Huarmey Valley, peanuts, maize (Greenblat 1968; Grobman 1982), and other plants reflect relations with intermontane valleys and the eastern slopes of the Andes.

Other than the areas mentioned above, there is a long list of early plant remains from other coastal and highland sites. Although the dates and contexts for many sites are questionable, enough reliable data exists to chronologically arrange the appearance of several domesticates. For example in the highlands during Period III, there are chili peppers, squash, and possibly lima beans, pacay, lúcuma, oca, and olluco, although the latter four may appear later. Further, in late Period IV, cotton appears. In Periods V to VI, maize, achira, and Chenopodiacea (probably quinoa) are adopted.

On the coast the plant inventory is much larger, largely due to good preservation of organics in sites. In Period IV, gourds and squash appear. In Periods V and VI, chili pepper, cotton, lima bean, common bean, achira, maní, pacay, quinoa, yucca, avocado, guayaba, several varieties of squash, and lúcuma occur. At the end of this period, maize, several fruits, potato, chili pepper, bean, and achira are found. In the case of maize, a debate continues about its chronology and context and whether it was derived from Mexico where it dates between 5,420 and 5,410 years ago (Piperno and Flannery 2001) or was developed independently in South America, where it possibly dates between 6,070 and 6,050 years ago (Bonavia and Grobman 1989b; Uceda 1987). Outside of the Central Andes, squash phytoliths and maize pollen are dated in the tropical lowlands of Colombia around 8,000 and 6,700 years ago, respectively (Pearsall and Piperno 1990), and in Ecuador around 9,000 and 8,000–6,000 years ago, respectively (Piperno, Andres, and Stothert 2000).

In regard to the domestication of camelids (llama and alpaca) and the guinea pig, there are no reliable defining characteristics. Archaeologists have suggested that animal domestication can be identified by studying several factors, including an increase in body size, morphological variation, survival curve, and the frequency of appearance of the bone remains of one species over others, and changes in age and sex ratios of individuals. For Andean camelids the most reliable indicators are survival curves, increase in the amount of bone remains in sites, dental morphology, increase in high-altitude corrals, and shifting utilization patterns. The domestication of the llama and alpaca in the central highlands of Peru probably began with generalized hunting of ungulates in the high puna between 7000 and 5200 B.C., then developed further with specialized hunting of guanacos (never domesticated) between 5200 and 4000 B.C., and finally the domesticated form between 4000 and 3500 B.C. (Bonavia 1996b; Wheeler 1999). Although more attention has been given to faunal data in the highlands of Peru, it is likely that camelids were domesticated in other areas as well. Little is known about the domestication of the guinea pig, although the bone remains of this animal appear early between 8000 and 7000 B.C.

in highland caves of Colombia (Correal and van der Hammen 1977) and later in Period III in the Peruvian highlands and Period V on the desert coast.

Before the chronology and the processes of plant and animal domestication can be better understood, more archaeological information is needed from various types of sites in different coastal, highland, and tropical environments. Although most emergent farming communities in Periods IV–V probably did not depend on a single crop, different regional specialties on the coast and in the highlands likely would have encouraged them to trade with one another, exchanging seeds or tubers for meat and other products, for instance. Trade was not a new idea in the Andes of Periods IV and V: obsidian, chert, and other materials for making stone tools had already been the subject of exchange several thousands of years before. Nevertheless, with the growth of farming there may have been a new and increasingly urgent need for the exchange of goods and for the development of animals such as the llama to transport these goods.

Increased Socio-Cultural Complexity: Periods IV–V

One of the most difficult and important challenges facing Andeanists is the task of disentangling the human responses to changes in both physical and social environments during the mid-Holocene Period (ca. 6000–1500 B.C.), when climates were generally warmer (Clapperton 1993). It has been assumed by most archaeologists that major climatic change was the primary stimulus for people to shift from a hunting and gathering existence to a settled agricultural life in an effort to adapt to a significantly deteriorated environment. The basic format of this explanation has been deterministic: in certain favorable coastal and highland environments, a radical change in climate led to a radical change in cultural complexity and social inequality. The most significant and widespread socio-cultural changes of this period appear in technology, settlement patterns, symbolism and exchange systems, burial practices, and the adoption and spread of different regional combinations of hunting and gathering, incipient agriculture, domesticated animals, and, along the Pacific coast, marine resources. Fancy and utilitarian textiles and pottery appeared, especially in burials, and assumed a social prominence beyond their technological value. Social differences were expressed consistently in burials to the point where we can infer greater distinctions among individuals. Settlements grew in size, permanence, and degree of residential aggregation: architecture became more widespread, substantial new building techniques were developed, and different types of public spaces were created (i.e., plazas, mounds, cemeteries). The cultural diversity and developments of these periods should not be surprising considering the appearance of large-scale monuments indicative of increased social complexity and economic synchronization throughout the north coast, central coast, and highlands by Period VI between 2500 and 1500 B.C. (Burger 1985; Kaulicke 1994a; Quilter 1991).

In considering the emergence of hunter-gatherer complexity in the Andes, it should be obvious that a rich resource base was not the sole condition involved.

The current data indicate that different social, technological, and demographic dimensions of complexity did not develop simultaneously on the coast and in the highlands, but that their timing, tempo, and connections often varied within and between regions. Complexity appears very early, around 5,000 to 4,500 years ago, if we define complexity as full-scale monumental architecture, primary maritime or agricultural economy, and a chiefdom-like society. The appearance of social complexity on the Peruvian coast has been a topic of debate for nearly three decades, with one side arguing primarily for a maritime society (Moseley 1975a) and the other stressing the importance of early agriculture (Bonavia 1998; Osborn 1977; Raymond 1982; Wilson 1981). The participants in this debate now admit that the truth probably lies somewhere in between and that the debate can be resolved only by more stratigraphic excavation and careful water flotation of cultural sediments in different domestic and non-domestic areas in more sites, and more careful comparative analysis of recovered materials.

The debate later shifted to types of complex societies. Feldman (1983), Haas (Haas, Pozorski, and Pozorski 1987), and the Pozorskis (Pozorski and Pozorski 1987) argue for state-developed urbanism based on the presence of multiple pyramids at Period VI sites such as Aspero, Caral or Chupacigarro, and Río Seco. Burger and Salazar-Burger (1991), Quilter (1991), and others argue for non-centralized communities. One possibility is that the multiple pyramids at these sites were independent structures and simply reflect the cumulative effect of long-term sequential building and abandonment in the same locality. Another possible interpretation is that the coincidence in the occupation of these structures may be due to periodic ceremonial activity by outlying groups that, thousands of years later, gives the impression of contemporaneity and urbanism. Alternatively, it can be argued that these structures are indeed contemporaneous and pertain to a single centralized urban population. These are all testable hypotheses and nothing more. The problem can only be resolved by detailed settlement patterns studies and by stratigraphic excavation and more precise dating and correlation of the multiple structures at these sites. Regardless of the chronology and degree of complexity, the Period VI emphasis of monumental architecture and public ceremony is a good indication that the newly evolved social and economic power, perhaps as a result of trade and synchrony of various economies and social activities, was focused on a religious ruling group who regulated public ceremony and increased contact among different communities.

We earlier mentioned a generalized hunter and gatherer adaptation to the coastal plains and adjacent western slopes between 10,000 and at least 9,000 years ago that resulted in a pattern of carefully scheduled, probably seasonal movements between coastal and upland locations, where various plants, animals, and seafood would be available at different times of the year. In some areas, this pattern of resource exploitation began to change between 7000 and 6000 B.C. For instance, between 7000 and 5500 B.C. in the middle and upper Zaña Valley, hunters and gatherers began a local permanent or semi-sedentary to sedentary life with larger organized communities, careful burial of the dead, separate small-scale open public spaces and domestic circular houses, and subtle social differences. The technology was dominated by unifacial tools, a varied ground stone technology, simple food storage, and a food economy based on the exploitation of a wide variety of plants and animals. Low frequencies of exotic materials (e.g., marine shell, carved stingray spines, quartz crystals, and raw stone material) suggest minor contact with distant coastal and highland areas. The following time span between 5500 and 3000 B.C. was marked by changes in house style (from small elliptical to larger, multiple-room rectangular) and the addition of cotton, beans, and coca (Dillehay, Rossen, and Netherly 1997; Rossen 1991). Although exotics disappeared, the separation of public and private space was more pronounced, as evidenced by small dual, stone-lined, multi-tiered earthen mounds at the Cementerio de Nanchoc site, where lime was produced in a ritual context for possible use with coca leaves or as a food supplement.

By 4000 to 2500 B.C., the pattern of movement between the north coast and highlands was modified by some groups who began to rely more on coastal resources year-round. La Paloma, on the central coast, was a small, permanent settlement focused on inland lomas resources and on nearby marine resources, including seabirds, anchovies, and other fish, as evidenced by bone remains and fishhooks and nets. Burial remains at La Paloma also suggest early social differentiation with ornaments and possibly female infanticide (Benfer 1990; Quilter 1989). At Chilca in Peru (Engel 1966a) and Camarones 14 (Schiappacasse and Niemeyer 1978), Pisagua, Quiani, and Punta Pichalo in Chile (J. Bird 1943) between 3500 and 2500 B.C., people apparently lived in permanent settlements where they consumed sea mammals, fish, shellfish, turtles, and sea birds and gourds, squash, and beans. Sometime between 2500 and 2000 B.C., some central fishing villagers began to grow cotton for weaving fabric, as evidenced at Huaca Prieta (J. Bird, Hyslop, and Skinner 1985), Asia (Engel 1963), El Paraíso (Engel 1966b; Quilter 1985), and other sites. Small-scale agriculture at other sites scattered along the coastal plains also furnished chili peppers, squash and beans as supplements to the primarily seafood diet (J. Bird, Hyslop, and Skinner 1985; Lavallée 2000; Quilter 1991). Also important is the Chinchorro tradition in southern Peru and mainly northern Chile (J. Bird 1943), which dates between 5500 and 1200 B.C., and is associated with an intense maritime economy, separate burial places for the dead, and extraordinary funerary practices focused on mummification of the dead. The mortuary evidence suggests that the mummies were socially differentiated, recycled as "ancestral statues" to participate in public ceremonies of the living, and related to community identity.

Between 3500 and 2500 B.C., coastal villages increased in size and subsistence expanded to include domesticates such as gourds, squash, and kidney and lima beans (Bonavia 1982; Fung 1988). At this time at Real Alto and other Valdivia sites on the south coast of Ecuador and at Huaca Prieta, Alto Salaverry, and Paracas in coastal Peru, there is evidence of increasing social complexity, as indicated by agglutinated domestic structures and small specialized structures such as pyramids or platforms and by elaborate textiles, worked gourds, or other objects.

On the arid south coast of Ecuador around 3500 B.C. hunters and gatherers using early Valdivia pottery focused their subsistence practice primarily on the collection of mollusks and other resources from mangrove swamps. The later occupants of Real Alto, the best-studied Valdivia site, built two long mounds that contained residential structures and formed a large circular village. The site inhabitants also widened their diet to include a wide variety of animals and both wild and cultivated plants. By 3000 B.C., additional mound structures and domestic units were placed in the site. After 3000 B.C., the specialized structures at Real Alto became increasingly large and sophisticated as occurred at Caral or Chupacigarro, Aspero, Piedra Parada, Bandurria, Río Seco, and El Paraíso (Fung 1988; Quilter 1991) on the central coast of Peru.

There also is evidence at these sites of a developing pattern of social stratification, in the form of differential size in ceremonial mounds and in houses. For example, Aspero, a large site covering 12 ha, has seven large and six smaller ceremonial mounds on top of which were constructed small temples that contained human burials (Feldman 1983). Around the mounds were open plazas and artificial terraces. A large resident population exploited the rich resources of the nearby coast. At Caral or Chupacigarro (ca. 15 ha) several large ceremonial mounds and plazas flanked by elaborate residential quarters suggest increased sophistication in community organization and social structure (Shady, Haas, and Creamer 2001). Both Aspero and Caral or Chupacigarro suggest social distinctions defined by small groups of elites and larger non-elite populations that most likely represent the initial formation of local polities. As earlier mentioned, because we do not know if the large mound structures and residential zones at these sites were contemporary, we cannot yet determine whether they reflect early urbanism and state development or simply large complexes formed by cycles of pyramid-building and abandonment.

By about 2500 B.C., coastal populations expanded into the interior, where more intensive agriculture would have been possible only with the construction of irrigation canals. Although no canals have yet been dated to this period, we suspect that people at this time probably utilized the alluvial silt in river deltas (Bonavia 1998) and/or first dug shallow irrigation ditches which they led from small, possibly dammed streams to enhance the growth of garden plant foods. As earlier discussed, this period is also marked by a dramatic increase in the significance of cultigens in the diet of the inhabitants. The success of these early maritime and farming practices is evident at later sites such as Las Haldas on the central coast of Peru (Fung 1969). Around 1800 B.C., several hundred residents lived at this site in a community that built a large terraced adobe-brick pyramid and plazas for ceremonial use. Finely crafted artifacts were made by specialists and included loom-woven fabric of cotton and objects of wood, stone, shell, and later ceramics. Similar settlements are found in other valleys during the period from 2200 to 1500 B.C., as well as others that continued to practice a varied foraging life until about 1500 B.C.

In the highlands, meanwhile, there were parallel developments. At Asana, a stratified open-air site located at 3,400 m in the high sierra and puna rim of the south-central highlands of Peru, Aldenderfer (1998) concludes that montane foragers of Periods I–VI shifted their use of the site through time by first using it as a temporary campsite for exploiting a wide range of plant and animal resources on a short-term basis to a permanent place with public and residential architecture around 5000 B.C. indicative of greater social complexity. Around 4500 B.C. this trend reversed with the public architecture abandoned and the site used temporarily by residents that gradually shifted to higher elevations to practice pastoralism of domesticated camelids. Besides pastoralism, maize farming and the domestication of other crops may have occurred initially in other areas of Peru above 1,500 m in elevation. For instance, the Mito phase (Izumi and Sono 1963) of the Kotosh site, at an elevation of 1,800 m in the north-central Andes, reveals an early religious mound complex associated with farming and the exploitation of camelids, deer, and guinea pig. The presence of tropical lowland influence is seen at the site, particularly with the later appearance of Amazonian-like ceramics around 1800 B.C. Another important highland site is La Galgada (Grieder et al. 1988), which is located on the lower western slopes of the Peruvian Andes with access to both the distant coastal plains to the west and the tropical forest to the east. The site is characterized by two mounds, elaborate funerary goods and several cultigens, and dated between 2200 and 1200 B.C. In other areas of the highlands in southern Peru, Bolivia, and Chile, people were gradually shifting from hunting and gathering to pastoralism and probably limited farming.

Other changes revealed in the archaeological record of Periods IV–V are increasing attention to the burial of the dead and to representational artwork on grave offerings and other objects. People were purposefully burying many of their dead, both mature adults and infants. Although there was no uniform method of burial, attention was paid to the positioning of the body and to the objects left with it. Ornamental objects adorn burials at Huaca Prieta, La Paloma, Chilca, Asia, and other sites. Representational artwork was expressed in several media, including textiles at coastal sites, clay figurines at Aspero, and carved gourds at Huaca Prieta. Whatever their meaning, these objects probably suggest increased attempts to understand, categorize, control, and reproduce the natural and social surroundings and, along with burial patterns, to express self and other identities. Although concepts of afterlives, the control of death, and possibly ancestor worship may be implied in these patterns, there is little evidence to suggest the employment of mortuary patterns to display social ranking.

In summary, many of the Period IV–V sites mentioned above have some of the familiar attributes of emergent complexity (i.e., nucleation, monumentalism, population growth, community planning, social differentiation, subsistence intensification) but not others (visible social ranking or stratification, ruling elites, and accumulation of prestige items). Most striking is the scarcity of evidence to suggest the rise of individual elites and leadership in the form of housing and burials and the accumulation of individual (or even group) wealth and prestige goods, although these came later. The current evidence suggests that the populations of Periods IV–V were focused more on horizontal peer-relations between similar and different types of societies than on vertical or hierarchical relations, and on small-scale corporate unity expressed in terms of separate but complementary public and private spaces and ceremonial landscapes, new corporate and household economies, and the development and refinement of new technologies. Defining ceremonial and sacred spaces on the landscape must have been as important as the development of local technologies and new resources.

A critical threshold was crossed by these societies in the fourth and third millennia B.C., when public and private spaces were separated and formal public structures were built at sites like Cementerio de Nanchoc, Asana, and others. These structures do not appear to be the residences of high-status individuals but ritual staging areas for small groups of individuals. The large multi-pyramid sites of Aspero, Caral or Chupacigarro, Piedra Parada, Kotosh, and La Galgada were built later but prior to the second millennium B.C. Although public ritual and ceremonialism at these sites also played extremely important roles, we do not yet understand how individuals and individual communities related to them. Although these types of sites do not appear to represent full-fledged chiefdoms directed by individual leaders, they may have been small-scale polities whereby power and authority were diffused, rotated, and situationally applied among small groups of individuals sequentially operating at large public sites. The creation and use of special ceremonial spaces such as dance plazas, small and large earthen and stone mounds, and other ephemeral features of Periods III–V were likely prototypes to the large ceremonial spaces and structures in the following Period VI, when evidence is clearer for non-elite and ruling elite relations.

Conclusions

Although the Pleistocene and Holocene environments of the Central Andes determined the resource structure and influenced the human response to the exploitation of these resources, Preceramic people created the conditions and structures in which they lived and, in turn, they were shaped by the institutions and beliefs that they either controlled directly or that were beyond their control. The first Central Andeans were general foragers, specialized maritime gatherers and hunters, specialized highland hunters, incipient horticulturalists, and other combinations in a wide variety of environmental contexts. These diverse economies entailed different degrees of technological innovation, planning, uncertainty and risk management, resource-sharing, mobility and territoriality, and social interaction. Not well understood by many archaeologists are the patterns of interaction operating among these societies, and how this interaction created new and different institutions and socio-cultural complexities. It is becoming more apparent that societies took different pathways to social complexity and to different scales of interaction between different types of societies differentiated by different social and economic combinations. It also is important to recognize that these regional developments did not fully emerge until plant and animal domestication occurred in Periods II–IV. Yet we cannot always look to domestication as the prime mover of social complexity. Also important are ideological changes oriented toward a restructuring and synchronization of different social and economic organizations. In many cases, the factors sustaining later, more complex ideological, technological, and subsistence developments in Periods V–VI and the subsequent Initial Period (ca. 1800–1500/900 B.C.)

are direct extensions of these developments, which are evident but not always dominant or materially conspicuous in the archaeological record of Periods IV–VI.

There is a tendency in Andean archaeology to homogenize society types and fit them into preconceived notions of progressive development toward ever-increasing complexity. That is, Andeanists often view a rather straight progression from mobile foragers to sedentary food producers with the implication being that spatial localization and aggregation fostered the kind of greater complexity documented at late Preceramic sites. But some Preceramic societies may never have fully reached a sedentary lifeway. Rather, a diversity of reduced mobile (such as pastoralists) to sedentary (such as fisherfolk) groups provided a certain socio-economic and demographic fluidity that generated even greater diversity and social complexity. This emergent complexity likely developed due to internal parameters such as population growth and intensification of land use and to social aggregation and greater attention to relations between the living and the dead. It also must have taken shape and changed as a direct outcome of the interactions of different populations in constant flux, especially where the crafting of complexity involved both material and invisible resources, such as the manipulation and invention of forms of meaning and abstract units of social organization.

In looking at the long Preceramic Period and its contributions to later Andean society, it is becoming more apparent that until Period VI social relations do not conform to the elite and non-elite dichotomy found in so many archaeological discussions of emergent social complexity in other parts of the world. We believe that Central Andeans of the late Preceramic periods were focused more on building a sense of social collectivity through ritual feasting, on the construction of both small-scale and large-scale monuments, and on interaction strategies than on the strategic pursuit of power or prestige through the accumulation of wealth goods. Such shared, distributed, public (corporate?) power systems were probably fueled more by socio-ideational factors than material wealth. Given the nature of the current evidence, we can only guess that this collectivity must have involved different categories of age, gender, descent, occupation, place, rank, and association, often simultaneously. We presently cannot identify any social loci, schism, resistance, and agency or institutional strategies in the archaeological evidence that may have constrained and counterbalanced the political role of elite groups (and less so individuals) and the pursuit of power through the accumulation of wealth goods. At some point in Period VI or the subsequent Initial Period, a critical moment was reached when more emphasis was given to wealth goods and individual leadership, as suggested at Las Haldas, Culebras, Aspero, and other sites.

Several new directions need to be taken so as to advance Preceramic studies. First, we need to use the ecological conditions of production and the resource structures of population distributions to explore the shifting organization and relationships through time of different scales of foragers, horticulturalists, agropastoralists, and pastoro-foragers. The result is a picture of widespread and systematic relationships between what is usually viewed as "separate" coastal, highland, and tropical peoples with separate maritime, agricultural or pastoral economies. In this regard models like ecological complementarity and the maritime hypothesis encourage us to look for development and control by a single economic mode when, in fact, elusive and less conspicuous forms of trade and exchange, economic synchronization and interaction also must have existed to link these various peoples. The shifting connections among these peoples surely have been a long-term feature in the regional dialogue through which ethnic identities were eventually fashioned and transformed into the corporate styles of later polities and state societies. Certain research questions can guide us in the ways these different societies operated in terms of their practical deployment of different material conditions, the way that practice reworked the structured social and economic principles of organization, the way practice and social agency mutually worked to meet historical contingencies (Dobres and Robb 2000), and the way they accessed different sets of material conditions and the mechanism of interaction operating between them. Another research direction should involve household or domestic archaeology, which has been a topic of increased research among archaeologists in later periods, but has received minimal attention as a social unit among Andeanists studying early maritime, pastoral, and agrarian societies. This is unfortunate, because it would help to counter the elite/ceremonial bias that plagues both the Preceramic and Formative Period (Initial Period, Early Horizon) archaeology of the Central Andes. Future work also needs to define better regional chronologies and to excavate larger areas in sites to identify and study activity areas and the internal spatial structure that make up local and regional systems. Above all, we need to identify the archaeological correlates of social identity and practice so as to apply new interpretative models (Preucel and Hodder 1996) before new myths are created about the Andean past that will require future generations of scholars to contemplate and likely reinterpret.

To conclude, all of the topics in this review are in need of more hard data to substantiate them, to ask new questions, and to develop more syntheses and theoretical analyses. Archaeologists working on the Preceramic Period are generally long on data and short on demonstrable explanations, especially from an anthropological viewpoint. Much of the existing data also can be made to yield new insights through systematic comparative analysis. Far too much archaeology in the Andes is carried out following a standardized, descriptive-evolutionary regional approach that is applied to single sites. We argue that a key to a better understanding of the Preceramic Period is to design research focused both on human ecology and on the meaning of culture, acquired – at least in part – socially.

ACKNOWLEDGMENTS

We thank Ricardo Fabio Srur for drafting the figure and table.

3
Cultural Transformations in the Central Andean Late Archaic

Jonathan Haas and Winifred Creamer

Introduction

The period from 3000 to 1800 B.C. was a time of momentous change in the Andean region. Known alternately as the Late Archaic, Cotton Preceramic, Upper Archaic, and Late Preceramic, this was the time of dramatic cultural transformation as people made a transition from nomadic hunting and gathering to settled agricultural villages. This was also the time when the Andean region set off on a developmental path that distinguished it from the rest of South America and eventually led to the much more complex and centralized cultural systems of Andean "high civilization."

This Late Archaic period (Arcaico Tardío as it is most commonly called by Peruvian archaeologists and is, thus, the term adopted here) has long been recognized by archaeologists as an important epoch of change in Andean prehistory. Two salient features of this period are the absence of ceramics and the presence of cotton textiles. Settled villages appear on the coast and in the highlands. Plant domestication is intensified and agriculture becomes a lifeway. Complex forms of social and political organization arise with centralized decision-making and social hierarchies. These cultural changes do not all take place at the same time in all parts of the region and early developments appear to have a significant impact on subsequent developments.

Although separate areas and events will be discussed individually below, it is worthwhile to present a brief précis of the Late Archaic to illustrate how all the parts fit together. At the beginning of the third millennium B.C. the Andean world is largely continuing the pattern of a transhumant hunting and gathering lifeway. On the coast, there are small semi-permanent fishing villages such as Huaca Prieta in the Chicama Valley and La Paloma in the Chilca Valley. The single exception to this pattern is to be found at the site of Aspero in the Norte Chico region of the coast. (The Norte Chico is a group of four valleys, Huaura, Supe, Pativilca, and

Fortaleza situated between what is traditionally referred to as the Central Coast and the North Coast: see inset, Figure 3.1.) In the first centuries of the third millennium B.C. Aspero was a substantial community with a variety of domesticated food crops, cotton and, significantly, communal architecture in the form of platform mounds.

By the middle of the third millennium B.C., while the rest of the Andean region continues in the preceding Archaic pattern, a complex of very large communities develops in the Norte Chico region. In contrast to Aspero, these other sites are all located inland in the valleys, away from the actual coastline. The earliest dates for these inland sites, 2600 to 2500 B.C., come from Caral in the Supe Valley and Vinto Alto in the Pativilca Valley, though a majority of such sites have yet to be dated. Thus far, surveys have located 26 Late Archaic sites in the Norte Chico all lacking ceramics and all with monumental communal architecture. These sites range from 50 to 250 ha in area, and have from one to six platform mounds ranging from 15,000 to over 300,000 m^3 in volume. The Norte Chico Preceramic complex then appears to have a "provocative" effect on other outside areas.

Historically, the first major developments outside the Norte Chico in the latter part of the third millennium B.C., ca. 2300–2000 B.C., occur further south on the coast at the site of El Paraiso (Chuquitanta) in the Chillón Valley and at the highland site of Kotosh. Both of these sites have significant resident populations and communal public architecture. It is no coincidence that these two subsequent manifestations of cultural complexity occur in regions adjacent to the Norte Chico. It appears from the available record that the Norte Chico complex represents the historical origins of complex societies in the Andes in the first half of the third millennium B.C. and that subsequent developments in the second half of the millennium were influenced or provoked by the Norte Chico system. This pattern continues in the first centuries of the second millennium B.C. with the appearance of even larger site complexes at Pampa de las Llamas-Moxeke and Sechin Alto in the Casma Valley, San Jacinto in the Chancay Valley, and Huaca La Florida in the Rimac Valley.

Later Initial Period and Early Horizon developments throughout the Andean region can ultimately all trace a historical line back to the precocious polities of the Norte Chico. Over time the spark of culture change extends further south along the coast to Lurín, then to Paracas and Ica and up into the highlands to Chiripa and Pukara. The northern sphere extends up the coast to the site of Caballo Muerto in the Moche Valley and in the highlands up to Chavín de Huántar. Along these same lines, it is significant to note that two separate pan-Andean religious elements also have their origins in the Norte Chico. One of these is the Staff God or Supreme Being, a central deity that appears widely in Early Horizon contexts and is resurrected in Middle Horizon Wari and Tiwanaku times. An archaic manifestation of the Staff God has recently been found in the Norte Chico and dated to 2250 cal. B.C. The other religious element is the sunken plaza, the earliest examples of which also are found in the Norte Chico centuries before they are manifested as an important religious architectural feature up and down the coast as well as in the highlands from Chavín de Huántar to Pucara in the Titicaca Basin.

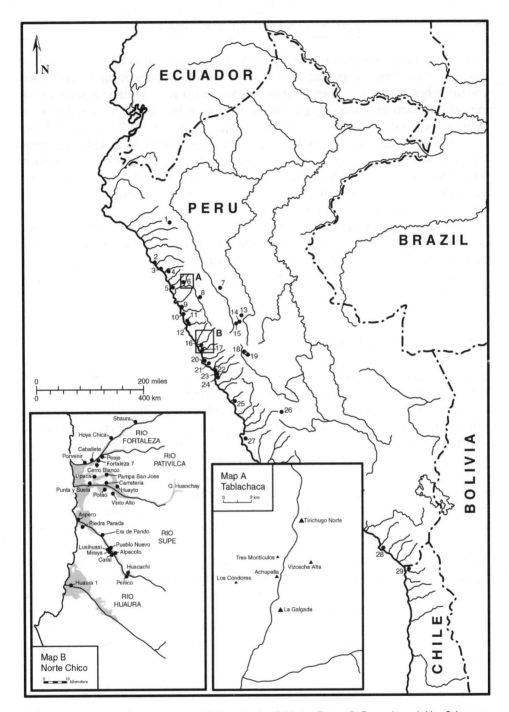

Figure 3.1. Andean Late Archaic sites: 1. Pandanche; 2. Huaca Prieta; 3. Gramalote; 4. Alto Salaverry; 5. Salinas de Chao; 6. La Galgada; 7. Piruru; 8. Huaricoto; 9. Huaynuná; 10. Las Haldas; 11. Los Gavilanes; 12. Culebras; 13. Waira-jirca; 14. Shillacoto; 15. Kotosh; 16. Aspero; 17. Piedra Parada; 18. Ondores; 19. Telarmachay; 20. Bandurria; 21. Rio Seco; 22. Ancón; 23. Ventanilla; 24. El Paraiso; 25. Asia; 26. Quispisisa; 27. Otuma; 28. Ring Site; 29. Azapa. (Map A, Tablachaca, is redrawn from Grieder et al. 1988)

As these surrounding culture areas to the north and south began to flourish at the end of the Late Archaic and the start of the Initial Period, the Norte Chico system dropped from the center stage of Andean prehistory. There were Initial Period and Early Horizon occupations in the region, but they were overshadowed by much larger developments to the east, south, and north. With limited land and water the valleys of the Norte Chico were not as productive as neighboring areas and were not able to compete effectively as irrigation and centralized organization spread outward on a broader landscape. Over the course of the succeeding 4,000 years, the Norte Chico remained as something of a frontier between the north and south Andean spheres of influence.

With this conjectural précis of history and process in the Late Archaic for overall context, it is possible to turn to the available data on Andean prehistory during the Late Archaic. Because highland and coastal occupations were quite different at this time, and the interactions between the two are difficult to define clearly, they will be treated separately.

Late Archaic in the Highlands

There were no panregional Late Archaic patterns shared by all parts of the Andean highlands. Some people held tenaciously to hunting and gathering lifestyles that had dominated the region during the preceding millennia, while others made a transition to full-time settled agricultural villages. Some of these differences are due to environmental variation from one area to another and others are due to differences in the agent-based adaptive strategies – tinkering (see Haas 2001a) – adopted by people in separate areas. Within a context of areal variability, the time from 3000 to 1800 B.C. in general witnessed a number of transformational changes: people came to depend much more heavily on domesticated plants; camelids, used initially for food and subsequently as pack animals and for wool, were fully domesticated; the first instances of centralized decision-making and political hierarchies arose. These changes were broadly interrelated, and ultimately laid the foundation for more than 3,500 years of subsequent cultural evolution in the Andes.

Broad geographic and environmental differences influenced the Late Archaic transitions of prehistoric populations of the highlands. In some areas, the archaic hunting and gathering lifestyle exploited deer as a primary meat source, while in others camelids were the primary meat animal. It was in the latter areas, quite naturally, that camelids came to be domesticated. In high-altitude puna areas, the people spent all or most of their energy on exploiting camelid herds. Excavations in the Junín area of central Peru, for example, have shown that, for most of the Late Archaic period, local people were heavily dependent on local wild camelids (Pires-Ferreira, Pires-Ferreira, and Kaulicke 1976; Rick 1980). During the third millennium B.C. local hunters appear to have reached an equilibrium that allowed them to remain sedentary in a single base camp over the span of multiple generations (Rick 1980:322).

This equilibrium involved selective hunting and culling of local camelid populations (particularly males) in a way that would not negatively impact the reproductive potential of the herd. This kind of selective hunting and herd maintenance is a first step toward domestication. With knowledge about the ecology and productivity of camelid herds, the highland hunters started to bring those herds under cultural control and by the end of the Late Archaic that process was complete (Wing 1978; cf. Aldenderfer 1998; Kuznar 1995; Wheeler 2000). This shift from hunting to herding was also accompanied by a shift in residence as people moved from stable hunting base camps to residential settlements near highland lakes where the diverse lacustrian ecology could be exploited all year (Moseley 2001).

Some mention must also be made of the consumption and domestication of guinea pigs or *cuy* in the Andean highlands. Wild ancestral lines of guinea pigs occur in highland puna areas, and their bones are relatively common in Late Archaic highland sites (Pires-Ferreira and Wheeler 1975; Pires-Ferreira, Pires-Ferreira, and Kaulicke 1976; Valdez 2000; Wheeler 1980; Wheeler, Cardoza, and Pozzi-Escot 1979). These small, tasty rodents would have been significant, adding fat to an otherwise spare diet, as well as providing an alternate protein source. However, the presence of large numbers of guinea pig bones does not translate into anything more than a supplement to the diet. Because the animals are small, they yield little meat but leave behind lots of bones.

In other parts of the highlands the annual round of hunting and gathering groups involved varying degrees of movement between the puna and lower elevation intermontane river valleys. In those areas where the hunters and gatherers were exploiting intermontane river valleys, the Late Archaic was marked by a gradual shift in emphasis from hunting and gathering to increasing reliance on domesticated resources and greater sedentism. As the Andean region stabilized into something close to the current environmental regime at around 3000 B.C., highland people were spending more time in the warmer, moister river valleys and less in the colder uplands where game was prevalent. There is a diverse list of plants that came under cultivation either during or just prior to the Late Archaic.

Archaeologists have recovered diverse samples of botanical remains that illustrate a limited assemblage of early plant domesticates. Part of this may be a reflection of the past reality, but it also may be due to limited research, and poor preservation of plant remains in highland archaeological contexts. Among the early edible plants grown by early highland farmers prior to 1800 B.C. are beans, squash, oca, lucuma, quinoa, tomatoes, aji, potatoes, achira (a fibrous root crop), coca, and possibly maize. There is also evidence for two industrial domesticated crops: cotton and bottle gourds (Pearsall 1992; Pearsall and Piperno 1998).

Unlike some other world areas, archaeologists working in the Andes to date have not tracked the physical domestication of specific plants in time and space (Pearsall 1992; Pearsall and Piperno 1998). Most inferences about the domestication of plants are derived from observations of the natural distribution of wild affines of particular domesticates. Based on these inferences, the domesticated plants found in the Late Archaic originated from a combination of highland locations (e.g., beans, some species of squash) as well as the lower and more tropical environments to the east (e.g., manioc, guava).

The question of when maize was first introduced into the Peruvian Andes has not yet been answered to everyone's satisfaction (R. Bird 1990; Bonavia and Grobman 1989a, 2000). Possible indications of the presence of maize in the highland area have been found in a number of different forms. In the central highlands, analysis of carbon isotopes demonstrated that human skeletal material from the Late Archaic site of Huaricoto is indirectly indicative of the presence of maize in the diet (Burger and van der Merwe 1990). The percentage of carbon probably derived from maize was 18 percent, indicating that maize was part of the diet, but not yet a dominant source of calories for the Late Archaic residents. In other areas, maize kernels have been found in caves in the Ayacucho Valley dating to the time between 4100 and 1750 B.C. Again, these represent a very small portion of the total plant diet (MacNeish et al. 1980; Pearsall 1992). In the northern Andes of Ecuador, cores taken from Lake Ayauchi contained maize phytoliths and pollen dating to as early as 3300 B.C. (Piperno 1990, 1993). All of these data are suggestive, but not absolutely convincing for the presence of maize in the highlands during the Late Archaic. What they do illustrate is that maize was clearly not playing the central dietary role it came to play in subsequent millennia.

The assemblages of plants at individual sites indicates that the Late Archaic people were moving toward full-fledged agriculture and pastoralism, but had not yet converged on a common, robust, balanced diet of domesticated plants and animals. There was also no single, dominant starchy food, such as potatoes or maize, that is characteristic of later cultures. The pattern as a whole is one of people who are still very much in transition from hunting and gathering to settled village agriculture or to stable herding.

In terms of social organization the Late Archaic in the highlands is again a period of transition. Over most of the highlands and for most of the period between 3000 and 1800 B.C., social relations are relatively egalitarian, community-focused, and decentralized. Against this broad backdrop, the appearance of a small number of large ceremonial centers with communal architecture stands out as a major societal turning point. How many of these Preceramic centers there may be in the highlands is unknown. The ones that are known about are all located in a fairly narrow band between 8°S and 11°S latitude in the north-central highlands. Because of their monumental architecture, these sites are not hard to locate. While there are most probably more of these early highland centers unrecorded/unpublished, it is unlikely that they were a common feature of the highland landscape outside this relatively narrow zone (see Terada 1985).

Three of these Late Archaic centers have been subjected to extensive excavation: Kotosh, Huaricoto, and La Galgada. Kotosh is situated near the modern town of Huanuco along the Higueras River, due east of the Fortaleza Valley on the coast. The site consists of two mounds that eventually reached a height of 8 m. This represents more than a thousand years of occupation, accretion, and rebuilding. The Late Archaic portions of the site, referred to as the "Mito phase," are at the bottom of these mounds. Communal constructions dating to the third millennium B.C.

consist of "temples" or quadrangular rooms 3–6 m across with thick side walls 2 m or more in height. These rooms share common characteristics, including finely plastered floors and walls, wall niches, a central sunken hearth, a ventilator, and a bench area for seating (Izumi and Terada 1972). At least some of these temples were built one on top of the other, suggesting ritual interment and symbolic renovation. Based on the number of structures excavated at the site and the portion of the site still unexcavated, it has been estimated that there could have been as many as 100 temples built at Kotosh during the Late Archaic occupation (Burger and Salazar-Burger 1986:70). A second large mound complex, Shillacoto, is located approximately 5 km east of Kotosh. Modern construction in the area prevents extensive excavation, but testing revealed two temple structures in a Preceramic context. Waira-Jirca, 30 km east of Kotosh, is smaller than Kotosh and Shillacoto, but also has Mito phase ceremonial structures (Bonnier 1997; Burger 1992; Izumi 1971; Izumi, Cuculiza, and Kano 1972; Onuki 2000).

At Huaricoto, located about 200 km to the northwest in the Callejon de Huaylas, thick layers of overburden prevented extensive excavation of the Late Archaic portions of the site. In the relatively small exposed areas where these earlier deposits were encountered, there were ceremonial hearths very similar to those found at Kotosh, but without signs of the enclosing walled rooms (Burger and Salazar-Burger 1980, 1985). These early features were deep in the mound and were not associated with large-scale construction at the site.

The site of La Galgada is situated at an elevation of 1,100 m in the valley of the Tablachaca River, a tributary of the Santa River. Its location places it in something of a transitional zone between the highlands and the coast. Unlike the other Late Archaic highland sites, La Galgada is in a very dry desert environment with low annual precipitation and sparse, drought-adapted natural vegetation (Grieder et al. 1988). It is important to note that La Galgada was one of 11 Preceramic sites recorded in a stretch of only 20 km along the river (Bueno and Grieder 1988).

La Galgada was extensively excavated. It is similar to Kotosh in having a superimposed series of quadrangular temple structures built one on top of the other. In this case, however, all of the structures appear to have been constructed on top of a large, terraced platform mound (Grieder and Bueno 1988). The main mound is approximately 40 m in diameter at the base, and while the total height of the mound is not reported, the excavated Preceramic features were built on top of at least 13 m of fill. The temple rooms at La Galgada are similar to those found at Kotosh in being roughly quadrangular (most have rounder corners than those at Kotosh), with thick walls 2–4 m high, wall niches, a central hearth, ventilator, and a bench going around the inside wall. Another interesting feature of the architecture at La Galgada is the presence of a walled circular plaza directly in front of the main mound. A staircase connected this circular plaza with the structures on top of the mound.

Because of the similarity and wide distribution of the Late Archaic temple form of architecture in the north-central highland rooms, it has been referred to as the Kotosh Religious Tradition (Burger and Salazar-Burger 1980). In using this descriptive term, it is important to recognize that there are no indications that the site of Kotosh was either the earliest site to manifest this ceremonial complex, nor that it was somehow a pan-regional center or "capitol" of this religious tradition. Rather, the widespread distribution of a common architectural feature in this area indicates quite clearly that there were indeed shared religious beliefs that integrated these highland communities in some kind of complex ideological system of communication and interaction. As yet, the nature of this communication and interaction has not been clearly defined, but, as we describe below, the highland system appears to be related to a similar emergent religious system on the coast at just about the same time.

In addition to marking the presence of a regional religious tradition, the temples and mounds at Kotosh and La Galgada also mark the first appearance in the highlands of centralized decision-making (see Onuki 2000). The concentration of large, non-residential temples at Kotosh coupled with the amount of labor involved in their construction is indicative of centralized organization and labor organization. This pattern is even more apparent in the Tablachaca Valley. La Galgada has significantly larger communal architecture than other roughly contemporaneous sites in the immediate vicinity. The large size of the main mound itself further indicates centralized organization of corporate labor. In both of these highland sites, it seems clear that some people were implementing the decisions of others. In terms of power, there were power holders within each of the communities who exercised a measure of power over a respondent population and these respondents recognized the authority of the power holders and implemented their decisions.

This development of a new kind of social relationship marks a major transformation in the trajectory of Andean cultural development (Haas 2001a). It is in trying to explain this transformation that archaeologists encounter some difficulty. The relatively small number of sites excavated, the lack of comprehensive surveys, and the problems inherent in dating these early sites make it difficult to describe in detail the sequence of cultural change and to explain why these particular Late Archaic societies in the north-central highlands took off on this new trajectory. The strong ceremonial/religious focus of the sites would indicate that ideological knowledge and probably access to the supernatural were key to the power bases of the leaders. The likelihood that irrigation agriculture was practiced at La Galgada also indicates that the local leaders could have had control over economic resources as part of their power base as well (Grieder et al. 1988).

There are also newly emerging data from the Andean coast that may indicate that cultural transformation in the north-central highlands was intimately related to a very similar transformation going on along the north-central coast at precisely the same time.

Late Archaic on the Coast

In some ways, the Andean coast is less complex than the highlands, as there is less environmental variability. Each coastal valley is similar to neighboring valleys: there is the ocean on the west, the coastline itself, the typically east–west running river valley watered by runoff from the mountains to the east, and desert on the north and south sides. In other ways, the apparent similarities can be deceptive. The water flow in each valley is different, as is the amount of arable land. Each valley has its unique topography, which has implications for irrigation, uses of ground water, defense, and settlement pattern. There are also general differences as you move north to south from one end of the chain of valleys to the other. Generally, the northernmost valleys on the north coast are bigger with more arable land. As you move further south, the valleys get smaller with less arable land. (This pattern is not absolute as there are exceptions.) The northern valleys are also subject to more frequent El Niño events than those further to the south (Billman 2001). These differences do not seem to be significant in the early occupations of the coast, but they begin to have an impact during the Late Archaic.

The first half of the third millennium B.C. has long been recognized as a time of transition and change on the Andean coast (Burger 1992; Fung 1988; Lanning 1967; Richardson 1973, 1992). During this time, there is some evidence of an environmental shift with the onset of El Niño events, along with the emergence of the current weather regime and approximate sea level (Sandweiss et al. 1996; cf. Wells 1987). There is some dispute as to whether there was a general drying up of lomas zones (cf. Craig and Psuty 1968; Lanning 1967). The nature and extent of environmental change on the coast has generally not been well documented. The evidence is spotty, coming from a small number of locations. There has been no broad attempt to gather multiple sources of environmental data from a mix of valleys on the north, central, and south coasts. As a result, it is presently not possible to document how the environment may have changed. The clearest indication of such change is manifested in shifts in settlement pattern and economic strategies suggesting that coastal populations responded to environmental dynamics at the end of the fourth millennium and beginning of the third millennium B.C.

The most widespread change taking place at this time is the appearance of stable, sedentary communities within the littoral zone of the coastal plain. Commonly found at the valley mouths where the rivers empty into the Pacific Ocean, at least one of these early maritime communities has been found in almost every valley along the coast. At least some data are available for numerous sites along the coast, including (from north to south) Huaca Prieta, Alto Salaverry, Las Salinas de Chao, Huaynuná, Culebras, Los Gavilanes, Bermejo, Aspero, Bandurria, Rio Seco, Ancón, Ventanilla, El Paraiso, La Paloma, Chilca 1, Asia, Ring Site, and different Chinchorro sites on the north coast of Chile. While this is not a complete list, it illustrates that there is a broad database for understanding coastal maritime lifestyles during the Late Archaic.

Subsistence at these sites is strongly oriented toward the ocean, with emphases on fishing, shellfish-gathering, and hunting marine mammals. The relative importance of these different maritime components varies from site to site depending on locally available resources. Analysis of human remains from the Chinchorro area in Chile shows that almost 90 percent of the diet consisted of fish, shellfish, marine mammals, and seaweed (Arriaza 1995:84). This extremely high dependence on marine resources would appear not to be representative of coastal residents further north. Where data are available for sites along the Peruvian portion of the coast, they show a highly eclectic combination of marine resources and cultivated crops. As we saw in the highlands, so, too, on the coast the range of edible plant domesticates lacks evidence of any dominant grain or starch of any kind (Feldman 1980; Quilter et al. 1991; Shady 1999). The identified edible plants from the Late Archaic period are: amaranth (*Amaranthus* sp.), achira (*Canna edulis*), three varieties of squash (*Curcurbita ficifolia, Curcurbita maxima, Curcurbita moschata*), sedge (*Cyperus* sp.), pacae (*Inga feuillei*), jicama (*Pachyrrhizus tuberosus*), Lima bean (*Phaseolus lunatus*), common bean (*Phaseolus vulgaris*), jack bean (*Canavalia* sp.), guava (*Psidium guajava*), lucuma (*Lucuma bifera*), chile/ají (*Capsicum* sp.), tomatillo (*Physalis* sp.), potato (*Solanum tuberosum*), cat-tail (*Typha angustifolia*), maize (*Zea mays*), oca (*Oxalis tuberosa*), ullucu (*Ullucus tuberosus*), sweet potato (*Ipomoea batatas*), peanut (*Arachis hypogaea*), avocado/palta (*Persea americana*), and chirimoya (*Annona cherimolia*). Not all of these plants are native to the coast and all are dependent on cultivation in the dry desert environment.

No single site has all of these food plants, but each site has a liberal mix of species. To date, there has not been an in-depth analysis of plant remains at any given site to indicate the relative importance of specific plants within the dietary regimen. The overall impression one gets from looking at the list is that the coastal peoples were "tinkering" with a wide variety of plants in an effort to achieve a balanced diet and adequate calories (Haas 2001a).

As in the highlands, there are questions about when maize appears on the coast. (Bonavia and Grobman 2000) have recently reviewed the evidence for the presence of maize in the Late Archaic throughout the Andes. Their conclusion is that maize is indeed present at least in small quantities. In coastal Ecuador, at the site of La Emerenciana (Tykot and Staller 2002) there is isotopic and phytolith evidence of maize by the end of the third millennium B.C. A growing body of evidence indicates that there was at least some maize being grown on the Pacific coast during the Late Archaic; however, it is equally clear that maize was never a primary source of calories in the diet during this time.

There are two additional domesticated plants in the botanical assemblage of the coast: cotton (*Gossypium barbadense*) and bottle gourd (*Lagenaria siceraria*). While not directly used as comestibles, both are elements critical to the coastal adaptation. Although the faunal portion of the diet of coastal peoples is a mix of fish, shellfish, and sea mammals, anchovies (*Engraulis rigens*) and sardines (*Sardinop sagax*) make up the primary protein source. Larger fish can be caught by angling, shellfish can be directly gathered by hand, and sea mammals can be hunted and trapped. But how to catch/harvest anchovies and sardines? These species can best be caught with nets, and on the Pacific coast during the Late Archaic there is abundant evidence of cotton used to make the nets and bottle gourds used as floats for the nets.

The overall picture of the coastal occupation, until recently, was one of maritime fishing folk who practiced auxiliary and highly diverse agriculture, probably on floodplain lands at the mouths of rivers. It was within this context that Michael Moseley (1975a, 2001) developed a "maritime hypothesis" to explain the development of centralized, complex society on the coast. Moseley was one of the first to recognize the precocious nature of cultural development on the Peruvian coast. He pointed out that there were a number of large maritime-based sites up and down the coast that dated to the third millennium or even before. He also was one of the first to highlight the fact that a number of these sites, such as Aspero in the Supe Valley and El Paraiso in the Chillón Valley had large communal architecture yet lacked ceramics in their cultural assemblages. This lack of ceramics would indicate that the sites antedated the introduction of ceramics in Peru at around 1800 B.C. Moseley went on to argue that maritime-dependent subsistence required central-ized coordination for the production, procurement, and distribution of resources. This centralization, in turn, "preadapted" these cultural groups to the subsequent development of even more complex, hierarchical and centralized forms of organi-zation based on irrigation agriculture.

The site of Aspero at the mouth of the Supe Valley is an important linchpin in any discussion of cultural development on the coast (Feldman 1980, 1987). Aspero, at 15 ha, is a fairly large site for the time period, and is distinguished by the pres-ence of six platform mound structures. The largest of these mounds is 4 m high and covers an area of 40 × 40 m. The other five measurable mounds are all smaller. As at La Galgada and Kotosh, architecture on top of the mounds has been interpreted as ceremonial. As in the highland sites, communal architecture is the physical man-ifestation of some degree of social hierarchy and political centralization/centralized decision-making. Radiocarbon dates taken from structures on top of the mounds extend back to at least 3000 B.C. and perhaps much earlier (see below). The suite of dates obtained from Aspero indicates that large communal structures were being built centuries before other known sites anywhere in the Andean region.

The Norte Chico

Recent work in the Norte Chico region is leading to a rethinking of the economic and social dynamics of the coast. As indicated above, the Norte Chico is a cluster of four valleys, Huaura, Supe (where Aspero is located), Pativilca, and Fortaleza (inset, Figure 3.1). These valleys often fall outside of the traditional coastal divi-sions: "North," "Central," and "South" (see Lanning 1967:31; Moseley 2001:22) – thus, the designation Norte Chico or "Little North." Since at least the 1940s, archaeologists have been aware of large sites lacking ceramics in the area (Kosok 1965; Shady 1997; Williams León 1985; Williams and Merino 1979). More recent work by Ruth Shady and her team from San Marcos University in the Supe Valley and specifically at the site of Caral begins to place these inland sites in a broader picture.

Caral is a large urban/ceremonial center 23 km inland in the Supe Valley. The site covers approximately 110 ha of contiguously occupied land including the main ceremonial and residential center and the adjacent mound/plaza complex referred to as Chupacigarro. The center of the site is dominated by six large platform mounds, two sunken circular plazas, numerous smaller platform mounds, an array of residential architecture, and various complexes of platforms and buildings (Shady, Haas, and Creamer 2001). The largest of the platform mounds, the

Piramide Mayor, measures 160×150 m and is 18 m high, while the smallest of the six is 10 m high and covers an area of 65×45 m. As with the coastal sites, all the faunal remains at the site come from marine resources, mainly sardines and anchovies, and the botanical remains are an eclectic mix of fruits, vegetables, and tubers (Shady 1999).

In addition to Caral, there are eight other major Late Archaic sites (not including Aspero) in the Supe Valley (Williams and Merino 1979). All of these sites are marked by monumental platform mounds, sunken circular plazas (with a single exception), secondary platforms, and large areas of residential architecture. Interestingly, there does not seem to be a consistent pattern in the layout of these sites. Caral, for example, has a ring of platform mounds around an open plaza; Miraya (2 km downriver) has a solid block of mixed mound and architecture; Era de Pando (8 km further downriver), has two widely separate main mounds, no plaza, scattered architecture, and a huge expanse of what appears to be temporary domestic architecture.

Supplementing this work in Supe, recent surveys in Pativilca and Fortaleza (Haas, Creamer, and Ruiz 2002; Ruiz, Haas, and Creamer 2003; Vega-Centeno et al. 1998) have located at least 15 major Preceramic sites with monumental architecture, sunken circular plazas, and associated architectural and residential complexes. Two Preceramic cemeteries have also been located. Early results from testing of the sites in the Pativilca Valley show that all of the architectural sites as well as the two cemeteries date to the period between 2600 and 2000 B.C. As in the Supe Valley, there is little patterning in the layout of these sites, though there are some similarities in having the main mounds and circular plazas facing out into a large open area that may have served as a public gathering place.

The complex of sites in the Norte Chico region is nothing short of extraordinary on the Late Archaic Andean landscape. While a very small number of contemporary sites with communal architecture, such as Kotosh or La Galgada, are present in other parts of the Andes, the concentration of at least 25 large ceremonial/residential sites in the valleys of the Norte Chico is unique. Metaphorically, most of the Andes is covered with granules of sand during the Late Archaic. In a few spots, there are anthills that clearly stand out from the loose granules. Then in the Norte Chico, there is a volcano.

The presence of this explosive early development along one short stretch of the Pacific coast requires some rethinking of developments outside the Norte Chico and subsequently throughout the Andes. There are two areas where the Norte Chico cultural complex appears to have played a formative role in the Andes: *political centralization* and the beginnings of a *fundamental Andean religion*.

Looking at the origins of political centralization and centralized decision-making takes us back to the place of Aspero in the broader picture. As noted above, Moseley used Aspero to support the theory that political centralization arose to facilitate the production, procurement, and distribution of resources in a maritime environment. The new dates from inland Supe sites, however, now show that Aspero was not alone in its precocious development. If dates are put aside just for the moment (see below for a fuller discussion), Aspero appears to have been part of a broader eco-

nomic system involving irrigation agriculture as well as fishing and shellfish collecting (Haas and Creamer 2001). Limited excavations at Aspero demonstrate that
cultivated crops, including cotton, gourds and comestibles, are found in even the
earliest deposits (Feldman 1980). But the land immediately around Aspero is all
salt marsh, and could not have been used for growing any of these crops. The only
arable land near the site is a small parcel of several hectares in size, fed today by a
kilometers-long canal. A preponderance of the available evidence indicates that
Aspero was getting its plant resources from inland agricultural sites, and the latter,
in turn, were getting their primary protein source – anchovies – from Aspero and
perhaps other coastal sites.

A symbiotic relationship between coastal maritime communities and inland
farming communities requires a reconsideration of the emergence of centralization
and social hierarchies. The nature of the relationship between the different parts of
the Norte Chico economic system is not clear. However, the fact that there are 25
inland sites, all with significantly larger monumental architecture than the small
mounds found at Aspero, indicates that leaders at the inland farming communities
were exercising substantially greater power than any leaders who may have resided
at Aspero. It is also important to note that, at Caral, excavations have revealed clear
status differences in architecture (Shady 1997, 2000; Shady, Haas, and Creamer
2001). Analogous architectural patterns are found at most of the other inland Late
Archaic sites in the Norte Chico, but are not apparent at Aspero. This regional
Norte Chico pattern indicates that the control over the production and distribution of agricultural resources played an instrumental role in the emergence of
leadership. Further research will be needed to better understand how leaders
came to exercise power in the Norte Chico system and the complex economic
interaction between the interior agricultural communities and the coastal maritime
communities.

A second area where the Norte Chico appears to play a precocious role in
Andean prehistory is in the beginnings of an identifiable Andean religion. There are
two religious elements found in the Norte Chico that appear to be antecedents to
subsequent pan-Andean patterns: ceremonial architecture and one of the principal
Andean deities. The first is the ceremonial structure referred to as the "sunken circular plaza" (Fung 1988; Williams León 1972, 1985). These structures occur in a
number of valleys outside the Norte Chico during the Late Archaic, but a concentration of more than 40 of these structures has been found in the valleys of Supe,
Pativilca, and Fortaleza. There is a circular plaza in front of the platform mound at
La Galgada and other early examples have been reported in the highlands as well
(Williams León 1985). The earliest firm date for a sunken circular plaza anywhere
in the Andes comes from an upper floor on one of the three sunken circular plazas
at Caral, with a calibrated radiocarbon date of 2450 B.C.

In terms of the trajectory of Andean prehistory, what is significant about the
initial appearance of sunken circular plazas is that they then radiate out from the
Norte Chico, both up and down the coast and into the highlands in subsequent
time periods. The Initial Period site of Sechin Alto in the Casma Valley (Moseley
2001), for example, has at least two of these structures, and there are three at the

Figure 3.2. Drawing of early Staff God image on gourd from the Pativilca Valley, 2230 B.C. (drawing by Jill Seagard)

site of Cardal in the Lurín Valley (Burger and Salazar-Burger 1991). There are square sunken plazas somewhat later at the site of Huaca de los Reyes even further north in the Moche Valley. In the north central highlands at the Early Horizon center of Chavín de Huántar, there is a sunken circular plaza remarkably similar to those found in the Norte Chico as well as a rectangular sunken plaza (Burger 1992; Lumbreras 1970). Further south in the highlands, sunken circular and rectangular plazas are found in the Formative sites of Chiripa and Pukara in the Titicaca Basin (K. Chávez 1988; Stanish 2001). Thus, an architectural tradition that appears first in the Late Archaic Norte Chico comes to be adopted and adapted by a far-flung array of later societies throughout the Andes and seems to play at least some role in the beginnings of formative Andean religious traditions.

A second line of evidence for the formative role of Norte Chico religion in the Andes comes from the recent discovery of two incised gourd fragments in the Pativilca Valley. One of the gourd figures depicts an individual in full frontal posi-tion with a fanged mouth, splayed, clawed feet, and holding some kind of staff or rod (Haas, Creamer, and Ruiz 2003; see also Figure 3.2). A radiocarbon sample taken from this first gourd yielded a calibrated AMS date of 2250 B.C. The second figure is very similar, but in the recovered portion no staff is apparent. Although simple in form, these two figures have the hallmarks of the Staff God that would come to play a central role in Early Horizon Chavín art, and take various forms in later traditions throughout the Andes: it eventually is fully resurrected as the pre-eminent Staff God of Middle Horizon Wari and Tiwanaku Empires (see Cook 1983), and evolves into Wiraqocha, the Creator deity of the Inca (Demarest 1981).

Whether or not a convincing link can eventually be established between the two Pativilca gourd figures and later Andean deities, the gourds offer tantalizing insights into the Late Archaic origins and subsequent development of a common religious iconography lasting millennia in the Andes. A fanged figure is clearly a super-natural being, and the presence of two very similar drawings from two different sites indicates that this is not a fluke, but a more broadly recognized and identifiable entity. Taken together with the sunken circular plaza, the iconographic figures indicate that at least the seeds of a core Andean religion began on the Peruvian coast in the Late Archaic.

Chronology

It is important to consider the state of absolute dating for the Late Archaic period (see Pozorski and Pozorski 1990; Quilter 1991; Rick 1987). Although method-ologically not very interesting, the high cost of having radiocarbon samples ana-lyzed has resulted in a relatively small number of dates for Late Archaic sites. The most dates for a single Late Archaic occupation comes from Caral with 18 (Shady, Haas, and Creamer 2001) followed by El Paraiso with 13 (Late Archaic dates only) (Quilter 1985), Aspero (Feldman 1980) and La Galgada (Grieder et al. 1988) with seven each. Others have fewer than five dates (Burger 1992). These dates are ade-quate for generally placing the sites in a broad chronological framework, but they are inadequate for assessing actual chronological relationships between sites and occupations.

Another problem with radiocarbon dates concerns accuracy. While seemingly precise dates are often cited in the literature (and have been so cited in this chapter), radiocarbon dating does not yield absolute dates with precision. Radiocarbon analy-sis yields a "B.P." or "Before Present" date (present being by convention 1950). This B.P. date is accompanied by a +/- figure indicating a date range for the sample. Thus, a date of 3900 +/- 75 B.P. would mean that the context providing the radio-carbon sample most likely fell between 3,975 and 3,825 years before present. But even this date is misleading, because radiocarbon dates need to be both "corrected" and "calibrated" due to differences in the kind of material analyzed and because of long-term fluctuations in the decay rate of radioactive Carbon 14 (see, e.g., Bowman 1990, 1994; Taylor, Long, and Kra 1992). Thus, radiocarbon measure-ments are not exact.

Until many more and better dates are available for a range of highland and coastal sites, it is not going to be possible to securely reconstruct the sequence of historical developments in the Andean Late Archaic. The chronological relationship between the emergent developments in the Norte Chico, Kotosh and surroundings, and La Galgada and surroundings cannot be determined based on available data. Likewise, the relationship between Aspero and the inland valley sites in the Norte Chico remains cloudy, as does that between El Paraiso and the Norte Chico sites. We basically cannot answer certain critical questions today. Was a complex maritime adaptation on the coast antecedent to the emergence of an irrigation-based agricultural society inland? Did the practice of erecting large ceremonial platform mounds arise independently in the Tablachaca Valley, Norte Chico, and the Chillón Valley (the location of El Paraiso)? Or did the practice originate in one of these areas and spread to the others? Is the Kotosh Religious Tradition of the highlands independent of the emergent coastal religious traditions? Answers to these questions are vital if we are to arrive at a basic understanding of the origins and initial stages of development of complex organization, power relationships, centralized decision-making, stratification, hierarchies, and heterarchies in the Andes.

Conclusions

The Andean Late Archaic is a period which will benefit greatly from targeted future survey, excavation, and dating. At the same time, a rich body of data is available with which to begin crafting a complex and provocative picture of cultural dynamics and innovation. In this chapter we have not engaged the question of whether any of the Late Archaic polities were organized as "chiefdoms" or "states." While these evolutionary categories remain useful analytical tools (Haas 2001b), they can distract from a focus on history and process (see Stanish 2001 for a good summary of recent considerations of the evolution of political organization in the Andes). Regardless of the labels used to categorize the societies, we can see that the centuries between 3000 to 1800 B.C. were a time of major transformation in Andean prehistory. The Late Archaic lays the foundation for a distinctly Andean tradition that coalesces and fluoresces in the succeeding Initial Period and Early Horizon. The cultural roots put down early on the Peruvian coast during the Late Archaic also lead to a better understanding of the multiple branches of Andean civilization that grow in different directions to the north and south, in the highlands and on the coast.

4

Building Authority at Chavín de Huántar: Models of Social Organization and Development in the Initial Period and Early Horizon

Silvia Rodriguez Kembel and
John W. Rick

Introduction

Turning to the archaeological record of the Initial Period (IP) and Early Horizon (EH), most Andean archaeologists would note two widespread conditions that become full-blown during these periods: regionally ubiquitous designs of monumental, probably religious architecture, and an associated art icon palette with strong commonalities in content, style, and material. Regarding the human organizations that were responsible for these patterns, however, the picture loses clarity. At the most general level, various scholars have referenced the concept of "civilization," putting its origins in these periods. Their definitions of civilization rotate primarily around the physical evidence – established and well-developed art and architecture, resulting from processes of specialization and labor control (Burger 1992:9; Lumbreras 1974c:61; Tello 1942:88). This perspective, however, leaves in question the nature and development of the underlying complex social organizations.

These periods establish material elements that were to last in the Andes, and thus are an important intermediate prior to the historically known Inca state and its immediate state-like ancestors. The alternative term "formative" for these periods more descriptively defines this intermediacy, but begs the question of whether the earlier organizations were simply less developed versions of the later states, or were qualitatively different in their central principles.

Clearly the IP/EH witnessed a transition to a society with significant wealth and power differences between those emerging to positions of control in the primary monumental centers, and the remaining population in and around these places. These elite individuals doubtless were involved in underwriting and directing the creation of the art and architecture we know from the period, but this in itself pre-supposes they had a mandate, justification, or controlling ability to do so. Unless we believe in a "bottom-up" directorship of early leaders by a commoner popula-tion, the change toward directed societies must at least partially involve self-interest strategies employed by those becoming elite. The central problem takes the focus, then, of how some individuals can convince the remainder of the group to accept and fund their decisions and plans. This likely is a long process, and con-tinues even today. Prior to the IP/EH a widespread, pronounced, and consolidated condition of established authority was absent in the Central Andes, but by the end of this time, there was rapid development toward highly politically differentiated and institutionally centralized systems. The emergence of authority in these time periods is thus our central focus in this chapter.

Generalizing about early authority in the Andean area for this long period of approximately 1,600 years is made difficult by the variation in the societies that existed across regions and between and around emerging centers. Relatively few sites are well enough known to build generalities. As an example of an early mon-umental center, we will therefore concentrate on the site of Chavín de Huántar, where we have been conducting investigations since 1994. We will make reference to the organizational developments not only between authorities and their local pop-ulations, but also between center-based authorities and distant populations as well as between peer centers. Specific authorities clearly interacted in what can be loosely described as an interaction sphere, which itself was highly involved with the broad similarities between architecture, art, and other aspects of these early periods.

The Archaeological Record of the Initial Period and Early Horizon

To address models of emerging authority in the IP/EH in the northern Central Andes, an understanding of the larger social contexts of this development is nec-essary. Comparisons of architecture, material culture, depictions, settlement patterns, and subsistence systems from the archaeological record highlight com-monalities of social development that occurred across environmentally diverse regions. Within these commonalities, local diversity emphasizes the dynamic quality of the development of increasing social complexity in the Andes during these time periods.

The IP and EH span 1800–900 B.C. and 900–200 B.C., respectively. While these two periods are defined and delimited chronologically, continuities connect devel-opments between them and link them with traditions originating in the Preceramic Period. Broadly speaking, the IP is the time in which ceramics first appear and in which agricultural production increasingly impacts people's way of life. Along with agricultural intensification, other major trends of the IP that also required much input of labor and planning, such as the proliferation of monumental architecture and the creation of highly developed art styles, had their roots in the Preceramic (see Chapter 3, this volume) and continued into the Early Horizon. During the Early Horizon, these diverse developments became increasingly linked through intensified regional trade and interactions. Innovations in metallurgical and other technologies that emerged in the IP were further developed in the EH.

During the IP, the incorporation of irrigation technology enabled people to expand the area in which crops could be grown. Canals channeled water from riverbeds into adjacent lands, transforming production capabilities of highland valleys as well as coastal deserts. With irrigation, the intensification of food crops – such as tubers, squash, legumes, and, in the highlands, maize – as well as industrial crops – such as cotton and gourds – complemented continued use of maritime resources on the coast and the domestication of camelids in the highlands. The accompanying initial appearance of ceramics facilitated the processing and storing of food. Other technological developments characterize the period as well: the use of cotton and highland camelid wool fibers increased production of products such as nets and textiles, while the first evidence of metallurgical technology appeared (Burger and Gordon 1998). Increased population growth accompanied these developments, both resulting from and further facilitating their continued elaboration. This growth occurred within numerous, widespread communities. Dispersed populations living in small villages, hamlets, and probably homesteads surrounded centers with varying degrees of monumentality in the highland and coastal valleys. In the highland valleys, both population and smaller monumental centers were more dispersed than on the coast, while in the high-altitude puna grasslands monumental centers seem to have been absent.

Construction of monumental architecture drastically increased in the IP, fostered by the multitude of communities resulting from increased agricultural yields and population growth. Architectural growth frequently continued over centuries of continuous occupation of surrounding communities. Forms that originated in the Preceramic Period continued through the IP, including the buildings of the Kotosh Religious Tradition in the highlands (Burger and Salazar-Burger 1985), and the U-shaped temple, the sunken circular plaza, and the stepped platform primarily in the coastal regions (Williams León 1985). In the highlands, the Kotosh forms continued from Preceramic constructions at sites such as Kotosh (Izumi and Sono 1963; Izumi and Terada 1972), La Galgada (Grieder et al. 1988), and Huaricoto (Burger and Salazar-Burger 1985). Other significant highland sites such as Pacopampa (Morales 1998; Rosas and Shady 1974), Huacaloma (Seki 1998; Terada and Onuki 1982) and Kuntur Wasi (Inokuchi 1998) grew significantly during this period as well, and some highland sites began to incorporate coastal architectural forms. On the coast, the U-shaped temple saw some of the grandest development, with expansion into huge complexes usually facing inland, toward the sources of rivers feeding agricultural production (Williams León 1980, 1985). Some of the many important coastal IP sites include San Jacinto (Carrión 1998), Huaca de Los Reyes (Conklin 1985; Pozorski 1980), Garagay (Ravines and Isbell 1976), Cardal (Burger 1992), Mina Perdida (Burger and Gordon 1998), Cerro Sechin (Samaniego, Vergara, and Bischof 1985), and Sechin Alto, Las Haldas, and Pampa de los Llamas-Moxeke (Pozorski and Pozorski 1987).

Many of these and other IP sites continued into the EH, along with similar settlement patterns, architectural forms, and art frequently containing images of entities with feline, serpent, avian, and anthropomorphic characteristics. Interactions between sites increased, with evidence for farther-reaching trade and sourcing of material goods between coastal and highland regions. An increased refinement of craft products such as ceramics, shell objects, mirrors, and textiles occurred, including elaborate metallurgical items such as gold burial masks from Kuntur Wasi and Chavín-style ornaments, suggesting an elite presence. Many coastal sites had declined by the middle of the first millennium B.C. (Burger 1981), and recent work has suggested a correlation of this decline with an increase in frequency and intensity of El Niño events (Sandweiss et al. 2001).

The investments in irrigation agriculture, monumental architecture, well-developed public art styles, trade relationships, and increasingly refined material objects during the IP/EH all suggest that large groups of people contributed to their development, and that smaller groups of individuals likely controlled the underlying processes to some extent. Clearly these patterns indicate that the IP/EH were periods of profound social development. The following discussion addresses some of the similarities between social groups of these periods, factors that affect emerging authority, and models that clarify the types of changes that might have occurred in social organization during these time periods.

Models of Social Organization in the Initial Period and Early Horizon

Before turning to specific data on the site of Chavín de Huántar, one of the key centers of this time period, it is worthwhile to clarify the social phenomena to be explored and explained. The material record of this time, summarized above, indicates commonalities in subsistence patterns, settlement patterns, architecture, objects, and images between highland and coastal valleys, along with the labor- and design-intensive nature of these characteristics. We have preliminary evidence to suppose that a number of locally evolving social and political systems were linked together by some sort of interaction, but we are left with a broad range of reconstructions that could account for these observations.

To build models of the types of organizations that might have produced this record it is helpful to take a first step away from the simple material record toward an inferred condition of the past – what are the likely fundamental dimensions of these societies? The following are logical and generally accepted features of the record.

First, the period's organizations were relatively *long-lasting and stable* in the sense that across time and space we see development of, but not radical change within or difference between, the emerging societies. Overall, this period may be as much as 1,600 years long – nearly as long as the time corresponding to all the later precolumbian societies in Peru. Thus, there is ample time for a tradition of early authority to have developed.

Second, the organizations appear to have a substantially *theocratic* nature: that is, the essence of the monumentality and spectacularly crafted material items appears to be religious, in the broad sense of the term. The architecture, art, and objects appear imbued with form and content that are highly structured as ritual settings and materials, carrying messages relating humans to a world of greater, natural powers. Human status appears intrinsically connected to these symbols of power, and we can guess that the monuments are contexts in which such status is encountered, negotiated, or conferred. Military paraphernalia and outcomes are notably less common in depictions than in the immediately succeeding Moche (see Chapter 6, this volume) and Nasca cultures of the Early Intermediate Period.

Third, at the same time, the monumental architecture and highly developed craft products imply the *presence of an authority structure* capable of designing, procuring resources, and organizing the production and construction of such endeavors. This authority and its products may have been funded by, but were not merely the result of communal efforts of, local populations; the impressive, highly messaged nature of the material culture seems intent on depiction of power-holding, and not merely the sum of collective efforts. The limited distribution of the monumental architecture and messaged materials implies that such authority was concentrated in centers. At the same time, we would qualify these as the products of an authoritative, rather than authoritarian, system: aspects of the system are of and for authority itself, but the authority does not appear to be pervasive or terribly widespread, or to have consolidated power.

Finally, the centers themselves seem highly *interactive* through their common participation in a developing tradition of architectural design and the messaging on objects and buildings referred to above. The particular pattern of this distribution is most telling: the different centers share identifiable design, features, and attributes, but the specific characteristics and combinations vary between center-based localities or regions. The result is an identifiable regionality, in which it is possible in many cases today to identify the location of origin of non-local items. For the better-known centers, however, there appears to be a long-term development of local traditions that draw strongly on the overall inventory of shared form and content. This is very unlike later distributions of messaged material – as in the case of Inca, in which we find identical imperial architecture and material in broadly distributed centers, along with an admixture of imperial and local styles. In the case of the IP/EH centers, there is no such core/derived structure, but rather the presence of many long-term localized traditions participating on a relatively equal basis in what can be best described as an interaction sphere of likely common function and meaning.

What could be the nature of the organization producing this record and congruent with these inferences? Our models must accommodate these data, but ideally should serve to elucidate the development of these systems, because many features, and presumably the authority structure itself, emerge in this lengthy period. Any model must also take into account relationships between both center authorities and their local populations, and between authorities at different centers and perhaps distant populations.

The evolution of authority systems must represent a series of circumstances that led to choices and actions through which increasing degrees of power were differentially and legitimately held by a limited number of people within IP/EH com-

Table 4.1. System-serving and self-serving processes in the evolution of authority under conditions of stress and abundance

	System-serving	Self-serving
Stress-generated	Authority as a response to environmental factors, demographic factors, or a need for conflict resolution, internal or external	Authority coming from promotion of self-interest when system is weak or during stress, or unwillingness to relinquish authority granted to resolve stress (especially if stress authority is based on force of arms)
Abundance-generated	Authority coming from a distributive function, leadership in a belief system, or the coordination and timing of agricultural or other production functions	Authority self-reinforced through disposal of surplus in underwriting monumental architecture, craft production, indebted specialists/retainers, and wielders of force

munities. These can be translated into two pairs of motivations that can help structure our model: circumstance of stress versus abundance, and system-serving versus self-serving intentions (Flannery 1972). Authority could serve as a coordinating or facilitating feature of society, capable of resolving problems generated within or through exterior relations of a society. Alternatively, authority could be developed in times of abundance, in which either the disposal of surplus is assigned to key individuals, or abundance itself allows the time (or underwrites the time of others) necessary for features of authority to develop (accumulation of knowledge or practice, investment in monumental structures, or creation of objects that accompany or identify authority). Similarly, authority could be developed due to a need for a leadership function, in which the overall system benefits from having an entity capable of making and implementing decisions. Alternatively, authority may come about because of self-interest, in which those in positions of accepted power have the ability to make decisions and take actions to benefit themselves. Table 4.1 summarizes some of the processes that may be involved at the intersection of these factors.

The development of authority might be due to any one or a combination of the factors listed here. Models could also be separated between those sufficient to describe the function of the ongoing system (operative models: how it worked) and those that explain the changes that occurred to bring that condition into existence in the first place (generative models: why it came about). There should be archaeological correlates that help distinguish both the pattern of origin and the nature of operation of the organization that actually existed. An important distinction to be made in any model will be the system that is served in any interaction pattern

– is it the local (or distant) population, or the peer or near-peer authorities at distant centers?

On a more specific basis, what are operational models that might logically conform to the situation of the IP/EH, and more specifically, the center of Chavín de Huántar? First, we discount models that suggest a multi-regional authority system – i.e., a large-scale political entity such as a state that strongly controlled major areas of the Central Andes. Any attempt to view sites from these periods as representing such an entity is contradicted by the variety of the IP/EH record, and the lack of evidence of direct control systems (administrative sites, military institutions, etc.) that such pervasive authority would have. A second model that does not appear generally applicable is a simple intercommunity warfare model, which would describe the organizations as small-scale raiding organizations. The lack of defensive features in the geographically exposed centers and the rarity of weaponry in IP/EH sites are primary evidence that military factors were not dominant.

In a simple system-serving model, centers primarily serve their local populations, drawing resources in return for guidance in ritual, agricultural, or other matters. It seems highly likely that centers did have importance to local people, but such a model hardly explains the interaction between centers described above.

The general current acceptance of religious or cult functions to IP/EH monuments focuses our models toward the roles that belief systems had in the development of authority. A number of factors seem to encourage thinking in this direction. The buildings of the centers seem to be primarily temple-like in function: they are free of use-period trash, bear no evidence of food storage or preparation, have few if any inhabited structures, show no resemblance to imaginable military function. Art or decoration from the period concentrates on strange deity-like animals or human-animal combinations, and when multiple individuals are present in scenes they appear to be involved in processions.

A number of current models address aspects of Table 4.1 within such a context. Burger (1988, 1992) argues that Chavín de Huántar, at least, may have served as an oracle-style cult center, similar to the coastal center of Pachacamac, an oracle known from contact times (see Chapter 11, this volume). In this case, a group of priests are acting as messengers between the gods and those consulting the oracle. Lumbreras (1993) elaborates the oracle concept to include the possibility that Chavín authorities may have predicted El Niño events. In particular, by interpreting signs in the environment, such as southward movement of tropical water species, priests could predict climatic changes yet to fully manifest themselves in the Central Andes. These situations would emphasize a system-serving function, probably related to stresses that stimulated consultation of the source of knowledge. The potential for center authorities to gain from the exercise of this function is undeniable, but under such a system any right to power is justified only by the service provided to some constituency.

Generative system-serving models have a difficult time explaining long-term change toward authority structures. If stress-induced, the authority should diminish when the stress has passed, unless there is some intrinsic need to maintain the stress-resolved features at all times. If stress generates technological or other advances that require organization or coordination, this could also explain why a system-benefiting authority might remain and evolve over time. For such an explanation to be viable in a strict sense, it must be shown that the addition of increased authority either increases the efficiency for the average person, or increases their security, giving continued impetus for change.

A more self-serving model would explain many of the characteristics of known centers as features intentionally designed to invent, promote, and sustain authority itself. In this view, the impressive, costly features of sites and artifacts reflect a strategy on the part of authorities to set themselves apart from local populations, justifying their right to demand resources by providing messages transmitted from sacred places by sanctioned individuals. The payoff for further development of the material accoutrements may be limited at the local level, with the possibility that income could be derived from distant sources in the form of obligations occasioned by inclusion of outsiders within the cult residing at the center. This assumes the inclusion of emerging authorities from other locations who are eager to become leaders in their own local systems, searching for the practices and materials that can reinforce their own claims to authority, and willing to contribute to obtain these things. In this model, authorities at both the donor and recipient centers are self-serving at the expense of local populations who are providing the underwriting for one or more centers. In effect, the authorities are finding ways to become consumers of production surplus in the investments made in sites, specialists, and products.

Maintaining a dominant donor position in the authority system would depend on having outstanding ritual elaboration, site monumentality, symbol recognition, and inimitability of the material items offered to cult initiates. Presumably there is an elaborate behavioral component accompanying the material record we recognize today, and the training of initiates in such ritual might have been important. In this sense the outstanding providers may have as much to offer in information as in material. If the donor center is to continue receiving income, there must be a lengthy relationship with recipient-contributors; one-time cult offerings would be little compensation for the major investments of a competitively elaborate ritual center. This suggests the possibility that, for initiates, cult status was cumulative and kept growing by repeated engagements at the preferred center.

This peer-to-near-peer relationship is in many senses mutually reinforcing self-serving behavior in regard to the populations that are increasingly contributing to the systems. What allowed or encouraged these populations to provide resources for the centers? We can guess that it was a continued belief that the function of the ever-more-authoritative priests was still to their benefit, combined with the increased ability of these emergent authorities to excite awe and appear different or superior, with a sense of godliness. Stress-resolving roles are possible ways through which such authorities might justify their access to power – including solving environmental problems, articulating successful defense against aggression, and the like.

Generative models for self-serving social development are easily conceived, because the impetus is implied in the name itself. While system-serving implies continued operation of the system due to dedication to it, self-serving suggests increasing benefit to an instigating subgroup. No increase in efficiency or risk reduction is necessary, because in a constant-sum game differential distributions of benefit toward an emerging elite can be seen as a powerful motivator. In this regard the development of self-serving systems may be mostly limited by the willingness of a population to put up with increasingly unequal distribution, and requiring either force or increasingly elaborate material or behavioral reinforcement and justification for the differentials. In the simplest terms, this describes the creation of a belief system designed to naturalize inequality. It is unlikely that such development starts with messages at all related to the display of wealth or privilege, but rather with those emphasizing system-serving and/or traditional aspects of the increasingly consumption-oriented authorities.

Evidence for Authority at Chavín de Huántar

Having discussed the theoretical elements and strengths of various models of emerging authority within social organizations of the IP/EH, we turn now to the archaeological record and examine characteristics of Chavín de Huántar and how they might fit within these models.

Site background

The site of Chavín de Huántar sits at an elevation of 3,150 m in a highland valley at the confluence of the Huacheqsa and Mosna Rivers, tributaries of the Marañon, immediately south of the modern town of Chavín de Huántar, Perú.

The monumental center at Chavín de Huántar consists of plazas, terraces, and stone-faced platform buildings (Figure 4.1). They form two contiguous U-shaped temples, one surrounding a large square sunken plaza and, north of this, a smaller one surrounding a circular sunken plaza. Within these structures lies an extensive system of internal stone-lined passages called galleries. The site was built in a complex sequence of at least 15 phases that can be grouped into five larger stages (Kembel 2001). These stages begin with the Separate Mound Stage, followed by the Expansion Stage, the Consolidation Stage, the Black and White Stage, and the non-monumental Support Construction Stage. The site's overall growth pattern is now known to have been much different than the previously postulated three-phase Old Temple–New Temple sequence (J. Rowe 1967). Additionally, the site appears to have been substantially larger than what is visible today, with large platforms west of the monumental center almost wholly buried over the centuries (Rick et al. 1998), and underground galleries existing south and north of the center.

The number and complexity of galleries at Chavín de Huántar are unique within known Andean monumental centers, although a few simple gallery-like features are present at IP/EH sites such as La Galgada and Cerro Sechín. At Chavín de Huántar, this complex network of passageways, rooms, and staircases, interconnected by a system of ventilation shafts and drainage canals, permeates the temple buildings,

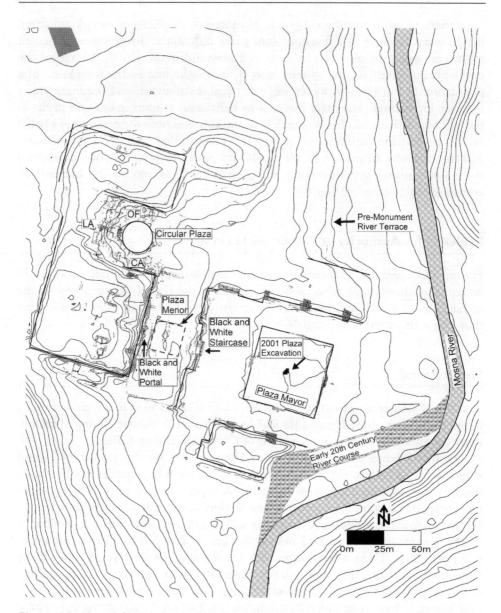

Figure 4.1. Map of Chavín, showing the placement of site relative to the Mosna River, and the major platform structures and plazas. Location of 2001 Plaza Mayor excavation is shown, along with old river terrace and the course that the Mosna River attempted to take in the early 20th century

terraces, and plazas. Galleries were built throughout Chavín de Huántar's long construction sequence and are intrinsic to the site's design. The functions of three of these have been relatively well investigated. The Lanzón Gallery houses the well-known Lanzón monolith in its cruciform central chamber (Figure 4.2), and has been proposed as the location of an oracle at the site along with the small Gallery VIII that once stood directly above (Patterson 1971b; Tello 1960). Excavations in

Figure 4.2. The Lanzón monolith in its cruciform central chamber (photo: John W. Rick)

the Ofrendas Gallery revealed over 600 ceramic vessels, many of them finely made and containing plant and animal offerings, accompanied by some human remains. The construction of the gallery entrance and the placement of items within the gallery suggest that the deposit was an offering that was sealed off permanently, perhaps placed to ritually initiate the use of the adjacent Circular Plaza, built in the same construction phase (Lumbreras 1993). Finally, our recent excavations in the Caracolas Gallery discovered 20 Strombus shell trumpets, many finely engraved, all resting directly on the original floor of the gallery. These heavily use-polished instruments were likely ritual gear that apparently was being stored, probably between usages, in this smallest of Chavín galleries. Thus, ritual, massive offerings, and sacred item storage all seem represented in these best-known galleries.

Art played a central role at Chavín de Huántar. Artistic styles displayed at the site were highly developed, and are epitomized by some of the fine ceramics found in the Ofrendas Gallery offering, the engraved shells of the Caracolas Gallery, and the incised stonework seen in the Lanzón monolith, the walls of the Circular Plaza, the columns and lintel forming the Black and White Portal, cornice stones that once encircled the buildings, and various stelae. Fantastic animal forms are represented on pottery and shell as well as on stone, where they frequently accompany larger anthropomorphic beings with feline, avian, and snake characteristics. These human-animal beings frequently seem to be performing some sort of ritual activity and tend to carry objects of significance, such as Spondylus or Strombus shells (Figure 4.3), or hallucinogenic San Pedro cactus. Remains of red, white, and yellow plaster in the galleries suggests that these spaces were vibrantly colored and perhaps even decorated with mud and plaster reliefs, as is seen at IP sites such as Kotosh, La Galgada, and Moxeke.

Chavín de Huántar's distinctive architecture and artwork inspired early researchers to view the site as the origin center of a Chavín style and indeed as the origin of Andean civilization (Tello 1960). Distant sites containing Chavín-style architecture and art were viewed as descendants of Chavín. Subsequent work of many researchers, however, showed that Chavín was preceded by a long sequence of Preceramic and early IP centers containing "Chavín-style" architecture and artwork (see Moseley 1985).

Previous studies in the Chavín monumental center proposed that the site spanned 1200–200 B.C. (Lumbreras 1989), while studies based on excavations outside the center postulated that the site spanned 850–200 B.C. and that its peak followed the decline, by 500 B.C., of other sites, particularly on the coast (Burger 1981, 1984b). Our recent detailed analysis of the architectural sequence of the center itself, however, suggests that the center reached its final monumental construction stage by approximately 750 B.C., and had physically declined and lost its organized ritual function by approximately 500 B.C. (Kembel 2001). This shift revolves around dates from the Ofrendas Gallery (Lumbreras 1993), which previously was viewed as part of the Old Temple. In the new architectural sequence, however, clear evidence indicates that the Ofrendas Gallery was built in the Black and White Stage, the site's final monumental stage, meaning its dates also correspond with this final stage.

Figure 4.3. Typical Chavín stone engraving showing a fanged human carrying a Spondylus shell, from a cornice fragment found in Chavín de Huántar in 1998

It therefore appears that Chavín de Huántar was one of many monumental centers that existed in the late IP and the early EH and that declined by the middle of the first millennium B.C., rather than one that developed largely after the decline of these other centers and flourished in the late EH (Kembel 2001; cf. Burger 1981). Accordingly, the following discussion views Chavín's interactions with other sites as occurring within a large interaction sphere involving many peer or near-peer centers, rather than as a late center whose dominance results from the collapse of the other centers.

Operational processes at Chavín

When discussing how Chavín de Huántar may have operated in the prehistoric past, the temptation exists to present the site's architecture in an idealized and pristine state, serving merely as the backdrop for ritual: visitors confronting the Lanzón oracle, priestly figures processing through space in the Circular Plaza or up the

Black and White Staircase, elaborately dressed figures appearing out of darkness into the sunlight of hanging staircases to crowds gazing below. While presumably these or similar ceremonies were important focal aspects of activity at Chavín de Huántar, such formal rituals likely comprised only a small subset of the total range of activities there, and occurred only on occasion. Two other realms of activities, not of a strict ritual nature, that likely occurred at the site demonstrate how Chavín de Huántar may have functioned and provide insights on emerging authority at the site.

Design and construction processes at Chavín
One such realm of activity is the construction of the temple buildings. The tendency to view archaeological sites as they may have appeared following completed construction stages overlooks the processes involved in construction, which must have consumed substantial amounts of time and energy. During periods of construction the site would not have been in a pristine state, ready and awaiting purely ritual activities, but rather would have been undergoing continual change. The volume and complexity of Chavín de Huántar's construction suggest that for substantial portions of the site's operation it was undergoing some aspect of the construction process: designing and planning, layout, preparation of the landscape, partial deconstruction of earlier buildings to accommodate new ones, acquisition and preparation of building materials, construction, and decorating with elements such as artwork and plaster, likely concluding with ritual initiation or dedication of the new structure. These processes clearly formed a significant component of activity at the site.

Viewing Chavín de Huántar thus not only as static stages of architecture forming the backdrop for rituals and oracular proclamations but also as a construction site undergoing frequent and prolonged periods of physical change raises many issues, especially related to the design process. Those who control the design process determine how the resulting construction operates as well as the messages it conveys. What forms should be created? How should new structures be incorporated with the old? What materials should be used, where should they be procured, and how should they be incorporated into the building? Presumably such decisions were – or eventually became – the responsibility and privilege of local authorities.

Control of the design and construction processes could provide those in authority with the opportunity to make new constructions self-serving. They could strategically design not only the final material product, but also the social processes behind the construction. Who would contribute the labor and how would it be organized and allocated? How could structures be modified or built to shape rituals and other important activities, direct the future of the site, and enhance their own roles? In answering these questions, the leaders in charge of the design and construction of the site could direct architectural growth to be self-serving.

Who actually carried out the construction process is important to consider. Was the local population continually responsible for the construction of new phases over time? Was labor partially or wholly supplied at varying times from distant populations, as a type of tribute or offering to the cult? Was labor required or willingly donated? At the oracle site of Delphi, Greece, populations from around the Mediterranean constructed monuments as offerings and dedications to the oracle (Andronicos 1993; Jacquemin 1999; Partida 2000), suggesting that contribution of labor from distant populations, perhaps organized by their own leadership, may be worth considering.

A final issue addresses how the processes of construction were incorporated with ritual activities at the site. Given the religious nature of the buildings as well as their probable ritual initiation upon completion, as supported by the Ofrendas Gallery and seen commonly throughout the ancient Andes, the construction process may have been integrated with more sacred and ritualized activities at the site, and perhaps itself imbued with sacred purpose. Thus, rather than an interrupting cost of temple expansion, the construction process could have been central to the site's operation, with rituals and construction occurring concurrently.

Did leaders at Chavín de Huántar capitalize on self-serving design and construction opportunities and leave their mark on its archaeological record? Two trends in the construction sequence are worth investigating. The first is a pattern of broader utilization of natural resources along with increasing alteration of the natural landscape over time. For example, early use of sandstone and quartzite for almost all building purposes shifts toward increasing use of granite and limestone later in the sequence. Quartzite and sandstone are available within 1 km of the site, while granite and limestone are located farther, at least 15 km and 3 km respectively (R. Turner, Knight, and Rick 1999), requiring much more effort in transport. Furthermore, while quartzite and sandstone were primarily used in blocks that were unfinished, the granite and limestone were finely worked and sometimes incised, largely used to create external focal points such as staircases and plazas. Another example regards a major feature of the external stonework called the coarse-to-fine transition (CFT), a horizontal plane separating coarse stonework below from fine stonework above. The construction sequence indicates that the CFT likely was not present on Chavín's initial buildings, but rather was introduced later and integrated into earlier phases by deconstructing and rebuilding portions of their façades (Kembel 2001). These examples of increasing utilization of varied types of stone materials originating from afar, worked into fine forms and decorations, and inserted into new as well as old architecture at strategic places suggests that leaders at Chavín de Huántar increasingly and purposefully manifested their growing authority by acquiring, working, and utilizing a broader range of natural materials.

An example of major alteration of the natural landscape is inherent in the construction of the Plaza Mayor, or sunken square plaza, during the Black and White Stage. Excavations in the Plaza Mayor indicate that the broad river plain in which the plaza sits was not the original landform but rather is an almost entirely artificial feature. Massive amounts of foundational stones and earthen materials were moved to build up this surface while simultaneously pushing the riverbed further to the east and constructing walls along this new channel to permanently contain the river (Figures 4.1, 4.4). So permanent was this effort that only in the early 20th century did the river significantly breach its banks and erode portions of the site's

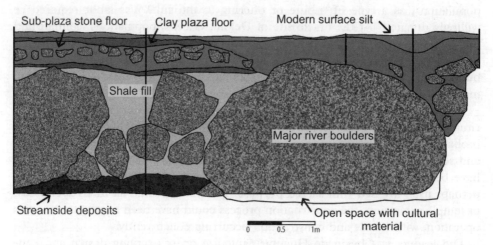

Figure 4.4. Profile of east side of 2001 Plaza Mayor excavation showing the major boulders and stratigraphic layers forming the plaza floor, and the bottom sediments indicating a riverside position prior to plaza construction

easternmost buildings (Tello 1960). Additionally, the plaza, although partly located on the previously wet land of the river channel, has maintained a nearly perfectly planar floor across multiple millennia, due to the carefully executed foundations. This major effort of planning, coordinating, and building created a large and flat area of land in the middle of this highland valley. Such land is limited in the highland valley environment, where easily worked valley-bottom land is highly desirable for agricultural purposes, and indeed the site of Chavín was used for agriculture according to 19th- and early 20th-century accounts (see Tello 1960). Yet the leaders did not build this plain for agricultural use, but rather lavishly and luxuriously used it for an ostentatiously large plaza. The massive work toward reclaiming this land, followed by its use for temple and likely ritual purposes, was a clear use and almost blatant advertisement of the authority of Chavín de Huántar's leaders and their ability to notably modify the landscape.

A final example combining broader natural resources use and increasing landscape alteration was the creation of the internal landscape of galleries using a range of natural elements to communicate a message of power to visitors. Twisting, disorienting, multi-level galleries, with walls encased in multi-colored plaster and decorated with niches, form the artificial setting for what we believe to have been a "multimedia" display designed to convince visitors of the power of the site, its deities, and their human representatives: anthracite mirrors strategically reflecting light into the galleries through ventilation shafts from the exterior (Rick 2002), smoke easily transferred from one gallery to the next via internal ventilation shafts, internal water canals purportedly sending roars of sound into the galleries (Lumbreras, González, and Lietaer 1976), and visually elaborate stone decoration and art, all experienced during ritual drug use (Cordy-Collins 1977) would have provided a full sensory impact – and probably overload. With these elements, the leaders at Chavín de Huántar gained control over the visitors' environment in a way not possible outside. The presence of galleries from the beginning of the sequence suggests that the roots of self-serving strategies may be quite early at Chavín, using the structural features of the galleries to promote the authority of the leaders. Smoke and mirrors aside, these efforts to not just guide but to manipulate a visitor's experience highlight a desire for control and an urgent need for leaving little to chance when convincing others of the site's power, and, in doing so, of their own authority.

Similarly, the conversion of the innermost space of the Lanzón Gallery from an open structure to an internal chamber (Kembel 2001) suggests that designers of this change desired full control over the experience of visiting the Lanzón. Through subsequent constructions, additions to the gallery simultaneously maintained access to this space, which presumably represented traditional associations of authority, and made that access more exclusive. By enclosing the space, the Lanzón and the activities that went on inside became even more restricted by being completely out of sight to those not allowed inside. By maintaining access through new constructions to a source and place of traditional, likely otherworldly power, designers simultaneously enhanced their own authority.

These patterns suggest that Chavín de Huántar's architectural sequence reflects increasing use and manipulation of nature, in order to reinforce the power of the site and its authorities. Major efforts go into the design and construction of buildings, art, landscape, and the experience of being at Chavín, and reflect back upon the leaders.

A second trend in the design and construction of Chavín de Huántar's buildings is a shift from an inward to an outward focus in the site's architecture. The galleries were an amazing system of technologically difficult-to-build structures, including staircases, drainage canals, and vents – and the early galleries were some of the most complex to be built at the site (Kembel 2001). Yet major efforts were made to hide them within buildings so that from the outside the buildings looked solid. The activities inside were also hidden, not advertised – they were only to be witnessed by participants and deities, not be a public spectacle or display of the temple's or the leaders' power. For the outsider, however, what went on inside was left to the provoked imagination, probably reinforcing the mystique of the cult and the separation between literal insiders and outsiders.

This private, interior focus for ritual interactions changed over time, adding a large external component with an increasing emphasis on finely worked and decorated stone later in the sequence, particularly in the Black and White Stage. Simultaneously, a reduction in gallery complexity occurred. Whereas early in the architectural sequence the galleries took complex forms requiring much planning and innovative construction techniques, by the Black and White Stage gallery forms were standardized to simple "E" or "H" forms (Kembel 2001). Significantly, substantial efforts were made to maintain access to earlier galleries through new additions, as in the case of the Lanzón Gallery, indicating that the use of galleries and their traditional associations continued to be integral to activities at Chavín de

Huántar. Through these shifts, leaders could further develop their authority by appealing to larger crowds in addition to small select groups, perhaps in part to compete with other centers. They were increasingly able to advertise rather than hide the labor that went into construction, promoting the temple as well as themselves by increasing expenditure of energy on external, showy features while decreasing the little-seen complexity of the internal galleries.

These two trends suggest that the construction process itself became a display and instrument of the authority of Chavín de Huántar's leaders, in relation both to local populations and to visitors. It could be used to strategically plan and implement this growth of authority, manifested physically as a utilization of increasingly labor-intensive materials and building processes, a pattern of increasingly manipulating nature, and a shift from an inward, intimate ritual setting to an outward, public display of ritual and authority. The massive new constructions and the labor contributing to them could communicate the power of the Chavín deities and the cult's leaders. Even tasks such as the incision of stone art could suit this purpose: such delicate work may have been performed in situ rather than transported in its completed state. Thus, inherent in the costly features of the site is the leaders' strategy to develop further authority.

Leaders' strategies may also explain why so many additions were built at Chavín de Huántar and why early structures were deconstructed, modified, and rebuilt. Leaders could increase their own authority by expanding the temple: the numerous changes and additions suggest that leaders actively used the design and construction of the buildings at Chavín de Huántar as a means to promote themselves. The whole process could become mutually reinforcing if contribution of labor towards building makes the conferral of benefits, such as a favorable oracular prediction, all the more likely. As in other belief-based systems, this contribution is a way to get supernatural entities – and their representatives on this earth – on your side. By making this demand and presenting it as beneficial for the contributor, the leaders could ensure themselves a labor force for continuing construction, while making the process of construction a means by which to exert and enhance their growing authority. This relationship may have helped develop and sustain an interaction sphere between leaders at peer or near-peer centers supported by local populations.

Chavín as a training center within an interaction sphere
The second realm of activity we discuss here is the operation of the site not merely as an oracle center, but also as an active training center for initiates within the Chavín religious system. While this function is more speculative than the clear physical requirements of the construction process, it helps explain important elements of the site's growth, layout, and relationships with the local population and other centers.

Oracle centers are, to a large extent, passive systems, in which those at the oracle center have only indirect control over or input into who will visit the site. Similarly, the visitor's quest for knowledge or other benefit imparted by the oracle deity may be a journey made once in a lifetime, or perhaps a handful of times. Neither of these characteristics is congruent with the evidence that Chavín de Huántar and many other centers of the IP/EH were large, complex sites continuously linked within an interaction sphere.

Additionally, the authority of an oracle is fundamentally based on intellectual capital. Information provided exclusively by the oracle is its product, and it is this product on which the success of the system relies. In a simple oracle system, perhaps tradition is sufficient to maintain visits to the site. But in a more complex system, perhaps one in which leaders are trying to promote the site and themselves at the expense of competing centers and leaders, the product of intellectual capital must be marketed. People must be convinced of the power and insight of this particular oracle or belief system variant so that they choose it, whether exclusively or in conjunction with others.

Such convincing requires that the system take an active rather than a passive role in gaining visitors. It is not enough for the livelihood of the system to rely on whoever may decide to visit during a particular day or season or year. The system must be advertised and actively promoted as providing unique and exclusive insight or products (material or otherwise), yet conforming within an overarching tradition of accepted and expected symbols, rituals, and architecture. In addition to this otherworldly insight, the worldly prestige of the center and the methods through which center leaders have achieved a self-serving condition can also become commodities that are acquired in visits to the site.

To actively promote a site, leaders may develop a number of different tactics. The first involves developing a system that encourages more than a single, short-term stay. This could include multiple visits that earn increased status in the system and access to more exclusive rituals. It could also include the selection of groups of people to become initiates into the "priestly" group at the site, and their long-term training in the rituals and information – the intellectual capital – of the cult, again increasing in status over time. Initiates could originate in both local and distant populations, and, upon completing their training, could return endowed with the information, status, and possibly material symbols gained in their training. In these ways, centers may have played an active rather than passive role in gaining visitors and promoting themselves.

Specifically at Chavín de Huántar, we see evidence supporting the idea of the site functioning as a multiple-visit or long-term training center. The leaders of Chavín de Huántar built a multitude of increasingly diversified external and internal spaces over time, suggesting a need for distinct activities and rituals for different groups of people. The construction of the three known plazas and their accompanying staircases in the Black and White Stage provided multiple spaces for gatherings and processions. This suggests that new activities occurred outside rather than almost exclusively inside, and that different rituals took place in each plaza, perhaps accompanied by people of varying status or used on different occasions. The presence of galleries within each building phase suggests that these spaces may have been created for additional activities and levels of initiates, providing space for more exclusive rituals. Similarly, with expanding numbers of visitors and initiates, less exclusive spaces than the galleries would have been needed – and built in the form of plazas made of labor-expensive materials and decorations. The appearance of art figures such as the Staff God, likely late in the sequence, suggests that, with expansion of buildings and audience, additional deities may have been worshipped, or an additional oracle or set of oracles may have been strategically introduced at the site, perhaps tailored to the varying needs and qualifications of their supplicants.

Similarly, the incorporation midway and late in Chavín de Huántar's sequence of architectural forms from different areas of the Andes, namely the U-shaped temple form originating on the central coast and the sunken circular plaza form originating in the north coast, suggests that visitors from these areas could have played an important role in influencing design choices, whether through active involvement or as the subjects of blatant appeals by Chavín designers. These forms could have been strategically incorporated by the Chavín designers, imbuing new constructions with associations of power and beliefs familiar to distant constituents, effectively expanding the temple's appeal to a wider audience. Rather than seeing Chavín de Huántar's ritual origins in the arrival of these forms and ideas, we suggest that Chavín de Huántar intercepts them when it is an already existing, calculating entity. A sharing of ideas was likely, as expected within an interaction sphere.

Examination of material culture found at Chavín de Huántar supports the idea of the site operating within a wide-ranging interaction sphere. Many of the fine, elaborate items found in the Caracolas and Ofrendas Galleries, both located in the terrace surrounding the Circular Plaza, originated outside of Chavín de Huántar. In particular, the twenty Strombus shell trumpets excavated from the Caracolas Gallery clearly came from tropical coastal waters, no closer than present-day Ecuador. They appear to have been highly valued ritual instruments that would have created stunning levels of sound when played in ensemble. The presence of these important objects within the site demonstrates not only that Chavín de Huántar clearly interacted with distant sites and populations, but also that these symbols of those interactions were highly regarded, used, and ultimately deposited at the center of ritual attention.

Seen in this light, Chavín de Huántar and probably other centers of the IP/EH look like more than simple oracle centers. Instead, it appears that leaders at Chavín de Huántar created a more complex system in which they could enhance their authority by actively controlling and directing their output of tradition, information, and ritual, as well as the income of materials, constituents, labor, and information. Such a system better explains the similarities in art and architecture between Chavín de Huántar and numerous peer or near-peer centers, and supports the idea of these centers interacting and perhaps competing within a framework of shared traditions.

This framework would form the foundation of an interaction sphere, in which cooperative inculcation of new concepts would create a domesticated population of both leaders and followers. In this type of system, similar concepts would be reinforced between groups whose basic ideas and symbols coincide. In particular, the invocation of traditional concepts, symbols, and modes of interaction in order to legitimize and transform new types of relationships between and within groups would be particularly effective. Any resulting initial cooperation between such groups could, however, give way due to developing competition for resources or followers over the long term.

The limits of self-serving authority and the role of tradition

Absent from Chavín's imagery and material record is clear evidence of military figures, suggesting there was little need for direct physical coercion. How then was the authority of the leaders enforced? In relations with other sites, obedience to the system likely was primarily derived through use of Chavín information by non-Chavín lower-level leaders. In their own distant communities they presumably were struggling to use visible iconography, kinship relations, limited status differences, and probably ritual activity to try to gain local loyalty and compliance. If some of the human-animal art images at Chavín reference the transformation of leaders into alternative entities, perhaps in drug-use situations, they would suggest a power, linked to deities or other supernatural entities, that would reinforce the leaders' authority. These experiences in alternative worlds of power, if made sufficiently evident or credible, may have led to respect both by distant leaders and Chavín de Huántar's residents.

Also of note within the archaeological record of Chavín de Huántar is the distinct lack, at least to this point in the time, of individual leaders represented in its cultural remains. While burials of Chavín-period individuals remain to be found within the monument, the substantial collection of images recorded on ceramics, stone, and textiles from Chavín de Huántar and Chavín-related sites shows what are presumably deities, animals, anthropomorphic figures, geometric patterns – but no images that obviously represent individual leaders. The human-animal beings perhaps representing leaders in altered, drug-induced states may have linked them to supernatural entities through indirect suggestion rather than direct and overly specific images. This suggests that leaders at Chavín de Huántar needed to focus their efforts on publicly promoting the site and its oracle, rather than themselves. So while archaeological evidence at Chavín de Huántar suggests that more than system-serving behavior and motivations were at work, it appears that a limit existed: the leaders at Chavín de Huántar were self-serving, but only to a degree.

Such a limit was likely due to distant and local forces that held the leaders' growing authority in check. Ironically, while development of an inter-regional system was boosted by competition within an interaction sphere, it was also limited by this system. By stepping widely outside these limits, leaders at Chavín de Huántar would cause the loyal base of visitors, initiates, and supporting populations to disintegrate and bring their loyalty and resources elsewhere. They could push the limits, eventually radically transforming the system, but changes had to be done gradually.

Closer to home, local populations who supported the site certainly placed limits on amounts of resources and labor contributed, limits that also could only be gradually expanded over time. Chavín de Huántar's residents to some extent may have willingly accepted the increasing authority differential of the site's leaders, for a number of reasons. They may have been aware of and benefited from an increased prestige due to their association with the site. Similarly, the site's income and prestige may have raised their overall quality of life, supporting some as craftspeople producing the site's fine pottery and stonework, and possibly creating living conditions better than those of other populations not associated with a large center. However, a primary factor likely was that they had increasingly bought into the system, with a belief that it worked in their favor reinforced by an ever-increasing recognition and conviction of the very authority the leaders were setting out to build.

It appears that to convince local and distant constituents and to expand these limits, leaders at Chavín de Huántar strategically manipulated traditional concepts. By referencing traditional elements present within the wider interaction sphere as well as those specific to Chavín de Huántar, they could justify profound changes, perhaps even presenting them as conservative. Incorporating traditional architectural forms, even those from the coast; maintaining access to traditionally sacred spaces or icons like the Lanzón, while limiting that access; harnessing different types of raw materials; continuing ritual practices while propagating their diversity and the spaces in which they were performed; combining traditional feline, snake, and avian figures with human forms to create new associations and links to those figures' traditional and natural power; even adapting the ages-old process of building itself to convey messages of authority – aspects such as these suggest that leaders at Chavín de Huántar purposefully calculated their use of traditional elements to shape new developments, gradually expanding the limits to their authority imposed by local populations and distant sites within the interaction sphere.

There also may have been a need for self-serving motives to be disguised or at least accompanied by system-serving results. Chavín de Huántar's leaders may have presented some changes as system-serving, to the extent that they benefited Chavín de Huántar's residents by promoting the site as a whole – for example by increasing the site's size in order to increase input from distant leaders and their populations into the overall system. In doing so, leaders could further persuade Chavín de Huántar's residents to accept these changes. In this sense, system-serving and self-serving would have converged; strategies that served the system would be selected in so far as they were also self-promoting. By strategically referencing tradition and apparent system-serving benefits, leaders could justify their efforts and gradually expand accepted limits, bypass the need for force, and increase their authority within a manipulated belief system.

Conclusions

We have focused on the IP/EH monumental centers, and one in particular, because this is where the greatest visible changes are occurring in these societies. A system-serving view would see the monuments as facilities for the expression of beliefs and perhaps as contexts for information transfer. If viewed as more related to self-serving on the part of emerging authorities, they would form part of a convincing system of ever-greater reinforcement involving impressive structures. But we need to explain both the functioning of IP/EH systems *and* their origins. Chavín de Huántar, like all similar sites, evolved as its residents changed their strategies for its use. The site's origins probably were as a communal space for collective action and observation, perhaps ritual related to agricultural, astronomical, and meteorological cycles, an early stage for which we have very little evidence. What would have led to the increase in size, complexity, and investment in this center? Is there something about a larger, more intricate Chavín de Huántar that improved the ability of local agriculturalists to practice their livelihood? Perhaps, but it does not seem to be the central explanation. The transformation of the center into a valley-dominating monument had a complex effect; it became a pan-regional place of importance, such that being at Chavín de Huántar had value in itself: for witnessing ritual, consulting an oracle, or entering a cult. This meant a flow of materials and information to Chavín de Huántar, which may have benefited the local population in some ways. But as the buildings grow to their maximum, and construction possibly becomes a process of importance in itself, it becomes increasingly difficult to accept that the motivations for growth were for benefits to the overall cultural system.

Did Chavín de Huántar originate or grow in response to stresses that were solved by a belief system, its leaders, and the information it contained? If these stresses demanded ways of controlling environmental uncertainty or its attendant variation in productivity, we would expect the Chavín center to show evidence of such a function – storage or technology capable of resolving local crises. In fact, the increasingly elaborate architecture seems to move further from any practically useful configuration, rather becoming ever more effective as an awe-inspiring precinct, especially when coupled with the evidence for sensory manipulation. Considerable care was taken in building orientation, and there are hints that horizon observation or other techniques may have been used in monitoring the passage of time; calendrically based ritual, perhaps involved with the agricultural cycle, may have continued through time at Chavín de Huántar, perhaps linking the evolving authority structure back to system-serving principles. Similarly, some galleries may indeed have been used for storage purposes. But the primary emphasis of the structures and art of Chavín de Huántar was to create a mindset that accepted arguments for the authority of those who created the monuments. The images are not of specific historical leaders, or necessarily even of humans divorced from natural sources of power. Rather, we seem to see statements linking architecture and art (and the authorities within and around it) with known, perhaps feared natural entities. We do not seem to see leadership justification based on human aggression or defense, so the element of force seems lacking from the beginning.

It is very likely that many, if not most, of the IP/EH centers of the Central Andes grew simultaneously, commonly benefiting from a far-reaching and perhaps fundamental change in belief systems. The ability of authorities all over this area to make increasing demands for labor and materials for their centers coincides with an apparently growing differentiation of privilege and wealth that they themselves enjoyed. The coherent and consistent elements, probably reflecting principles of belief that the centers shared, albeit in regionally differentiable form, argue that an evolving formula had been found for effectively harnessing the widespread Andean communities through an alteration of mindset. This is apparently effective, since it creates the impressive archaeological record, with monuments that compete with those of any time period in the Peruvian past. The support for these centers was, however, somewhat voluntary, or at least not obtained under constant threat of force, as best we can tell. With the simultaneous expansion of many local systems, there was undoubtedly competition between them, which seems largely to have taken place within the norms defined by the interaction sphere – by developing larger temples, more sophisticated convincing behavior, spectacular adornment or costume. This would have worked as long as all major players competed by reinforcing the cultic principles. Continued increase in material and labor costs at the centers would have had some expected outcomes. First, centers may have started to exceed the willingness of local, non-coerced populations to support them; second, they may have become less flexible to adjust to major environmental or other exogenous changes; and third, competing on an aggressive, rather than semi-cooperative, basis may have become a less expensive option such that large-scale coercion, perhaps in the form of warfare, may have started to play an important role.

While the redesign of Andean belief systems that occurred in the IP/EH was in many ways radical, it probably was not portrayed or perceived as such. As we have presented here and elsewhere (Rick 2002), there was a consistent appeal to tradition in architectural forms, art content, and execution. The architecture at Chavín de Huántar, while certainly not static in design, does maintain forms over hundreds of years, and galleries themselves served in part to access earlier important spots and objects which became buried by the incessant growth of the center (Kembel 2001). In this case, access is not only to the objects, such as the Lanzón, but to their original locations, suggesting that direct links to the past may have legitimized the trajectory of the authorities. Even the use of drugs, argued to have shamanistic features in Chavín imagery, may be a way of relating esoteric practices, themselves aimed at reinforcing new ideas about social structure, with a widespread, credible tradition of shamanism that had probably already been practiced for thousands of years. The Chavín belief system made assertions about the relationship between a world of natural power and some humans; shamanistic traditions would be a source of ready-made belief about such a powerful world. Chavín authorities skillfully edited the message to change from a system-serving function (shamanistic problem-solving in realms of health and social relations) to a self-serving argument for exclusive access to, and retention of, such natural powers.

What explains the growth and longevity of Chavín and the IP/EH period? Considering our original models, it seems it was primarily driven by self-serving impulses from a ritual sector that maintained system-serving overtones to reinforce its highly calculated convincing message about the authorities' increasing right to power. While there may have been elements of problem-solving, such as weather

prediction, the overall evolution does not seem driven primarily by crisis resolution. Most probably the portrayal of system-serving function was a smokescreen for
a balance shifting towards self-serving, reinforced by the mutual, cooperative interests of broadly distributed emerging elites characteristic of the period. In all probability this growth was primarily fueled by abundance from an increasingly effective
production system.

We have examined the nature of organizations in the IP/EH periods of the
Central Andes, and come to the conclusion that we are dealing with long-lasting
theocratic organizations with a leadership that is increasing in its authoritative and
self-promoting character. In summary, what would we call this organization?
Archaeologists often have taken shelter in simple terms for developmental stages of
increasing societal complexity or inequality, which in the case of this period would
fall into the realm of "chiefdom"; there is clear evidence of authority and organization, but Chavín clearly falls short of the size, population, administrative complexity, and coercive foundation of true states. Yet the term "chiefdom" does not
seem to accurately characterize Chavín or the other center-based peer organizations
of the time. Chiefdoms imply a secular or semi-secular authority in which the chief
is a pivotal individual whose standing, based on economics, kinship, or religion, is
paramount within a local or regional system. Classic definitions of chiefs rarely
imply a principally religious/ideological system that authorities operate within and
develop their power from. For Chavín society we do not yet know for sure who the
ultimate authorities were – but the current, reasonable supposition is that they were
religious authorities who were heavily and consciously manipulating a belief system,
including the architecturally complex centers and esoteric cult practices, in an evolution of authority itself. This may be parallel to at least the Olmec of Mexico, and
perhaps other cultural systems in similar world circumstances.

At the same time, we believe that the IP/EH is somewhat unusual in its extension of an apparently ritualistic, theocratic basis into a surprisingly complex society,
with highly developed architectural abilities and impressive artistic achievements in
ceramics, textiles, and metals. Rather than be satisfied with the term "civilization,"
we would return to the idea of the Formative Period, in which the foundations for
authority were being explored, and conceive of Chavín as residing in the very Upper
Formative – perhaps this could be termed the Overextended Formative. Was the
Formative intrinsically different from later, state societies in the Andes? We think
the answer is an overwhelming yes, in the reinforcing peer-peer principles between
centers, and in its concentrated efforts at convincing its population of the ideas of
authority through symbol and monument. In the relatively delimited segments of
the primary natural environments of the IP/EH – the coastal and highland valleys
– it was possible for surprisingly complex organizations to develop – not at all in
isolation, but rather in distant semi-cooperation and exchange with each other. Yet,
there may not have been, in most cases, the immediate adjacency between centers
which might lead to conflict and increasing use of force that in itself might have
fueled the coercive basis common to states and their growth.

Arguably in the Central Andes this is a time in which exceptional levels of human
ingenuity and comprehension about how to gain credibility are applied to the

problem of naturalizing authority. Interestingly, belief systems that are usually conservative and norm-reinforcing are being used to promote a major portion of the transcendental change away from egalitarian societies that is the hallmark of later human history. That these systems were viable for well over a millennium is testament to their fit to human credibilities and realities; that they disappeared fairly rapidly in most places during the EH makes us realize the susceptibility of non-coercive systems to environmental or social-political problems.

ACKNOWLEDGMENTS

Our research at Chavín de Huántar was supported by the National Science Foundation, the National Geographic Society Committee for Research and Exploration, the Stanford University Morrison Institute for Population and Resource Studies, and various other sources of support from Stanford University. We extend our thanks to Luis Lumbreras, the late Marino Gonzáles, authorities of the Instituto Nacional de Cultura, the people of the town of Chavín de Huántar, and our research teams.

5

Life, Death, and Ancestors

Lisa DeLeonardis and George F. Lau

Introduction

Following the demise of Chavín a lengthy transformation of Central Andean societies occurred. New types and scales of production and redistribution emerged, as did innovations in art, architecture, and technology. Vigorous changes in regional economics promoted novel social arrangements and forms of political centralization that responded to and accommodated larger social groups. Extraordinary art styles emerged that distinguished various regions of the Andes.

Scholars of the late 1940s characterized this dynamic time as the "Florescent," "Classic," or "Mastercraftsmen" in recognition of these achievements. John Rowe later proposed the less descriptive term Early Intermediate Period (ca. A.D. 1–700) to refer to the intervening time between the Early Horizon Chavín cult and the expansion of the Middle Horizon Wari state (J. Rowe and Menzel 1967). Here, we adopt Rowe's terminology but recognize a more dynamic relationship between temporal and social developments.

There has been a trend in Andean studies to view Early Intermediate Period developments as expressive of "ideologies of power," or belief systems which naturalize the relations of a dominant class over less potent social groups. Here, we suggest that funerary practices and associated visual culture served to promote social cohesion and kinship ties as well as political-economic ends. Different processes of continuity and innovation occurred during the Early Intermediate Period and multiple interpretations will be needed to probe their character.

In many ways, the great Peruvian archaeologist, Julio C. Tello (1880–1947), represents the starting point for this study. Tello's indefatigable studies of ancient and contemporary peoples and cultures throughout the Andes culminated in general syntheses on Peruvian civilization of unprecedented breadth, intellect, and imagination. Among his many endeavors, Tello's archaeological fieldwork included pioneering coverage of major Early Intermediate Period cultures such as Paracas and

Nasca (Tello 1917, 1928, 1931, 1959), Lima (in Shady 1999), and Recuay (Tello 1923, 1929, 1942). His intellectual legacy continued through devoted students, who took up his exposition of Recuay (Carrión Cachot 1955, 1959; Espejo 1957; Mejía 1941, 1957) and Paracas (Carrión Cachot 1949; Tello and Mejía 1979).

Tello was one of the first scholars to point to ancestor veneration as a vital cultural dimension of ancient Andean civilization (Tello 1929, 1942). By the 1920s, some investigations had already focused on cemetery sites, furnishing insights on funerary practices, cultural distinctions and chronology (e.g., Reiss and Stübel 1880–87; Uhle in Menzel 1977). It was Tello, however, who synthesized a model of ancestor veneration that linked prehistoric cultural patterns to religious traditions pervasive in ethnohistoric accounts and among contemporary Andeans. He argued that many elements, such as funerary and public architecture, stone sculpture, and iconography, could be explained as components of a coherent program of religious ceremony focused on ancestors, fertility, and community reproduction (Tello 1929, 1942).

In this chapter, we examine new archaeological data concerning the regional cultures of Recuay, Lima, Paracas, and Nasca to elaborate and recontextualize the themes introduced by Tello over 70 years ago. We find that diverse but interrelated patterns of ancestor veneration are manifest in burials, tomb architecture, mortuary treatments, stone sculpture, and ritual practices associated with post-interment contexts. We propose that general innovations in religious practice and related artistic production were linked to a widespread proliferation of leadership ideologies used to establish and maintain relations of political authority. Moreover, we understand the evidence for funerary practices in groups of differing sociopolitical complexity not only as elite rhetoric, but also as cultural expressions of community and kin-based integration.

Ancestor Veneration in the Andes

Ancestor veneration concerns the religious practices and beliefs centered on specific deceased kin (Fortes 1965; Hardacre 1987). As the domain of families, kin groups, or lineages tracing descent from known deceased, it is thought that specific progenitors maintain supernatural abilities that can directly affect the living. Ancestral spirits can be both beneficial and malevolent. Their temperament can often influence health, success in warfare or economic production, and bestowing of ancestral wisdom (Classen 1993:88–91; Newell 1976; Salomon 1995:328–329).

The bond created between the ancestor and his/her descendants involves as its basis a historical memory that encourages formal rites of commemoration that frequently extend beyond interment and associated funerary rites (Morris 1991; Whitley 2002). Expressions of these ceremonies may entail offerings, prayers, consultations, and feasts. Ritual objects, ancestor effigies, and special buildings are important elements in these activities, frequently serving as references to specific ancestors, kin relations, and historical or mythical accounts.

Ancestor veneration, in a given context, can also be considered a malleable social field in which individuals and groups participate, maneuver, and benefit. Because ancestor veneration tends to uphold the authority of elders, it can be considered a conservative institution that reinforces traditional sociopolitical arrangements and expectations of filial responsibility (Calhoun 1980). Scholars also contend that ancestral relationships frequently provide domains of individual action legitimizing political succession and resource entitlement (Helms 1998; McAnany 1995; Morris 1991).

A long-held belief in the Andes rests on the premise that deceased ancestors continued to have active social lives (Sillar 1992). Unlike the finality and stark conceptual break between life and death common in Western funerary culture, the portability and accessibility of ancestors guaranteed that they could be revisited, handled, and revered well past the time of physical death. This is best expressed in Colonial Period accounts of the Inca practices of storage, display, and active engagement with esteemed royal mummies. Retrieved from their repositories, these mummies were circulated in processions, feasts, offerings, consultations, and dances as objects of reverence as well as active participants (Isbell 1997a; J. Rowe 1946). Indigenous chroniclers such as Guaman Poma de Ayala (1980) identified distinct funerary practices within each of the four regions of Tawantinsuyu (the Inca Empire). Guaman Poma took care to identify the importance of mummies and the monuments that were dedicated for their housing. Notably, Guaman Poma's famous drawings of regional mortuary ritual privilege the practices of the living as much as they treat the dead. The artist paid special attention to their handling of the deceased – including dedicatory libations, mourning by women, the mannered seated position and apparel of the corpse, and carrying of the funerary litter (e.g., Guaman Poma de Ayala 1980: folios 288–297).

Many Andean people believed that ancestors wielded remarkable powers of provision. The achievements attributed to ancestors commonly center on irrigation, the establishment of local social groupings, or the introduction of certain crops (Salomon and Urioste 1991; Sherbondy 1988, 1992). Many groups also regard ancestors as having ongoing influence over former property, which affects the inheritance or use of critical resource rights to land or water (Sherbondy 1992). The veneration of specific deceased kin remains important where resource rights continue to be defined on the basis of descent (Allen 2002; Dillehay 1995; Platt 1986).

More broadly, we might envision that Andean funerary practices related to certain perceptions of human and agricultural regeneration. The cultural association between death and agricultural livelihood is predicated on the notion that the landscape is a provider and a source of life (Allen 2002). In this sense, the practice of interment – as the corpse is inserted into the earth/tomb – reenacts cultivation and human fertilization (Bastien 1995; Gose 1994). Like sexual reproduction and farming, ancestor veneration plays on a trope of repetition – ancestors were periodically brought out, revered, and reinserted into the tomb on a cyclical basis. These are comparable objectives to foster agricultural success, family reproduction and community well-being.

In different regions of the Andes, one finds homologies between agricultural work and mortuary ritual. In his study of Apurimac, Gose (1994) identifies similar behaviors, language, and attitudes for the consideration of souls of the deceased and seeds. Ancient burials may very well express conditions of transformation and nurturing, along the lines for "seed states" described for religious beliefs in Maya and Olmec cultures (e.g., Frame 2001; Tate and Berdersky 1999). Clearly, the common flexed, fetal position, juxtaposition of bundles, and practice of wrapping textiles around mummies suggests similar conceptual beliefs among ancient Andeans. Following this line of interpretation, Sherbondy (1988) draws parallels between cultivated trees and mallki – a Quechua term signifying both "ancestor" and "cultivated tree." The ancestor-as-tree is perceived as one with deep roots in the earth that reproduces life in the form of fruit. Sillar (1996:269) links the process of making chuñu (dried potatoes) to the process of the mummification of ancestors. Long deceased and therefore desiccated ancestors – "grandmother dust" (laq'a achila) and "grandfather dust" (laq'a awilita) – are considered a potential source of fertility for the earth.

The concept of transformation or becoming an ancestor is an underlying tenet of ancestor veneration. Ancestorhood is a status or role to be achieved, first by one's behavior and respected longevity in life, followed by a conscious, public effort on the part of the ancestor's descendants to remember. Implicit in this concept of transformation is the belief in a corporeal and spiritual body, elements of which remain and others of which transmigrate after death. Citing the Colonial extirpation of idolatries documents, Tello (1929) emphasized pacarinas, origin places to which the spiritual body returns. In the Andes, there is often a deep-seated association between tombs, special geographical features, and places of group origin (Urton 1999). Not surprisingly, caves, grottoes, and associated grave constructions often held interments (Isbell 1997a; Kauffmann-Doig et al. 1989; Muscutt 1998). As we will describe, many groups of the Early Intermediate Period appear to have stressed that ancestors hold potential for transformation that can be kindled by attention, nourishment, and veneration in their earthly setting.

Archaeological referents for ancestor worship

In the absence of written texts, our assessment of ancestor veneration relies upon inferences from the archaeological record and iconographic readings of visual images. Drawing from wider examples of ancestor veneration and particularly Andean contexts and traditions, we examine several material referents collectively to better distinguish the treatment of ancestors from general funerary traditions and practices: mortuary patterns, shrines, caches and offerings, iconography, evidence for feasting and celebration, territorial expressions, and public displays. We recognize the difficulties in attempting to identify specific personages in the archaeological record, especially where consistent data are lacking. Moreover, we acknowledge that some ancestors may be conceived by ancient Andeans as ideal or mythical; hence, the correlations we seek may not be manifest in specific material forms.

Mortuary patterns
Here we are concerned with cultural practices associated with interment and especially those that may specify esteemed ancestors. Analysis of mortuary patterns provides both indications of a cultural group's norms and aberrations in terms of spatial patterning, treatment of the dead, and variations in tomb constructions. The presence of intrusive burials is of particular concern. We consider instances of "funerary displacement," a practice that involves the intentional removal, disruption, or destruction of an interment in a cemetery by others who wish to appropriate that space. We propose that it represents an aberration of custom as most ancient Andeans interred their kin in specific places and respected the cemeteries of other groups. To get at the question of whether intrusion reflects a need for space (e.g., population increase) or a conscious reordering of ancestral space requires additional lines of supporting evidence.

A second source of interest is evidence for tomb reentry. Descendants would be expected to access the dead for the purpose of renewing offerings or removing the body (or some of its parts). In this vein, secondary burials or skeletal materials that have been moved to a new location are instructive. These may take the form of bundles of disarticulated bones or the interment of individual body parts (heads, hands, feet). A related practice of prolonged or protracted burial may also provide supporting evidence for special attention devoted to an ancestor.

Shrines
Ancestor shrines may take the form of an individual mummy, a household commemorative relic, a grave marker, or a place or huaca honoring the ancestors. We recognize that shrines may be distinct from actual burial locations and that the two may have a disjunctive spatial relationship. We consider "cult objects" which may take the form of figural sculpture, as well as ritual space in which veneration activities may have occurred.

Caches and offerings
The practice of caching special objects (including plant materials, skin and hair) for purposes of propitiation is a long-held Andean tradition. These may be buried, burned, or interred under water in any number of contexts. We consider some offering caches which occur in funerary contexts as episodic events following the completion of original interment (Carmichael 1995; Lau 2001; Makowski 2002). We also include others that do not directly relate to funerary constructions or human burials but appear in offering contexts to commemorate specific historical personages or achievements (Verano 1995; see also Cook 1992a).

Iconography and images of transformation
Images of transformation may represent ecstatic shamans in trance, masked personages mimicking actual dance ceremonies and mythical reenactments. Here we are concerned with visual referents of humans portrayed as persons of importance

as well as mortuary images (scenes portraying death, interment, mummies), and images that might commemorate mythical events pertaining to human origins. We also consider works of art and architecture that implicate the efforts of groups to commemorate particular individuals.

Celebration and feasting

Feasting and celebration are associated both with mortuary ritual and ancestor cult activities. Various lines of supporting evidence are necessary to distinguish one from the other in the archaeological record. The location where feasts are held or the type of the structure (or plaza, pampa) in which they occur provide some indications of the nature of the feast. Drinking cups and liquid storage containers, musical instruments and their attendant iconography lend support to these distinctions. We also consider the amount and kind of feasting refuse to better assess whether food consumed in honor of the dead differs from that of other celebrations.

Expressions of territory

We suggest that land claims among ancestral cults or lineages may be expressed in various forms. Manipulation of burials or interment in unusual locations (away from customary cemeteries or residential sites) may indicate a purposeful association or claim by one group to real or mythical ancestral land. Intentional acts of appropriation may involve the displacement of tombs by new ones or the establishment of ancestor huacas or theft of others. Lineage or ancestor cult territories may be visually demarcated by individual or clusters of ancestor shrines or mortuary monuments, such as chullpas.

Public display

Here we are concerned with public displays that may involve exhibiting mummies in plazas, courts, and open spaces. We also consider monumental art such as stone sculpture and wood monoliths that call attention to ancestor groups or individuals.

Recuay

Recuay culture emerged in northern Peru during the early centuries A.D. and flourished at least until the rise of the Wari state, at about A.D. 700. The highlands of Peru's Department of Ancash formed the heartland of Recuay culture, especially along the upper drainage of the Río Santa, better known as the Callejón de Huaylas. Recuay peoples held strong influence in coastal regions, the western flanks of the Andes (Cordillera Negra), and neighboring highland zones.

The Recuay are best known for their distinctive art that developed following the demise of Chavín. Despite the geographic overlap, Recuay ceramics and stone sculpture lack continuity with Chavín in terms of style or representational content. Unlike Chavín art, Recuay art, strictly defined, is known primarily from funerary contexts.

Ceramics are the hallmark of Recuay culture (Figures 5.1 (top row) and 5.2). Innovations in technology and artistic elaboration are evident: thin oxidized pastes, polychrome and resist painting and hand-modeled sculptural decoration (Eisleb 1987; Grieder 1978; Reichert 1977). Ceramic vessels sometimes employ white kaolinite clays or slips. Compared to regular clays, sources of kaolinite are more limited in distribution in Peru and the clay requires a higher firing temperature.

As shown by stylistic similarities, Recuay people held diverse cultural relations with other peoples of the Early Intermediate Period, most notably those represented by the Moche, Gallinazo, Cajamarca, Lima, and montane forest cultures (e.g., Bankmann 1979; Church 1996; Daniel Julien 1988). Interaction with Wari became especially prominent later in Recuay development (Lau 2001; Schaedel 1993). Located centrally in northern Peru, the Recuay participated in cultural interchanges linking different parts of the highlands, coast, and Amazonian headwaters.

It seems reasonable that Recuay peoples brokered some economic transactions for these regions. In addition to raw materials and prestige goods (e.g., marine shell, salt, metals, fineware ceramics, bird feathers, coca, and other commodities), exchange probably included products such as camelid meat and staple tuber crops, complemented by fruits, vegetables, and maize from lower elevations. Some high-altitude communities processed camelid fiber, probably for Recuay-style textiles (Lau 2001:416–419).

Not surprisingly, many Recuay settlements occupy strategic locations on vital routes of exchange, commonly as defensible settlements or as hubs of core areas (Proulx 1982; Topic and Topic 1983). In key trade and production zones, important regional centers developed in various parts of the Recuay heartland. Perhaps best exemplified by the settlement of Pashash (Grieder 1978; J. Smith 1978), these centers were probably the seats of powerful regional chiefdoms.

Recuay warfare and political authority

As in other Early Intermediate Period cultures, warfare is a recurring theme in the interpretation of Recuay groups. Although there is little physical evidence for actual intergroup hostilities, settlement planning, architecture, and iconography indicate that warfare played central roles in shaping Recuay society. The wide majority of known Recuay sites can be characterized as small hilltop settlements, often with restrictive access, strategic positions, and fortifications. It is likely that most Recuay peoples lived in areas closer to their fields and pastures, but convened at these hilltop locations as refuges during periods of aggression. Larger settlements often feature massive perimeter walls, baffles, parapets, and moats. Investigations at some Recuay hilltop sites have also recovered weaponry, such as slingstones, axes, mace-heads, and projectile points. These Recuay patterns coincide with the widespread emergence of fortified settlements throughout the north highlands, including the Alto Chicama, Huamachuco, and Cajamarca regions (D. Julien 1988; McCown 1945; Pérez 1988, 1994; Terada 1979; Topic and Topic 1982). This defensive and

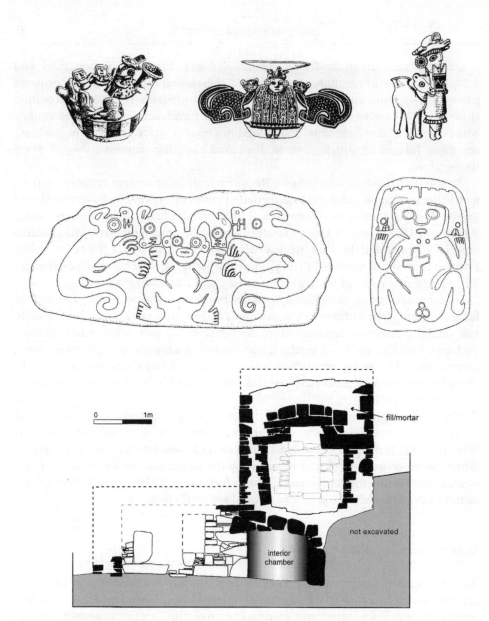

Figure 5.1. *Top left*: Recuay jar showing scene with drinking and revelry (adapted from Carrión Cachot 1955: lámina XVI-j)

Top center: Recuay jar showing "central figure scene" (rollout). Two profile felines flank the frontal human figure, probably an important Recuay leader. He is dressed in an elaborately decorated tunic, earspools, and headdress, from which the jar's short cylindrical spout is attached (adapted from Carrión Cachot 1955: lámina XV-c)

Top right: Recuay vessel of panpipe player, dressed in elaborate regalia, leading a llama. The representation may refer to the presentation and sacrifice of camelids in Recuay ceremonies (adapted from Carrión Cachot 1955: lámina XVII-b)

Middle left: Horizontal slab sculpture (s11), from Chinchawas (Ancash), showing central figure scene. Height 88 cm, length 203 cm

Middle right: Vertical slab sculpture (s9), from Chinchawas (Ancash), showing splayed male ancestor figure. Height 102 cm, width 68 cm

Bottom: Superposition of tombs at Chinchawas, Ancash. Chullpa Tomb 8 is built directly above an oval-shaped subterranean chamber, to which is attached another rectangular chullpa structure (CT-8sub). Small eastern-facing thresholds facilitated access to the chullpa and interments

Figure 5.2. Recuay ceramic vessel showing ornate multi-storied funerary structure. Above-ground mausolea, known as chullpas, were dedicated to housing ancestor bundles and commonly adorned with sculptures. Human tenon-heads flank either side of a threshold, topped by four statue-like ancestor figures (photo courtesy Staatlische Museen zu Berlin-Preussischer Kulturbesitz Ethnologisches Museum)

militaristic posturing reflects a sociopolitical milieu in the north highlands in which the threat of intergroup violence, apparently, was pervasive.

Recuay art also reflects a preoccupation with warfare. Some ceramic sculpture features scenes of large fortified enclosures with armed sentries positioned along the walls (Lumbreras 1978:113). Moreover, in both ceramic and stone sculpture, Recuay artists depicted highly individualized male warriors armed with clubs and shields. Differences in rank or status may have been marked by formal regalia, such as distinctive headdresses, adornments, and insignias. Disembodied heads or "trophy heads" are common motifs, appearing as neck adornments and clutched in bags (Schaedel 1948: figs. 56–57; Tello 1929:75–80). In addition, human hands and feline paws and heads often adorn the headdresses worn by Recuay warriors (Disselhoff 1956). As symbols of hunting or combat success, the taking of trophies must have been an important practice by which males in Recuay groups negotiated social acceptance, prominence, or rank.

Curiously, other implements of warfare like bows and arrows, spears and spearthrowers, or scenes of siege or killing are uncommon in Recuay art. As in Moche iconography, this may reflect small-scale fights or staged one-on-one contests that may have been centered more on the performance of the matches or the capture of opponents and trophies, rather than large-scale battles involving armies and territorial conquest (Donnan 1978; Hocquenghem 1987; Topic and Topic 1997). Wider-scale conflicts between groups almost certainly occurred, but Recuay artists, like their Moche counterparts, chose not to render them or render them literally.

It is worth noting that some painted scenes from Moche vessels may represent Moche and Recuay combatants in conflict (Donnan 1978:49). Disselhoff (1956) and J. Smith (1978) identified that some features of the non-Moche figures, such as facial treatment, weaponry, headdresses, and accoutrements, had parallels in Recuay art (cf. Reichert 1989). It is unclear, though, whether such scenes commemorated real events or treat a general, perhaps idealized or mythical theme of coast–highland conflict.

Recuay visual culture also expresses clear social differences in status, position, and wealth (Gero 2001; Lumbreras 1974a; Reichert 1977). Ceramic and stone sculptures often depict a single male who is accorded privileged treatment: central placement, a larger size, and more elaborate attire and accouterments. The figure is often accompanied by a number of ancillary figures who perform activities around him, in architectural settings or in groups (Figure 5.1 top left). Many are women carrying drinking goblets or textile and infant bundles, held out with both hands as part of a series of "presentation" themes (J. Smith 1978:63–64). As in Moche iconography, individual scenes or images may form parts of a larger narrative (Donnan 1978; Quilter 1997). Given the complex and individualized treatment of the figures, these "presentation" scenes may very well treat life-history events, such as the birth of an heir, political ascendancy, public appearances, or funerals.

Traditions in mortuary architecture

Recuay peoples interred their dead using a variety of constructions. Subterranean tombs form one category, with different types of elaboration. Cist graves are a very common type occurring in many parts of the Callejón de Huaylas. They typically consist of a small, rectangular chamber capped by large stone slabs or natural boulders. More elaborate examples bear stone-lined side walls and antechambers which connect the entrance to the main burial chamber (Lau 2001; Ponte 2000).

Subterranean galleries comprise another type, and were used both as locales for interment and also as accessways into larger multi-compartment chambers. They are especially common at funerary sites near Huaraz (Bennett 1944). Formed by lining the side walls and roof with stone slabs, some galleries extend up to 20 m, but most measure between 3 and 10 meters in length, and about a meter or so in height and width. The most elaborate Recuay burials consist of multichambered complexes, like those of Jancu, Katak, and Pashash. In this type, a main chamber connects a series of compartments, presumably for multiple individual interments. In the case of Jancu, flat stone slabs, arranged perpendicular to the floor, partition the interior chamber into a number of distinct burial compartments (Wegner 1994).

Another category of north highland burial practice uses above ground constructions, or chullpas (Figure 5.1 bottom). These are rectangular in floor plan, with the façade of the building typically one of the longer ends (Bennett 1944). Chullpas may have one or more doorways that face cardinal directions, but there exists a preference for eastern exposure to the rising sun (Isbell 1997a). Basic chullpas have just one chamber, while more elaborate examples are partitioned into multiple chambers through use of interior walls or columns. Most chullpas in the north highlands were one-story, but the largest known examples have additional levels. Wilkawaín, the largest known chullpa, measures roughly 15 × 20 m in plan and contains three stories with at least 21 chambers. To heighten their prominence on the terrain, these chullpas also lie on top of raised platforms. Chullpas often appear in clusters, and are sometimes enclosed by perimeter walls.

At Chinchawas, excavations in chullpas recovered materials dating after A.D. 800 (Lau 2001). This is consistent with other chullpa sites of the north highlands bearing imported ceramics of mid–late Wari cultural influence (Bennett 1944; Isbell 1991a). The tradition of subterranean tombs therefore likely pre-dates chullpa structures. Nevertheless, there is at least some temporal overlap, regional variability, and functional similarities in both practices to interpret the chullpas as terminal components of a broader Recuay funerary tradition.

Despite temporal and general physical distinctions, both the subterranean and chullpa mortuary traditions employ comparable practices and address similar principles about how to treat their dead. Both traditions appear to be able to accommodate multiple individuals. Larger tombs especially are mausolea intended for the interment of many individuals, perhaps organized on the basis of kin relationships or other group affiliations (Isbell 1997a). Multiple chambers in chullpas likely served to house separate interments in the same manner as the compartmentalized spaces of subterranean tombs.

In addition, there is a strong focus on reuse. In chullpa tombs, small doorway openings facilitated reentry. This served a number of functions, including the retrieval and veneration of certain individuals, maintenance of the tomb, and new interments (Lau 2000). Along the same lines, entrances and key access points in subterranean tombs are often not sealed by walls; rather, they are closed off temporarily by movable stone slabs that can be repositioned in place, thus permitting intermittent access to inner chambers (Bennett 1944; Wegner 1994). Niches in both chullpas and subterranean chambers probably functioned to hold sources of light and store ritual paraphernalia or grave goods.

Reuse also characterizes central cemetery areas where local peoples maintained distinct burial practices through time. In these key zones, morphologically discrete mortuary constructions occur in the same general area over a period of time. This is clearly the case for the numerous constructions at Katak (Bennett 1944; Tello 1929). The clustering of chullpas also belongs to this tradition of locating or adding new tombs next to older ones, perhaps as ways to map kin-based associations to certain ancestors. Interestingly, at Ichik Wilkawaín, and Chinchawas, chullpas are built intentionally above subterranean tombs in key cemetery zones (Figure 5.1 bottom). In so doing, chullpa builders superimposed a different mortuary program that was compatible with earlier practices. We further explore the practice of "tomb displacement" below.

Finally, there is geocentrism in both mortuary traditions. Subterranean tombs and chullpas frequently exploit natural depressions or fractures in bedrock, boulders, and hilly outcrops to comprise parts of walls. Large monolithic slabs, moreover, are used in both traditions as capping or roof stones over the interment chambers. In the case of Jancu, a gigantic lenticular boulder serves as the main roofing element, while rock overhangs sheltered Recuay funerary compartments at Aukispukio. Subterranean constructions were not always hidden to prehistoric peoples, as large stone uprights or boulders were often positioned above the tomb to mark their location at ground level, such as at Jancu, Roko Amá, and Chinchawas.

Recuay peoples co-opted natural topographic features into funerary architecture for a number of reasons. First, the builders sought permanence and stability in these special constructions. Durability is noteworthy because highland Ancash is prone to earthquakes and other types of natural disasters. In addition, it is clear that both the subterranean and chullpa mortuary traditions of Recuay culture allied ancestors with natural features of the landscape. This appears to be an early expression of indigenous highland beliefs, described in ethnohistorical and ethnographical accounts, of the close connections between ancestors, the physical terrain, and fertility/renewal ritual (Allen 2002; Bastien 1995; Gose 1994). The rich associations between topographic features (especially springs, caves, and mountains) and cosmological places for emergence, death, and group origins appear linked to broader cultural traditions manifest in many parts of the New World (Heyden 1981; Roe 1982; Salomon 1995). It follows that dotting the region with mortuary monuments establishes enduring visual cues for the dependency between land and ancestry, and may have marked territorial boundaries of Recuay communities, social groups, and their lands.

Stone sculpture and ancestors

Richard Schaedel (1952) first recognized that small and large settlements in highland Ancash actively produced stone sculpture in the Recuay tradition. Although Recuay stone carving is best known from core areas (e.g., Pashash, Aija, and Huaraz), production occurred in many pockets of highland Ancash with little overt evidence of permanent elites (Lau 2002). Further, Recuay stone sculptures show considerable variability in their style and execution, although the representational content is fairly restricted (Wegner 1994), suggesting that various groups of different means were responsible for their manufacture. Thus, interpretations about their production must include agency at different levels of sociopolitical complexity. We believe that many stone sculptures constituted key objects in Recuay ancestor cults, and can be best understood as components of a flexible religious tradition organized along kin-based affiliations.

The Recuay were inheritors of a prominent Ancash practice, made famous at Chavín de Huántar, of using tenon-heads to embellish the façades of walls (Burger 1992:132). Sculptures were attached to walls by cantilevering the opposite end, a long projection known as a "tenon," into holes in the wall. This produced the effect of suspending the sculpture from the wall face. Most Recuay tenon-sculptures depict the heads of humans and felines, but there are also rarer examples of owl heads and full-bodied warriors. Many of the human examples have a distinctive headdress of male leaders/warriors bearing trophy hand motifs (Disselhoff 1956). Where contexts are known, tenon-heads adorned above-ground chullpa mortuary constructions (Thompson and Ravines 1973). Miniature human tenon-heads also appear on the architecture of modeled ceramic vessels (Figure 5.2).

Many Recuay sculptures are worked only on one side, typically on a large flat panel of the stone block. Given their irregular form, most were probably either structural members or propped against walls of special ceremonial buildings. In his investigations at Chinchawas, George Lau found three in situ examples as jamb sculptures on a tomb and high-status residence, and numerous others associated with chullpa mortuary structures (Lau 2001).

Some Recuay statues, which are sculpted in the round, portray individual men and women (Tello 1929). Most are seated, with legs crossed or turning inwards, and arms bent inwards, as if rendering the flexed or tightly tucked positions of mummy bundles (Lumbreras 1974a:116–117). In addition to the conventionalized positions of the body, the flat ovoid face, wide eyes, and prominent jaw resemble masks and other facial representations characteristic of ancestor effigies in late prehistoric Peru (Kauffmann-Doig et al. 1989). Almost all the vertical slabs at Chinchawas depict a single, frontally positioned individual, sometimes with a cross over a diamond-shaped torso (Figure 5.1 middle right). Each figure wears a headdress or has two appendages emerging from the top of the head that arc to either side of the head. The tips of the appendages terminate usually at shoulder height as serpent or feline heads. The legs and feet can either turn inwards or, more commonly, spread outwards in splayed position. Arms are usually bent at the elbow, with the hands held high up. Horizontal slabs, or lintels, in Recuay art frequently portray a similar individual, but who is flanked by two profile feline creatures (Figure 5.1 middle left).

The males on Recuay sculptures often clutch paraphernalia associated with warfare, like clubs and shields. The warriors also wear trophy head images on the belt or around the neck, or carry them in bags hung over the back. Male genitalia are often rendered as two or three raised dots, while female genitalia may be portrayed as a narrow groove in the pubis (Carrión Cachot 1959:12–13). Breasts are not commonly depicted. Certain types of clothing, headdresses, and activities also distinguish women in Recuay art (Tello 1929; see also Gero 2001). It seems possible that some Recuay sculptures could have been wrapped or covered using textiles – such as the bundling of cotton, vegetal materials, logs, stones, and other objects found in coastal cemeteries (Stumer 1954a; Tello and Mejía 1979).

The variability of human representations seems consistent with the notion that these sculptures represent individual personages. Further, their architectural contexts, such as at Chinchawas, suggest that they may have been important people associated with specific tombs and enclosures for ceremonial gatherings, perhaps the founders or heads of certain lineages (Lau 2001, 2002). Ceramic depictions also show Recuay statuary poised as omnipresent, protecting guardians of important structures (Figure 5.2). In these settings, we can expect that ancestor representations in Recuay ceremonial spaces were pervasive references to descent and entitlement for participating individuals and groups.

The human personages of the central figure scene and the vertical slabs bear resemblances to common designs on funerary pottery and painted burial shrouds wrapping late Middle Horizon mummy bundles from the central coast. The Sky God is a frontal anthropomorph often depicted with a serpent headdress or bifurcating head appendages, while the Sky Serpent is a bicephalic creature, often rendered with a serrated body (Menzel 1977). These figures have associations to water, lightning, and supernatural influence over fertility and renewal. Carrión Cachot (1959) argued that these figures, and the natural forces they influenced, were paramount in the Andean religions of the central and north coast.

It seems reasonable that certain attributes of Recuay stone sculpture (head appendages, torso cross, or zigzag designs) were meaningful in the cosmology of transformation from deceased to ancestor. Ethnohistorical sources contain references identifying stone monuments as specific ancestors and landmarks (Doyle 1988). The purposive depiction of nudity, serpent headdresses, and trophy heads in Recuay sculptures may be related to the unique identity or achievements of specific personages – e.g., irrigation works, establishment of territory, or exploits in warfare (Doyle 1988; Salomon 1991).

The felines in Recuay stone sculpture most likely portray pumas. They are commonly rendered in profile, with prominent genitalia (Figure 5.1 middle left). Their juxtaposition to human figures in Recuay art probably reflects an ideology of authority that valued feline virtues (Lau 2002). This would be in keeping with other cultures of Mesoamerica and South America, which make reference to the virility, strength, cunning, killing prowess, and supernatural abilities of felines, especially jaguars and pumas (Benson 1972; Saunders 1998; Tello 1923). Quechua traditions of the Callejón de Huaylas also articulate that pumas are considered to be representations of the recently deceased (Walter 1997).

Ceremonial architecture

Recuay ceremonial architecture, including shrines and temples, is fairly rare in the archaeological record and none has ever been researched systematically. Perhaps the best known are unusual circular structures of concentric walls, with arc-like compartments formed by radial partitions. Such structures are found typically at the highest points of hilltop settlements. Excavations date these constructions to the Recuay period; one structure contained significant amounts of camelid bones and burnt offerings (Lau 2001; Terada 1979).

Tello (1929) likened the form of such buildings to an "Inti Watana," alluding to circular tower constructions of the Inca associated with worship of the sun. Recuay groups certainly accorded their circular buildings special importance, but the hypothesis of astronomical significance cannot yet be substantiated. Similar hilltop constructions occur in other parts of the highlands, such as at Ñawinpukio in Ayacucho, suggesting that similar ceremonial practices and beliefs may have been shared by Early Intermediate Period groups.

Tello also called attention to special architectural constructions on ridgetops throughout highland Ancash. He wrote,

> Apart from the numerous corrals that are seen in all parts of the puna as remains of herding, there exist other corrals, patios, or enclosed plazas – of differing sizes, in rectangular or circular form – located near shrines or at the foot of glaciated peaks as sacred locales or places. The construction of these corrals required the cooperative effort of an organized populace, given that they are formed with large stone uprights and located in columns in the style of the Kalasasasaya [sic] enclosure in Tiwanaku. These corrals were sacred places where the Indians gathered for the celebration of ceremonies. (Tello 1929:45–46, translation ours)

Tello alludes to ceremonial practices that centered on the veneration of ancestors (Doyle 1988; Isbell 1997a). John Rowe (1946:308) describes similar Inca practices: "The mummy-bundles of dead Emperors, who were also regarded as divinities, were brought out with the images. Most ceremonies included elaborate sacrifices, dances, and recitations, during which all present consumed enormous quantities of chicha."

In the Callejón de Huaylas, archaeologists have identified walled patio enclosures similar to those described by Tello above. These constructions are basically open spaces enclosed by walls, measuring between 15 and 20 m, and appear to form parts of high-status architectural complexes on hilltop settlements. Unlike residential buildings, however, these enclosures seem to have been mainly used for special corporate gatherings. At Queyash Alto, near Marcará, large densities of food and serving pottery remains, panpipe fragments, and evidence for high-status goods are consistent with large-scale feasting and displays of wealth (Gero 1990, 1992). At Chinchawas, in addition to dense remains of meat consumption and serving pottery, archaeologists have found that the enclosures featured sub-floor drainage works, elaborate masonry, and ancestor sculptures (Lau 2002).

These constructions provided special settings where corporate groups could reaffirm their kin ties. These were also settings where leaders could reinforce their authority and build prestige by sponsoring festive ceremonies, in practices sometimes known as "commensal politics" (Dietler and Hayden 2001). Also, the festive provisioning of food and drink, especially intoxicants, in return for labor is a common social strategy in the Andes (e.g., Gero 1990; Godelier 1977; Hastorf 1993; Mayer 2001). Andean festive reciprocity may be best known from Inca administrative centers, where great feasts of food and chicha corn beer were sponsored to exact labor obligations from the provinces (C. Morris and Thompson 1985).

Discussion

Ancestor veneration and mortuary ritual, in general, were significant fields for cultural elaboration for the Recuay. In addition to offerings such as finely made sculptural ceramics, Recuay peoples invested considerable effort in mortuary structures and carved stone monuments to honor the deceased. Through comparison of archaeological and historical evidence, we now have information to contextualize these objects and settings in order to reconstruct some of the activities in Recuay mortuary ritual.

As in many parts of the Andes, the offering of drink, especially chicha, was an important component of Recuay mortuary practices. Nearly 50 years ago, as part of a cross-cultural study of water and fertility cults, Carrión Cachot (1955) drew special attention to Recuay funerary vessels, known as pacchas, which were used for libations and offerings of chicha. Many of these vessels are sculpted with scenes that may portray dedicatory ancestor ceremonies. The focus is on a central figure presiding over a number of individuals often holding cups and engaging in formal acts of presentation, toasting, and celebration. Elaborately attired individuals are rendered in the act of drinking, presenting a toast, or receiving cups from subsidiary figures. As noted for highland groups in the south-central Andes, the living enter into relations with the dead, with the expectation of recompense. Gose (1994:137) argues, "when people 'do ayni' [reciprocal transactions] with the dead by providing alcohol at the burial, the dead repay them with water in the rainy season."

The presentation and sacrifice of llamas, as an obligation of a generous host, was also probably common in festive ceremonies. This may be the subject treated in well-known ceramic vessels showing a Recuay warrior or musician dressed in elaborate apparel and headdress, while leading a camelid by a rope (Figure 5.1 top right). At Chinchawas, large amounts of camelid remains were found adjacent to enclosures with ancestor sculptures, suggesting that consumption of camelid meat also figured prominently in public feasts (Lau 2002). The playing of musical instruments, dancing, and other social activities, all portrayed in Recuay pottery (Carrión Cachot 1955), likely reinforced the appeal of such occasions.

Recuay ancestor ceremonies served to stress the authority of local leaders and played key roles in personal aggrandizement. Like other societies of the Central Andes, leaders sponsored public celebrations that were premised on kinship relations, feasting, and conspicuous displays of highly symbolic sumptuary items. These activities acted to promote community cohesion, but also conferred individualizing benefits to the leaders, such as tribute, labor obligations, and legitimation of their authority.

Lima

The Lima culture of Peru's central coast, like Recuay, has long been recognized as part of the important regional developments of the Early Intermediate Period (Gayton 1927; Jijón y Caamaño 1949; Kroeber 1926; Strong and Corbett 1943; Tabío 1965; Uhle 1903[1991]; Villar Córdoba 1935). During the time of early scholarship, the Chillón, Chancay, upper Rimac, and Lurín Valleys were day excursions to the shore and countryside outside Peru's capital city, Lima. Today, these valleys are fully integrated into the city's growing suburban sprawl.

Indeed, the recent swelling of Lima as an urban center has both facilitated and limited our understanding of the central coast in prehistoric times. While the push to populate outlying zones has uncovered important archaeological finds, urbanization continues to threaten the very integrity of the sites, especially in terms of their destruction by development and illicit looting (Ravines 1995; Stothert 1980). Many of the key type sites for Lima culture no longer exist (Stumer 1953; Willey 1943). At the same time, the growth of Lima and burgeoning archaeology programs have cultivated an active professional interest in Lima culture and local patrimony, especially on the part of universities and cultural institutions.

Scholars in Peru are at the forefront of the archaeology of Lima culture and related developments of the central coast. Many studies have grown out of research programs and university field schools focusing on sites around the Lima area (Cárdenas 1999; Dulanto 2001; Makowski 2002). New studies emphasize representation in iconography (Escobedo and Goldhausen 1999; Falcón 2000; Goldhausen 2001), architectural patterns (Canziani 1987; Paredes Botoni 1992), economic orientations (Shady 1982), sociopolitical patterns in settlement systems (Silva 1996), and cultural transformations vis-à-vis Wari influence (Guerrero and Palacios 1994; Shady 1982).

The first studies of Lima culture – known variously as Interlocking, Pachacamac Interlocking, Playa Grande, inter alia – focused on the culture history and mortuary practices of Lima groups (Jijón y Caamaño 1949; Kroeber 1926; Strong and Corbett 1943; Stumer 1953, 1954a, 1954b; Uhle 1991). Patterson (1966) proposed a nine-phase Lima ceramic sequence that spanned the Early Intermediate Period and the early portion of the Middle Horizon; earlier components include Miramar, Baños de Boza, and other white-on-red styles. Recent studies employ a more conservative terminology, preferring "early," "middle," and "late" Lima designations (Escobedo and Goldhausen 1999; Falcón 2000; Makowski 2001). Currently, scholars refer to post-Lima components, sometimes including Lima Phase 9, under the stylistic term Nievería, previously known as Proto-Lima, Cajamarquilla, Pachacamac, and Maranga (Fernández 1960; Shimada 1991). Menzel's stylistic analysis (1964) situates Nievería during Middle Horizon 1 and Pachacamac as Middle Horizon 2. More recently, Shady (1982:20–21) argues that Nievería likely begins to be used during the late Early Intermediate Period and continues into Middle Horizon 2 (cf. Guerrero and Palacios 1994).

The interpretation of the sociopolitical implications of Lima culture remains at a nascent stage. On the basis of settlement pattern data, Earle (1972) postulated the expansion of a Lima state, driven by demographic pressures, into Lurín by the end of the Early Intermediate Period (also MacNeish, Patterson, and Browman 1975:52). Drawing upon models of zonal complementarity, Dillehay (1979) argued for the coexistence of different ethnic groups occupying mid-valley production zones simultaneously. Like Moche and Recuay territoriality, Patterson, McCarthy, and Dunn (1982) identified a mid-valley frontier zone separating different cultural groups – for example, coastal Lima vs. highland traditions. By the end of the Early Intermediate Period (Lima Phases 5–8), the lower valley "social formation," as reflected in cultural expansion, had pushed into the frontier zone, apparently incorporating highland groups and settlements (Patterson, McCarthy, and Dunn 1982:69). Despite these contributions, there remains no consensus regarding complexity in Lima society, especially in regard to regional variability and change through time.

Although arguments for a centralized Lima state continue, some Peruvian scholars have problematized this interpretation (Silva 1996). At least for the early portion of the Early Intermediate Period, Makowski (2001) prefers the identification of confederations of small ethnic groups sharing strong similarities in material culture and religious customs centered on funerary practices and community integration (see Stothert 1980:295). Only later, with the growth of Maranga and Cajamarquilla, is there evidence for powerful multi-ethnic, multi-valley polities (Canziani 1987; Falcón 2001; Shady 1982).

Funerary practices

Lima is best known for its huaca structures and cemeteries such as Pachacamac, Cerro Culebras, Cerro Trinidad, and Playa Grande. The huaca constructions are essentially mounded structures or terraced platforms constructed of adobe or poured clay tapia. Some exhibit polychrome murals. Lima shares with other coastal Early Intermediate Period groups a renewed emphasis on huaca construction after the decline of Chavín.

Lima period huaca complexes show considerable variability in content and activity contexts. The variability probably reflects functional versatility at the synchronic level as well as unique histories of use (Canziani 1987; Sestieri 1971:101). The complexes no doubt functioned for high-status residential and secular activities, although exact correlations remain difficult to isolate (Paredes Botoni 1992; Silva et al. 1988; Stumer 1954b). Falcón (2000:60) argues that Playa Grande was an important religious center because of its proximity to offshore islands. Elite ceremonial occupations at Pachacamac can be established as early as the Lima period temple and nearby structures (Franco 1993; Jiménez 1985; Paredes 1985; Shimada 1991; Strong and Corbett 1943). It seems clear that Lima and related groups also frequently used huacas, and more commonly the surrounding complexes, as settings for burials (Sestieri 1971; Stumer 1953, 1954b).

Like some Early-to-Middle Moche examples, Lima interments often show extended burial positions, placement below litters of wood/cane construction, and rich offerings of pottery and textiles (Kroeber 1926). At least in Playa Grande and Chillón, orientation is typically north–south, with the head face down. Large portions of pots, typically plainware, often cover the head (Stumer 1953, 1954a). Funerary litters appear at least by the "Banos de Boza" White-on-Red occupation of Chancay (Willey 1943:176) and continue into Nieveria (e.g., Kroeber 1954; Sestieri 1971:102). In contrast, burials associated with later Middle Horizon materials are typically mummy bundle interments or fardos, with flexed body position (Ravines 1981; Sestieri 1971).

Based on differences in grave offerings and architecture, high- and low-status individuals can be discerned by Lima times. Some of the richest Lima tombs, often with multiple interments, were found at Playa Grande. Stumer (1953:45–46) identified graves in which individuals were given different funerary treatments: the "master" often occupied a litter and was lavished with camelid fiber textiles with Lima interlocking designs and necklaces, while the "servants" were naked or wrapped only in a simple cotton textile. Grave offerings of fineware ceramics, figurative effigies, Spondylus shell, precious stone jewelry, and rare items from tropical forested regions like birds, monkeys and chonta wood probably reflect social differences in prestige and the ability to access rare goods (Stumer 1953, 1958:13).

Major differences in social ranking may also be manifest in a massive interment of over one hundred humans underneath the Temple of the Sun at Pachacamac, perhaps a dedicatory event for the temple during late Lima times (Strong and Corbett 1943:41). Similarly, Shady (1982:56) reinterprets human and monkey remains found in burial excavations at Cajamarquilla's Huaca Tello as immolations accompanying a higher-status Nieveria mummy bundle (Sestieri 1971).

Changing funerary patterns

Long-term scientific investigations at Lima cemeteries are beginning to recover important evidence for ancestor cults that emerge following the weakening of Chavín influence on the central coast (Makowski 2002; Stothert 1980). In the Tablada de Lurín cemeteries, early graves employ shaft and chamber tombs; later, subterranean chambers become more prominent. Although individual burials were present, the majority of the graves were composed of multiple interments.

Archaeological patterns indicate that Early Intermediate Period cultures of the Lurín Valley reused funerary spaces in different ways. Reuse first describes the episodic post-mortem treatment of the dead. It is clear that both the early (Tablada-style shaft and chamber tombs) and later practices (post-Tablada subterranean stone chamber) involved periodic reentry into the tomb. Periodic access, especially in the later phase, enabled additional interments and offerings, tomb renovations, maintenance and cleaning, secondary burials, and care/removal of the dead in the form of mummy bundles (Cárdenas 1999; Makowski 2002; Stothert 1980). At some time, presumably when there were no more interments or when treatment ceased, each grave was sealed.

Reuse certainly describes the intrusive placement of subterranean chamber tombs over earlier shaft and chamber tombs (Cárdenas 1999; Makowski 2002). No doubt, this reaffirmed the continued significance of the cemetery space. This is interesting because some of the later post-Tablada graves intentionally destroy parts of earlier burial structures and their bundles, what Makowski (2002) describes as a firm "lack of respect" for earlier groups. There is, therefore, continuity in the valuation of the zone as a sacred mortuary area, despite the cultural and stylistic discontinuities in mortuary architecture and pottery. Makowski (2002) argues the patterns derive from two regional traditions – the earlier from the local lower valley, and the later from the mid- to upper-valley/highlands – which may have some temporal overlap.

Discussion

Lima culture funerary activities exemplify the practice of tomb displacement, a deliberate shifting, crowding out, or appropriation of older materials/burials to privilege new ones. The Tablada de Lurín pattern of placing younger tombs over older ones is apparently a purposeful appropriation of sacred space (Makowski 2002). In many ways, the practice resembles the deliberate superpositioning of chullpa mausolea over subterranean tombs in the Recuay area. Notably, the pattern appears to occur regardless of chullpa size, implying that groups of different scales and status participated in this practice. Because of the latitude in scale, such practices were probably organized and carried out along the lines of corporate groups based on common descent or affiliation. If these tombs with multiple interments were the mausolea of kin groups, as seems very likely, then the practice of funerary displacement appears to co-opt the ritual prestige of the older tombs and express a new territorial authority.

These central coast patterns also encourage reevaluation of the character and significance of other Early Intermediate Period funerary practices. For example, the presence of elaborate mummy bundles at Lurín for Early Lima corresponds temporally to the Necropolis burials on the south coast and may reflect a wider coastal phenomenon following the collapse of Chavín (see Paracas section, this chapter).

The Playa Grande excavations recovered evidence for a "simulated burial," where a large portion of a thick wooden log occupied an actual corpse's position on a litter. Stumer (1953:45), citing similar finds at Ancón, conjectured that such interments may have commemorated important individuals lost at sea. The extended burials of Middle Lima correlate with key cultural changes associated with "classic" Lima polychrome styles (e.g., Interlocking, Playa Grande). Additionally, there are central coast mortuary patterns for which no clear parallels are evident.

Finally, the fact that mummy bundles proliferate again during the Middle Horizon indicates another series of important transformations associated with Wari influence (Ravines 1981). Local peoples apparently found it worthwhile again to participate in previous style cults, reconfigured with Wari symbolism and rhetoric. Did Wari affiliates, as part of state political strategy on the central coast, advocate a return to older, but familiar, religious traditions as a conscious rejection of Middle–Late Lima elite ideology? After the florescence of Lima culture, local peoples apparently grew increasingly dissatisfied with the ideology responsible for what Stumer called "primitive elegance" on the central coast, and apparently more receptive towards new religious emblems bearing strong Wari influence (Menzel 1964, 1977; Shady 1982).

Poorly understood but concomitant socio-religious changes may have facilitated the Middle Horizon growth and transformations of use in major centers, such as Cajamarquilla, Pachacamac, Maranga, and Copacabana. Sestieri (1971:103) indicates that an intrusive mummy bundle (Tomb VIII) was buried at the Huaca Tello in Cajamarquilla, pushing away but not completely destroying an earlier Nievería extended interment with a cane litter. This seems an outward rejection of earlier funerary practices but is also in keeping with the local tradition of funerary displacement at a highly esteemed burial locale.

Paracas

The vestiges of Paracas (900 B.C.–A.D. 1) cover a 350 km strip that encompasses the coastal valleys of Cañete, Chincha, Pisco, Ica and Acarí, the Río Grande de Nazca Drainage, and the Paracas Peninsula for which the culture and art styles are named. In contrast to the barren, windswept landscape of the south coast, Paracas visual expressions celebrate life and the fertile earth. An array of images rendered in ceramic, cloth, and gold convey messages about the Paracas conceptual universe – the continuum of life and death, the transformative qualities of that continuum, and the mythical ancestors who must have figured actively in daily life. We know that Paracas cultural practices also reinforced the relationship between the living and the dead through mortuary rituals in which seed-like bundles were interred in the earth, and by way of ritual specialists and leaders who provided guidance in the affairs of agriculture and economy – transforming the desert into a fertile ground for maize, gourd, and cotton cultivation and making available the resources of the sea.

Archaeological investigations have centered both on establishing settlement patterns and interpreting mortuary complexes. Inferences drawn from the patterning of where people lived, the nature of their settlements (e.g., households, cities, ritual centers, and cemeteries) and how and when they were abandoned suggest a sociopolitical organization loosely defined as a complex chiefdom, centered in the Ica Valley heartland. In conjunction with the Ica Valley chronology or ten-phase Ocucaje sequence, early, middle and late periods of development are recognized.

Paracas society and sociopolitical developments

Of principal concern to the present discussion is the period in which Late Paracas society flourished (500 B.C.–A.D. 1). It is during this time that large, highly visible communities such as Tajahuana, Cerro Max Uhle, Animas Altas, and Chongos developed. Platform pyramidal structures, few excavated, are the most evident feature of these agglutinated centers which are configured with precincts for ceremonial activities, residences, workshops, and cemeteries. At Tajahuana, some buildings coincide with landscape features and others appear to be oriented with celestial alignments. Clearly, populations had increased from earlier times as Late Paracas settlements are notable in all south coastal valleys including Ica (Cook 1999; DeLeonardis 1991, 1997; Massey 1986, 1991), the Nazca Drainage (Browne and Baraybar 1988; Reindel, Isla, and Koschmieder 1999; H. Silverman 1994), Pisco (Peters 1987–88, 1997; H. Silverman 1997), and Chincha (Canziani 1992).

Innovative art forms and styles distinguish Late Paracas from its earlier visual traditions. Fineware ceramic styles include a traditional painted and incised form historically grounded in Ica, complemented by the monochrome fineware Topará style of Pisco. New figures, including humans and the wide-eyed Oculate Being, appear in the iconography. Massey's (1986, 1991) work at the temple complex of Animas Altas also points to the introduction of sculpted wall friezes on the interior of at least one temple. Production of finely woven cloth reaches its zenith and is best articulated by the garments and wrapping cloths of Necropolis, discussed below. Embroidered figures, distinct from the ceramic repertoire, include masked personages, grinning back-bent creatures, and individuals holding or tasting severed heads (Figure 5.3 top left, right).

Earlier settlements (900–500 B.C.) are characterized by small villages with associated cemeteries largely found in Ica. Elite huacas or shrines such as Cerrillos and smaller domestic settlements are known in Chiquerrillo and Callango (DeLeonardis 2003; Wallace 1962). While lacking the monumental grandeur of the later period, Early Paracas society is not thought to be an insular hinterland. Analysis of plant, marine shell, animal bone, and obsidian remains suggests fluid interaction between inland settlements with their highland and coastal neighbors. Ritual practices included offerings to the dead in the form of grave goods, and careful interment of structures at the time of abandonment. Household rituals involving the burning of seeds and rock crystals were likely offered to propitiate the gods to assure fertile and abundant crops (DeLeonardis 1997). Larger shrines such as Cerrillos may have served as regional pilgrimage centers.

We know less about early interment practices, although the fineware ceramics recovered from some graves points to differential types of grave offerings. We may

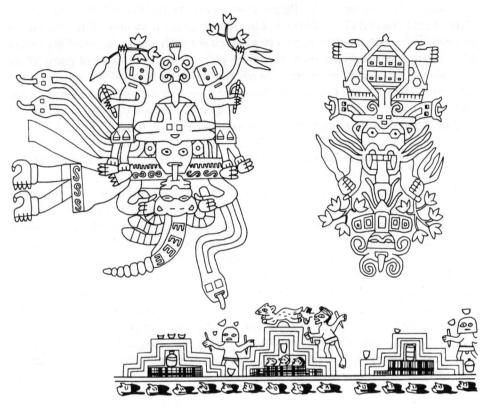

Figure 5.3. *Top left*: Detail, Paracas embroidered textile showing central masked back-bent figure grasping and "tasting" inert feline. Displaying rooted plants, two auxiliary backbent figures flank the central figure (Brooklyn Museum, New York)
Top right: Detail, Paracas embroidered textile showing central, splayed backbent figure holding rooted plants and "tasting" the insect-like diadem of a stylized severed head (Brooklyn Museum, New York)
Bottom: Detail, Late Nasca polychrome double spout and bridge bottle showing altar, officiates, and ceremonial paraphernalia associated with head-caching ritual (Museo Nacional de Antropología, Arqueología e Historia, Lima)

hypothesize that some tombs held elite burials, but in the absence of comparative data we lack the ability to establish rank or to define social roles. Moreover, we will never know whether the graves contained single or multiple burials, nor the age or sex of the deceased. Reindel and Isla's (1999:184–185) systematic excavations in Palpa suggest that, prior to the late period, Paracans were interred in deep graves containing multiple individuals in extended positions.

Head-taking and caching

It is during Late Paracas times that the practice of decapitation and conservation of human heads is observable in the archaeological record. The best evidence for this practice was recorded by Pezzia (1968:99–101) for the neighboring sites of Cerro Max Uhle and Cerro de la Cruz in Ocucaje in the Ica Valley. Here, two caches of heads were excavated in cemeteries associated with the sites. The Cerro Max Uhle cache contained two heads that were placed on a thick layer of pacae (fruit tree) leaves. An offering of ceramic sherds and tiny cobs of maize accompanied the interment. Both heads exhibited an elongated type of cranial deformation. The age and sex of the individuals were not recorded. The Cerro de la Cruz cache contained 13 heads, arranged face up. Some heads were placed atop others. The entire group was covered by a cotton cloth. Small holes were present in the forehead of at least some heads. The holes allowed a cord to be inserted for the purpose of portability and display.

The practice of taking heads and the art of portraying them are most pronounced among the Nasca, discussed in the following section. With regard to ancestor veneration, it is unlikely that the head caches encountered in Ocucaje or elsewhere were taken from the bodies of revered ancestors. Among the heads analyzed by physical anthropologist John Verano (1995:214), a majority represent young to middle-aged men (under age 50). The heads were likely severed at or around the time of death, a practice that differs from removal of the skull long after the body is fully desiccated. It is reasonable to propose that, in some cases, formal caching and secondary burial of heads was a gesture of offering designed to propitiate or "feed" the ancestors. We have previously noted a fruit tree–ancestor link, and the interment of pacae with one head (and there are other Nasca examples) may be one of the earliest expressions of this association.

Places of commemoration

Several aspects of Paracas cemeteries permit us to assess mortuary practices and to highlight the factors critical to ancestor veneration: first and foremost the attention attributed to preparing the dead overall and the differential attention to some, the presence of intrusive burials, evidence of tomb reentry, movement of bodies (secondary interments), the burial of elders, the interment of body parts, and the location of burials relative to their place of origin.

Paracans interred their dead in formal cemeteries and provided offerings of food, ceramics, textiles, and other culturally meaningful objects. During Late Paracas times, the deceased were wrapped in cloth and interred in a seated and flexed position in deep tombs or pits. In the Ica Valley, some of the better-known cemeteries are associated with Cerro Max Uhle, Cerro de la Cruz, and La Peña in Ocucaje, Olladon in Callango, Chiquerrillo, Tajahuana, and Juan Pablo at Teojate. Others documented are Pachinga and Chongos in Pisco (Peters 1987–88, 1997; Pezzia 1972) and various cemeteries in Palpa (Reindel, Isla, and Koschmieder et al. 1999). Few of these cemeteries have received the research attention necessary to make inferences about specific ancestors. For example, consistent data are lacking regarding the age and sex of the deceased or excavation details that would imply reburial or tomb reentry for the purpose of renewing offerings to the dead. We can say that all Paracans were meaningfully interred and that mortuary practices involved burial of both physically whole (mummy or articulated skeleton) and partial bodies (head, or bundled incomplete remains).

Necropolis of Wari Kayan

Perhaps the most spectacular, yet equally understudied, necropoli known for ancient Peru are the Paracas Peninsula cemeteries. Research begun here in 1925 by Julio C. Tello resulted in excavations of hundreds of well-preserved mummy bundles (Tello and Mejía 1979; Yacovleff and Muelle 1932, 1934). Since their discovery, the mummies have received considerable attention because of the exceptional textile garments associated with many of the bundles. Debate continues as to whether the deceased were local inhabitants or bundles brought in from elsewhere to the sacred huaca location of the Paracas Peninsula. Certainly the number and concentration of elite burials in one place is an aberration of custom. The debate is partly fueled by the question of whether the environment (low on sources of fresh water and arable land) would have been able to sustain a resident population. These issues are raised in Tello's excavation report (Tello and Mejía 1979) and are addressed in a number of excellent syntheses of ongoing interpretive problems (Daggett 1991, 1994; Dwyer 1979; Dwyer and Dwyer 1975; Paul 1990; Peters 1997; H. Silverman 1991, 1996a, 1996b).

There is a general consensus that at least two related cultural groups (Cavernas and Necropolis) are buried among two principal cemeteries: Necrópolis de Wari Kayan on Cerro Colorado and Arena Blanca or Cabeza Larga about 1 km to the west. Discrete spatial patterning is lacking – both groups were interred in a disorderly fashion in both cemeteries. Cavernas boot-shaped tombs are associated with Paracas painted and incised ceramics; these tombs pre-date the Necropolis tombs. Cavernas tombs contained single and multiple burials (up to 37 in Caverna V), partial burials (including severed human heads), and secondary burials. All age grades and both sexes were represented. Some tombs were vacant. Others appear to have been reentered and sequentially re-used in ancient times.

Necropolis tombs intruded into the earlier Cavernas habitation refuse, although some bundles (in both cemeteries) were situated in or below chamber-like tombs where they were covered in clean sand. Tombs were marked with posts extending from the base of the tomb to the ground surface. One question that has been raised is whether these structures were intended as burial cists or had previously served some other function.

Necropolis bundles, associated with Topará-style ceramics, are the best known for their size and quality of the textiles. Four hundred twenty-nine small, medium, and large conical-shaped bundles were excavated by Tello on the northern slopes of Cerro Colorado. Only a fraction of the bundles have been unwrapped, but these indicate that hundreds of objects, organic material, cloth, gold ornaments, basketry, and garments accompanied the large (1.5×1.5 m) mummies. Anne Paul (1990:32) estimates that up to $100 \, m^2$ of cloth were utilized in some bundles and as many as 30,000 hours of labor were invested in the production of cloth contained with a single mummy. Among the largest bundles, 33 (about 8 percent) are considered high-status individuals. Carrión Cachot (1949) notes that these individuals were males of advanced age.

Images of transformation

It is uncertain whether the peninsula burials represent local or imported bundles. Nor can we name lineage heads and hence specific ancestors among the Necropolis burials. But we need not limit the discussion to actual bodies when considering archaeological expressions of ancestor veneration. Paracas visual sources abound with references to transformation and the process of becoming an ancestor. A few of the most compelling examples are drawn from icons embroidered on the textiles that accompanied the Necropolis bundles (Tello 1959). One group, known as "back bent" or "flying" figures, has been analyzed by Frame (2001). She presents a convincing argument that some of these latter figures are conceptual representations of ancestor transformations. The figures appear in several progressive variants which Frame proposes are narratives of mythic transformations. In their most basic form, they are shown naked with long hair and exposed ribs, usually holding a fan/knife in one hand and a baton/staff in the other. In another variant, the skirted figures show wounds from bloodletting or autosacrifice. In a yet more progressive variant, the fully clothed figures eat/taste and are eaten/tasted by other back-bent figures (Frame 2001: fig. 4.24). Frame considers the back-bent figures to be a prototype "transformation figure" which also includes complex renditions of composite humans-as-predatory birds, sharks, and felines.

Many of the Necropolis textiles bear images of these intricate figures holding or tasting severed heads. Paul's (2001) analysis considers over 300 of these images. She distinguishes between those pictured with a carrying cord and those carried or held by their hair. The distinction is important because these differences are also reflected among actual heads found in the archaeological record. Based on Tello (1917), Paul suggests that the heads symbolize repositories of the vital essence of life after death. Citing a preponderance of heads shown at the mouth or tongue of whole figures (Paul 2001: fig. 23), she draws analogies between early Colonial accounts of ancestor (mallki) cults and rituals, whereby mummy priests would summon the spirit or upani into his speech (mouth) and temporarily reconstitute the ancestor to invigorate the living.

Discussion

Paracas mortuary ritual and its complementary visual program acknowledged and celebrated the transformative qualities of death. Proper interment was inclusive of all members of society. In a general sense, living generations prepared their dead for the afterlife – essentially a preparation to ensure their rebirth after death. Wrapping or bundling was basic to this process. The body, secured in a womb-like casing, was planted "as a seed." The process of its transition to dust thereby insured continued fertility of the earth (Sillar 1996).

In extreme cases, the process of preparation for the dead may have spanned a lifetime and was likely the work of collective hands (Dwyer and Dwyer 1975; Paul 1990). Moreover, the number of bundle layers appears to be a meaningful gauge of one's status in society. Some of the Necropolis burials are particularly suggestive of lineage heads – esteemed elderly males whose graves were marked and who literally bore the paraphernalia, garments, and thereby the symbolic images of ancestorhood. This is further supported by the fact that not all Paracas burials (particularly in non-peninsula locations) are as sumptuous as the select Necropolis group.

Whether these Necropolis elites were former peninsula residents or transplants is of less concern because, in either case, they assumed dominion of the peninsula cemeteries – perhaps displacing their own ancestors, possibly establishing a new social order.

Paracans also wrapped or bundled and interred other fertility symbols. Mummified severed heads were wrapped or covered in cloth and interred separately or tucked into the wraps of bundles containing whole bodies. At Cabeza Larga, two bundles that at first glance appeared to be infants instead contained cradle boards used to deform the heads of Cavernas children. Even one of Tello's Wari Kayan bundles (Category I-91) was shown to contain not a cadaver, but 12 kilos of black beans (Daggett 1994:57). Apparently this was not the only one of its kind. In fact, the bean bundles are instructive, considering the amount of effort attributed to create a single bundle. Clearly these forms must have served as surrogate mummies similar to the log burial at Playa Grande (see Lima section, this chapter). Moreover, the substitution of beans – a seed that will become a vine, reproducing itself when planted – emphasizes conceptually the regenerative qualities of interment.

Nasca

Once thought to be a state with its capital at Cahuachi, Nasca (ca. A.D. 1–600) has been reevaluated to be a powerful Andean social formation more akin to a theocracy, with Cahuachi serving as a cultural axis (H. Silverman 1993). Archaeological investigations have identified a core development of residential sites and cemeteries in Ica and all of the Río Grande de Nazca Drainage associated valleys. A nine-phase chronological sequence has been developed and refined to seven phases (Nasca 1–7) that include several substyles. An early, transitional phase, or Nasca 1, is contiguous with Late Paracas, while two later phases (Nasca 8–9) are affiliated with the Middle Horizon (H. Silverman 1988). According to both the sequence and on-ground archaeological investigations, scholars recognize early, middle, and late developments.

Early Nasca society is best understood from the perspective of the Río Grande de Nazca Drainage. Its onset, intertwined with Paracas and Topará societal developments in Ica and Pisco, remains the subject of ongoing research, yet continuity between Late Paracas and Early Nasca cultural remains at Ica Valley and Río Grande de Nazca Drainage sites is recognized. Early Nasca marks the florescence of Cahuachi and the proliferation of geoglyph constructions. A second site of note, currently under investigation, is Los Molinos in the Palpa region (Reindel, Isla, and Koschmieder 1999:372; Reindel and Isla 2001). According to preliminary analysis of the site, the most significant occupation, during which large adobe ceremonial complexes were constructed, appears to be Early Nasca. Reindel and Isla (2001) call attention to the similarities between Los Molinos and Cahuachi, although each center is thought to have served different functions, as discussed below.

Middle and Late Nasca mark a clear change in Nasca society accentuated by the abandonment of Cahuachi and a reordering of social institutions and cultural practices. Schreiber and Lancho (1995) have carefully detailed the development of a system of subterranean water canals and wells, or puquios, which would have revolutionized accessibility and distribution of water in the region. Evidence for ranking and social stratification becomes apparent in archaeological contexts including burials. Large, urban centers such as La Muña are established (Reindel and Isla 2001; Reindel, Isla, and Koschmieder 1999:372), and some sectors of Los Molinos are reestablished as cemeteries of a completely different nature than their Early Nasca counterparts. Internal conflicts and competition are proposed for these times, as are interactions and involvement with the wider Andean sphere (Proulx 1994; H. Silverman and Proulx 2002).

Much like Paracas, Nasca presents a colorful, enlivened visual arts tradition. Nasca artists conceived of the landscape as their "canvas," creating linear rock designs or geoglyphs, some stretching for kilometers across the desert pampa (Aveni 1990; Reiche 1974; Reindel, Isla, and Koschmieder 1999; Reinhard 1988; H. Silverman 1990). In contrast to these monumental ground drawings, Nascans also excelled in miniatures – garments, figurines, and hammered gold sculpted to form three-dimensional figures including tiny heads (Lechtman 1988). Polychrome painted ceramics depicting both repetitive plant and figural designs, severed heads, and spectacular narratives of the supernatural are widely considered the hallmark of Nasca visual arts (Blasco and Ramos 1980, 1991; Proulx 1968, 1970, 1994, 1996; Schlesier 1959; Seler 1961[1923]; Townsend 1985).

Nascans at death

Mortuary practices during Nasca times are variable in nature and differ significantly from those of the Paracas tradition. Like Paracans, Nascans interred their dead with the same attentiveness to preparation for the afterlife. While interments overall are less sumptuous, similar attention is devoted to protocol whether the burial is that of an infant, an elder, or a victim of sacrifice (Carmichael 1988, 1995; DeLeonardis 2000). Even criminals receive their due – heaved face forward into the earth, they receive neither a cloth nor other offering (H. Silverman 1993:195–196, 215).

Over the course of time, particularly after the abandonment of Cahuachi, a movement toward commemoration of elite individuals is evident. This is notable for the

Middle–Late Nasca cemetery at Los Molinos, where elaborate and excessively deep funerary chambers have been identified (Reindel and Isla 2001). At Puente de Gentil, Isla's reevaluation of Tello's 1927 excavations indicates the interment of 46 fineware polychrome vessels associated with a single individual, a pattern unprecedented for earlier graves (Isla 2001).

Carmichael (1988, 1995), Kroeber and Collier (1998), and H. Silverman (1993) offer the best recent synthetic sources that address the range of Nasca mortuary practices. Unlike the multiple burials of Cavernas, individual burials were a far more common form of interment. Nascans were wrapped in simple cotton cloths, but rarely in layers like their Paracas counterparts. Carmichael (1988) has systematically recorded the contents of a number of graves. These typically include modest offerings of ceramics and may include human hair wads with feathers, braids, cloth and turbans, and maize and pacae seeds. His analysis of graves that contained offerings of human hair (clippings and braids) suggests that a number of persons, possibly relatives, contributed to an individual's grave (Carmichael 1995:173–174). Carmichael also recorded a few instances of secondary interments, high-status tomb reentry and protracted interment (Carmichael 1988, 1995:176–177). Burials in non-cemetery settings are also known. In Ica, DeLeonardis (2000) has documented the interment of an Early Nasca headless individual at Paracas Site D-13. Given the close proximity of a Nasca cemetery to the site, she suggests the individual may have been interred at what was conceived to be an ancestral huaca. It is also possible that Nascans in the region strategically interred the body away from their cemetery in order to claim or acquire new territory.

Centers of celebration and ritual

In view of the cultural achievements of Nasca society over time it is clear that certain activities were carried out by corporate groups. Membership in some groups may have been flexible and based on the task at hand. For example, specialists were likely involved in the engineering of at least some of the Nasca geoglyphs as well as the systematic design of the puquios, yet any number of groups structured by kin relations or other criteria may have been responsible for their construction and periodic maintenance.

Group participation is equally evident in ritual associated with ancestor veneration. One of the most visible domains of group activity is Cahuachi and its associated sacred terrain. Here, strong inferences can be made about how social groups operated in the public arena of propitiating and celebrating the ancestors.

Cahuachi

The ceremonial center of Cahuachi has intrigued scholars for well over a century; continues to be the focus of ongoing research and interpretive debate. Sprawled across the desert pampa are the ruins of over 40 platform pyramids and countless cemeteries. The history of Cahuachi, paralleling other developments in Nasca social history, began during the early period where it served as the focus of cultural activities including rituals, musical celebrations, and seasonal pilgrimages. Such ritual may have included public mortuary ceremonies and human sacrifice judging by the number of burials interred at the apices of platform mounds. Several other features of the site, discussed below, firmly suggest rituals involving ancestor veneration. Cahuachi is thought to have reached its apogee during Nasca 3, after which time it was abandoned. It continued to function as a sacred burial ground or huaca for centuries. In fact, most cemeteries postdate the apogee (H. Silverman 1993:108).

As a regional pilgrimage center, Cahuachi drew thousands of Nascans from dispersed valley settlements. It served as common ground to unite neighbors (families, clans, lineages), exchange information (possibly items), and to reinforce social and political group relationships though sponsorship of dance, feasting, and public display. The number of musical instruments found at Cahuachi alone – ceramic panpipes and drums – and the images that support an emphasis on ceremonialism, underscore this interpretation (H. Silverman 1996c; H. Silverman and Proulx 2002). Helaine Silverman (1993:315–316) attributes the lack of refuse such crowds would have generated to a concerted clean-up effort after these reunions.

Wooden posts and ancestors: the room of the posts at Cahuachi
Rituals commemorating ancestors are strongly suggested by one of the most unusual discoveries at Cahuachi known as the Room of the Posts. The room is situated at the base of a platform mound ("Unit 19") excavated by Helaine Silverman (1993). Roughly 10×12 m in size, the room consists of a walled space in which 12 wooden posts (huarango, a local fruit tree) emerge vertically from the floor. Eleven of the posts are unmodified; one has been planed. Four small pits surrounding the posts may have held the (edible) pods and seeds of huarango judging by the excavation of one. Various images were incised on the plastered walls – panpipe flutes, a rayed face common to ceramic iconography, and a pattern of over 50 circular impressions. Twelve Spondylus shell pieces were recovered from depressions within a niche carved out of the east wall. Judging from the remnants of an eroded feature in the room's center, a raised platform or altar likely occupied the space. The room was constructed sometime during the early period but may have been continuously used for several centuries. During the late period, it was filled with ceramic offerings and interred in clean sand, effectively sealing the room from further use.

There is little doubt that the room represents ritual space. Drawing from the work of Zuidema (1972) and Sherbondy (1988), H. Silverman (1993:174–194) argues that the posts are possibly the earliest expressions of trees-as-symbolic ancestors. The commemorative rites that would have taken place in the room may have involved manipulation of the posts; their final arrangement mimics an enclosed "orchard." We do not yet understand the symbolism of the number 12 – although it is indicated by the number of posts and pieces of Spondylus in the room. Among larger Nasca antaras, 12 tubes are present (see Stone-Miller 1995: fig. 59). At Estaquería (see below), huarango posts were arranged in 12 rows. It may well represent the number of mallki or significant Nasca ancestors recognized at the time the room was buried.

Fruit-bearing trees figure in both Nasca and Paracas mortuary practices. For example barbacoa tomb constructions involve the horizontal arrangement of huarango logs and may hold a deeper significance than simply structural concerns. Isla (2001: fig. 9) illustrates one example that contained 15 huarango logs laid side by side to form the roof of a sumptuous Nasca tomb. Helaine Silverman (1993: figs. 14.6–14.14) illustrates variations of these roofs at Cahuachi (see also Kroeber and Collier 1998; Strong 1957: fig. 13a). Carmichael (1988:491) also notes that logs are often found leaning against the interior walls of deep, high-status tombs. The presence of cane markers or cane bundles is well documented for many Nasca graves (Carmichael 1988; H. Silverman 1993), and may relate to a similar idea about trees, death, and commemoration. Moreover, the presence of pacae, either associated with individual mummified heads or as a common fill material of barbacoa tomb construction, also supports this fruit tree–mortuary link.

Wooden posts at other sites
Two other post configurations constructed during Nasca times are known outside of Cahuachi. Little can be said about one of them. Strong (1957:34) recorded a "wooden-stake temple" at Tres Palos I in the lower Grande Valley. Helaine Silverman (2002:49) believes she has reidentified this site but notes that "it is in significantly worse condition than when Strong recorded it."

A colonnade of 240 huarango posts – 12 rows of 20 posts, each spaced 2 m apart – originally characterized the Late Nasca site of Estaquería, located on the westernmost edge of Cahuachi. Kroeber (1944:26–27) initially surveyed the site in 1926 and suggested that this "place of stakes . . . a most impressive Stonehenge" did not pertain to the Nasca culture, an error later corrected by Strong (see Kroeber and Collier 1998:82, figs. 76–77). At the time of Strong's (1957:34) excavations in 1952, only 47 posts were found upright. Fewer posts remain in situ today. Each log was burned at the base and notched at the upper end. From the surface of the colonnade, Strong recovered a wood plaque (48 cm in height) carved from huarango in the form of a human face. It is unknown whether the carving was displayed on the posts or had been dug out by huaqueros.

The posts at Estaquería are considerably larger than those at the Room of the Posts and a more permanent arrangement is indicated (see Kroeber 1944: fig. 4, plates 9–10). It is likely that Estaquería represents a Late Nasca expression of an earlier practice begun at Cahuachi. A greater number of wider, taller posts representing older trees are also suggestive of an enduring, public monument in contrast to the setting at the Room of the Posts. Wooden heads or masks may have embellished the posts or may have comprised ceremonial offerings buried at the shrine.

Feeding the ancestors: caches as offerings

Caching and offering of specific objects, particularly those indicative of transformation, has been linked to the wider practice of ancestor veneration. In the overall context of mortuary practices, as discussed above, Nascans cached various items singly or with the dead. One type of offering that epitomizes transformation, for which the Nasca culture is best known, is the mummified head. The practice of taking human heads is widely debated in the literature and is variously associated with warfare and ancestor veneration (Baraybar 1987; Proulx 1989, 2001; Verano 1995, 2001a). Here, we depart from a focus on the act and instead draw attention to the contexts in which caching occurs and the process of final disposition.

As we discussed previously, mummified heads appear in south coast contexts as early as Paracas and are profusely illustrated in the visual imagery of the Early Intermediate Period, particularly among the Nasca (see Recuay, Paracas, this chapter). On the south coast, most interments involve one head interred singly in cemetery settings. DeLeonardis (2000) has shown that both mummified heads and headless bodies receive proper burial treatment, particularly during Late Paracas–Early Nasca times. Caches of human heads, while infrequent, are more common during Middle and Late Nasca. It is also during this later period that a greater number of images depict the act of decapitation between human pairs (see Blasco and Ramos 1980, 1991), including a very limited number of human head caches (Lapiner 1976: fig. 513; Tello 1959: fig. 123).

Head caches associated with Middle and Late Nasca are best illustrated by two archaeological contexts: the Cerro Carapo cache in Palpa (Browne, Silverman, and García 1993) and the Chaviña cache from Acarí (Baraybar 1987). At Cerro Carapo, 48 heads were recovered from a shallow cist without cloth cover or other offerings. The Cerro Carapo cache is the largest single cache known to date. At Chaviña, 11 heads were cached at subsoil level along an adobe wall. Each was wrapped separately in a plain white cotton textile. Two were interred in jars. Offerings were found within the wraps of five heads. These included semiprecious stone as well as edible plants and fruits such as maní (peanut), ají (hot pepper), and pacae. Each example presents a completely different manner of interring large numbers of heads.

Of the two images that have been published of head caches, both depict scenes in which two groups of three heads are interred or kept in altar-like structures on cloth (Figure 5.3 bottom) (Lapiner 1976: fig. 513; Tello 1959: fig. 123). Representations of birds, common to decapitation scenes, are shown, as well as pairs of human figures holding batons or knives. In both images consumption of liquids is implied judging from the number of vessels and cups shown among the heads. In one image, San Pedro cactus, a psychotropic, is depicted. In another (Figure 5.3 bottom), llama sacrifice is performed atop the altar where the heads are held. The depiction of heads in groups of three may hold significance in terms of numbers. In a third widely published example of Late Nasca head-taking, three pairs of men participate in the act (shown on both sides of the vessel) (Amano 1961: plate 41).

These images provide potent insights into caching rituals and direct attention to a process that preceded the final interment of mummified heads. It has been pointed out that caches need not be considered the heads of ancestors but rather the food that nourished them. In Andean cosmology the head or uma is conceived as the locus of a powerful spiritual essence or upani, offering protection to the possessor. In Nasca society and cosmology heads are inextricably linked to fertility and regeneration of life, and their final disposition, like mummy bundles, is analogous to the planting of seeds. As suggested by images of the Necropolis textiles, we must consider that the heads, as blood offerings, provided a conceptual link between living and past ancestors. We may reasonably assert that caches of heads, like those of cloth or precious metals, must have represented symbolic wealth that could have political ramifications in the realm of land acquisition and resource control.

The little people

While public ceremonies served to reinforce clan and lineage ties, it is worth considering less visible rites and practices that were carried out in honor of the ancestors. A corpus of Nasca figural sculpture is suggestive of objects that may have served commemorative ritual, either as objects that were manipulated or the focus themselves of veneration. These portable objects were rendered in clay, tooth, and cloth. Silverman and Proulx (2002: figs. 6.5–6.6) also illustrate small stone statues (20 × 35 cm), some of which appear to have been attired or wrapped in cloth. Variously described as fertility idols (Morgan 1988), supernaturals (Lyon 1978), and dolls, they may also have played an integral role in ancestor veneration, serving as amulets, shrines, and symbolic portable bundles.

The ceramic group is broadly characterized by hand-modeled standing and seated figures, predominantly female (e.g., Lapiner 1976: figs. 479–483; Lothrop and Mahler 1957: plates IVa–b, VIe, VIIIa, IX). Female standing figures share several characteristics: corpulent, naked bodies, slightly forward-leaning posture, legs pressed together, presence of tattoos or body paint, and flattened heads indicating cranial deformation. Small (4–10 cm) standing figures are common throughout Nasca history, while large (15–32 cm) standing figures (including males) are limited to Middle and Late Nasca.

Seated figures (14–30 cm), entirely female, assume a slightly reclined posture with open legs and outstretched hands that rest on the knees. Large tattoos or body paint often cover the buttocks and groin area. Common Nasca icons are featured: severed heads, stars, and marine symbols such as the killer whale. In one example, a seated figure is adorned with shell and bone necklaces and attired in a (removable) gauze weave shirt (Lapiner 1976: figs. 478–479, 481). Seated females appear during Middle and Late Nasca.

Ceramic figurines have been recovered from various archaeological contexts. At Chaviña, three ceramic figures were excavated from burials (Lothrop and Mahler 1957:24–25, plates IVa–b, VIe). In one of the burials (Cist I), two male figurines accompanied an adult female. A seated female figurine accompanied a second adult interment whose sex has not been verified. A partial figurine was recovered from the floor of the Lower Eastern Room excavations at Cahuachi (H. Silverman 1993:260, fig. 17.1). The figure lacks a head and left leg. At Huaca del Loro, Strong (1957:40) excavated over 22 fragments from architectural fill and refuse deposits.

These examples suggest the figures were variously cached for burial, manipulated (decapitated?) in ritual, and discarded.

Exactly how the figurines were used is uncertain, although they may well have been set out, adorned, and fed. Lothrop points out that few of the standing figurines support themselves in an upright position (Lothrop and Mahler 1957:24). It is likelier that the figures were positioned on their backs, back legs, or stomachs. Some may have been wrapped or held in a cloth pouch.

A second group of small (3–8 cm) hand-held figures carved from whale tooth, closely resemble the posture of the smaller standing ceramic figurines. Eyes are inlaid with shell or other stone. Both males and females are represented (Lapiner 1976: figs. 505–508). This group is associated with the Late Nasca–Wari transition and may be an early expression of small stone ancestor figurines (see Cook 1992a).

Cloth figures, produced during the early period, range in size from 7 cm to 17 cm and have the outward appearance of dolls. Horié (1990–91:90) cautions against this interpretation, citing their fragility and the impeccable preservation of the garments that do not indicate repeated handling. Ann Rowe (1990–91:93–94, fig. 1) has discerned that the interior of at least some consisted of a cross-shaped wooden apparatus stuffed with plant material (dried leaves) or cotton that was covered with cloth and stitched closed. Tiny woven garments were created for the figures by the same conventions that guided life-sized apparel. Some figures bear finely braided human hair wigs embellished with colorful feathers. One cloth figure was recovered from excavations at Cahuachi in association with a cist burial, possibly a child (H. Silverman 1993:199, 265, fig. 18.3).

Discussion

Nascans interred their dead in cemeteries but kept the ancestors alive through gifts of human sacrifice and rituals designed to propitiate and commemorate. In two contexts we called attention to ancestor commemorations distinct from the general feasting and celebrations associated with mortuary activities. At the Room of the Posts and Estaquería we are compelled to consider that the symbolic relationship between tree posts and ancestors has its earliest expression in Nasca times. As important symbols of life, trees are conceptualized as the embodiment of the family (Sherbondy 1988). Ancestors possess the qualities of an old tree. In life, their experiences are enduring and the fruit they bear – their descendants – ensure that new life will emerge from the earth in keeping with the cycle of renewal (Sherbondy 1988:108). Conceived as a walled compound of trees or enclosed orchard, the Room of the Posts and Estaquería must have served as huacas or pacarinas where periodic rites were performed and perhaps common ground where social group identity was reaffirmed. The association of orchards and ancestral dwellings is also manifest in Maya cosmology (McAnany 1995:66–102).

It is critical to point out that an ancestral relationship existed between Nasca and Paracas and hence a likely source for Nasca ancestor shrines would be former

Paracas territory. Two recent discoveries in the Ica Valley support this observation. We have mentioned DeLeonardis' (1997, 2000) work in Callango. In this case, an isolated Early Nasca interment was discovered at a (then) abandoned Paracas site. Curiously, an Early Nasca cemetery located some 100 m away was not utilized. Recent excavations at Cerrillos, a Paracas shrine in the upper valley, are also illuminating in this respect. Within a room atop a terraced structure, Dwight Wallace recovered a large (ca. 2 m in height) effigy bundle or idol fashioned from a feathered mantle with a false head and wings resembling a bird. A 20–35-year-old female was found tightly bundled within the chest of the bird. Preliminary analysis of the idol suggests that the inner mummy may have been exposed and wrapped at periodic intervals, implying prolonged rites prior to its (her) final interment. The idol dates to the Late Nasca–Middle Horizon transition (Dwight Wallace, personal communication, 2002).

During Nasca times head caches must have held particular significance as ancestor offerings. Singly, the head represented a highly charged symbol of life and its transformation. In large numbers, or caches, heads must have been conceived as a concentrated source of upani or life essence. Surely this translated into power for the possessor, whether it be an individual or corporate group. After removal, heads may have been subjected to any number of uses including display before their final interment. Some, perhaps all, caches were subject to rites of passage. We have called attention to ritual depicted in two Late Nasca images where groups of three heads are cached in altars in the presence of officiates. Ceremonies enacted about these altar caches involved drinking and llama sacrifice, as suggested from the images. The Chaviña cache closely mirrors these images – heads wrapped in cloth accompanied by food and amulets for the afterlife. In contrast, the Cerro Carapo cache that pre-dates the images lacks cloth and accouterments. Hypothetically, some ritual may have preceded the interment. We do know that the Cerro Carapo cache was intrusive to an Early Nasca residential site and cemetery. In this respect, like the cases mentioned above for Ica, Middle Nascans may be returning to Early Nasca territory to commemorate and/or to reclaim ancestral land.

In the realm of visual arts, Nascans possessed the extraordinary ability to transform their vast surroundings with rock designs of a monumental scale while miniaturizing their universe in thumbnail-sized objects of exquisite detail. We reviewed a sample of these miniature human figures that may have formed personal ancestor "relics" or small-scale representations of significant members of society. Nascans are hardly alone in their creation of human figurines and their portrayal as females. Examples from Mesoamerica and the Andes abound (Di Capua 1994; Joyce 1993; Lesure 2002; Marcus 1998). Judging from the Late Nasca ceramic seated figures, Nasca women held prominent positions of authority in society and must have orchestrated ritual and possessed landholdings. As a group they were culturally exempt from head-taking activities – osteological evidence suggests they were rarely victims. That figurines are predominantly female stands in contrast to other Nasca gender-specific ceramic forms, such as the jars on which males are exclusively portrayed. These contrasting forms of gender representation allude to the roles each may have assumed as ancestors.

Conclusions

Ancestor veneration is centered upon specific ancestors whose living kin memorialize them through gifts, rituals, and ceremonies. Our overview of Recuay, Lima, Paracas, and Nasca suggests that the ancestors were alive and well in the practices and cosmology of ancient Andeans. It is beyond our scope to name individuals or to specify cults, yet different types of archaeological evidence and iconography leave little doubt that the living engaged in activities to support and celebrate the dead that extended beyond routine funerary rites.

Judging from iconographic sources, ancestors appear to have been an idealized or mythological group. We suggest that, conceptually, ancient Andeans differentiated between the "recent dead" and the "mythological" or idealized ancestor, each having a distinct visual referent for the stages of transforming or "becoming" an ancestor. We envision a visual program that reflects the transformation cycle from seed state, to established ancestor, to pacarina (the origin place to which the spiritual body returns). In some cases, these stages of death's journey may well have been expressed in corresponding media that culminated in the enduring, permanent monuments of stone and posts known for Recuay and Nasca, respectively. We called attention to a range of Recuay stone statuary depicting male and female elites positioned in a fetal crouch closely mirroring the mummy bundle posture. Recuay vertical stone slabs associated with specific tombs may well bear the "transformation insignia" of crosses and appendages that characterize lineage founders. Similarly, some Necropolis bundles were virtually enveloped by cloth bearing the icons representing states of ancestor transformation. Nasca figurines, clothed and bundled, perhaps the objects of veneration, are suggestive of the "portable ancestor."

That the deceased ancestors continued to have active social lives required unremitting obligations and responsibilities on the part of their descendants. Among the cultures we reviewed, tomb and shrine constructions, celebrations, sponsored feasts, and public displays are evident and appear to be collective endeavors. Nasca and Paracas peoples are unique in creating caches of mummified heads, yet the practice of acquiring the heads, the enactment of rituals, and their eventual burial clearly involved the participation of many. It has been amply demonstrated that weaving and embroidering the finest Necropolis textiles represented the work of countless hands over an extended time period. We also recall the Lima and Paracas practices of interring elite surrogate or simulated ancestors – symbolic in nature yet requiring nearly an equal investment of energy to create as a bundle.

Collective veneration is also implicit in the creation and placement of ancestor shrines. The towering chullpas of Recuay and the huacas of Lima and Nasca present monumental testaments to the revered dead. Recuay stone sculpture and the monolithic posts of Estaquería provide comparable statements about the enduring nature of the ancestors and of the social order. The Paracas mummy bundle, itself a "stratified hill of cloth" (Paul 1990:115), may be considered a shrine, huaca, or cult effigy. We also noted a correspondence between shrines and particular landscape features.

Mountains, islands, peninsulas, and rock outcroppings as loci of shrines were observable and likely relate to the conceptual link between the fertile ancestor and the earth as a provider and a source of life. By extension, this fertile earth–ancestor link is supported by the repeated presence of trees and fruits – huarango and pacae – that figure in Lima, Paracas, and Nasca ancestor shrines and funerary practices.

Careful nurturing of the dead, understood by the practice of ancestor veneration, is apparent in the prolonged funerary rites suggested by our review. Tomb reentry for the purpose of visitation and renewal of offerings was common to the four cultures under study. The structural characteristics of Recuay mortuary architecture permitted tomb reentry and may have facilitated removal of the body for display. Our data for Lima indicate that both Tablada and post-Tablada traditions involved tomb reentry for purposes of offering renewals. Tello (Tello and Mejía 1979) demonstrated that objects were often placed above the Necropolis bundles after interment, indicating a similar tradition. Prior to final interment, the mummy may have received additional wraps, a custom suggested by the bird idol at Cerrillos. These temporary visitations may have been carried out in tandem with calendrical cycles corresponding to agricultural activities – the planting of seeds and reaping of successful harvests brought about by ayni with the ancestors.

Feasts and celebrations honoring the ancestors may have been held expressly to satisfy the reciprocal obligations of ayni. The archaeological evidence for Recuay and Nasca supports that these activities were carried out in various social contexts. Compelling evidence from Chinchawas points to feasts held adjacent to enclosures associated with ancestor sculptures. Sacrifice and consumption of camelids during these banquets are supported by dense archaeological remains. There are also indications that ritual libations of chicha were offered by way of pacchas, paraphernalia common to ancestor cults. Llama sacrifice and drinking are also pictured in Nasca rituals associated with the interment of mummified heads. At Cahuachi, llama sacrifice and consumption is evident in numerous contexts in and about the pyramid complexes (Silverman and Proulx 2002:102). Moreover, Cahuachi presents a veritable celebration center where public displays involving dance and music were enacted during valley-wide group pilgrimages. It is here in particular, at the Room of the Posts, that we find ritual space devoted to ancestor veneration set apart from burial or feasting contexts.

Fulfilling the obligations and responsibilities to one's ancestors was surely thought to ensure the approval of the ancestor while strengthening the prestige of the lineage. These activities must have generated some degree of competition between lineages or social groups in their efforts to maintain the cycle of propitiation. Periodically, it is likely that some groups invoked ancestral claims to property, water rights, trade routes, or other privileges by negotiating and manipulating ancestral alliances. Our analyses suggest that social groups appropriated space in a number of contexts and by various methods.

We examined the development and continued use of a cemetery area, or "necropolis," a remarkable process that has seen little treatment in the archaeological literature. The activity or sequence of activities that leads to the formation and evolution of a multi-cultural necropolis is usually taken to be an inert or natural process of culture history – for example, of simple superposition. Our data suggest that cemetery formation reflects complex social practices that express cultural values and relationships. As in Recuay and post-Recuay funerary patterns of the Callejón de Huaylas, Tablada de Lurín's distinct clusters of tombs or interments may literally map out kin and ethnic relationships as sections of the cemetery. The Tablada de Lurín cemetery reflects, in this sense, a constantly changing social field comprised of miniature communities for the dead. More broadly, the development of cemeteries based on kin-based funerary practice might be employed to compare highland developments, such as the cliff mausolea and necropoli in the northeastern Andean flanks, the subterranean Recuay cemeteries, or the ubiquitous chullpa clusters throughout the north highlands.

Funerary displacement, or appropriation of sacred burial space, was an effective means for groups to assert change in the ancestral order. In the north highlands, above-ground chullpas, visible and accessible, were strategically placed upon former Recuay subterranean tombs. A similar pattern is evident for Lima cemeteries where the placement of subterranean chamber tombs over earlier shaft and chamber tombs marks a break in the old pattern. Later, post-Tablada interment is blatantly destructive since earlier burial structures and their bundles are intentionally destroyed in the process. Paracas Necropolis bundles equally characterize the intrusive and destructive nature of funerary displacement especially at Wari Kayan where they are literally enmeshed in the bones of their predecessors. Such practices may be more meaningful if we follow Isbell's (1997a) plausible interpretation that by the Early Intermediate Period, many groups viewed tombs as the origin places of corporate kin groups. In a sense, tomb displacement resembles the rationale behind "huaca capture" and trophy head-taking. Each type of practice seeks to acquire supernatural properties or efficacy through physical appropriation from the "other."

Appropriation of ancestral space is also manifest in non-cemetery settings. The interment of a Late Nasca-Middle Horizon idol at Cerrillos, a Paracas shrine, exemplifies the concept of a historical memory for an ancestral huaca temporally distinct by nearly a millennium. Similarly, the interment of a Nasca burial at a Paracas residential site signals an aberration in custom likely related to the appropriation of sacred space. We must also consider the interment of Late Nasca head caches in Early Nasca space as a powerful expression of ancestral continuity between groups.

More research is needed to enable comparative analysis between Early Intermediate Period cemetery populations. Studies of human skeletal evidence provide fundamental data on sex, age, the causes of death, post mortem treatment, and health during life (e.g., Verano 1995, 2001a). Lamentably, there are very few Recuay human osteological remains for study. Because of lack of research and poor preservation in the highlands, even in intact tombs (e.g., Bennett 1944; Grieder 1978), we know comparatively little about the physical characteristics of Recuay peoples. Our data for Lima, Paracas, and Nasca clearly indicate sumptuous burial treatment for select elderly elite males, a finding that encourages further inquiry into the role of men and women as lineage founders.

Additional archaeological studies are also needed to explore the variability and character of ancestor cults during pre-Inka times. Archaeological investigations in the future will almost certainly find new graves and associated paraphernalia. But it seems worthwhile to continue to look beyond the burial context and treatment for wider cultural ramifications between ancestors and the living, as Tello (1929, 1942) alluded to years ago. We expect that further research on how Early Intermediate Period societies articulated with their deceased will enhance our understanding of ancient Andean religions and cosmologies of the afterlife.

Our comparative review of four Early Intermediate Period cultures emphasizes a number of commonalities between groups as well as diversity in expression within each. One of the strengths of assuming a diachronic perspective is that it enables us to observe changes in mortuary practices, iconography, and other cultural patterns germane to identifying activities associated with ancestor veneration. These observations suggest that the Early Intermediate Period was not a static interval of Andean prehistory dwarfed by the onset of empire. Rather, we conceive of the epoch as dynamic and multifaceted, marked by innovations in art and economic programs and by the active efforts of regional groups to establish, negotiate, and redefine social and political boundaries. We have viewed these cultural processes through the lens of ancestor veneration and suggest that its practice served as a unifying mechanism by which kin-related groups ordered their social universe.

ACKNOWLEDGMENTS

George Lau gratefully acknowledges the support of the National Science Foundation and the Wenner–Gren Foundation for Anthropological Research that enabled the Chinchawas investigations under awards 9612574 and No. 6066, respectively. Permission for his fieldwork was granted by the Instituto Nacional de Cultura, under Resolución Directoral Nacional 419-96/INC. Craig Morris and Sumru Aricanli of the American Museum of Natural History are thanked for facilitating the study of Wendell Bennett's North Highlands Collection. Lisa DeLeonardis acknowledges the Fulbright Commission and the Robert H. Smith Fellowship Program for funding excavations in Ica and subsequent analysis of the Early Nasca burial in Callango. Her excavations were undertaken under Acuerdo No. 132-94 - CNTCICMA/INC. She gratefully acknowledges Jeanette Sherbondy and Dwight Wallace for their insights and contributions.

6
The Art of Moche Politics

Garth Bawden

Introduction

In the later Early Intermediate Period (ca. A.D. 100–700), a people on the north coast of Peru became the dominant political power of the region. They created a florescent society that we know as Moche, named after a local river of that name (Figure 6.1). The Moche heartland encompassed the Moche River and thirteen other small rivers that flow westward from the ever-visible Andes Mountains across a harsh desert into the limitless Pacific Ocean, watering the lands immediately bordering them and creating the spectacular environmental stage upon which coastal people played out the drama of their individual and collective lives.

Understandably, this dramatic natural setting profoundly affected the material and spiritual lives of its inhabitants. When benign, its diverse features yielded a rich subsistence in which plentiful marine resources of the Pacific Ocean supplemented intensive agricultural harvests of the irrigated fields to nourish large coastal populations. However, the Peruvian north coast also possesses a very destructive quality. Lying in one of the most volatile tectonic regions in the world, the land and its people experience tremendous earthquakes in which whole towns can be destroyed in an instant. Similarly, the usually predictable climate is subject to dramatic disruption. In periodic El Niño events the prevailing oceanic winds change course and the offshore Humboldt current warms, with cataclysmic effect on marine life. At these times violent storms inundate the desert plains, severely interrupting the normal life and activities of human communities. Ironically, the region is also prone to periodic droughts when the mountain rains fail and the rivers that they generate shrivel, bringing reduction of crop yield and hardship to the inhabitants of the desert coast.

The physical world played a major role in molding the cultural expressions of all Andean groups and the belief systems that they constructed to order their social and political lives. Given the powerlessness of coastal inhabitants to materially control the destructive forces of their world, it is no mystery that they confronted

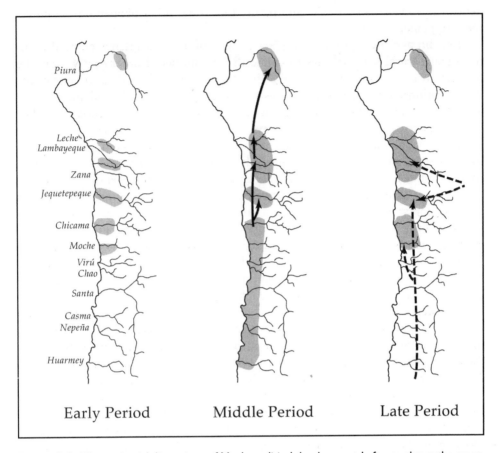

Figure 6.1. The territorial dimensions of Moche political development. Left map shows the emergence of earliest Moche Valley polities. Center map shows Middle Phase emergence of the southern conquests of the Moche Valley-centered polity and consolidation of several northern counterparts. The arrows indicate the traditional view of a pan-coastal state, now largely discredited. Right map shows Late Moche loss of the southern territories and Lambayeque political conquest of the coastal Gallinazo territories. Arrows show the direction of coastal Wari and highland Cajamarca influences into the region

them in the supernatural sphere. Powerful natural phenomena were innately accepted as manifestations of spiritual force and were mediated through religious conception and practice. Myths explained the origins and meaning of the ever-present environmental forces and ordered their relationship with human society. Rituals repeatedly manifested these myths in daily life, reaffirming and enacting the cosmological system in which humans and natural world alike had appointed places and mobilizing supernatural forces on human behalf. In the precolumbian past visual symbols affixed to public monuments and crafted on portable objects codified these organizing concepts into standardized messages that ensured general recognition and continual reinforcement of their accepted meaning. Ultimately this integrated conceptual and material scheme infused a sense of balance and mutual dependency between humanity and nature that could never happen on the purely physical plane.

How did ancient north coast leaders draw upon their distinctive cultural traditions and natural surroundings to create the vibrant social order that we call the Moche? More specifically, what were the strategies used by rulers to consolidate their positions, to mediate their interests, and to maintain their social and political identities? Scholars undertaking to answer these questions are fortunate for they have access to a rich body of material resources that originally played a central role in the Moche political arena. Architecture is the most prominent of these resources, its particular form and setting signifying its social meaning and political function. Moche architects designed the great adobe platforms that still tower over the coastal valleys, their great size and permanence inspiring awe and asserting the power of their creators. Similarly, portable items suffused with specific social meaning complemented the actions of their human users and conveyed information about their contexts of activity. Moche artisans utilized a wide variety of media to produce one of the world's great art styles. Moche art displayed the iconography of power. It is largely through the window provided by this wealth of human creativity that we glimpse the social and political structure that gave it meaning.

The successful analysis of the thematic content of Moche corporate art has proven fundamental in understanding Moche political structure and its ideological foundations. Scholars have been able to identify the ceremonial complex that lay at the center of political practice (Berezkin 1983; Castillo 1989; Donnan 1976, 1978, 2001a; Donnan and McClelland 1979; Hocquenghem 1987; Kutscher 1954, 1955; Quilter 1990). In the arena of burial excavation, scholars have documented Moche funerary practices (Donnan 1995, 2002; Donnan and Mackey 1978; Narváez 1994; Tello, Armas, and Chapdelaine 2002). They have conducted valuable osteological research on the status, mortality data, and nutrition of the interred (Nelson 1998; Nelson and Castillo 1997; Verano 2001a, 2001b). And by utilizing the knowledge gained from analysis of iconography, archaeologists have identified the actual rulers who participated in the religiously charged ceremonies depicted on Moche art (Alva and Donnan 1993; Donnan and Castillo 1992, 1994). This recent work has inspired further study of Moche political ideology and symbolism that includes investigation of the major Moche centers (Alva and Donnan 1993; Castillo 1993; Castillo and Donnan 1994; Chapdelaine 2000; Franco, Gálvez, and Vásquez 1994; contributors to Pillsbury 2001; Shimada 1994, 2001; Uceda 2001; contributors to Uceda and Mujica 1994, 2002), and theoretical works on the nature of Moche political structure and its development (Bawden 1995, 1996, 2001; Canziani 2002; DeMarrais et al. 1996; Dillehay 2001).

Political Inequality, Ideology, and Symbolic Discourse

At its most basic level, political power denotes the ability of an agent to advance partisan interests in the face of opposition. As such it is a universal accompaniment of human society, exercised in all aspects of social discourse. However, at the governmental level political power utilizes a set of institutions and positions that serves to facilitate its effectiveness and formalize its existence. Unless imposed from outside, the structure of a political system is shaped by the unique combination of internal developments and external interactions that constitute the particular historic experience of its parent society. This distinct history provides the shared perception used by individuals and communities to negotiate social relations and to define specific interest groups.

A more common characteristic of political society is its integration of two conflicting forces. On one hand a broadly shared concern promotes cooperation and collective identity. On the other hand intra-societal differences inevitably coalesce around contesting interest groups. It is this paradoxical combination of broad social cohesion and internal competition that creates the dynamic for the construction of formal systems of political power while also embedding the seeds for their continual negotiation and change. Comparative research indicates that all social traditions contain qualities that dispose them to emphasize one of these opposing tendencies over the other (Dumont 1980, 1986; Turner 1969), ideally contrasting societies that promote a differentiated and hierarchical organizing structure against those that resist such order and foster communal, kin-ordered authority.

The ways in which individuals construct political influence significantly differ in these two social contexts. While it is demonstrable that individuals frequently make influential decisions that cannot be purely explained by reference to the prevailing social milieu in which they act, it is equally true that historically engendered conceptual and behavioral norms shape the degree to which they can negotiate change. It follows that their opportunities are greater in a society that encourages achievement than in one where collective equality is the standard. Andean social structure has, quite correctly, been characterized as conforming to organizing principles of communal kinship with real and fictive relationships paramount in assigning status and influence. This structure functioned on both spatial and temporal planes to locate people within a balanced social universe, tied to traditional lands, peopled by the entire living and ancestral community, and maintained through rituals of supernatural mediation and reciprocity. Andean political systems had necessarily to manifest the local communal beliefs and historic experiences in which they were constructed. North coast political leaders clearly succeeded in this enterprise, consolidating their power bases within the context of a broader belief structure that naturally resisted such development. Their strategies reveal the structural dynamic underlying Andean and Moche political formation.

Political power can be maintained through a continuum of strategies that range from non-violent persuasion to physical coercion. While Moche leadership occasionally utilized force to achieve its ends, it is important to understand the ideological component of power that underlay political formation, and the material symbolic system that affirmed it.

Ideology is that special formulation of social discourse that promotes the interests of its advocates in the wider community. Within this broader framework, dominant ideology, which seeks to promote cohesion in the interests of the established social order, represents its most prominent expression. Dominant ideology achieves its impact by condensing the conceptions that represent reality for its adherents and affirming these to the public at large through codified visual symbolism and par-

ticipatory ceremonies. The Marxist view of dominant ideology as a beneficial construction used by rulers to mask repressive reality has been rightly criticized because
of its assumptions of deeper hidden truth and the passivity of people in the presence of doctrines that oppose their interests (Abercrombie, Hill, and Turner 1980).
Actually, history makes clear that when dominant ideological discourse and communal interest fall into opposition, the former may be speedily discarded. When
successful, ideology successfully reproduces notions of social reality and advantage
espoused by society as a whole. In such instances prevailing discourse does not
mask deeper truth. Rather, shared perception *makes* it social reality for all.

Visual symbolism, often fashioned in elaborate artistic forms, acts to affirm its
related ideologies of power. Ruling groups usually dictate the creation and public
display of politically charged symbols through their control of the resources and
specialized skill required for their production. It follows that the symbolism of dominant ideology is much more visible in the archaeological record than are the
symbols of resistance (but see Bawden 2001 for one clear example of the emergence of resistance ideology in opposition to a weakening Moche elite). So it is with
the Moche, where it is now generally accepted that a vibrant art style represents a
powerful symbolic instrument of central authority, not a "cultural" diagnostic
(Bawden 1995; Castillo 1993). Moche art displays a relatively narrow range of
complex narratives (Donnan 1978) that articulated the shared cultural memory of
north coast people with the rituals of political and religious power. By codifying
these familiar themes as dictated by the ruling elite, art symbolically communicated
the partisan discourse of leadership. While the non-elite population could not fail
to be familiar with the ideas symbolically attached to great architectural centers of
power and enacted in the rituals of political authority, they were passive receivers
rather than active creators of this central aspect of dominant ideological discourse.

Origins of the Moche Political System

Moche ideological symbolism was both a product of and an innovation in the long
tradition of north coast political structure. We can trace its origins to the early
hydraulic societies of the Initial Period (second millennium B.C.) when small
coastal societies coalesced around impressive platforms whose façades were embellished with the symbolism of authority. Initial Period iconography provides a precise
symbolic precedent for Moche imagery and affirms the same essential principles of
social integration that persisted throughout north coast history. Thus its feline and
composite human/animal forms have been persuasively identified with shamanistic
transformation (Burger 1992:96) while the Cupisnique "Decapitator" figure and
its variants underscore the importance of sacrifice. The large number of Initial
Period centers together with the absence of any widespread cohesive artistic style
suggests that the regional political pattern was one of small autonomous societies
occupying restricted ancestral lands. Leadership in such society is embedded
in local tenets of communal belief codified as political ideology. This pattern
embodies the peculiar Andean form of inherent structural tension between

collective and individualizing conception of authority that played a persistent role in shaping political formation throughout north coast history. Significantly the subsequent Early Horizon period reveals the attempt by local rulers at a time of decline, repeated in the Moche period, to break the limiting bonds of communal organization. By adopting the tenets of the pan-regional Chavín ideological discourse as the basis for their doctrine of rule they created a broad but short-lived elite network based on widespread economic and religious links and created the potential for a more differentiated domain of exclusive power.

By the end of the first millennium B.C. the parameters of north coast political configuration had been set. It is from this pattern of differentiated local authority and intermittent broad alliance that Moche political society emerged. Archaeologically the first part of the Early Intermediate period saw the emergence of a number of related, yet distinct, ceramic styles that include Salinar, Gallinazo, and Moche throughout the region and the enigmatic Vicús in the far north. We should be cautious of advocating the view that these archaeological units represent smooth cultural succession as required by the traditional need for archaeologists to equate art styles with distinct human groups, and to order them in neat evolutionary sequences. Castillo (2001), Kaulicke (1992), Shimada (1994) and Shimada and Maguiña (1994; also see Ubbelohde-Doering 1967, 1983) have recently noted chronological contemporaneity of the Gallinazo and Moche styles. Also, recent research supports Rafael Larco Hoyle's early observation of close links between Gallinazo and Vicús styles in the far north (see Kaulicke 1992), while it now seems that Salinar, instead of being separated from Moche by a significant Gallinazo interlude, in fact may have been its direct antecedent, connecting it with the rich Cupisnique/Chavín tradition of modeled and painted ceramic wares (Kaulicke 1992).

While, this complexity appears to introduce confusion into the cultural and chronological picture, it fairly represents the actual sociopolitical configuration of the region. The four Early Intermediate Period styles are actually material signifiers of distinct and sometimes contending political systems that were constructed from a common cultural base. By the beginning of the first millennium A.D. the Moche and Gallinazo systems had differentiated from their Salinar and Vicús north coast counterparts with Moche ultimately emerging as regionally dominant. Nevertheless, Gallinazo, Moche's rival, maintained a presence throughout the period. Archaeologically, Gallinazo and Moche are characterized by great adobe platforms located throughout the region (for Gallinazo centers see Bennett 1950; Fogel 1993; Hastings and Moseley 1975; Kaulicke 1992, 1994b; Moseley 1992; Moseley and Mackey 1972:165; Shimada 1994:69–41; Shimada and Maguña 1994; Willey 1953; Wilson 1988:160–1. For Moche centers see Alva and Donnan 1993; Bawden 1982a, 1982b, 2001; Castillo and Donnan 1994; Chapdelaine 2000; Donnan 1972; Haas 1985; Hastings and Moseley 1975; Kaulicke 1991, 1992, 1994b; Russell, Banks, and Briceño 1994; Shimada 1994; T. Topic 1982; Uceda 1995; Uhle 1913; Willey 1953; Wilson 1988). Similarly, residential occupation and the artifacts of domestic use are identical (Bawden 1990, 1995; Fogel 1993; Willey 1953), as are general burial practices (Fogel 1993:281–292).

Only in the sphere of elite craftsmanship is there significant difference. Moche art, with its rich narrative texts, locates leaders at the center of the rituals of power and emphasizes their individual importance in the social order. By contrast, Gallinazo symbolism eschews the narrative form of Moche art. I suggest that this difference mirrors the contrasting forms of social authority that characterized the two systems. Gallinazo was rooted in time-honored communal kinship principles, thereby conforming to the pattern that I have traced to the Initial Period. By contrast, Moche leaders created a potent political ideology that synthesized dramatic public ritual, regalia, and symbolism to assert their central role in maintaining social order. This strategy constitutes innovation in regional tradition and offers us an ideal opportunity to examine leaders actively constructing political power within a context that fundamentally resisted their ambition.

The Geopolitical Context of Moche Symbolism

The geopolitical configuration of the north coast during the Moche period manifests the conflicting qualities that are so apparent in the tradition. It is understandable that, in a region extending across 13 distinct valleys, each at least partly isolated from its neighbors by the intervening desert and with its own specific historic and cultural history, leaders would continue to maintain the pattern of local authority that we have already noted. Apart from adherence to a common political ideology with its accompanying convergence of interest at the governing level this pattern persisted throughout the Moche period. In spite of earlier acceptance of a pan-coastal Moche state in the middle of the Moche period (Figure 6.1), scholarly consensus now suggests that only temporarily in the south was there any multivalley political integration. Recent archaeological research supports this diverse geopolitical picture. Thus, the famous portrait vessels are limited to the south (Bawden 1996, 2001; Donnan 2001b); certain mythical themes appear to be valley-specific (Castillo 1993, 2001); there is greater emphasis on the use of precious metal in the north (Alva and Donnan 1993; Jones 2001); formal difference exists in platform construction between north and southern valleys (Bawden, 1996; Kroeber 1930); there is considerable geographical variation in stylistic development across the region (Castillo and Donnan 1995; Kaulicke 1991; Shimada 1994); and major local differences occurred in the response to Late Period disruptions (Bawden 1996; Castillo 2001; Castillo and Donnan 1995). Powerful ideology and magnificent artistic symbolism bridged this internal regional variation at the elite political level and that created the vibrant material expression of Andean civilization called Moche, as we shall now see.

The Context of Moche Ideology

Two important qualities of Moche political discourse are essential to understanding its effectiveness. First, in spite of its innovative nature, it is grounded in a set of myths and practices deeply rooted in north coast cultural history. On the general level the fundamental importance of the shaman as arbiter between humans and the supernatural is apparent in Initial Period art. Here images of animal mediums – often feline – combine with human forms in dualistic compositions that convey the transformative power of the shaman to meet with the supernatural on behalf of the human community. Discovery of the actual paraphernalia of shamanistic hallucinogenic ritual further suggests that this persistent aspect of Andean religious conception prevailed many centuries before the Moche. Moreover, specific elements of Moche symbolism are traceable to earlier times. Images of the "Decapitator" in sacrificial scenes and the ritual combatants in the "Confrontation Scene" appear in ceramic iconography as early as the Cupisnique period (Burger 1992:95–97; Cordy-Collins 1992, 2001; Jones 1979; Roe 1974: fig. 34).

The second vital feature of Moche ideology is that its accompanying narrative symbolism depicts real human activity. Archaeologists have recently recovered the remains of dignitaries clad in the garb and regalia of the various participants in these mythic scenes, interred at the very centers of power at Sipán and San José de Moro (Alva 2001; Alva and Donnan 1993; Donnan and Castillo 1994), revealing that such events were enacted as the ceremonial of social and political integration. In this important context these elite individuals played important roles in death as in life in the perpetuation of the dominant order in a society where ancestral reverence constituted a core essence of communal cohesion.

In addition to understanding the underlying structure of Moche political ideology, we can also trace its evolution through the development of artistic content. While Early Moche art (ca. A.D. 100–300) sometimes depicts the symbols of traditional belief noted in the previous paragraph, the principal constituents of the fully evolved style do not yet appear. Similarly the earliest burial accouterments of Moche rulers, while identifying them with sacrificial activity, do not mark them as recognizable officiants of later, fully evolved ceremonial. Consequently, we can assume that Moche political ideology assumed its mature character after a formative phase during which it identified and developed those principles of historic north coast belief that were to become its central elements. It is only with the imagery of the Middle Moche Phase (ca. A.D. 300–600) that a ritual complex centered on human sacrifice entered the artistic inventory as the well-organized symbolism of fully formed political ideology. It was then that the "Sacrifice Ceremony," with its central officiant and his attendants, clearly identified by their accouterments of role, became central to political ceremonial (Figure 6.2) (see Alva 2001; Alva and Donnan 1993; Bawden 1996; Bourget 2001; Donnan 1978; Verano 2001b). Accompanying themes such as combat between mythic heroes and the ritual hunting of anthropomorphized deer – metaphors for combat and sacrifice – became similarly integrated into an organized symbolic system. It is important to stress, however, that even in this mature phase, regional artistic depiction reflected local variation. The most elaborate representations of the full ritual cycle appeared on ceramic art in the south. Elsewhere, although these variations collectively communicated the pervasiveness of sacrificial ritual as the central manifestation of the dominant ideology, there was differential local emphasis on architectural

Figure 6.2. Fine-line drawing of the Sacrifice Ceremony (redrawn from Kutscher 1955:24–25)

murals, burial content, and portable non-ceramic art as the preferred symbolic medium.

Moche Symbolic Expression in the Context of the Mature Moche Political System

The florescent Middle Period reveals Moche political strategy at its most success-ful. During this period political hegemony expanded through most of the region, replacing its Gallinazo rival with a multi-valley conquest polity in the south, and elsewhere restricting it to lower portions of the large northern valleys (Figure 6.1) (see Shimada 1994). Great Moche architectural centers displaying the symbolism of central authority accompanied the expansion, while portable art displayed a quality and variety of creativity and craftsmanship never surpassed in precolumbian America. It was a time of plentiful subsistence, environmental quiescence, and social stability. Archaeology indicates that the political order, together with its belief system, was embraced by the overwhelming mass of the population. People of all social levels attended great rituals of power where leaders performed rituals that ensured communal well-being. After death they incorporated symbols of prevailing ideology in their burial goods, revealing a sharing of belief indicative of a success-ful order.

However, the fact of its acceptance does not tell us why most north coast people apparently accepted the dominant ideology so readily. While the overall success of Moche political and economic society with its attendant benefits clearly encour-aged acceptance of leadership, the real answer to this question lies in its successful activation of cultural conception as political agency. I have previously noted that dominant ideology is most successful when it proclaims a system of central author-ity that is regarded as advantaging the population as a whole and when its tenets and forms are drawn from the familiar cultural memory of the entire group. It appears that this is the pattern that characterized the Moche system, at least through its Middle Phase.

At the core of Middle Phase ideology was the vital ritual of sacred gift-giving through sacrifice, an act of religious and social integration that remains a central component of Andean social conception to this day. Central to this practice is the role of shamanism. In general the Andean shaman, whether Moche ritual practitioner or modern-day *curandero*, is an individual possessing special ability to directly communicate with the supernatural world on behalf of the community. The shaman interacts with the ancestral and nature spirits of his society in order to effect healing, to ensure collective well-being, and to forecast coming events. In the Moche context, leaders appropriated this ancient role and expanded it to further their political interests. Most prominently, in elaborate public ceremonies they entered sacred ritual space to animate the mythic stories that created the structure of north coast social identity and to mediate the antagonistic forces of the cosmos whose balance was essential for wider group welfare. This formalization of basic Andean religious practice and the conflation of the roles of shaman and ruler had two effects. First, through their participation in transformational drama leaders separated themselves in ritual status from their subjects. Second, by locating the sacred renewal of communal cohesion within the context of political ceremonial rulers acquired supernatural sanction for their positions of social authority and for perpetuation of the sociopolitical order that they represented.

The specific content of these ceremonials of state, abundantly materialized through a rich symbolic inventory of portable media, architectural mural, and elite burial evidence, helps us to understand the nature of the Moche political system. While there is considerable variation in the representational styles of the various valleys the core content is fairly clear and comprises a series of distinct events, including combat between warriors, both human and supernatural, defeated combatants stripped of their dress and weaponry, arraignment of captives before elaborately garbed dignitaries, images of decapitation, and sacrifice performed on the summits of platform mounds. Human combat is invariably limited to a pair of combatants whose elaborate garb and ornate earplugs and headdresses identify them as warriors of elite status. Moreover, the desert setting within which they habitually fight reveals that this event was confined to a designated location beyond the boundaries of the river valleys. Subsequent removal of the signifiers of personal and group identity suggests eradication of their social status and position. The culminating scene depicts the ritual killing of prisoners on the summits of platforms by individuals wielding the crescent-bladed "decapitator" knife, their blood then offered to the principal practitioner (Figure 6.2).

This narrative and its attendant ritual graphically articulate myth, the human cosmos, and political statecraft. At the outset we must reject any notion that it represents general warfare. Rather, combat represents a ritualized act, conducted in a circumscribed desert location and restricted to members of the elite warrior stratum. The purpose of combat was to obtain "prisoners" and prepare them for the subsequent dramatic culminating ceremony. These sequential stages combined to convey immense social significance to Moche communities. At its core the cycle incorporates the essential elements of sacrifice in its capacity of precious gift-giving. To traditional Andean people ritual offering comprises the central act in a sacred contract between the human and supernatural domains of their cosmos. Blood, regarded as life force in earlier periods, as in contemporary ritual, was the most powerful category of gift. It follows that in the crucial event that ensured continuing social vitality, the life essence of elite human warriors would be the most fitting gift possible. Blood was offered to Pachamama with the expectation that an equally powerful life-giving substance – water – would be returned in the form of mountain rains, this reciprocal transaction ensuring fecundity for the earth and social balance for humanity. Given the ceremony's fundamental sacredness, all participants were ritually charged for their entry into its liminal space and time. Thus, officiants became the mythic figures of Moche communal integration, while their sacrificial partners entered the transforming presence of ritual already unencumbered by the identities and rank of daily life, as befitted their consecrated status at the threshold of the supernatural.

We should briefly note the significance of the physical setting of the sacrificial ceremony. Moche myth and ritual reflect the impact of a dramatic natural environment with its alternation of barren desert, cultivated valley, dry flat plain, and soaring snow-capped mountain. The tall platforms, oriented toward the mountains, architecturally replicate those life-giving sacred places where the rivers had their origins and where coastal shamans communicated with powerful apu gods and conducted rituals of social integration. Fittingly, the culminating event of the sacrificial cycle reproduced the setting of these important links between the human and divine worlds and complemented their rituals of spiritual interaction, fertility, and balance.

The Shape of the Moche Regional Political Configuration

Thus far we have examined the internal structure of dominant Moche ideology, emphasizing its character as a specialized extension of deeper cultural conception. Now let's shift our focus to study its vital practical role in maintaining regional political relations. We have seen that an important genre of symbolic art depicts pairs of elite Moche fighters, wearing their elaborate garb of rank, engaged in formally staged conflict. The significance of this specialized combat lies in the fact that it represents controlled opposition between members of a single dominant regional group, not between local and foreign warriors. Also, I earlier noted that the regionally diverse archaeological record suggests persistence of the traditional pattern of local political autonomy. It follows that the regional network of dominant interest represented by Moche ideology supported several distinct and sovereign centers of power (Figure 6.1). Shared ritual provided the means by which their various ruling elites brought this paradoxical pattern of ideological unity and political fragmentation into complementary alignment. Thus, the fundamental principles of Andean social being required that religious practitioners offer the sacrificial gifts that brought reciprocal benefit to their communities. The tenets of political discourse drew on this belief to transform the elite warrior into the subjugated hero of familiar north coast mythic combat, and consecrated him as the most potent sacrificial gift. Ritual combat provided a culturally sanctioned means whereby these vital sacrificial offerings were distributed in the context of mutual political dependency. On a practical level, ritualized combat foreshadowed today's highland tinkuy (ritualized combat) festivals by engaging representatives of distinct groups as dependent partners rather than warring enemies while concurrently emphasizing their separate identities. The culminating sacrificial ceremony placed leaders at the center of an act whose effects transcended local differences, reinforced their own positions, and supported the system that they embodied.

This, then, was the system of beliefs and practices that underlay Moche political power at its zenith. Its fundamental strength resided in affirmation of a body of beneficial cultural ideas, myths, and practices rooted in the shared identity of north coast people. Middle Moche ideology gave cohesive structure to these familiar principles and embellished them with a prescribed set of visual symbols and ritual practices. By taking the roles of the shamans and mythic heroes of cultural memory in these rituals of group renewal leaders explicitly placed themselves at the axis of religious belief and communal leadership. By so doing they created a potent ideology that at once provided for the emotional needs of their people, legitimated their own authority, and addressed the peculiar geopolitical exigencies of the north coast centers.

The End of the Moche Political System

As might be expected, the particular form of structural vulnerability of this potent political system shaped its decline. Until recently we viewed the end of Moche civilization as a singular event of collapse initiated either by invasion from the highland Wari Empire or by severe environmental disruption. However, the results of recent research have caused us to recognize a much more complex process of innovation and response in the Late Period (A.D. 500–750) that prepared the way for the emergence of new cultural and political florescence in the Late Intermediate Period. The causes of this transition are far from clear. However, it is probable that conditions within Moche society contributed significantly. Thus, while ice core analysis and geomorphic research show convincing evidence for a series of destructive droughts and El Niño events around the end of the seventh century A.D., it is unlikely that this alone precipitated the period of major change that followed. Rather, environmental problems should be viewed as exacerbating a process marked by the withdrawal of the southernmost Moche polity from its Middle Period dominions south of the Moche River (Figure 6.1).

There is no indication that this major retreat was caused by invasion. It is better understood as a result of innate contradiction between fundamental Andean communal social conception and hierarchical political construction, which developed to its greatest extent in the southernmost Moche polity. Here alone we see a move toward creation of an expansionist, centralized state with its capital dominated by the largest architectural monuments ever constructed by the Moche, the Huaca del Sol and the Huaca de la Luna. Here alone we see the one clear episode of conquest in the Middle Period: the southern expansion into valleys previously dominated by the Gallinazo. Here alone, communicated through ceramic portraits, the symbolism of political ideology depicted rulers as individuals rather than solely illustrating the roles that they played in the rituals of government. It follows that it is also here that rulers most closely linked the maintenance of a beneficent social and cosmic order to their individual prowess. By so doing they elevated their personal control of power to an unparalleled degree. However, they also raised the danger that they would be held personally responsible for unresolved disruption such as that which occurred at the end of the Middle Period, and would be discredited, together with the system that they headed.

Change in the south affected all major aspects of life and accompanied a process of settlement abandonment, demographic reorganization, economic decline, and social confusion. In the political domain the great Huaca del Sol site was abandoned, although a reduced settlement persisted around its sister Huaca de la Luna (Chapdelaine 2000, 2002); rural dwellers were concentrated into the new urban settlement of Galindo (Bawden 1996); traditional platforms were replaced by new enclosed compounds as central architectural symbols of power; portrait vessels disappeared from the symbolic inventory; and new elite ceramic forms inspired from outside of the region eschewed the mythic narratives of earlier times (Bawden 2001). Elsewhere in the region change was less dramatic but still substantial. Disruption in the south almost certainly forced the withdrawal of the affected polities from the ritual alliance that had sustained their elite ideological network. Consequently, local rulers were unable to sustain the core rituals that had physically asserted their tenure of authority and had given it unified meaning. With the collapse of the only substantial links between the otherwise separate Moche polities, leaders addressed the crisis in ways that were shaped by the peculiar historical development and local circumstances of their own areas.

In the areas to the north of the Moche Valley a variety of local innovations replaced the relative standardization of rituals and symbolism that had characterized Middle Period political structure. In the Jequetepeque Valley, rulers attempted to vitalize their ideological base by introducing new foreign-derived forms into the weakening tradition (Castillo 2001). Innovative narrative rituals were newly portrayed in fine-line ceramic painting and symbolic art was adopted from the ascendant Wari style, reflecting modification in the political system. Still further north in the Lambayeque Valley rulers reacted to threat by initiating an unprecedented degree of political centralization. Overthrow of the last Gallinazo centers and resettlement of their populations in the sprawling new urban center of Pampa Grande marked the imposition of a Late Moche state in which rulers evoked traditional ideological support by erecting a huge platform as its focal symbol of power. However, here too further change was inevitable, the new conquest bringing with it the seeds of internal strife and the ultimate overthrow of the last Moche administration (Shimada 1990, 1994).

Everywhere the discourse of power changed. Late Moche leadership progressively disengaged its roots from familiar north coast cultural and political discourse and came to rely on locally modified tenets and symbols of transcendent Wari political ideology. While this attempt to replace the failed Middle Moche Period ideological network brought short-term advantage to threatened leadership, it effectively divorced the non-elite population from their previous access to the rituals and symbols of authority and had the effect of replacing structural paradox with social contradiction. This latent social tension inevitably generated an inexorable process of negotiation, adjustment, and change that ultimately led to the demise of the ruling stratum and the material symbols through which it had asserted authority. While the process took different courses and speeds in the various localities, with southern collapse accompanied further north by much greater degrees of continuity, by the end of the Late Moche Period there was no longer a coherent Moche elite art "style" on the north coast, nor presumably a singular Moche political system. With the breakdown of the Middle Moche Period ritual network and concurrent fragmentation of its ideological system, successor polities evolved according to their own needs until, with its meaning lost, Moche political structure no longer existed and the transition to Late Intermediate Period society was complete.

7
Clothing the Social World

Ran Boytner

Introduction

Historical and ethnographic records clearly show that textiles were crucial elements for Inca administration. Murra (1989:293) summarized this reality saying, "no political, military, social or religious event was complete without textiles volunteered or bestowed, burned, exchanged or sacrificed." In addition, textiles were markers of ethnic identity, useful in the ready identification of subject peoples. Thus, Guaman Poma de Ayala (1978:53) recalled that "no member of any tribe shall wear clothing other than what is customary in the tribe, on pain of 100 strokes of the lash." And Cobo stated that

> the men and women of each nation and province had their insignias and emblems by which they would be identified, and they could not go around without this identification or exchange their insignias for those of another nation, or they would be severely punished. They had this insignia on their cloths with different stripes and colors, and the men wore their most distinguishing insignia on their heads; each nation was identified by the headdress. (Cobo 1979[1653]:196)

Textiles were used as payments for services – a soldier serving in the Inca military received two pieces of garment annually. Textiles were also used as means to accumulate and distribute wealth – cloth was produced and stored, to be redistributed in special events. Textiles were one of the most important means by which subjects paid their taxes – the Incas ordered the production and storage of vast numbers of textiles, storing them in an extensive network of specially designated facilities. Indeed, many scholars believe that textiles were the most important cultural object in the Inca Empire. Clearly, textiles merit the attention they have received in the scholarly literature.

The Inca divided textiles into two distinct categories. The first consisted of plain or marginally decorated garments, termed awasqa. These textiles were used by ordinary people in domestic settings for normal daily activities. The second class encompassed finely woven and elaborately decorated textiles, termed cumbi. The ownership of these textiles was restricted to people of higher status and was used for the performance of administrative or ceremonial activities. Elaborately decorated textiles were acquired by commoners, probably as gifts bestowed in recognition of significant acts or service to the empire (Guaman Poma 1978: plates 342, 344, 346). Much thought and resources went into the creation of cumbi textiles; their superb artistic form would make them objects of desire in any culture.

Textiles were important in other Andean cultures as well. But for the pre-Inca period we must rely almost exclusively on the archaeological record to learn about them. Fortunately, the extreme dry conditions along the central and southern parts of South America's Pacific coastline are favorable to the preservation of perishable materials, and textiles are among the best-preserved artifacts. Thousands of textiles have been recovered from excavations – mostly from burials – creating the world's largest body of archaeological textiles in existence.

Almost since the beginning of modern archaeological work on the coast, excavations revealed vast quantities of textiles. In the early 20th century Julio C. Tello and Max Uhle commented extensively on the superb quality of these textiles, in terms of both their technical sophistication and the complexity of their designs (Tello 1923, 1956, 1959; Uhle and Grosse 1903; Uhle and Kroeber 1924). Elaborate textiles have now been recovered from every period and from almost all major Andean cultures, beginning with the Chavín and Paracas textile traditions and continuing throughout Andean prehistory (see Bird and Bellinger 1954; Conklin 1971; Kaulicke 1997; King 1965; Paul 1990; Reiss and Stübel 1880–87; Wallace 1960; Willey and Corbett 1954). The level of weaving quality and sophistication of design suggested the investment of vast resources – both raw material and time – in their creation. Clearly, Andean people made a great cultural investment and commitment to their creation.

Typical coastal Andean burials consist of one or more bodies wrapped in textiles. Some of these wrappings are over a hundred meters long, and many are finely decorated with complex designs. Despite differentiation in the amount of pottery, metals, or other objects deposited in burials, textiles were almost always present and seem to be the most crucial element in mortuary practices. Although organic preservation in highland cemeteries is typically poor, the few pieces of surviving evidence show a similar central role of textiles there as well.

In addition to wrappings, textiles also have been recovered as significant items of offerings. Many burials include quantities of ready-to-be-woven threads and complete garments deposited near the deceased or inside the mummy bundle. Frequently, weaving implements were important enough to be buried with individuals for their benefit in the afterlife. Indeed, many high-status burials include a number of weavers, evident from the large quantities of colorful threads and other weaving implements deposited with them (see Heyerdahl, Sandweiss, and Narvaez 1995; A. Rowe 1980).

Textile miniatures are one of the most spectacular forms of offerings. Recovered from burials as well as from middens of temples and other ceremonial structures,

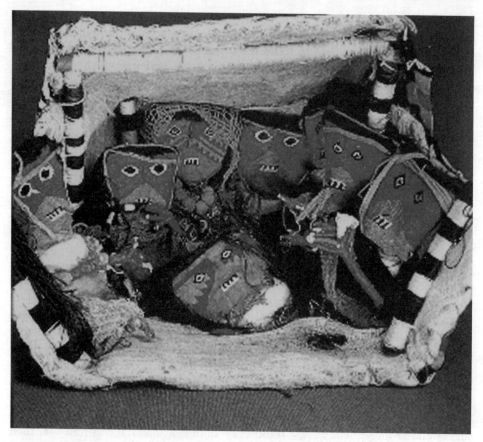

Figure 7.1. Chancay textile dolls, ca. A.D. 1400 (Museo Amano, Lima)

miniature textiles imitate the form and decoration of full-scale garments. Miniature textiles include tunics, headdresses, even loincloths. They were used independently or to cover small figurines made of wood, clay, or metal (e.g., Bruce 1986; A. Rowe 1990–91). But, arguably, the most spectacular are the three-dimensional textiles, depicting complete individuals or even entire social scenes (Figure 7.1). Some Chancay miniature textiles even depict groups of weavers making miniature textiles (see Tsunoyama 1979).

It is impossible to know whether the Incas' two-tier division of textile types existed previously in other cultures. But many Andean sites do include plain and elaborate textiles. Unfortunately, only a few sites have been excavated where textiles were collected in relation to internal social divisions. The site of Pacatnamu at the north coast of Peru is one of the few where spatial location could be correlated with social class. Analysis of textiles there showed that most plain textiles were recovered from low-status contexts while most decorated textiles were recovered

Figure 7.2. Maitas belt from excavations in the Azapa Valley, northern Chile, ca. A.D. 900–1400 (photo by Marissa Schleicher, Vicki Cassman, and Ran Boytner)

from high-status burials (see Boytner 1998a, in press). A similar distribution of textiles was identified from excavations in the Azapa Valley in Chile (Cassman 1997; Figure 7.2), and less controlled samples elsewhere suggest that such correlation holds across time and space in the Andes.

The archaeological evidence clearly shows that the role textiles played in the Inca Empire was not unique. Textiles were highly valued objects, embedded with social meaning, across time and space in the Andes. It is possible that textiles had such prominent standing due to the significant role they played in the establishment of Andean complex societies. Cotton threads were used to create fishing lines and nets that generated the needed surplus so central for the emergence of complex societies in the Andes. In addition, recent discoveries at Caral – one of the first urban and ceremonial centers of the region and dated to the Preceramic Period (2600–2000 B.C.; see Chapter 3, this volume) – showed that textiles were made into nets that contained small units of building materials. Put together, these units were used to create the large ceremonial structures dominating the site (Solis, Haas and Creamer 2001). We could say that textiles were the building blocks of complexity in the Central Andes.

The Economics of Textiles

Andean textiles are made from a variety of raw materials. Some are made from human hair, others from a range of shrubs and roots. But the vast majority of textiles are made from two primary sources: cotton and camelid wool. Cotton – primarily *Gossypium barbadense* – is native to the coast and has been extensively cultivated there since early in Andean prehistory. Cotton cultivation became so sophisticated that Andean farmers were able to produce cotton in a wide range of colors, from white to dark brown.

Four different camelid species were the sources for wool. Llamas were likely the source for the coarser wool, alpaca for the finest, while little is known about the use of guanaco or vicuña. Ethnohistorical records describe the presence and cultivation of vast herds of domesticated camelids, where their wool was a significant source of wealth to local, regional, and state elites. Although coastal burials frequently contain camelid remains, most scholars agree that the production of camelid wool was done primarily in the highlands, where climatic conditions are more suitable for the herding of these animals.

Since highland preservation conditions of perishable materials are poor, most of the information about trade in raw material or finished textiles comes from coastal sites. Many of the coastal elaborate textiles were made with cotton base, but many of the decorative elements were made with dyed camelid threads. Commenting on such structure and the consistency of camelid wool thread technology, Ann Rowe wrote,

> Considering that [a]lpacas thrive only in the highlands, it is reasonable to assume that the fiber was imported to the coast. But the extreme uniformity of the yarns and the lack of spindles with [a]lpaca yarn at Chan Chan and other coastal sites suggests that they were also spun and dyed in the highlands for export purposes, and that this production was on an industrial scale and centrally controlled. (A. Rowe 1980:87; but see Shimada and Shimada 1985, 1987)

The idea is that highland yarns were exported to the coast to be woven by local craftsmen in the style of their particular society. In the past two decades, many spindle whorls with camelid yarns have been discovered in various coastal sites. The arguments about the creation of camelid thread in the highlands, however, are based not only on thread characteristics alone, but also on the type of dyes identified from these threads. Camelid threads are typically dyed with materials native to higher elevations and not with dyestuffs found in coastal habitats. In contrast, cotton threads are typically dyed with dyestuffs native to the coast (see Boytner 2002, in press). Combined, consistency in thread spin and ply direction and dye choice are strong indications that Rowe was correct in her observations and that dyed camelid wool was exported from the highlands to the coast.

Analysis of thread material from the few surviving highland textiles reveals that almost all highland textiles were made solely from camelid wool; cotton is rarely present. Trade in camelid wool threads from the highland to the coast was not reciprocated by the shipment of cotton threads back. It is still not clear what highland communities desired or obtained in exchange for their wool, but evidence suggests that shellfish and other marine products were highly valued and were transported from the coast in significant quantities. Other goods may have also played a role in this trade. Until further research, however, it is impossible to speculate what these products were.

Sign, Symbol, Text

In his seminal work, Martin Wobst suggested that styles may be viewed as a strategy of information exchange (Wobst 1977:317). The appearances of objects (aesthetics), as well as the shared methods for their production (traditions) convey significant and deliberate messages about those who made them and those who use them. It is beneficial to think about these messages as a dynamic two-way system. Messages are displayed through the use of specific style, and in turn solicit responses and reactions from spectators. As Wobst discovered from his work in the former Yugoslavia, textiles are particularly embedded with information and meaning. They are prominent, large in size, used by all members of community, and one of the first items observed in the initiation of any social interaction. Echoing such observations, Bean suggested that "cloth and clothing animate the most elaborated systems of representation in social and cultural life" (Bean 1998:115).

In the Andes, textiles fulfilled functional needs (clothing) but were also rich with cultural meaning. Such meaning was presented through the use and alteration of fibers, and through the incorporation of exotic materials. Coastal textiles were sometimes decorated with feathers, creating spectacular patterns and configuration. Other elaborate textiles also had metal additions: gold and silver plaques were sewn to textiles to maximize light reflection and visual impact. More typically, patterns were created with colored threads – natural and dyed – which craftsmen wove into complex designs ranging from geometric to naturalistic themes. Andean dyers used some of the best organic dyes in existence and were able to achieve a range of over a hundred colors and hues.

The use of elaborate design schemes employing a wide range of materials resulted not only in some of the ancient world's most spectacular works of art, but also a sophisticated method of communication. Lacking writing systems, textiles were one of the most visible methods to create messages, express social standing, and declare cultural and ideological affiliation.

Three elements were used to convey meaning: form, composition, and design. Combined, this was the visual language shared by all Andean societies. On one level, meaning was derived from the form (or shape) of a particular textile. In the Inca Empire, long tunics are associated with females while short ones are associated with males. Long flaps of loincloth in Chimú textiles are associated with high status while short flaps are associated with lower status (A. Rowe 1984). On another level, the composition of different sets of garments also transmitted cultural information. Perhaps the most striking example is the stripping of captured enemies. Moche fineline drawings and Chimú iconography show naked captives, with their hands bound behind their backs, indicating that the lack of clothes is the ultimate humiliation one can inflict. Cook suggested that, in the Wari social hierarchy, higher status was marked by the number of clothing layers individuals were allowed to wear (Cook 1992a). Finally, the complexity and quantity of design elements served as indicators for individual access to power and resources. Wari elaborate textiles include highly abstract and sophisticated designs, commonly associated with high-status individuals (Menzel 1964). Similarly, Paracas textiles, expensively decorated with fantastic embroideries, are indicators of the social standing of their owners (Paul 1990).

Considering the strict control over and management of textile production, it is surprising to discover that Andean textiles were rarely uniform. It is difficult to find two similar textiles, made by the same method, constructed in the same shape, and decorated with the same designs. Instead, the Andean vocabulary of uniformity is loose, where only broad guidelines were observed. Within each cultural sphere, design elements appear following only a general order of visual organization. The specifics of each element, its color composition, or its relations to other elements in the design matrix are unique for each textile. For example, elite Wari tunics are typically decorated with four broad vertical bands, each a repetition of a single design unit (see Conklin 1986; Frame 1999; Stone 1986). Although the general organization of vertical bands is consistent, the choice for individual elements, their color and orientation varies from textile to textile. Some elements are abstract, while others are naturalistic. Color combinations are inconsistent, and elements associated with a certain design on one textile may be absent from or different on another. It is possible that this diversity reflects temporal changes. Yet the vast quantities of available textiles indicate that these patterns reflect actual Andean practices and not random preservation of the textile record.

Although different in details, the overall visual organization within cultural groups is consistent. In this sense, individual Andean textiles speak the same language but may be different in grammar. Not all spectators may have understood the entire meaning associated with any specific textile and its particular visual organization, yet they could easily read its overall message. In this sense, textiles were used as signs, symbolizing general information about the owner's cultural affiliation and social standing, but the full narrative associated with each textile may have been completely understood by only a few.

Individual cultures may have unique styles and may have chosen specific images to be repeatedly depicted in their designs. But certain themes, artistic conventions, and traditions are common across the Andes. They include a front- or side-facing figure holding one or more staffs, upper sections of felines (particularly their facial features), serpents, interlocking teeth, and winged creatures. In addition, many of the Andean textiles were created following similar principles of duality, bilateral symmetry, and anatropic organization (see Conklin 1986; Kubler 1975). This shared image, vocabulary, and organization suggests that some basic principles of meanings and transmission of information were similarly codified across the Andes. Many scholars believe this to be an indication that basic principles of belief systems were shared across time and space in the Andes (for discussion, see H. Silverman and Isbell 2002:7; Tello 1923:204–311).

Although it is possible to observe similarity in design patterns (etic), detailed studies of the specific meaning of textile iconography (emic) have just began. Much is still missing from our understanding of the embedded messages. Yet, some initial works are promising and may prove essential for understanding knowledge organization and transmission. Gail Silverman suggested that the iconography was not understood merely because it was symbolic, but that it generated narratives that could be "read" by members of society (G. Silverman 1988, 1998, 1999). Silverman did not suggest that motifs could be combined to make written, pictographic language, but rather that individual motifs had conceptual meaning and that assemblages of motifs could present a complex message to viewers. These ideas have gained support from recent work by Margaret Jackson, who examined evidence of Moche proto-writing at the site of Cerro Mayal (see Jackson 2000, 2002; but also see Paul 1997). Although Jackson focused primarily on Moche pottery and ceramic iconography, the same systematic organization she observed there appears on textiles and in other Andean traditions as well. Considering how sophisticated Andean iconography is, whether on ceramics, textiles, or murals, it is surprising that a full-fledged writing system did not evolve. Jackson suggested that, although a writing system may have been the next logical evolutionary step, the material context for the presentation of symbols was as important as the message itself. Symbols may have gained meaning similar to signs, but an important part of this meaning was derived from the cultural and material context and placement of their presentation. She wrote,

> Although the [artists] seem to have developed a codified system of visual notation, the social institutions surrounding feasting, gift reciprocity, and other ritual activities would continue to demand the production of certain kinds of objects . . . given the larger ritual functions of specialized pots in Moche society, one would not expect the notational system to replace the actual objects in production. (Jackson 2002:130)

Textiles and Power

Power can be defined as the ability of some to control, influence, extract, force, sway, or otherwise dictate actions to others. Power can be translated to the physical and social realms in ways that are typically inclusive. Power can be translated into the physical control over resources, technology, or space. But power can also be translated into social control over people and their actions through the use of conviction or force. Whether physical or social, power relationships frequently translate into ideologies of legitimization. These ideologies manifest themselves not only in social interactions but also as symbols of domination and servitude (see Cohen 1979; Hodder 1982a, 1982b; Kus 1982; Tilley 1999). Symbolically charged artifacts, features, and designs are used to reinforce and otherwise support a social order that legitimizes dominance and relationships of inequality.

In a key publication, Elizabeth DeMarrais and colleagues suggested that power relations and particularly their symbolic expression are directly translated into the material realm (DeMarrais et al. 1996). As such, it is possible to reconstruct power relations from the archaeological record, carefully examining the distribution of materials, technology, and iconography within cultural spheres.

Andean textiles are an ideal medium for the symbolic presentation of power. Weaving technology allowed for the easy creation of patterns and forms. Availabil-

ity of superb dyes in a wide range of colors enabled the creation of colorful presentations. And the use of textiles as garments, headdresses, and accessories guaranteed the constant presentation and easy mobility of symbols by their owners.

Lower-class Andean burials are usually found with simple, typically undecorated
textiles. Andean iconography typically depicts commoners with plain or marginally
decorated textiles. Elite burials, on the other hand, are rich with highly decorated
textiles. Similarly, iconography on pottery, murals, and other media frequently
depicts elites dressed in elaborate garments with sophisticated designs.

The number of social tiers within each Andean society varies and depends on
the level of social complexity. With little ethnographic evidence and no written
records, it is difficult to reconstruct detailed social hierarchies from the archaeological record alone. Yet it is possible to distinguish between broad differences of
social classes. These differences are clearly observed in textiles and can be seen in
textile quantity, quality of weaving, quality of garment, choice of raw material, and
selection of design patterns.

Early in the history of Andean textile analysis, scholars noted and investigated
elaborate elite textiles only. Burials from Ancón, Paracas, and Pachacamac yielded
highly decorated and sophisticated textiles, found in large quantities in single burials
(Reiss and Stübel 1880–87; Shimada 1991; Tello 1959; Tello and Mejía 1979; Uhle
and Grosse 1903). Even in recent years, excavations of important sites focused on
the descriptions of elite textiles (Alva and Donnan 1993; Castillo 1997). Few plain
burials or textiles were investigated, and only in the early 1990s has careful recording and focus on class differences as expressed through textiles begun to emerge
(see Clark 1990; Horta 1997; Paul 1990; Peters 1995, 1997). In her study of textiles from the Azapa Valley (Figure 7.2), Vicki Cassman devised a method to score
the overall quality of textiles recovered from three different cemeteries (Cassman
1997:127–140). Termed Q-score, Cassman calculated numerical values for fabric
density, quantity of repairs, number of colors used, and quantity of garments recovered. Her inter-site Q-scores correlated positively with differences in quality and
quantity of pottery and proved an effective tool to differentiate social status based
on the textile record alone.

Work in the lower Osmore Valley in southern Peru yielded similar results. Based
on their association with pottery and architecture, textiles from the Late Intermediate Period Tumilaca and Chiribaya occupation phases were divided into lower-
and higher-status groups (Buikstra 1995; Lozada 1998; Owen 1993). Lower-status
burials consisted of a single plain textile, while higher-status burials included two
or more textiles, decorated in a variety of colors and sophisticated designs (Boytner
1998b).

The chroniclers discussed the strict control of textile production in the Andes in
Inca times. These controls applied not only to quality of weaving or quantity of textiles, but also to the right to display particular design elements and their combination. Elite textiles typically include complex designs charged with cultural meaning
(see J. Bird 1963, 1964; Conklin 1983; Donnan 1986; Paul 1979, 1991; Paul and
Turpin 1986; A. Rowe 1979, 1980; J. Rowe 1986). These designs were intentionally selected, reflecting the divine right and legitimizing the claim for power.

Control over textile production also included their distribution and right of ownership. Elaborately decorated textiles were sometimes given to lower-status individuals as a reward for service or recognition for loyalty. The frequent discoveries of elaborate textiles in low-status burials suggest that the practice was common across the Andes. How esteemed these textiles were is evident from observations of their use prior to burial. Elaborate textiles from elite burials are typically new, with little mending. Elaborate textiles from lower-status burials frequently show high levels of wear and frequent events of mending. Elaborate textiles in the possession of lower-status individuals were probably displayed frequently, demonstrating recognition by the authorities and, therefore, increasing the social standing and power of their owners. Extensive wear suggests these textiles were so important that in some instances these were heirlooms, transferred from one generation to the next to ensure continuation for the symbolic possession of power they represented.

The tight controls over textile production and ownership are evident not only through their design and iconography, but also through the materials used to make them. Historical records mention the attachment of a special class of weavers to Inca elite households and distribution of textiles during special events (Guamán Poma de Ayala 1978). Specialized textile production areas were discovered in Chan Chan, where textiles were produced for consumption by Chimú elites (Moseley and Day 1982). But control over textiles began even before the first warp was put on the loom. Work at Pacatnamu, a Lambayeque center in northern Peru, shows that elites not only controlled the weaving quality of textiles, but also the raw materials used for their production (Boytner 1998a, in press). While most textiles were made from locally available cotton threads, design elements in elaborate textiles were made with imported camelid fibers. Elite textiles were made with large quantities of camelid threads while lower-status textiles rarely had a single camelid thread in them. In addition, dyes used in elite textiles were from highland origins, while those used in low-status textiles were from local sources. The Lambayeque elite at Pacatnamu controlled the entire spectrum of textile production. Pacatnamu may be the only site thus far where textile analyses were able to fully document class differences, but fragmentary evidence from Chan Chan, El Brujo, Nazca, and San Pedro de Atacama suggests that similar patterns are present there as well.

Textiles and Ethnic Identity

The chroniclers documented the existence of many Andean cultural groups. These groups differed in their adaptation to different environments, languages, ideologies, and social and political organizations. These differences were translated to the material realm, expressed through differences in design, as well as in production methods. Each group created its own style, serving as an essential reference point for group identity.

James Sackett described style as "a highly specific and characteristic way of doing something which by its very nature is peculiar to a specific time and space" (Sackett 1982:63). Amy Oakland suggested that "different cultures can live side by side and do the same things, interacting yet maintaining their distinctiveness, or conversely members of one culture can live far apart and maintain their similarity" (Rodman 1992:318–319). Style symbolizes shared values, tradition, and, frequently, ideology. It is a reflection of group identity – their ethnicity. Ethnicity does not necessarily suggest shared biological heritage, and ethnic identity can be acquired, adopted, or bestowed through various social institutions such as marriage, religious conversion, alliances, and conquest.

Cross-cultural research has shown that textile style is commonly used as the basis for expression of social identity. Polly Wiessner (1984) found that the Kalahari San express their identity through beaded headdresses. Ian Hodder (1982b) described how costume changed in three different African tribes as a result of marriage. Martin Wobst (1977) noted that textile style is commonly used in Yugoslavian folk culture as a definition of group affiliation. The importance of textiles for ethnic identity in current traditional Andean communities also has been widely documented. Christine Franquemont (1986) described how important the choices of material, technique, and appearance of textiles are for the Chinchero in the Peruvian highlands. Elayne Zorn (1990) documented how cloth proclaims a separate ethnic identity for the Sakaka of Bolivia.

In her investigation of the Calcha region in southwest Bolivia, Ann Medlin documented the tensions between tradition and innovation as reflected in textiles (Medlin 1986, 1991). The young people of Calcha are not interested in producing or wearing traditional textiles, but are instead adopting European clothing. Despite the shift in daily use to European dress, traditional Calcha handwoven cloth is still necessary for proper social interaction in significant social events, such as marriage, plantings, and festivals. These findings echo Lewis Binford's conclusions that symbols of group identity and ancestor affiliation are expressed most strongly during rites of passage. He claimed that symbols are especially relevant in mortuary contexts (L. Binford 1971:17).

In the Andes, most archaeologically recovered textiles come from burials and other mortuary contexts. Relating to Ann Medlin's work, these textiles may not reflect the daily dress, or the intensity of presentation of ancient Andean identity. They are an expression of extreme conditions, where the value of identity and its relations to ancestral help is most needed. Yet, despite the extreme nature of presentation in textiles from mortuary contexts, they are valuable indicators of ethnicity and ethnic relations in the Andes.

The expression of group affiliation in textiles proved important for regional investigation of ethnic composition. Examining the textile record at the Azapa Valley, Cassman found that textile technology and iconography differ little between sites and across time. She concluded that, although she can isolate characteristics associated with status differentiation, only one textile style can be identified, and therefore a single ethnic group resided in the valley for most of its human occupation (Cassman 1997). The case is dramatically different at the site of Pachacamac on the central coast of Peru. Early chronicles wrote that the site was the seat of an important Andean oracle, where entire communities and individuals from across the Andes came to seek advice. Among other types of material record, Max Uhle excavated and documented textiles belonging to diverse and different ethnic groups, providing independent evidence for the importance of the site and its function as a pilgrimage center for many ethnic groups (Shimada 1991). The site of Pacatnamu was initially believed to be also a pilgrimage center, a sister site to Pachacamac (Keatinge 1977; Keatinge et al. 1975; Schaedel 1951). Recent examination of the textile record there, however, showed that not to be the case. The textile style represented a single, local ethnic group, and no evidence for the presence of other groups and pilgrims was detected.

John Murra described a unique Andean phenomenon where a community residing in one environment built a satellite community in a different environment as means to maximize extraction and transportation of diverse resources to the center (Murra 1975, 1985). Termed "Vertical Archipelago," the model illustrates how the center and its colonies are geographically apart but socially united. Maintaining coherent and shared cultural affiliation and identity, colonies in distant areas did not assimilate or integrate with local cultures, but lived as culturally isolated foreigners in distant lands. Amy Oakland's examination of textiles from San Pedro de Atacama in northern Chile showed how clear and distinct local textile tradition was from the textiles of the Tiwanaku colony, despite the sharing of similar cemeteries. These differences did not disappear through time. To the contrary, each group maintained its own symbols and textile decoration tradition, keeping to its own part of shared cemeteries. Oakland suggested that textile distribution patterns and textile decorations clearly demonstrate that foreign Tiwanaku groups coexisted with local populations, but maintained cultural isolation and separate affiliation to the Tiwanaku center (Rodman 1992).

The creation of foreign colonies in otherwise culturally homogenous landscapes may have resulted in political tensions and outright animosity between local and newly arrived communities. In times of danger and increased hostility, demand for intra-group solidarity increases and expressions of group identity are emphasized. Identities are frequently displayed through symbols, and textiles are the perfect mode to present group affiliation and loyalty. Potential for hostilities also has an impact on the size of symbols. When warfare technology requires close contact – as is the case in the Andes – it is important to distinguish between friend and foe from a safe distance so that options to engage or flee will be open, and rational decisions assessing the situation can be made. Large displays of group identity are vital in such conditions, and textiles are the natural mode for such presentation. When symbols are small, group affiliation can be detected only from short distances, indicating that inter-group relations do not require identification over large distances; this implies cordial relations. In this sense, size does matter (Wobst 1977). Exploring textile iconography using this model allows the evaluation of group adherence to traditional values, as well as of the nature of relationships between different groups coexisting in similar geographical settings.

The model was recently applied to the examination of Tumilaca and Chiribaya textiles from the lower Osmore Valley (Boytner 1998b). Although distinct and clear differences in textile technology and iconography were found between the two groups, these differences were visible only from a short distance. It was impossible for one individual to identify the ethnic affiliation of another from a long distance since the differences were located in the decoration of small elements on tunics and bags. These distinct but small-scale differences were interpreted as strong intra-group identity but a peaceful coexistence of both groups in the valley, leading archaeologists to develop a new understanding of the nature of human occupation there.

Textiles and Gender

Great advances in gender studies and in research into textile and gender issues have been made in the past few decades (Barber 1994; Gero and Conkey 1991; Meskell 1999, 2001, 2002; R. Wright 1996). Yet Andean gender-focused research rarely moves beyond description. What little was done followed primarily second-wave feministic theory, with limited geographical and temporal scope (Gero 1992; Hocquenghem and Lyon 1980; Lyon 1978; Silverblatt 1987; but see Costin 1993, 1998). Despite these shortcomings, enough data have been collected to allow initial insights into gender relations in the Andes.

Ethnographic descriptions of gender relations, gender divisions, and gender func-tions are articulated in some early chronicles. Their readings, however, must be bal-anced against the contemporary biased European view of female inferiority and binary gender divisions. Despite these biases, the chronicles do provide some sig-nificant information. They describe that, within the Inca Empire, awasqa textiles were produced at the household level, most likely by females as part of their domes-tic work (Costin 1993:4). In contrast, cumbi textiles were produced by specialists of two kinds. Female specialist weavers were part of the aclla class, but a male spe-cialist class also existed, called cumbi kamayoq. Murra wrote that, although women were primarily responsible for awasqa cloth production in the Inca Empire, those men not engaged in military or other labor service (mit'a) were also required to spin threads and weave textiles (Murra 1962).

Independent verification of producer gender identity has proven to be a difficult task, particularly when attempting to compare information from chronicles against data from contemporary traditional Andean communities. Division of labor asso-ciated with textile production, including spinning and weaving, is not consistent across traditional Andean communities today or in the ethnographic record from the last century. Although Ed and Christine Franquemont described weaving in Chinchero done mostly by females (Franquemont and Franquemont 1988), Joe Fabish described exquisite textile weaving in Huamachuco region done mostly by males (Fabish 2003). In a photograph taken by Hiram Bingham while leading his Yale Expedition through Cotahuasi, a large vertical loom is present with at least two male weavers (see Frame 1997–98: fig. 11). In their examination of traditional Ecuadorian textile production, Ann Rowe and colleagues found that designated genders for both spinning and weaving are not only region-specific, but also depended on the type of textile made. They observed that, although some tasks may be ideologically feminine, practice is different and both genders participate as economic and other conditions dictate (A. Rowe and Meisch 1998:24, 36–39). While working with the Q'ero of Peru, Ann Rowe and John Cohen described both males and females spinning threads while only females wove textiles (A. Rowe and Cohen 2002:82–84).

Not only are we not sure about the gender identity of producers, we are also uncertain about the manifestation of gender identity through textile form or iconography. Guamán Poma de Ayala illustrated traditional dress of Inca elite, where males wear short tunics and females wear long tunics held by a wide belt and covered by a shawl that is held over the shoulders with a tupo (metal pin) (Guamán Poma de Ayala 1987: plates 1132, 1153). Some scholars have concluded that further divisions of form are possible. They suggest that it is possible to assign gender identification to tunics based on the orientation of their neck and sleeve slits. Tunics with horizontal neck and sleeve openings are for females, while tunics with vertical neck and sleeve openings and sometimes with short sleeves are for male use. Other attempts to define gender-specific textile form were made. Mary Frame described detailed division between male and female Chuquibamba textiles, identifying gender-specific tunics, shawls, loincloths, belts, and bags (Frame 1997–98:34–25; also see Desrosiers 1992). Unfortunately, these divisions were not based on the correlation of excavated textiles with gender identification of their associated human remains but on previous, untested assumptions about the form of male and female textiles. In fact, evidence from a variety of Andean sites shows that it is impossible to identify a pan-Andean distinction between male and female textiles based on slit orientation, tunic size, or any other characteristic. In the Azapa Valley – where good correlation between human remains and textiles exists – Cassman found no significant gender difference in tunic style or form (Cassman 2000:264). Examining collections of miniature Wari figurines, Cook concluded that, despite her ability to identify gender based on body features, differences in garments' form or style resemble regional, not gender, attributes (Cook 1992a:354–355). Attempts to engender Moche textiles from Pacatnamu were based on correlation between textile motifs and ceramic art, and not between textiles and human remains, raising some doubts about the interpretation of the textile attributes (Donnan and Donnan 1997:224–225).

Traditionally, gender division follows a biologically based binary distinction – male or female. Yet recent anthropological literature recognizes the possibility for the cultural construction of more than two genders and the archaeological record from the Andes shows that we must entertain such possibilities there. While examining Moche fineline drawings, Christopher Donnan recognized a religious theme repeated on most Moche ceramics (Donnan 1976). Recent finds at Sipán, San José de Moro, and Dos Cabezas revealed that the fantastic deities depicted in Moche art were actually impersonated by members of the Moche elite in their lives. Moche elite were dressed in the clothing and paraphernalia depicted in their art, making them the living incarnation of supernatural deities (Alva and Donnan 1993; Castillo 1997; Donnan 2001b; Jiménez Díaz 2001). Those individuals were both males and females, but their appearance on iconography and their rich burials suggest that their role as representatives of the mythical world surpassed their mortal gender identity as normally practiced within Moche society. It is possible that they were viewed outside the typical gender hierarchy and power relations, or that they represented some mythical equality of genders since they represented equally important deities.

The association of gender-specific textiles and their representation of gender power and status are further confused by evidence from Chimú and Chimú–Inca burials. Excavations at Las Avispas at Chan Chan, Huaca Larga at Tucume, and, recently, at Farfan, revealed that burials of females with richly decorated textiles accompanied burials of elite males (Heyerdahl, Sandweiss, and Narvaez 1995:90–97; A. Rowe 1980; Carol Mackey 2002, personal communications). Alfredo Narváez suggested that the women buried at Tucume were acllas sacrificed in an attempt to appease the gods in times of great distress (Heyerdahl, Sandweiss, and Narvaez 1995:96). But were their textile form and iconography representing their status as females, as elite-attached weavers, or were the textiles appropriate to the specific ceremony performed to alleviate the problem that caused their sacrifice? Although the answers to these questions are open, the mere existence of such cultural phenomena presents a challenge for the cultural interpretation of textiles as representations of gender role not only for the Moche, Chimú, or Inca, but for the entire sweep of Andean cultural history as well.

Conclusions

The data show that textiles had special significance to the people of the Andes almost from the beginning of sedentary life there and possibly even earlier. Cassman has stated that relishing textiles and clothing

> was a pan-Andean phenomenon, although one would not know this from the low number of large-scale archaeological textile analyses carried out until recently . . . Given the level of importance prehistoric Andean peoples placed on their textiles and the frequency of these remains in household, midden, and mortuary contexts in Andean coastal sites, I urge archaeologists to develop a greater understanding of textile analysis . . . and the significance of problem-oriented textile analyses in archaeological research. (Cassman 2000:256)

As textile analysis becomes more relevant to mainstream Andean archaeological research, sustained efforts must be made on two fronts. Textile research must move beyond description and should dramatically enhance its anthropological context and interpretation. Considering the rich archaeological record, the vast museum collections, and the consistent discoveries of textiles in current excavations, it is one task that can be easily achieved. But general field archaeologists must also do their part. It is essential for them to recognize and actively pursue the cultural meaning embedded in this class of artifacts. Particularly in coastal sites, research investment and interest in textiles should be at the same level as that dedicated to ceramic and architectural research.

Fortunately, textile research is moving forward on both fronts. New research is more cognizant then ever of anthropological issues, and more projects are dedicating resources for textile analysis and publication. These efforts are most apparent in the increasing number of textile-related papers presented in regional and international conferences, although publication in journals is still lacking. More can be done and, given their availability and importance, textiles should – and will – become one of the primary sources of information about the social life of the ancient inhabitants of the Andes.

8
Wari Art and Society

Anita G. Cook

Introduction

The Middle Horizon (A.D. 550–1000) was a period of tremendous shifts in power and wealth accumulation. Wari dominated the political scene in the central and southern Andean highlands and coast (Cook 1992a, 1994; Isbell and Cook 2002; Isbell and McEwan 1991; Lumbreras 1974a; Menzel 1964, 1968, 1977; Schreiber 1992; Tello 1970; Williams and Nash 2002) while Tiwanaku ruled a smaller expansive state in the Titicaca Basin and southern altiplano (Browman 1985; Goldstein 1993; Janusek 1994; Kolata 1993; Lumbreras and Amat 1968; Mujica 1985; Ponce 1969; Posnansky 1945; Wallace 1980) and colonies in adjacent areas including the far south coast of Peru and northern Chile. Each polity produced remarkable monuments and mural and portable art. Monumental architecture and ceramics reveal most of the big picture, while crafted portable objects occur in various media, some of which are primarily recovered on the arid coast, such as wood, textiles, and other more perishable items. Occasionally, these are also encountered in sealed tombs and dry cave finds in the highlands, but preservation is biased in favor of coastal conditions.

Most researchers agree that Wari was an expansive state, an empire that consolidated power rapidly (Isbell and McEwan 1991; Isbell and Schreiber 1978; Schreiber 1992). Centrally administered from its eponymous capital in the Ayacucho Valley of the central highlands, there was a four-tier site size hierarchy in some valleys (Isbell and Schreiber 1978). This is most evident in Ayacucho with the capital of Wari, second-order provincial centers, towns, and villages.

Wari did not develop in a void. Rather, close connections existed between the central highlands and the south-central coast prior to the emergence of Wari. Huarpa communities dotted the landscape during the Early Intermediate Period along tributaries of the middle Mantaro Valley including the entire Ayacucho Basin and Pampas River drainage. Huarpa social organization has been described as a

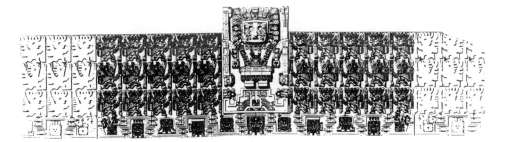

Figure 8.1. Gateway of the Sun at Tiwanaku

loosely connected confederacy or as a series of complex chiefdoms (Isbell and Schreiber 1978; Lumbreras 1974a; Schreiber 2001:79). Huarpa peoples of the Ayacucho and surrounding areas had already adopted tricolor (red, white, and black) ceramic slips, and during late Huarpa times polychrome painting appears due in large part to close connections with south coast Nasca potters. It may have taken as little as one or two generations to popularize the polychrome tradition. By the early Middle Horizon, ceramic designs combine south coast and Ayacucho local styles in innovative trends that are found in distant lands and provide some of the initial indicators of the first wave of Wari state expansion.

In addition, it is well known that a new figural assemblage of circum-Late Titicaca origin arrived in the Ayacucho area. But – and this is very important – Wari expansion occurred early, and prior to the far-flung popularity of this foreign iconography. In fact, Ayacucho had already developed a sophisticated iconography that was assembled locally from earlier contacts with the coast and the north highlands. The integration of local Ayacucho and south coast styles and imagery was tremendously important and the mechanisms and people responsible for this art were most likely those who moved between these two regions developing an economic, social, and eventually a political co-dependency that would last centuries. If the mytho-histories of those living in such different environments were brought together as they were during late Huarpa and early Wari times and depicted in vivid color, this was certainly something to emulate. The only medium that could compete and did so successfully for millennia, prior to the ceramic polychrome tradition, was that of textiles. In fact textiles have been recognized for years as the mechanism by which the religious iconography was spread (see discussion in Chapter 7, this volume).

It would take several more generations for the Staffed Deity and Profile Staffed figures of Tiwanaku origin (Figure 8.1) to populate the scenes on regular and oversized vessels in Ayacucho (Figure 8.2). Here I am referring to an all important iconographic cluster known as the Staffed God theme (Cook 1983, 1987, 1994) which is accompanied by staffed profile figures as known in monumental form on the Gateway of the Sun (Figure 8.1) at the site of Tiwanaku in the Titicaca Basin (Isbell and Cook 1987). Throughout this chapter I will refer to "gateway icono-

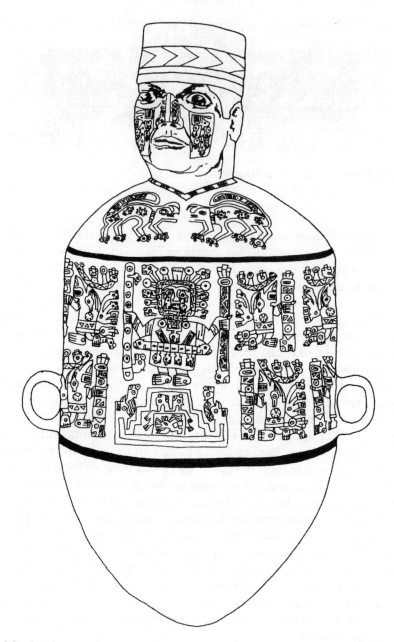

Figure 8.2. Conchopata offering vessel depicting the Staff God theme, from the 1977 excavations. Compare to Figure 8.1

graphy," although this reference will include design registers also found on the monoliths that include a larger number of figures than those identified exclusively on the Gateway of the Sun (see Posnansky 1945).

The arrival of Tiwanaku imagery set the stage for a popular religious base, founded on an ancient core paradigmatic image of a human being gazing forward and grasping staffs or other implements in both hands (see Chapter 3, this volume). The full-frontal body posture, forward demanding glance, feet pointed outwards and firmly situated on an elevated platform mound or mountain was easy to replicate, a statement of power and wealth, perhaps even of divinity through time, in the Andes. The image went in and out of popularity but continues despite these interruptions to be manifestly present in the Middle Horizon.

Major Problems in Wari Studies

Andeanists vigorously debate the origins, interactions, and the strategies employed by Wari and Tiwanaku lords to achieve economic and political supremacy. In large part the debates have historically focused on theocratic origins at both centers, with Tiwanaku religious architecture and iconography spreading through religious/cult mechanisms to the central highlands (Lumbreras 1974a; Menzel 1964, 1968, 1977). Wari adopted a similar imagery and reoriented its use to more secular ends through militaristic expansion, with religious overtones, basically a Crusades model of religious proselytization.

Other models emphasize the economic dimension. For instance, Schreiber (1992) discusses how fertile lands were reclaimed by the Wari and transformed into productive terraces in the central highland Sondondo Valley with sites moving to lower elevations to tend to these new imperial agricultural demands. A switch to intensification of maize cultivation ensued (see also Browman 1981; Isbell 1977).

There was an abrupt political expansion in the first epoch of the Middle Horizon (Schreiber 2001) to the far south coast (Moquegua: see, e.g., Williams and Nash 2002), south highlands (Pikillacta and Huaro: see McEwan 1991 and Glowacki 2002, respectively), north highlands (e.g., Viracochapampa and Honco Pampa: see Topic 1991 and Isbell 1989, respectively), central coast (Pachacamac: see Schreiber 1992:106) and south coast (Pacheco and Huaca del Loro: see, e.g., Schreiber 1992:107 and Paulsen 1983, respectively). The second epoch illustrates some unfinished building projects at several boundary sites (Viracochapampa and Pikillacta), and a more inward looking empire that was focused on economic issues and agricultural production and storage (e.g., Azangaro in the Huanta Valley near Ayacucho: see Anders 1986). All this came on the heels of what had been a more dispersed village economy.

How often this happened has yet to be fully evaluated, but settlement surveys indicate that the valleys in which the Wari had greatest interest, and where extraction of goods was essential, are the areas where these changes are most pronounced. Wari material remains and architecture are abundantly present at the center and they tell a story of occupation and significant social organizational reform in the heartland. There are nuances in the archaeological record when individual valley systems and Wari sites are examined in detail. Was religion part of an expanding state ideology and the dominant form of Wari hegemony? How did the political economy and the tribute system work? Did a documented drought in the sixth century prompt seasonal population migrations or even movements involving several generations? Could these then have motivated more enduring contacts between valley systems and an expanded kinship network across diverse environments? Should we be examining the question of environmental degradation due to overexploitation in the Wari heartland that prompted expansion measures? Why and when did the Wari appropriate the Tiwanaku gateway iconography given that Wari had already established hegemony at home using its own visual language to integrate populations under Wari control? All of these issues are actively under investigation. Here I focus on the last question.

Re-presentations of Political Inequality in Material Form

Political inequality exists in all forms of human social organization, but it is most visible to the archaeologist in tangible material forms such as human-made objects and buildings. An equal challenge is to focus on the agents of change, in other words, the people who made and used these objects and places.

Consequently, the following discussion examines material culture and architecture, taking into account that events may have occurred within and between the still-standing remains of ancient buildings and in the unbounded spaces between communities. More specifically, my aim is to examine the pictorial histories, as preserved in various media, and focus on the way human depictions express particular social identities. The mannerisms, interactions, and juxtapositions among humans and the particular plants, animals, buildings, and objects with which they are displayed offer unparalleled insights into how artisans viewed particular individuals, the sexes and class from the mid-sixth to tenth centuries A.D.

Objects, dress, gesture, posture, and glance, to name a few, are attributes that convey knowledge about the age, class, and sex of the actors in *pictorial presentations*; while the context, form, color, size, and even frequency of *objects*, in close archaeological associations, provide insights into their life histories. It is not solely a question of understanding whether things are made at home, in a cottage industry or in a workshop context; or whether they were commissioned by a family as opposed to a wealthy lord (a patron of the arts); objects are shaped through an inseparable weave of culture and technology (Lechtman 1977, 1984): by this I mean that we cannot separate the technology or steps in production involved in making an object from its producers, and the logic and choices that are employed in the process. Furthermore, objects have cultural biographies (Gosden 1997) or life histories – they are made for a reason, certain individuals partake in their production over others, and they circulate according to particular shared norms; occasionally they are elevated to special status. This is usually the product of finely made and highly valued pieces: heirlooms are often in this category.

Earlier studies focused on description and the classification of artifacts into groups that might reveal significant patterns reflective of past behavior. Using ecology, taxonomy, and cultural evolution, questions of artifact style and function as well as more structuralist approaches were emphasized. These studies of material culture included work on prehistoric technologies, ethnoarchaeology, and replicative or experimental studies resulting more in methodological advances than a richer understanding of the past (see also Carr and Neitzel 1995; Conkey 1990; Hegmon 1992). In general, many of the results were focused on the group with little appreciation for the interactive role between makers and users. Artifacts are not frozen in time, and much of their significance is lost when taken out of context and removed from the larger system of social meanings in which they were created and circulated. Humans populate their world with objects, which they need to live with, and which structure sets of meanings that change over time. This active role of artifacts is central to understanding social identities in the past.

A groundbreaking study by Heather Lechtman (1977, 1984) on how prehistoric metals were made in the Andes revealed that metallurgy was far more complex than was functionally necessary. In other words, metallurgists developed technologies that could not be attributed simply to practical and functional needs. Instead, a series of sophisticated metallurgical smelting practices were developed to allow a preferred color to be present both on the surface (where we would expect it) but also within the object. In this way, it was revealed that metallurgy, and probably other technologies in the Andes, such as textile production (Lechtman 1996, 1999), might contain value-laden information. Furthermore, these are not necessarily static patterns; in fact, technological practices are historically contingent and will actively respond to new indigenous or internal developments, and outside influences, thus revealing how particular ways of doing things resist or absorb change. In other words, a strictly functional and a need-based approach to material culture is inadequate; we need a broadened consideration of the nature of production and consumption patterns as well as the material symbols they contain. We need to look at the many facets of production and end uses of material remains. Practices are adopted, transformed, and contested over time in individual historical settings. The view that reality is a social construction, and that it is continuously reconstituted in the past as it is in the present, provides a historically dynamic backdrop for a perspective on changing class and status markers during the rise of empires in the Andes. These markers will help reveal the social identities of those making, possessing, and disposing of materials and the symbols they convey.

Who made the objects, embellished the structures, and painted the images as Wari coalesced as a state and empire? Andeanists are challenged to answer this question because writing did not exist in precolumbian times. With no formal writing system in the Andes, scholars rely on the multivocality of *iconography* and *material symbols* because they express and embody forms of past knowledge. They should be viewed as fulfilling critically important communicative roles, as significant as those associated primarily with texts in literate societies. Imagery and objects not only reveal a rich way of accessing information in the Andean past, but they inform new ways of looking at imagery where writing has been privileged. In our case the focus is on the rise of political elites whose accumulated wealth and power ushered in a privileged class.

The complex intercultural setting that was assembled by the emergence of Wari elites in the sixth century A.D. set the stage for a radical change in political discourse and ideology. At no earlier time in Andean prehistory was there such a far-reaching impact on material remains. Was this due to direct or indirect political control? Were politicians actively engaged in disseminating a core state ideology under the guise of a religious imagery that was focused on human interactions with the supra-natural world? If so we would expect centralized places where production took place and individuals charged with controlling the content of images on objects, in our case, particularly ceramics, which remain among the least perishable of human made artifacts. Who were the producers and consumers? These are the questions frequently asked when studying the state and the very rare occurrences of empire in the archaeological record.

Ceramic styles purportedly offer information on degrees of contact, assimilation, and diffusion of motifs that express, in symbolic form, information and even aspects of ideology. Moreover, new questions are being asked of these same style categories. For instance, can assemblages from distinct sites express local concerns, mythologies, and even dissension? Do individual agents or groups assimilate foreign designs, and who is responsible for the integration of local traditions with foreign influences? From contemporary ethnographic contexts in the Bolivian highlands, migrant artisan specialists have been observed, charged with bringing their clays and the tools of their trade to make their pottery in places distant from their home and clay sources (Sonia Alconini, personal communication, 2002). This type of situation poses some serious problems for the archaeologist, because we are prone to examine clay sources and ceramic mineralogical compositions in order to assess whether pottery was locally made or imported. We suspect this type of activity will leave poor archaeological signatures, but it should not be ignored.

Of greater potential is the study of individual communities and the nature of production activities at single sites, such as at Conchopata, a Wari site where I have been working for several years. How much power lay in the hands of Conchopata's artisan ideologues, for if they did exist, they brought with them a language of images that became almost commonplace even among the elites of such impenetrable societies as the north coast Moche. Was this a new religious ideology that belonged to a new class of wealthy elites? If so where did they reside and was their purpose to disseminate or to make inaccessible and sacred the images that were emulated throughout the central Andes? In a strange twist of fate, the sharing and dissemination of a trademark, that of slip polychrome painting, was so powerful that it may have accidentally led to the emulation of the biggest and the best. By A.D. 600 one of the major centers of prestige ceramic production had shifted from the south coast to the Ayacucho Valley, and the styles linked to this center were found over 1,300 km through the Peruvian highlands and parts of the coast (Schreiber 2001:80).

Approaches to material culture are varied. Some view the remains as the literal embodiment of past knowledge. This suggests that an in-depth study of the object will provide technological, social, economic, political, or even ideological information about the society in which it was produced. Some may start as a raw material and are transformed by craftspeople with different skill levels and expertise into final products. These are then circulated, some are used and discarded, some are lost, and others are reworked into new artifacts with new life histories. I am inclined to the view that social values can be studied by careful study of what is and is not represented in sculptural or painted forms from good archaeological contexts. Conversely, individual and community practices are more readily revealed through the art of making objects, in other words specialized crafts. In brief, technologies are practiced to achieve particular end products and they also embody commonly held behaviors and assumptions about how an object should be manufactured, community preferences, the right versus the wrong way of making desired artifacts (Dobres 2000).

Some artisans specialize in one medium, while others might adapt their expertise to suit the material (e.g., stone tool producers may have also carved figurines in semi-precious stones, or been involved in modifying recycled potsherds into tools). One challenge we face as archaeologists is how to identify the specific activities of producers, the value attributed to their work within complex political settings, and the nuances of their daily lives and annual cycle. For instance, how important were age, sex, and class in particular craft activities? Was mentoring important, and can we detect the work of apprentices? Were producers engaged in their craft full-time or seasonally? Were their talents applicable to other media, suggesting they may be engaged in one craft for part of the year, while the remainder was dedicated to a second craft activity? What is meant by the distinction drawn between full versus part-time craft production? For instance, making pottery at the household level, within communal facilities or within workshop contexts (where special-function pottery or mass-produced wares might be produced) implies distinct work conditions, labor pools, and resources. If certain materials can only be obtained from distant places, or are available exclusively in specific seasons (e.g., seasonally available dyes for yarns) then preparation and resource procurement become part of the scheduled activities of full-time work. Conversely, in state-sponsored or commissioned contexts, resources may be accrued through collecting the goods and labor as revenue (best documented for the Inca Empire).

Crafting and Elite Artisans

In Quechua, one of two indigenous languages still spoken in the Andean highlands, there is no word for art, artist, or artisan. The Quechua term quellcay translates as drawing, painting, sculpting, and embroidery or the embellishment of textiles. In fact all words that deal with a particular art form include the term quellcca, as in the word for sculptor, rumiqquellcaycamayok, which literally translates as specialist of the stone canvas. All words that relate to specialization in a trade include the word camayok or specialist. There is a word that refers to painting a garment (quellcascappacha in Holguín 1989[1608]:301). From a linguistic perspective, an artisan's skill includes inscribing information in or on particular media.

Crafting, which I use as synonymous with art and artisanship (Glassie 1999), is a social activity that involves learning through imitation and practice. Craftsmanship assumes a degree of expertise that would not have been available in every household. There may have been opportunities for apprenticeship experience in the recycling and rejuvenated life histories of artifacts. For instance, working with stone and pottery would have been commonplace by those responsible for reshaping discarded materials, such as broken pottery sherds, and transforming them into useful ceramic production tools. To accomplish this, stone tool artisans would share their expertise in reducing technology with others, perhaps male and female apprentices or even children. At sites where ceramic production was a major activity, discarded potsherds and misfired vessels are available in quantity and would have been a safe arena for trial and error. Recycled ceramics were made into standard shapes (e.g. rectangular, trapezoidal, triangular, circular) that were used by the potter as smoothing and scraping tools, and disks of various sizes which were possibly used to spin a vessel during the construction process. Some recycled sherds are shaped into disks with holes at their center. These have usually been exclusively interpreted as preforms of spindle whorls used for spinning yarns into distinct thicknesses, but potters are ingenious and wear patterns suggest these preforms had multiple functions. Another arena that is under-explored is game tokens or counters of standardized weights, and what these may have looked like. This diversity of pots, tools, and recycling illustrates how ceramic production was intimately woven into the fabric of crafting on many levels in the Andes and elsewhere.

I am interested in how we have configured the social identities of craft producers: their gender, status, and class and how the production process may shed light on these issues. This comprises one side of the equation. The other concerns representations of men, women, children, and other subject matter common to the iconography of empire during the Middle Horizon (A.D. 550–1000). We are fortunate to have highly decorated vessels of different shapes and genres. What can be revealed through a study of the conventions used to convey the sexes and the activities in which they are engaged? Can we infer who was painting vessels from the technique, individual style, and content of images? All these questions will remain open to debate for many years, but the case study presented in the following pages is intended to address both sides of this equation and explore answers to some of them.

Thus, it may be wise to rethink some of our assumptions about where specialists reside and how they interacted. Teotihuacan in the Valley of Mexico has served as one of several possible production models in the Americas. At this ancient city distinct workshop areas were identified as well as ethnic barrios. In contrast, this separation of skilled labor may not be as applicable to the Andes, where we have good examples of craft sectors at sites like Chan Chan dating to the Late Intermediate Period (A.D. 1000–1400). John Topic (1990:155–158) found that there were several different types of crafting in single locations at Chan Chan. Furthermore, developed market systems were prevailingly absent in the Andes, which may account for the striking dissimilarities between Mesoamerican and Andean craft production, relations between producers, and the circulation of finished goods (e.g. craft barrios at Mesoamerican sites like Teotihuacan).

Conchopata

Conchopata is situated in the Ayacucho Valley heartland of the Wari Empire. The question of who lived at the site has been intriguing. Early work was largely culture-historical in nature and concerned the definition of ceramic styles and iconography. Menzel (1964, 1977) proposed a stylistic seriation for the Middle Horizon based on ceramics. From this work she inferred that the speed with which these styles spread was indicative of an aggressive military conquest campaign that used the gateway iconography or Staffed Deity imagery as a means for spreading an imperial message. Menzel conveyed the idea that the religious imagery offered an overarching cosmology that softened the blow of conquest and integrated far-flung ethnic groups into the political fold. She argued that the religious iconography was borrowed in one form or another from what is today the Bolivian altiplano.

Early studies by foreign investigators (Bennett 1946, 1953; Menzel 1964; J. Rowe, Collier, and Willey 1950) included surface collections, but the focus was on fancy wares, whole pots, and well-preserved textiles from burial contexts and museum collections. Peruvian archaeologists interpreted Conchopata differently. They have focused on local styles, namely Huamanga, and vernacular architecture with an emphasis on the economic underpinnings of social and political complexity, interpreting Conchopata as a community of specialized potters (e.g., Lumbreras 1974a; Pozzi Escot 1991). Seen from this perspective it is not surprising to find different views of the site.

After four seasons of excavation, new data from Conchopata reveal that the site consists of an amalgam of urban activities, showing that this was a center of prestige second only to the imperial capital of Wari (see Isbell 2001c; Isbell and Cook 2002; Ochatoma and Cabrera 2002). The site consists of grand monumental buildings. Two types that are considered signatures of Wari imperial presence are the D-shaped temple and the patio group that contains a large rectangular plaza at its center, and is surrounded by narrow galleries on all sides (Isbell and McEwan 1991; Isbell and Schreiber 1978; Cook 2001; Cook and Glowacki 2003). Later constructions included residential and crafting compounds surrounding the civic-ceremonial structures with below-floor burials and mortuary areas.

During the earlier part of the 1900s, before the city of Wari was well known, it was widely believed that the images on Tiwanaku ceramics, stone architecture, and sculptures had influenced styles in what is today Peru. Several scholars Bennett 1946, 1953; Lumbreras 1960, 1974a; Menzel 1964, 1968; J. Rowe, Collier, and Willey 1950) revisited this question and determined that the city of Wari, not Tiwanaku, was the major contributor to broad regional stylistic trends in the central highlands and coast. Conchopata was important to these re-evaluations.

At Conchopata, the size, quality, and beauty of painted oversized vessels were originally considered to be of great importance, because they displayed figures also found in the gateway iconography from Tiwanaku sites in Bolivia. The iconographic similarities prompted a great deal of confusion, particularly because Tiwanaku is situated more than 600 km southeast by the way the crow flies from the Ayacucho Valley.

The ideology of emerging elites: dedicatory events and feasts

Rituals of power and expressions of emerging elite ideologies unfolded at Conchopata unlike any other Wari site currently known. In 1942 and again in 1977 two buried caches of broken pottery were found at Conchopata. The first, excavated by Julio C. Tello and subsequently published by Menzel (1964, 1968), contained huge urns. The second, the result of emergency excavations at the site (Cook 1987, 2001; Isbell and Cook 1987), revealed a corpus of oversized face-neck jars. These contexts contain what Menzel called "the Middle Horizon offering tradition," which consisted of votive events that prescribed the local production and consumption of huge ceremonial vessels that were covered with polychrome iconography. For reasons that were not fully understood, the vessels were smashed and buried together at sites like Conchopata, prompting the interpretation that these were offerings.

Excavations resumed in 1997. These new excavations have revealed new "offerings" and more of the materials that Julio C. Tello excavated in the 1940s. The offerings are all located in close proximity to one another, suggesting this area had special votive importance (the special nature of the votive area was accentuated by a thick stratum of pink river sand that was laid down to seal the offerings and several Early Intermediate Period Huarpa burials; see Isbell and Cook 2002; also see Tung 2003; Tung and Cook in press). Food and drink was served from vessels made by skilled artisans at Conchopata on occasions that appear to have ended in events where vessels were ritually killed, and then were buried or disposed. The cycle was then ritually renewed at the next major ceremony.

This Middle Horizon offering tradition, particularly the urns found in 1942, was situated early in the Middle Horizon sequence by Menzel (1964). New data from Conchopata and radiocarbon dates (Isbell and Cook 2002) place these urns considerably later in the sequence, prompting a re-evaluation of the chronology for the site and valley that is currently underway.

The offering tradition played a central role in constructions of Wari culture history, but these magnificent vessels can be recast in a more socially active context. I suggest these pots were among the most prestigious Wari imperial culinary vessels and that they were intended as serving utensils for food and drink at special politically charged ceremonial feasts (Cook 2000; Cook and Glowacki 2003).

Women were likely important in those activities. In highland communities today women continue an ancient practice, which is control over the production of chicha (corn beer), which is the most highly regarded ritual drink in the Andes. During Inca times the acllacuna ("chosen women") were the exclusive elite chicha producers for the ruling Inca. For the Wari Empire one of our tasks is to unravel the gestures that signal emerging elite ritual practices that may have had gender specific associations. This is indeed a challenging task because males and females have been very difficult to identify in the archaeological record of the Middle Horizon (Cook 1992a; Isbell 2002).

Expressions of excessive eating and drinking are still practiced today and have direct links to the ancestors. One often says that one is drinking also for a deceased relative on ritual occasions. Chicha, when consumed, causes frequent urination. It is widely believed that human bodies, the earth, and mountains have similar hydraulic systems (Allen 2002:241) that unite the individual to the cosmos through the flow of water (Skar 1987:284–285). In Huaquirca, Gose (1994:123–140) reports that water is expelled from the land of the dead below the mountain Qorop-una and water is vital to agriculture and life itself. The intimately close ties between life, death, and regeneration pervade Conchopata material remains, and women, who are the biological reproducers of society, appear to have played a greater role than previously assumed.

Were elite women living at Conchopata? Could they have been engaged in the special role of making chicha? If so what is the evidence? I briefly present insights to women's work, their presence and elite status at Conchopata, and finally some of the roles they are conveyed as fulfilling in the iconography. This reconstruction is brief but serves as a good case study for situating women in Wari society.

Several functional classifications of Wari pottery have been extremely useful in reassessing the contexts in which they were made, used, and deposited (e.g., Anders 1986; Brewster-Wray 1990; Cook and Glowacki 2003; Glowacki 1996). Oversized vessels occur in archaeological assemblages, but they are usually intended for storage of liquids or dry goods and are not decorated to any appreciable extent. At Conchopata these ceremonial vessels received extraordinary attention and were beautifully painted by skilled artisans. The designs were not simply repetitive geometric motifs; instead they conveyed figures in elite dress in various poses. In contrast to Menzel's contention that these were dedicatory vessels ritually broken after little use for ceremonial reasons, I suggest that their shape and iconography convey a somewhat different picture. Based on their size and volume, these were most likely used to serve large numbers of people in what may have been state-sponsored feasts held within the walled patio groups at the site (Cook 2000; Cook and Glowacki 2003). No doubt they were the result of labor skills that reached far beyond the household level and were simultaneously the canvases of scribes involved in the transfer of local ritual into national symbols. These same carriers of powerful visual imagery were the centerpieces for large state-sponsored feasts. The conspicuous consumption of food and drink may very well have been the arena for ritual battles, competitive games among intermediate elites, and rituals of death and regeneration: all are themes that can be detected in the iconography.

Following the feast these vessels were ritually "killed" and deposited in a number of sealed contexts, some of which were recovered and identified as offerings by Menzel. Not all were sealed as votive events. In the case of the 1942 pottery we found more of the same strewn across an open pavement and not sealed in a subterranean cache as the 1977 jars were encountered. In fact, Isbell (1987) reconstructed where Julio C. Tello excavated, and it corresponded to where we found more of the same material in our 1999 excavations. Furthermore, we have huge accumulations of ceramics that look like offerings, but their composition is mixed with production tools and they conform more closely to artisan dumps (Cook and Benco 2000). Perhaps this was the proper way to dispose of vessels that were originally intended for ritual use. Whether plain or painted, the vessels that were not good enough for use in celebrations due to design errors, misfiring, and other kiln mishaps were apparently still treated with care and ceremoniously buried.

In summary, the general chronological outline originally presented by Menzel has remained relatively intact. The most pronounced changes result from new radiocarbon dates that are now available from provincial Wari sites and from Conchopata (Isbell and Cook 2002; Williams 2001). The last five years of intensive research provide a much larger corpus of material for study. Some highlights of our research have changed our perspective on the Middle Horizon. Wari did grow at a remarkable speed, but it lasted far longer than previously believed. Instead of a 200-year span (approximately A.D. 650–850) during which time the empire flourished, the time frame has doubled (approximately A.D. 550–1000).

The impact of a longer chronological yardstick has led to some important changes in our thinking about Conchopata. First, it flourished before altiplano motifs became popular in Wari assemblages (Isbell and Cook 2002). Several distinct styles flourish in Ayacucho, while some imports are found in the provinces; most are imitations of Ayacucho styles. Second, in recent excavations, an early Ayacucho figurative imagery was identified on oversized urns (Cook and Benco 2000; Isbell 2001c; Isbell and Cook 2002) from architectural fill and other contexts. Some have both interior and exterior decoration; on other vessels decoration is confined to the exterior. These vessels are the earliest large urns recovered in Ayacucho and they set a precedent for what would most likely later become state-sponsored feasting utensils. Images painted on the later feasting vessels change focus and integrate the altiplano gateway theme with older familiar Ayacucho culture heroes, legends, and mytho-histories. This unique ability to integrate foreign prestige symbols seems to have paved the way to Wari ideological expansion. While Wari imagery embraced foreign themes, its architecture placed visible constraints on intra-site mobility and restrained physical access to Wari leaders.

In the early Ayacucho assemblage, narrative scenes have been partially reconstructed on large urns and face-neck jars. The main figures include the depiction of high-ranking men and women, warriors in boats, and persons in elaborate garments with human heads dangling from their necks. Numerous individuals are displayed whose pose, size, gesture, dress, and jewelry convey recognizable activities, class, age, and sex distinctions. This early narrative genre largely lacks altiplano influences. Furthermore, scenes of this nature are not common to the later gateway iconography.

There are good indicators that the circum-Titicaca iconography was introduced gradually, taking on greater importance after A.D. 800 in the Ayacucho Valley. This radically changes the popular understanding that Tiwanaku engendered Wari state imagery. Instead, the impact was late, probably once Wari colonies were firmly entrenched close to or in Tiwanaku territory (e.g., Moquegua Valley). In Moquegua, on the far south coast, the span of occupation of sites such as Cerro Baul parallels the dates at Conchopata. Both sites experience reorganization around A.D. 800.

The eighth century is most likely when Tiwanaku imagery is fully appropriated by Wari, but it is one of several coexisting pictorial programs in the Wari heartland. In addition, almost all of the Wari Middle Horizon ceramic styles, defined by Menzel (1964) in her classic work on Wari relative chronology, have been found in our excavations at Conchopata. This underscores the fact that the site had a long history. Several styles continued side by side at sites like Conchopata. One of these styles was Huamanga, the local Middle Horizon style of Ayacucho, which Menzel referred to as less fancy Viñaque. It consists of a variety of jars, bowls, cups, and spoons with geometric and figurative motifs (Anders 1986; Lumbreras 1974a; Ochatoma and Cabrera 2001c). It has also been identified in areas outside of Ayacucho, for instance in Cusco, where a Huamanga imitation style, called Araway, occurs when Wari penetrates the valley during the Middle Horizon (Bauer 2003:15; Glowacki 1996); it is made up principally of decorative bands of geometric designs.

In Ayacucho, the gateway iconography eventually enters the area, appearing on painted and incised prestige drinking and serving wares associated with state feasting halls (Cook and Glowacki 2003), on effigy vessels in votive and mortuary contexts, and on textiles. Architecture in the form of enclosed patio groups, and conspicuous production and consumption of oversized vessels covered with the material symbols of an emerging empire, provide two forms of evidence that festive and somber rituals most likely occurred at the site. I now turn to who the participants may have been.

Evidence of upper-class women at conchopata

At Conchopata, one of the first bioarchaeological studies to be conducted on Wari highland populations has provided the identifications of 188 individuals and 31 trophy heads from burials and offering contexts excavated between 1977 and 2001 (Tung 2003; Tung and Cook in press). These individuals were found in a number of distinct tomb types (Isbell and Cook 2002). Variation in tomb architecture increases over time from a late Huarpa/pre-Wari phase when three types are identified to over eight Wari tomb forms. This increase is interpreted (Tung and Cook in press) as evidence of increased stratification and greater diversity in the community during Wari times with the appearance of intermediate elites in richer and more elaborate tombs. The best-preserved tombs housed what we interpret to be extended family burials with multiple individuals interred over time. Demographically women outnumber men almost two to one, even in contexts with single-sex adult burials (Tung 2003; Tung and Cook 2002 in press).

Turning to the women buried at Conchopata, we have found that the personal funerary artifacts associated with them included Wari blackware face-neck jars, miniature vessels, copper tupu pins, worked Spondylus, and turquoise. Some of the senior females likely represent secondary burial practices. It appears that cinnabar was applied after soft tissue had decomposed (Tung 2003, personal communication). These associations were absent among the male burials, leading us to interpret that senior women belonged to a wealthy intermediate elite class of individuals who were afforded greater mortuary prestige.

In one particularly rich burial a miniature structure of adobe was built over the capped cist in which the female was buried. Although the tomb had been looted we recovered the osteological and remaining artifacts. The first impression of the bioarchaeological remains suggested this was a male until the pelvis was located, clearly revealing that this was a "robust" female. The physical remains suggest that this was a particularly strong and imposing individual. Was she viewed as female or did she fulfill a different gendered role at Conchopata?

The role women fulfilled at Conchopata remains to be fully determined, but the data suggest that their elite position raises new questions. Were they involved in provisioning the corn beer and managing the production and perhaps the consumption of prestige ceramics for which the site is so well known? Although the question is speculative, were these women elite artisans? Were they responsible for the pictorial content on oversized ceremonial pots? Hints of this are revealed in iconography and portable art media, such as figurines. Can elite women be identified in Conchopata art? How are they framed and referenced?

Few stylistic and iconographic studies embrace the problem of the social identity of males and females in Wari art. In part, this is because they are often difficult to identify. Two-dimensional figures are usually fully clothed and we have little recourse, short of an in-depth study of dress, to gain insights to marked differences in attire based on sex. The representation of female supernaturals has received most attention (Lyon 1978; Menzel 1964), but these studies rely on the assumption that elements such as projecting canines or fangs, split eyes, and wings, features of probable altiplano origin, separate humans from preternaturals.

Unlike other media, Andean three-dimensional sculptures display sexual attributes far more frequently than two-dimensional images. Stone figurines reviewed from controlled excavations and museum collections reveal an attention to anatomical and garment detail that is unparalleled, yet sexual characteristics are generally subsumed or ambiguous. Figurines that are not made of stone, on the other hand, are far more prone to exhibiting sexual characteristics. Was stone as a sacred medium the locus where male and the female essences combined in an androgynous discourse? Did other media have specific gendered associations, and are these revealed in what and how things were conveyed as well as their contextual associations?

One significant breakthrough in recent research is the ability to at least identify some males and females in Wari material culture. Most attempts to do this in the past have failed because we lack associations from excavated contexts that would allow these identifications to be more easily made, and because Wari artisans employed genres that defied easy recognition of the sexes. In part this ambiguity was intentional, yet as I have argued elsewhere (Cook 1992a, 1997b), the ambiguity conveys gender categories we have yet to unravel.

The clearest examples at Conchopata are mold-made figurines of men and women, both dressed and in the nude. Some are crude, perhaps even made by children playing with clay; others are made from elaborate molds and painted. These, in addition to a few examples of stone, turquoise and Spondylus carvings, comprise the bulk of three-dimensional figures at the site. Textiles can be considered three-dimensional, because they contain within themselves the spun yarn and a matrix of warps and wefts resulting in a two-faced cloth with surface designs. Unfortunately, all we have left at Conchopata are carbonized fragments, although a beautiful example from the site of Wari is on display at the site museum (Rodman and

Fernández 2000: fig. 9B), and others are known from dry cave finds in the region. Most contain mythological scenes. Few textiles include human depictions; those that do have no clear anatomical or gestural attributes of either sex (e.g., Angeles and Pozzi-Escot 2000: figs. 9a, 9b, 10a, 10b; Conklin 1970; Cook 1996).

Mold-made figurines come in different sizes; the largest was found among the funerary objects in a multiple extended family tomb. Although nude, she may have been originally dressed in textiles that have now decomposed (Figure 8.3b left). She represents the prototypical female: hair is parted in the middle and falls down either side of her face, a common way of representing hair on coastal Nasca figurines as well. Breasts, belly button, and genitals are painted and molded. But the breasts and belly button appear as circles with dots of comparable size outlined in black. Breasts were not emphasized, whereas her hair and fingernails are painted in black with white paint. Cheek designs descend from her eyes, painted as two elongated rectangles with a similar swash of paint down the ridge of her nose. Equally present is the posture common to most female figurines: arms are bent at the elbow, palms flat against her rib cage and belly. Joints are also indicated by a small protrusion that is painted black. Most of the figurines at Conchopata share these anatomical details even when they are just a few centimeters tall (Figure 8.3b right) and hand-made. One exception is a small figurine that has one arm down by her side and the other crossed over her belly (Figure 8.3b right).

The figurines are particularly interesting because females are represented as sculptures in the round much as the famous clad green stone figurines from the Wari site of Pikillacta near Cusco (Cook 1992a). At Conchopata women are not represented as mothers, holding or breastfeeding infants. They are also not portrayed in a submissive role vis-à-vis the opposite sex, or engaged in erotic scenes. We cannot at this stage discuss the activities with which they were associated, but the lack of visible indicators is significant because it places them on a par with male figurines, imparting the idea that equivalent social value was assigned to male and female representations. An in-depth study of the distribution and contexts in which the figurines are found is underway and will lead to further insights.

Do men and women occur on painted ceramic serving vessels, particularly the oversized urns and jars that were used for large festivities? As in the case of figurines, identifying men and women has been difficult. In fact, social class and identity as expressed in clothing and associated symbols of sovereignty are far more apparent than sex or age. A few rare but important examples of females have been recovered from recent excavations. The first example was reconstructed from several fragments and found where the potters dumps and offerings are clustered. The vessel is an oversized urn with both exterior and interior designs. Although difficult to detect, on the interior face is a female in profile with one hand raised and the other flung back (Isbell and Cook 2002: fig. 9.13). Loose black hair frames her face, like that of the figurine described above. She is clearly of elite status bearing an earspool and nose plug, yet most remarkable is her nude torso. A jaguar cub, with claws extended, is depicted upside-down suckling at her breast. At present, it is the only clear image of a female on oversized urns and it forms part of the early Ayacucho iconography that pre-dates significant altiplano influence in the area. Part of a

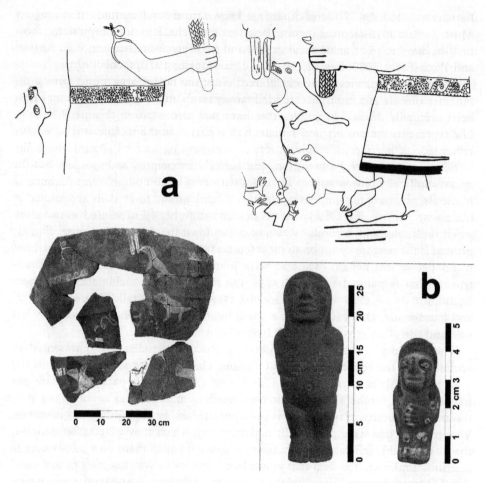

Figure 8.3. (a) Photograph of the body of a partially reconstructed oversized jar (excavated in an open kiln within Architectural Space 106B, Locus 2041, Special Find 1697) and a black line drawing of the cross-mended pieces. Two females in long wrap-around dresses and one visible tupu pin face each other. They each grasp an elongated object that may be a painted wooden implement or a thick piece of cordage. Between the figures are juvenile wolves and a young condor nibbling at a human foot and the lower portion of a skull. In the lower right-hand corner of the photograph is a more complete skull that belongs to another part of the vessel. It is interesting to note that the feet of the women are executed in similar manner to those found in later Moche murals. (b) *Left*: Nude hollow female figurine (from a multiple burial in the Architectural Space 105, Locus 2095, Special Find 1905). *Right*: Nude and painted female figurine with one hand along her side and the other on her chest (from Architectural Space 106, Locus 1945, Special Find 1491)

much larger narrative scene, the interior and exterior designs depict mythical figures, warriors with bows and arrows, and elaborate feather headdresses.

One more fragmentary example is known; it also can be considered part of the early ceremonial Ayacucho urns, completely lacking in gateway and Tiwanaku-related motifs. Two women face one another, with arms raised. Their dress identifies them as females. They each wear a long wraparound garment gathered by copper tupu pins at the shoulder and belted at the waist. It is difficult to detect how the different parts of this scene assemble and their heads are missing. The participants include juvenile foxes and a young condor feeding at detached human limbs. We know that human skulls or trophy heads received post mortem treatment from remains found in a circular temple at Conchopata (Tung and Cook in press; Isbell and Cook 2002; Tung 2003). Ropes are attached to the two human skulls. These women are proportionately larger than all the other figures and are associated with the sacrifice.

There are a number of other examples that probably represent women, but these appear in the Huamanga style in rather rustic form (Isbell 2002) and are identified by their long dresses and the association with children.

The study of representations of women is therefore still in its infancy and the two definite examples are part of the early iconography of the Ayacucho Valley. In some striking ways the representation of women in sacrificial scenes is strongly reminiscent of late Moche murals and vessel iconography. Could the burial of a "robust" elite female covered in cinnabar be related in any way to the activity represented in these iconographic scenes? Surely a great deal more analysis will be required to answer this question but it opens new areas of investigation.

Conclusions

A discussion of the many facets of production and the end uses of material remains was presented. Additionally attention was focused on the visible and less tangible or more ideological aspects of material symbols that are conveyed in portable media such as figurines, and on painted pottery in complex political settings.

Interpretations need to go beyond a functional or needs-based approach and address the materiality of objects, how they were produced, and their life histories as well as by extension their non-material social and symbolic values. This is the general goal but only a few issues were directly addressed in this chapter. These were examined through a historical overview of Wari studies in light of work recently conducted in the Ayacucho Valley at Conchopata, a site second only in importance to the capital of Wari situated a short distance away.

Within this historical overview I reinterpreted the Middle Horizon offering tradition somewhat differently than originally proposed by Menzel (1964), primarily because we have greater chronological control and a longer period of ceramic production and use than previously understood. I suggest that large gatherings, where food and drink would have been served, were the settings in which the vessels were used. Although feasting is likely to have taken place on these occasions, the vessels were produced largely for internal consumption. They were also too large to transport. The esoteric knowledge, in the form of registers of narrative imagery richly displayed on the early urns, reveals that these were in use before the gateway iconography became popular in the central highlands. I would argue that the early history of emerging elites is signaled by the entrepreneurial aspects of adopting a south coast popular polychrome tradition, while combining this with complex forms of representation that were more characteristic of northern cultures such as the Moche and related highland societies (Topic and Topic 2000[2001]). The representation of ritual activities on pots made by specialists underscores an organization that had both religious and political overtones.

Face-neck jars were also part of the "offering tradition" and they seem to have been intended as representations of lineages, or possible age grades. The sexual amorphism on these anthropomorphic jars and the very rare depiction of females on the oversized ceramic vessels stand in stark contrast to three-dimensional figurines. Among the figurines we can detect sexual as well as social differences that display a form of visual dialogue distinct from those found on ceremonial serving vessels.

A more agency-oriented perspective was introduced in a reconsideration of the widely recognized Middle Horizon offering tradition as a series of distinct ceremonies. Isbell (2001c) has interpreted Conchopata as the locus of an old and a new palace. He has also suggested that the vessels were smashed on the occasion of the death of a ruler. The succession ceremonies may have involved destroying the old china dedicated to the deceased ruler, and the initiation of a new set of china for his/her successor. This palace model will need considerable refinement. Part of Isbell's conceptualization is that there were male rulers actually living at the site, with attached specialists producing the oversized wares. This scenario will need to be re-evaluated in light of the intensity and variations in ceramic production evidence at Conchopata, the contrast between the lavish and esoteric iconography painted on these oversized serving vessels, and the remarkable stylistic variability present in our ceramic deposits suggesting many different styles and shapes were tolerated and used at the site. Furthermore, there is considerable architectural variability within the walled perimeter of the site. Vernacular architecture, circular or D-shaped temples, and feasting halls are all present at the site; moreover a demography skewed heavily in favor of females, inclusive of elite females, significantly alters our preconceptions of a male ruler and his family.

Without writing the conditions that prevail in prehistoric contexts shift our focus to the material conditions of production, the producers, and their social values. To accomplish this focus on how objects were made, who made them, and their pictorial histories sheds light on the way human depictions express particular social identities.

The pictorial histories that abound in both early and later Middle Horizon depictions focus on elites, and the taking of elite captives, perhaps symbols of conquered peoples as the empire annexes new territories. If the urns could be fully reconstructed one would be able to walk around the circumference of them and view a cycle represented as a procession that leads to physical transformations between the human and supra-natural and celestial worlds by means of human sacrifice and decapitation. In almost every instance of decapitation there is a narrative that is not entirely clear to the modern viewer, but the storyline was accessible and widely understood by those for whom the paintings were intended. Scenes of capture and bloodletting, and a close association of death with regeneration in the form of cultivated plants, insects, reptiles, raptorial birds, and felines, is repeatedly conveyed, at times in great detail and at other times in abbreviated fashion. Who were the participants: men, women, children, the young, the middle-aged or the mature? Sexual traits and age grades are difficult to identify in Wari art, with the possible exception of differences in dress and the extremely rare instances of nudity. In the case study presented, we discover that women appear to have been ritual specialists and involved in acts of sacrifice as depicted in Figure 8.3a.

Gender roles are blurred for the modern viewer, yet there are unexpected parallels between the performances identified with the few females identified in Wari vessel iconography and the Moche. Despite enormous differences in painting genre between the Moche bichrome fine-line pictorial narratives and the Wari polychrome depictions, there are general themes, such as human sacrifice and blurred gender roles, that are similar. A female ritual specialist who is involved in human sacrifice scenes has been identified in north coast iconography.

The Moche are also described as having a relatively closed political system with a focus on social control and careful management of how ideological content was displayed (DeMarrais et al. 1996). Elite and commoner assemblages circulated largely within their own spheres, as though separate bodies of knowledge pertained to each. This system begins to break down as Moche monumental architecture and fine-line drawing are on the wane.

Like the Moche, the Wari adhered to a close relationship between rulership and ideological themes in their art (Russell and Jackson 2001:159). Interestingly, however, it is highland Wari symbols of sovereignty that are appropriated by late Moche elites (Castillo 2001). As puzzling as this may seem, Wari foreign policy included a strong ideological component whose content embraced ethnic differences and successfully elevated them to considerable levels of prestige. This is a system that seems to have been antithetical to the Moche, who resisted external or foreign influences for most of their history. In fact, during the early period of Wari vessel painting there is a preponderance of diverse figures and themes, and a couple of figures that remind one of Moche murals (Donnan 1972; Gálvez and Briceño 2001).

Differences increase over time and the result is a Wari visual discourse that is repetitive and redundant, despite a popular undercurrent that defied elite themes and continued to display local Huamanga designs that had been in use from previous generations. These two counter-currents may seem contradictory. In fact, the persistence of local traditions side by side with elite ritual vessels is sometimes seen as an indicator that the state did not mandate that the populace use, eat, or drink out of vessels that were recognizably Wari in shape or design. Wari potters emulated the kaolin pots from the north, the polychrome wares from the south, and the effigies and narrative iconography of the Moche as well as the emblematic theocratic symbols of Tiwanaku. It was a truly cosmopolitan taste, allowing the pursuit of exotic wares that were held in high regard and even incorporated into state rituals at the capital.

By the time the Wari empire restructures during its later history or Epoch 2 of the Middle Horizon, ceramic styles have more in common and include some new symbols of sovereignty that are embedded in local design traditions. A good example is the face fret design, the Grecian fret band, and figures commonly associated with the gateway iconography and other Tiwanaku profile figures. If the vernacular and the elite were accepted side by side it conveys the resilience and power of local elites and traditions, despite what we might anticipate to have been considerable tensions between competing groups, even within the heartland. What remains interesting is that distinct visual discourses were permitted on Wari vessels. Artisans often inter-mingled elite and vernacular designs, disguising the elite motifs within a stylized geometric venue, e.g. Chakipampa, Okros, and secular Viñaque also called Huamanga (Menzel 1968:92). Initially this conveys a greater degree of tolerance vis-à-vis local ritual practices, a situation that changes in the later empire.

ACKNOWLEDGMENTS

Many of the insights that are presented in this chapter are the result of lengthy con-versations with many colleagues to whom I am deeply indebted. Most importantly this research is largely a result of collaborative efforts by members of the faculty at the Universidad San Cristóbal de Huamanga and collaboration with Willliam H. Isbell and all the participants on our project, only a few of whom could be per-sonally mentioned in this piece. Many thanks to the Instituto Nacional de Cultura for granting permission to conduct research at the site of Conchopata and for declaring the site part of Peru's protected patrimony. Funds were granted to Anita Cook and William H. Isbell from several generous sources. The success of this project was made possible by two Dumbarton Oaks Summer Projects (PI: Anita Cook), five National Geographic Society Grants(PI: William H. Isbell), H. John Heinz III Foundation (PI: Anita Cook), the Brennan Foundation (PI: William H. Isbell) and Sponsored Research at the Catholic University of America (PI: Anita Cook).

9

Experiencing the Cities of Wari and Tiwanaku

William H. Isbell and Alexei Vranich

Introduction

Archaeologists make inferences about the past based on interpretations of material remains from antiquity. In addition, ethnography and cultural evolution furnish information about human behavior as well as theories about how cultures change. Archaeology in the United States, at least during the last 30 years, has been shaped by processual evolution, a school of archaeology that argues that human culture change is constrained by certain regularities. It posits that all societies develop by evolving through very similar stages – ideal cultural types abstracted from ethnography. Processual archaeologists' inferences about the past are informed by expectations set forth in theory, including the assumed ideal cultural types.

In this chapter we adopt a different perspective and different bases for inferences. We employ a phenomenological and landscape perspective more characteristic of postprocessual archaeologists such as Julian Thomas (1996; see also Tilley 1994). Our questions are not about the regularities of cultural evolution, but how prehistoric people experienced their world – what was their sense of place, a prerequisite for building identity? We focus on archaeological information about ancient landscapes and built environments, assuming there are certain regularities in the way humans experience their surroundings in much the same way that processualists assume regularities in the way cultures change.

While it may be impossible to precisely reconstruct past experiences of place we can at least gain broad insights into these experiences from material remains, including spatial metaphors and symbolic assertions. Perhaps most reliably, we can show similarity and difference in the ways several societies constructed and experienced their respective worlds. With that goal in mind we have selected two related and contemporary Andean societies for comparison, Wari and Tiwanaku. How did the people who produced these two cultures differ in the way they experienced their material universes?

Wari and Tiwanaku were two great cities that dominated most of the Central Andes between A.D. 500 and 1000, a period called the Middle Horizon. They shared complex religious art so there can be no doubt that they had much culture in common. But the people of these two centers felt profoundly different about the most basic things of life: the places they built, the materials of daily living, and the landscapes on which they conducted their activities. What were these two early Andean cities like for their residents and the people who came as visitors? How did they differ?

At Wari and Tiwanaku one sees the same highland Andean sky, especially after dark. The dry season night sky is vast with stars that accompany the sprawling Milky Way as it tumbles from horizon to horizon. But the horizons, the land, the people, and the experience of place are different. Wari's Ayacucho Valley is one of many narrow and jagged ravines formed by deep slashes between rocky mountain chains. The horizon is close; land is steeply inclined, and commanding panoramic views from high peaks reveal craggy valleys with finger-like peaks reaching into the sky. Seen from high, human settlements and surrounding farmlands appear delicately tucked into sheltered places across the scarred earth.

Tiwanaku lies on the flat altiplano (high plain), 20 km from the south shore of Lake Titicaca. Much higher than Wari, the receding horizon is far away in this rolling landscape that is surrounded by spectacular but distant mountains. Much of the land is too high for agriculture. There are tall grasses where herds of llamas and alpacas graze, migrating rhythmically with change of season. Commanding views of settlements are rare, and travelers come upon places suddenly. The feeling of the land is different.

Rain comes to the Andean highlands in October and November. In the Ayacucho Valley, water quickly runs down the inclines, eroding new pathways. By February and March the soil is saturated and land begins to slide, destroying anything below. But in the altiplano, water rises. Colossal Lake Titicaca fills slowly, but tiny depressions are much quicker to respond, as seasonal lakes, puddles, and swamps appear across the landscape, often becoming a sea of mud by March.

Certainly the ancient people of these places experienced them differently, both physically and culturally, but of course, physical and cultural experience cannot be separated. Being in the world encompasses body and mind, integrating intention with feeling, power with desire, and always accommodating to coercion with compliance and resistance. All constitute the human experience of being. As archaeologists we can experience some aspects of ancient landscapes as they remain today. We can also reconstruct features of the places that ancient people constructed and inhabited, trying in our imaginations to recreate their experiences. To achieve this, we employ structural generalizations about Wari and Tiwanaku material culture, architecture, and landscapes, based on the archaeological information currently available, creating a representation of the past. Then we try to imagine how local inhabitants as well as foreign visitors might have experienced such places and things. Of course, this requires well-informed imaginations, that benefit from analogies.

The City of Tiwanaku

The Tiwanaku realm was dominated by the city of Tiwanaku, an urban center many times larger than any other site in its sphere of influence (Figure 9.1a). Certainly, it must have presented an overpowering experience for visitors, for even in ruins it inspired Spanish chroniclers and European travelers to write about its grandeur. Unfortunately, today, it is difficult to appreciate the ancient appearance of Tiwanaku. Understanding Tiwanaku is hampered by severe destruction of the site, combined with archaeologists' errors, both in excavation and reconstruction. Invading Spanish priests considered Tiwanaku's sculptures an expression of paganism that must be destroyed. Subsequently, the spectacular stones from Tiwanaku's façades became highly desirable building materials. For centuries, thousands of blocks were carted away for churches, civic buildings, and private houses, as far as La Paz. With the coming of the steam engines, a railroad was built through Tiwanaku, initiating pillage of even greater magnitude. Huge stones were taken for building bridges. Smaller blocks and even earthen fill were mined from Tiwanaku's monuments by the railroad workers. Stones too big to be moved were dynamited and their pieces transported by rail to distant construction sites. New stone façades revealed by the first archaeological excavations quickly disappeared. Some may have been taken to European museums, but most of them went into new buildings or railroad construction. Without stone facings to protect them, earthen fills within the great pyramids eroded into deformed hillocks, spreading broader with each torrential rain.

As damaging to Tiwanaku's spatial order is a misunderstanding of the dynamics of precolumbian ceremonial cities. Modern scholars tend to imagine Tiwanaku at a hypothetical moment of apogee, an essentially static vision, when all the monuments and buildings were completed, and functioning at full capacity. In the mid-20th century, Bolivian excavators wanted to present Tiwanaku as the equal of ancient cities in the old world, a goal that promoted a severe case of "monumentalism." This is an infirmity of archaeologists and architects in which the chief symptom is an obsession with the monumental at the expense of more ephemeral remains. Entire sections of architecture were dismantled and removed from around Tiwanaku's major monuments because they were judged too modest to have participated in the same landscape. Tiwanaku was physically reconstructed as a symbolic whole composed of spectacular architectural monuments, all conforming to the same structural ideal and frozen at an imaginary moment of site apogee.

But precolumbian cities were processes, constantly becoming, and constantly transforming (Isbell 2001c; Vranich 1999). The authority of antiquity was certified by the existence of buildings in ruins, and the future of the city was probably experienced by contributing labor to never-ending construction projects. Witness the comments of the first Spaniards to visit the great oracle and pilgrimage center of Pachacamac, on Peru's central coast, where Tiwanaku/Wari style art has been excavated. They noted buildings in ruins and experienced the intended effect – verification of the antiquity and authenticity of the power of that place (Zárate

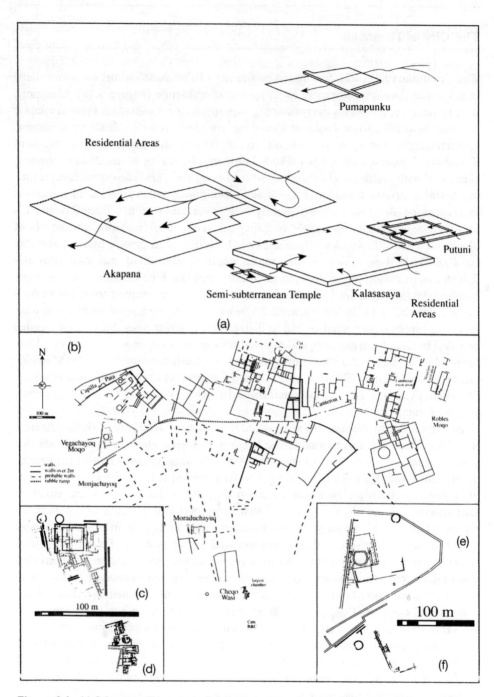

Figure 9.1. (a) Schematic illustration of the principal monuments of Tiwanaku. Large arrows represent major routes of access. Small arrows represent secondary or restricted routes. (b) Map of Wari showing major walls and compounds in the core of the city. (c) Inset map of Moraduchayuq Compound (Wari). (d) Inset map of Cheqo Wasi Complex (Wari). (e) Inset map of Vegachayoq Moqo Compound (Wari). (f) Inset map of Monjachayoq Royal Tomb Complex (Wari)

1968[1556]). Cieza de León (1976[1553], n.d.) personally visited Tiwanaku in 1549 and was perceptive enough to notice how some of the monuments were completely ruined while others were clearly unfinished. Cristobal de Polo concisely summed up his experience of Tiwanaku, stating that "they build their monuments as if their intent was to never finish them" (Polo de Ondergardo 1916[1571]). Our goal is to experience Tiwanaku as it was for visitors in the Middle Horizon, so we must eschew European ideals as well as recent reconstructions. We must seek to understand the site as it was without post-colonial despoilment, a goal that requires much more archaeological research than currently available or reported, but one that we will attempt nonetheless.

Tiwanaku was a site of great monuments that, like coastal Peruvian huacas, were characterized by enormous size and volume. Visitor and resident alike must have felt dwarfed and insignificant before the great Akapana pyramid, and its lower but equally massive neighboring platforms. However, height and volume were not the only dimensions employed by Tiwanaku's architects to astonish viewers. The façades of Tiwanaku's platforms and pyramids were revetted with megalithic stonework of unequalled proportion and precision (Protzen and Nair 1997, 2000). Some areas were probably even covered with burnished metal sheets. Monumental gateways and other architectural appointments were cut with an exactitude, including perfect right-angles. Perhaps this precision expressed some secret and arcane domain of perception, for it exceeds anything that can be fully appreciated by ordinary inspection. Surely these sculptures possessed the power of mystery in their day.

One of the most impressive aspects of Tiwanaku is its location between the shore of the traditionally sacred Lake Titicaca to the west and the equally revered snow-capped mountains – particularly Illimani – to the east. Visible across the southern Titicaca basin, the glaciated peak of Illimani acts like a beacon for people walking towards Tiwanaku from the heavily populated lakeshore. Furthermore, Tiwanaku's wedge-shaped valley would have funneled travelers toward the great ceremonial center. As one approaches Tiwanaku, the snowcapped mountain appears to crown the first monument at the western margin of the site, the Pumapunku platform, a four-tiered stone-faced dais with a large plaza in the east and a sharply graded approach on the west (Vranich 1999, 2002).

Pumapunku acted as the official entrance to Tiwanaku, channeling visitors in their eastward quest toward snowcapped Illimani. In the process it packaged an experience in spatial metaphors and symbols of Tiwanaku religious ideology. Significantly, as the traveler nears the Pumapunku complex, the mass of the platform blocks the view of Illimani, and the mountain disappears from sight. Pumapunku is a unidirectional concourse, channeling visitors up into the volume of the platform, through a sequence of narrower and broader spaces defined by ramps, steps, stone façades, decorated gateways, paved courts, and megalithic chambers. Suddenly, the spacious western plaza is reached, upon exiting the pyramid's interior passageway. The monuments of the city, its sprawling residential buildings, and snowcapped Illimani Mountain appear instantly before the viewer. For Middle Horizon pilgrims visiting Tiwanaku, the simultaneous appearance of the legendary city, with Illimani looming above it, would have been miraculous.

Standing in Pumapunku's eastern plaza, the viewer's attention was drawn further east, toward the impressive snowcapped Illimani, and toward the center of the city a scant kilometer away. This view of Tiwanaku, at least after about A.D. 700, would have been as impressive as any city in the ancient world. To turn around or to wander about Pumapunku would have revealed the extent to which the platform was a façade designed to impress visitors arriving from the west. The southern and northern faces of the pyramid may never have been completed, and at the very least, they were under construction and renovation for decades and perhaps centuries. Recent excavation confirms similar experience at the core of the city, where some monuments were climaxing, old buildings and spaces were in various degrees of decay and collapse, and newer structures or renovations were just beginning (Couture 2002; Janusek 1994; Vranich in press). The Semi-subterranean Temple (Figure 9.1a) was originally a Yaya-Mama structure, probably dating to the final centuries B.C. (Karen Chávez, personal communication, 1999). It apparently remained sacred, albeit heavily modified and embellished by the Tiwanaku, with new sculptures and other appointments. But its low profile, open demeanor, and small interior space were relics of the city's early pre-urban history – when it was no more than a local center of assembly and ritual, like so many other sunken courts of the Yaya-Mama religious tradition (K. Chávez 2002; S. Chávez 2002). Yaya-Mama semi-subterranean temples promoted solidarity among the residents of a few hundred square kilometers, but they were not pilgrimage centers for great areas.

Tiwanaku's Kalasasaya platform (Figure 9.1a) was probably the monument that replaced the Semi-subterranean Temple as the primary focus of the emerging ritual city. It was much larger than the sunken court, permitting many more participants. However, its interior space was also deeply depressed, carefully shielding the main ceremonial area from view, suggesting that access differentiated initiates, or a group of elites, from the rest of the population. What was the dominion from which the Kalasasaya drew participants and pilgrims? Whatever this area may have included, the orientation of the Kalasasaya was the reverse of the temporally later Puma-punku. Its monumental entrance faced east side, so the building channeled people from east to west – from Illimani toward sacred Lake Titicaca.

Around A.D. 700, Tiwanaku underwent a period of "urban revitalization" (Kolata 1993) which dramatically increased the city's monumentality as well as its resident population. This probably relates to new ceramic styles and the religious symbols Tiwanaku shared with Wari. Surely it also implies a significant increase in the range from which Tiwanaku attracted pilgrims, and to new kinds of religious and political powers. The Kalasasaya and poorly understood Kerikala complex were selectively dismantled (Couture 2003) to build new structures such as Putuni, Kantatayita, and, most visibly, the towering Akapana pyramid (Vranich in press). Pumapunku had been begun only slightly earlier, and it probably became the official entrance to the transformed city at this time (Figure 9.1a).

Within the jumble of construction, deconstruction, and reconstruction, the 18 m tall revetted Akapana pyramid (Figure 9.1a) surely became the center of attention. Centuries of quarrying its stone façade, and large-scale looting, have reduced it to little more than its earthen core, obscuring its stepped pyramidal form.

Nevertheless, there are clues suggesting that, like Pumapunku, Akapana was a monumental platform within a more extensive architectural complex. Aerial photographs and geophysical survey suggest the existence of a large court to the west of the pyramid, in front of a double set of stairs ascending its flank to a broad summit.

A great courtyard to the west of the Akapana pyramid would have provided an area for feasting, and for observing theatrical rituals on the summit. This ample top includes the remains of numerous structures, among them a U-shaped room complex, monumental gateways, raised platforms, and perhaps an immense sunken court. Certain parts of this area would have been visible to people standing at the base, while others remained out of view. Were visitors permitted to ascend the summit, and continue on beyond, or did they remain in the courtyard area?

Certainly, some of the spaces on the Akapana summit were too small to accommodate more than a select few visitors, but there are some ethnographic points in favor of procession beyond the courtyard to the top. Until the recent ethnographic past, the summit was the primary gathering point for the villagers of Tiwanaku during one of their festivals (Bandelier 1911). Furthermore, an ethnohistorical reference to a standing gateway a few meters east of Akapana (Cobo 1990[1653]:102) suggests that, like Pumapunku, the pyramid was flanked on both sides by bounded spaces intended to sculpt the flow of visitors. Another factor to consider is that, like Pumapunku, the pyramid was never finished, though it was clearly in use for a long while (Manzanilla 1992). If participation in building activities was an essential part of some kinds of pilgrimage experiences, then the Akapana was an important objective for visitors.

A huge cache of smashed keros (drinking vessels) was excavated on a lateral terrace of Akapana by Linda Manzanilla (1992). Originally the entire collection was interpreted as one great offering marking the abandonment of the pyramid, smashed in place. However, re-examination of the context shows that this location is actually fill between double-walled retaining constructions that contained the volume of each stepped layer of the pyramid (Vranich in press). It now appears more likely that trash from ritualized feasts held at Akapana over an extended period of time was swept up and used as fill in the rising mass of the monument. The act of building was part of Tiwanaku ritual, and conversely ritual was part of the construction process. Perhaps completion of the pyramid was dependent on ascent and subsequent labor contributions by a huge number of visiting pilgrims. Be that as it may, during at least a century of Tiwanaku's late development, Akapana must have been a hive of activity, with huge numbers of workers toiling in construction. The pilgrimage experience, at least for some, included a stint of hard labor. Perhaps other pilgrims brought food for feasts to which the volunteer workers were treated. It is reasonable to think that women were among the visitors and that they assumed responsibility for preparing food and drink, possibly supervised by resident administrators.

Around this period, Tiwanaku's resident population reached urban proportions. At least some of city dwellers followed the rural tradition of building houses composed of individual, free-standing rooms made of sod or adobe (Janusek 1999). Such homes are surprisingly modest and ephemeral. In Tiwanaku's hinterland communities, and at least some urban areas, profound concern with ritual, pollution, and purity is manifest in the clean floors of abandoned houses, and surrounding activity areas. Refuse was carefully placed in pits and covered, out of sight and out of the sunlight. In fact, residential trash is so uncommon on house floors that buildings must have been cleaned before abandonment. Then they remained virtually untouched until the adobe melted back into the earth. Whatever the ideology behind such cleanliness, it reveals a world with formidable prohibitions, where discards of quotidian life must have been charged with dangerous powers.

Residential architecture immediately surrounding Tiwanaku's monuments consisted of multi-roomed compounds. Perhaps this was an innovation that occurred in housing for elites. Putuni is often called the "Putuni Palace" reflecting the consensus that it was a residence with highly restricted access for nobles. It is also the most monumental and elaborate of the residential compounds.

The platform of Putuni was made from sandstone and andesite ashlars cannibalized from older monuments. The main entrance on the east side is truly spectacular and its flanking masonry revetment is arguably the finest at Tiwanaku. Small stairways, at least five in all, permitted ascent from the crowded sides of Putuni to the interior of each bank of rooms on the rectangular platform. On the basis of a large amount of melted adobe excavators we believe that tall mud brick or sod buildings were constructed on a megalithic platform surrounding a shallow, open courtyard (Ponce 2001). Putuni's monumental entry, spacious plaza, and surrounding labyrinth of small and more specialized rooms of restricted access are repeated throughout the Andean world. This pattern probably indicates palaces whose residents were responsible for hosting feasts and theatric rituals (Bauer 1991; Isbell in press; Moore 1992). A central courtyard, slightly sunken, but of substantial dimensions, allowed visitors to be hosted by residents, who employed food, alcoholic drinks, hallucinogenic drugs, ritual paraphernalia, retainers' labor, and probably elaborately costumed elites appearing from narrow lateral stairways, to produce the intended effect of awe-struck support for Tiwanaku.

Fairly well preserved residential complexes east of Akapana are modest adobe compounds (Janusek 1999). Tall enclosing walls and a single entrance opening onto narrow passages made it difficult or impossible to see into residences, except perhaps from Akapana summit. Architectural organization and artifact contents indicate permanent residents, perhaps of distinct ethnic affiliations. It seems likely the residents of these compounds also hosted gatherings, for smaller groups than the celebrations at Putuni and Akapana. Perhaps they hosted individuals of the same ethnic origins, who may even have been kin.

The archaeological record implies that Tiwanaku had many buildings that were constructed for feasting as well as hosting theatric rituals. It remains unclear whether most of Tiwanaku's residents were involved in hosting, with pilgrimage visitors serving as guests. But it does seem apparent that Tiwanaku was a city that was designed to receive and impress visiting travelers, almost certainly pilgrims of some sort, from a vast surrounding area. At least after A.D. 700, these pilgrims approached from the west, from the shores of Lake Titicaca. Upon reaching the city, they first experienced the spectacular Pumapunku. Subsequently, they traversed the civic center of the city to witness rituals at Akapana, and they probably retired to private residential compounds where they were hosted with extravagance by permanent residents of the appropriate ethnic group and probably also by the corresponding social class. Perhaps the most wealthy and powerful were invited to the supreme feasting location that must have been Putuni for a considerable time. Of course, we also suppose that the pilgrims brought gifts, probably rural produce and raw materials, without which urban residence would have been short-lived.

The City of Wari

We know less about Wari's overall form than Tiwanaku's, but more about certain aspects of it, including residential buildings, ceramic styles, and chronology. It is clear that the differences between the Tiwanaku and Wari built environments were profound. Wari people made little use of volumetric monuments, building instead high walls of rough stone, whether for houses, temples, or palaces. Consequently, all their architecture is quite similar, whether a rural home or an urban palace. What differs is scale. There are neither the ephemeral residences of Tiwanaku's hinterland nor the megalithic pyramids of the capital city. Also, abandoned Wari buildings were filled with domestic trash. Clean floors and surfaces are so infrequent that it is apparent that Wari people experienced domestic refuse as benign and unthreatening. Their quotidian world seems to have been relatively free of ritual pollution and spiritual threats.

The Wari state (whose capital was the city of Wari) built several great provincial centers. These share many architectural features, notably "orthogonal cellular architecture" (Isbell 1991b). Orthogonal cellular architecture at Pikillacta in Cuzco (McEwan 1991 inter alia), and to a lesser degree at Viracochapampa in Huamachuco (McCown 1945; J. Topic 1991) and Jincamocco in southern Ayacucho (Schreiber 1991a inter alia) is very regular, less overgrown, better preserved, and more completely described than the vast architectural sprawl of Wari (Isbell, Brewster-Wray, and Spickard 1991). Consequently, some of what has been generalized about Wari and its built environment is based more on these provincial sites than on Wari itself.

Wari's neighbor and contemporary second city, Conchopata, has been intensively excavated during the past few years (Cook and Benco 2000; Isbell 2001c; Isbell and Cook 2002; Ochatoma and Cabrera 2001a, 2001b, 2001c). Importantly, its built environment possesses features in common with the provincial capitals, but it is also much less rigid in plan, and more organic in its development than provincial capitals like Pikillacta. In this Conchopata was probably more like the Wari capital.

Wari lies at mid-elevation on the east flank of the deep and narrow Ayacucho Valley. Descending from the valley lip in any direction the city was displayed before the traveler long before it was reached. However, its location is not particularly prominent or arresting. Rasuwillka, the only snowcapped (or periodically snowcapped) mountain visible from the Ayacucho Valley, can be seen behind Wari if one approaches from the southwest, but it is unlikely that tricks of vision could have been developed around an entry into Wari, as we believe to have been the case with the western approach to Tiwanaku. The land surrounding Wari is so irregular that the city must have appeared and disappeared from view many times as one followed any of the possible roadways.

Whereas viewers experiencing Tiwanaku surely focused on massive pyramids spread against a background of residential compounds and sacred horizon markers, particularly Illimani Mountain, the architects of Wari, by contrast, sought to accentuate the experience of enclosure and redundancy, emphasized by building repetitive, modular cells organized in high-walled geometric blocks – at least in later architectural stages of the city. Furthermore, Wari seems an unlikely destination for many pilgrims for it appears to have lacked both pyramidal monuments and vast plazas where enormous numbers of visitors could have been hosted. Wari temples and palaces are similar to residential houses, consisting of high walls of field stone forming complexes of rooms and small courts enclosed by perimeter walls. Wari must have been a very different kind of city and political center than Tiwanaku.

Although much like houses in appearance, Wari's palaces and ceremonial buildings include a unique building, the D-shaped temple. Examples of D-shaped temples are known at Wari, Conchopata, Honcopampa, and Cerro Baul. They are not very large, ranging from about 10 to 20 m in diameter. Well-preserved examples have doorways in the flat side, and the buildings were probably very tall, like towers (Cook 2001; Isbell 1989, 1991a; Williams 2001). But D-shaped buildings did not stand in isolation. They were located in large, walled enclosures, associated with numerous rectangular and trapezoidal rooms and courts.

The most diagnostic feature of Wari architecture, employed with virtually all kinds of buildings, was the great walled enclosure. In Wari's provincial centers the perimeter wall was neatly rectangular, but in the capital city there are examples that were trapezoidal and even irregular in form. But all great enclosures shared walls of significant dimensions, usually much more than a meter thick, and as much as 8 or 10 m high. These enclosures were the first thing visible to travelers approaching Wari.

A traveler approaching Wari early in the history of the city would have seen only a few compounds, unpretentiously clustered at the tip of an arid ridge, surrounded by stone-walled houses, and high above well-watered canyons. But by A.D. 700 great enclosures of diverse shapes and sizes stretched for a kilometer along the edge of the ridge, paralleling a small ravine through which a road entered the city from below. By A.D. 800 or 900 enclosure complexes covered the entire ridge, spreading over several kilometers. There must have been some spatial order to the city, but no convincing order has been detected (Figure 9.1b). Spatial order probably changed frequently through progressive additions. Visitors approaching the city were surely confounded by its spatial confusion, but profoundly impressed by the city's brilliant expanse and density.

Wari architects built with rough stones set in clay mortar, but they apparently did not expect the stones to show in their building façades. Rather, stone walls usually were coated with clay, and often finished with brilliant white plaster. In a few cases, and particularly in ceremonial buildings, red paint was applied. So during the Middle Horizon the great enclosures were shining white or shockingly red, probably with an occasional tower, and they sprawled across the crest of a steep-sided ridge. The city must have looked like a vast mouth full of shiny irregular teeth, gleaming in the sunlight, each tooth a uniquely shaped compound cleverly inserted among its neighbors.

Wari appears to have coalesced between A.D. 500 and 600 from a collection of four or more villages located within the area of the later city. We believe that inhabitants from several of the villages began to resettle their families in the lowest and easternmost community of the old enclave. Before long this community spread upward and across the ridge. Eventually it covered several square kilometers with semi-orderly enclosure complexes.

We do not know why people decided to leave old hamlets and crowd into a single expanding village. One possibility relates to the low elevation of the growing center, at the edge of a steep canyon. Perhaps this site was most easily defended, but more likely it was closer to valley bottom land irrigated by systems of canals. Perhaps irrigation was expanded at this time, and people moved in order to reside close to new fields.

It is also likely that the area where the Wari city began its growth became a core of temples and palaces. So perhaps the early city developed around a ceremonial complex, or a political focus. Thus, the cause of Wari's growth may have involved several factors, all of which seem to share a common theme of organizational developments associated with increased centralization of power.

Wari was more than the urban concentration. Traces of terraces and irrigation features imply that the surrounding valley sides, and the hills in front of Wari, were carefully tended gardens. So Wari was probably nestled into a manicured, cultural landscape, not the wild, thorny brush one sees today. On several of the surrounding hills and ridges were individual enclosures, large and imposing. They were probably villa-like estates of powerful nobles, or perhaps temples where pilgrims might have arrived.

Perched on its ridge, Wari was entered from the southeast, or below, but probably also from the west, and above. The southeastern ascent was through a small canyon, the Quebrada de Ocros, which reached far into the city before the traveler emerged among the compounds. Both sides of the ravine lip were lined with buildings, so anyone ascending was in full view, and at the mercy of arrows and slingstones for half a kilometer's march. Entrance from the west must have been very different, hiking down through grasslands into cultivated fields, and then into suburban residential neighborhoods, with the city frequently in view.

Wari's streets were narrow and canyon-like. There were avenues less then 2 m wide, with walls on both sides 4 m or more in height. All a pedestrian could see was fellow travelers in front of them, and the sky above. So any sense of direction probably relied on distant views of the city, from above. However, the narrow streets were few, so in places there may have been nothing but margins of varying width between compound walls. Indeed, traffic through Wari remains something of a mystery. Perhaps it was even intended to by mystifying. Where there were no streets, how did people get from one place to another? Perhaps there were paths on the tops of the thick walls, that range from 1 to 5 m wide. The alternative would have been passing from room to room, a confusing experience for anyone not raised in the labyrinthine city. These two solutions are radically different. Walking on wall tops would have presented the city spread out below the pedestrian. Order and disorder would be revealed, and one could peek into patios where quotidian life was unfolding without participating in it. Walking through doorways connecting rooms and courts would prohibit panoramic views, and visitors would have been cast among the residents, in all their daily activities.

Within the city's great enclosures were complexes of rooms surrounding courtyards, but these varied greatly depending on the nature of each great enclosure. Many buildings were two and perhaps even three stories tall, so each courtyard, with its surrounding rooms, became a tiny world of its own. Many people probably spent most of each day in their respective courtyard complex.

Rooms and walls surrounding the patio had small doorways that admitted little light. Even with brilliant white walls and floors, the rooms were dark and cool – attractive in the midday heat, but somber and uninviting for work at other times. Lamps (a ceramic or a carved bone container for grease, with a small wick) could be placed in a wall niche a couple of meters above the floor, but these lamps are rare in the archaeological record, suggesting that the normal condition inside was darkness. On the other hand, the courtyards must have been teeming with light and activity. Long eaves probably overhung the front of each tall building, and low earthen platforms or benches ringed the court where residents could squat in the shade, or avoid the rain, while doing chores. A communal hearth may have been located on one of the benches, but smaller kitchens were also found in some ground-floor rooms. Perhaps heat from cooking fires warmed the rooms above, but if smoke filtered through upper stories they may have functioned more for storage than as living quarters. Physical enclosure and sharing scant living space must have promoted solidarity within each residential group, which was probably already composed of kin. But what of privacy for bodily functions, and where was fecal matter dumped in this glittering city?

Vegachayoq Moqo (Bragayrac 1991; González et al. 1996; Isbell 2001c) is the most extensively excavated of Wari's big compounds (Figure 9.1b, 9.1e). It is located in the early sector of the city where palaces and temples seem to have been concentrated. This enclosure complex has been called a temple, but it is more likely that it was the palatial residence of a ruler, at least in the early part of its history. Vegachayoq Moqo may be the only Wari building that employed a platform with earthen fill to define a plaza. Perhaps it represents an early stage in the development of Wari's multi-story urban architecture. It had a sizeable patio, at least 40 or 50 m long but of unknown width, for later remodeling transformed the original layout. A mound 8 or 9 m high surrounded the east end of the patio. The mound was faced with two broad terraces, one above the other, like stories of a building, which were under one great roof. This space was probably similar to the throne room of Old World palaces, a location for the royal court with enough space for a substantial assembly, although hardly large enough for hordes of pilgrims. The ruler would have officiated from the upper terrace, in full view of the patio below, protected from the elements, but physically and metaphorically above the ruled. Behind the terraces and on the top of the mound was a residential area for elites. Here polychrome painting decorates rooms, the only such example reported at Wari.

The Vegachayoq Moqo patio was transformed by the construction of a large D-shaped ceremonial building, with 18 huge niches and a north-facing doorway in its flat side (Figure 9.1e). This seems to relate to a later moment in the history of the compound, when it probably served as a mortuary monument for the deceased ruler. We do not know if the building compound continued to be occupied by royal descendants. Be that as it may, the compound soon changed function again. A broad wall more than 2 m thick was built across the patio to the west. Perhaps it was part of another enclosure compound, but its primary function appears to have been mortuary. Many looted tombs were found in this great wall, some constructed when the wall itself was built, and others cut into its masonry at later times. A row of meter-square niches on the east side of the wall, facing into the old palace patio, may also have had mortuary functions, for one of the niches was sealed up and contained several secondary burials. Vegachayoq Moqo had become a popular cemetery, probably its final function before abandonment. Small rooms along the base of the mortuary wall have niches blackened from lamp smoke, perhaps associated with funerary rituals conducted for the deceased. But the goods associated with these burials show that the many dead were not high or wealthy nobles. Who were these dead, and who came to mourn them in the dark little rooms? Certainly the experience of Vegachayoq Moqo was very different when a ruler was officiating over crowds in the open courtyard, from a hundred or so years later, when the great wall bisecting the old courtyard was a cemetery with adjoining chambers where mourners met.

Across the street from Vegachayoq Moqo is Monjachayoq (Figure 9.1f), an architectural compound that contains what is best interpreted as a royal tomb, even though severely looted. Consisting of three floor levels below the ground, much of the tomb employed huge cut stones. Megalithic constructions have also been documented at one of the Wari's hinterland villas, named Marayniyoq (Valdez et al. 1999, 2000). Although there is no question that megalithic construction was more characteristic of Tiwanaku than Wari, it is becoming apparent that Wari architects were more familiar with stone-cutting and with the use of monumental ashlars in construction than previously thought. Did the Wari learn this building technology from Tiwanaku architecture? How common was megalithic construction at Wari, and was it restricted to certain time periods? How did it impact the experience of Wari? In contrast with Tiwanaku, most of Wari's megalithic constructions appear to have been tombs that were hidden below ground, or inside buildings within great enclosures. They may have been experienced by only a very few of Wari's residents.

Half a kilometer to the east of Vegachayoq Moqo is the Moraduchayuq compound (Figure 9.1c; Brewster-Wray 1990; Isbell 1997b, 2001a, 2001b; Isbell, Brewster-Wray, and Spickard 1991). It was a residential apartment building, probably occupied by middle-level nobles responsible for administrative activities

within the city. Late in its history its planned orthogonal cellular architecture clustered around patios of 10 to 15 m on a side, and the residential density may have
reached 150 persons per quarter of a hectare. Indeed, this was crowded urban life.

At an earlier moment, Moraduchayuq had been a temple. At the beginning of
its architectural history a semi-subterranean court was built. It was a square of
megalithic polygonal blocks constructed in a deep natural hole. Perhaps its technology and form were influenced by the old Yaya-Mama tradition at Tiwanaku.
However, it was soon filled in to make way for the orthogonal cellular compound
of patio groups similar to the kind of buildings found at the provincial center of
Pikillacta, except smaller in size.

Continuing farther east through Wari one reaches the Cheqo Wasi area (Figure
9.1d). It was probably never a great enclosure compound of its own, but appears
to represent the intersection of several enclosures. Be that as it may, many of its
rooms contain megalithic stone chambers, probably tombs for Wari nobles just
below the rank of king. But these spectacular chambers were not presented to the
public like Tiwanaku's cut stone buildings. They were deep within walled enclosures, and partially hidden below floors. Wari's highly enclosed and segmental architecture seems to have been associated with a ceremonial life that emphasized private
ritual for deceased ancestors.

Understanding the Wari city will require the definition and study of entire enclosure compounds as well as relations among them. Were there workshops and storage
facilities, or were all of Wari's great compounds residential in function? How did
pedestrians move about the city, and who were the people who lived in Wari? Did
the residents commute to agricultural fields to farm, or were city dwellers occupied
in specialized activities? Wari appears not to have been the objective of pilgrimage,
unless we have failed to identify great assembly areas. Or perhaps the Wari pilgrimage experience ended at a temple in a villa in the suburban periphery, overlooking the city. Many questions remain to be answered by future research, but we
have begun to gain at least some ideas of what the Wari city was like, and how much
it differed from Tiwanaku.

Conclusions

Tiwanaku and Wari appear to have been very different kinds of cities. They were
constructed to promote very different experiences, and their occupants felt very differently about their respective worlds, down to such mundane things as quotidian
refuse. If Wari was intended for large-scale pilgrimage – seemingly unlikely – most
pilgrims probably never entered the city. Instead they ended their quest at special
compounds overlooking the metropolis from surrounding hilltops. If some continued into the city, the experience was surely one of humiliating confusion, shuffled
from one compound to another through a maze of walled streets, doorways, passages, and courtyards. As a city Wari was densely occupied, but even though only
meters apart, each compound was spatially and architecturally separated from its
neighbors. There was no obvious civic center. The sense of enclosure and of sepa-

ration must have been very strong, perhaps promoting a security and a sense of belonging, but possibly also encouraging feelings of imprisonment. Was there any privacy at all? Compound residents, probably some type of kin unit, must have remained the group of orientation for Wari's people.

Tiwanaku, on the other hand, or at least its civic center, was a experiential catechism tutoring visitors in the Tiwanaku world view. Perhaps it should be recognized as the hemisphere's first theme park, conceptualized and built as a set, within which pilgrims and residents became actors in a cosmological passion. Viewers experiencing Tiwanaku surely responded to massive pyramids set against an expansive background of residential compounds and sacred horizon markers, particularly the Illimani Mountain.

At Wari, temples and palaces were almost indistinguishable from residential buildings. Wari's elites seem to have been content with palaces and ceremonial monuments that were little more then big versions of traditional stone-walled homes. When they did indulge in megalithic building, they seem to have kept it private, or secret, to be experienced by only a select few, deep within the confines of great enclosure compounds. There can be little doubt that the "house" was the primary symbol of Wari kin groups.

Small and ephemeral Tiwanaku homes of adobe or sod stand in sharp contrast to massive megalithic monuments of the capital. Early in the evolution of altiplano culture the temple became a permanent feature impossible to melt away – semisubterranean courts in Yaya-Mama times. Soon these were followed by larger mounds, and by the time of full urbanism at Tiwanaku, altiplano people were building some of the most massive megalithic monuments ever constructed in the Andean world. They were not symbols of resident kin groups contained within, but statements about nationalism and cosmic structure, attracting and funneling enormous numbers of visitors through a choreographed experience. Tiwanaku's kings and priests apparently reveled in displays of megalithic precision and monumental permanence that contrasted absolutely with the adobe and sod homes of their followers. Perhaps this served to mitigate the centrifugal pressures of a pastoral way of life.

Experientially, Wari and Tiwanaku were so different that we doubt that the two cities and cultures were ever one people, even though they shared religious images. Their inhabitants and rural supporters resided in different landscapes, each constructing places that made little sense to the other.

ACKNOWLEDGMENTS

William H. Isbell is responsible for the sections in this chapter dealing with Wari. Alexei Vranich is responsible for the sections dealing with Tiwanaku. The two authors worked closely to produce the final draft. Isbell wishes to acknowledge the National Science Foundation, National Geographic Society, and the Brennan Foundation for financial support, as well as the Peurvian Instituto Nacional de

Cultura, and the Bolivian Ministerio de Cultura for research permissions. Vranich wishes to acknowledge the support and collaboration of the Ministry of Culture of Bolivia, and UNAR, the National Institute of Archaeology of Bolivia. Since 1996, financial support for Vranich's research has been provided by Kurt Bost of the Coca Cola Corporation, the Brennan Foundation, the Landmarks Foundation, and Engel Brothers, Inc.

10

Household and City in Tiwanaku

John W. Janusek

Introduction

On the windswept altiplano south of Lake Titicaca, the ancient site of Tiwanaku reached a size of at least 6.5 km² by A.D. 800. It was both a prestigious ceremonial center and a bustling city with extensive residential populations projected at 15,000–30,000 inhabitants (Figure 10.1a). City residents juggled diverse interests, trades, and social identities while playing significant roles in the emergence, transformation, and, ultimately, collapse of Tiwanaku.

Tiwanaku has been the focus of intensive and extensive excavations, notably in the past 20 years. Recent attention paid to its non-monumental areas is of particular interest for the information provided on domestic life at the site. Indeed, Tiwanaku can be used as a case study for an approach to the study of households in past urban settings that emphasizes continuity and change over the long term. In this chapter I interpret the data from my own excavations in Akapana East, an extensive residential sector just outside of Tiwanaku's central monumental complex (Figure 10.1a), and I compare the changing patterns of domestic residence in various areas of Akapana East with those in other residential areas of Tiwanaku, including Putuni and Ch'iji Jawira. I consider these data in relation to changing patterns of ritual activity and monumentality in Tiwanaku, as well as settlement and land use outside of the center. From such an analysis comes a fascinating new perspective on the dynamics of identity formation and power relations in the history of an Andean polity. I seek to demonstrate that a comparative understanding of residential patterns at an emergent urban center such as Tiwanaku, considered in relation to other aspects of prehispanic complexity, can provide a far more nuanced view of state development and collapse than is typically generated in studies focused strictly on monumental structures or settlement patterns.

In this chapter I first discuss some general problems and benefits of household archaeology, including some of the key challenges presented by such a project in

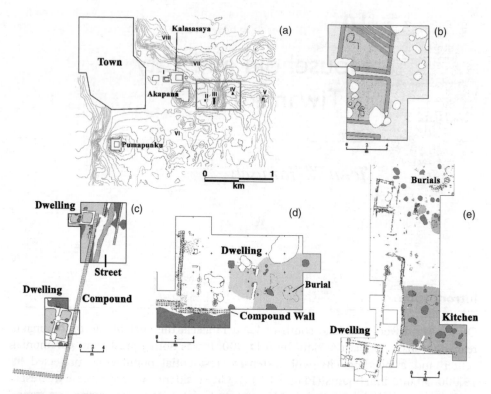

Figure 10.1. Relevant excavation areas mentioned in the text. (a) Map of Tiwanaku showing the location of Akapana East (gray box) and areas mentioned in the text, including: Putuni (I), Akapana East 1M (II), Akapana East 1 (III), Akapana East 2 (IV), Ch'iji Jawira (V), Mollo Kontu South (VI), La Karaña (VII), and Kk'araña (VIII). (b) Plan of the first floor in the Late Formative 2 occupation in Akapana East 1. (c) Residential features in the Tiwanaku IV occupation of Akapana East 1M. (d) Residential features in the Tiwanaku IV–Tiwanaku V occupation in Akapana East 2. (e) Features in the Tiwanaku V residential and feast production contexts of Akapana East 1

an urban center like Tiwanaku. This leads into a theoretical discussion that establishes a framework for interpreting urban residential patterns in light of a historically grounded focus on social identity and various domains and expressions of social power. Following, the theoretical discussion turns to potential expressions of identity, power, and ritual in prehispanic cities, drawing on relevant examples from Mesoamerica and the historically documented highland Andes. The rest of the chapter investigates Tiwanaku residences in relation to other aspects of complexity over Tiwanaku's phases of incipient statehood (Late Formative), development (Tiwanaku IV), consolidation (Tiwanaku V), and collapse (Late Tiwanaku V – Pacajes). I conclude by suggesting that such a research focus, grounded in large-scale excavation, offers much toward understanding past Andean societies.

To anticipate my conclusions: I believe that Tiwanaku urban populations were diverse. They lived in bounded compounds and neighborhoods that maintained coherent identities and had vibrant social memories, unique interaction networks, and in many cases specialized trades. Urban formation and state integration involved highly complex strategies, institutions, and productive enterprises involving intentionality and agency on the part of various groups, including those considered non-elites. Local identity played an important role in the multi-centered power relations that forged, consolidated, and eventually fragmented the Tiwanaku polity, and residential patterns at Tiwanaku help elucidate the trajectory of these complex processes.

Household Archaeology in Complex Societies

Research around the world has demonstrated the enormous value of household archaeology in investigating social, economic, and ritual activities in past complex societies (Allison 1999; Ashmore and Wilk 1988; Flannery 1976; Hendon 1996; Manzanilla 2002; Palka 1997; Santley and Hirth 1993; Smith 1987; Stanish 1989b; Wilk and Rathje 1982). It has encouraged archaeologists to complement studies of monumental grandeur and regional settlement with deeper investigations of the practical rhythms of daily life.

The original framework of my fieldwork at Tiwanaku was to do what archaeologists typically call "household archaeology." A basic goal was to recognize the household unit, defined as a minimal co-residential social group with corporate functions. However, there are problems in applying the concept of household to the archaeological record. For example, the household is an ethnographic concept with unclear material correlates (Wilk 1991; Wilk and Netting 1984). Adapting the concept to archaeological study, most scholars agree that archaeological households, identified as repeating units of dwellings and their associated activity areas, were minimal co-residential groups that shared common tasks, including production, consumption, distribution, and social reproduction (Stanish 1989b). Further, households were dynamic groups that experienced regular domestic cycles (Hirth 1993; M. Smith 1992; Tourtellot 1988), and so varied greatly over time. They were open systems of membership – at least as much as they were bounded kin groups. That is, they were variable domains of social identity integrally tied to wider communities (Brumfiel 1991). Kinship ties may have been fundamental, but other aspects of identity and group activity, such as specialized occupation or ritual affiliations, also may have been significant or even as prominent.

Recent critics urge archaeologists to consider the past household as "a symbolic construct defined and contested through practice" (Hendon 1996:48; Joyce 1993; Tringham 1991). This view is in keeping with the approach I develop here. Rather than a homogeneous social entity with singular corporate goals, a household "consists of social actors differentiated by age, gender, role, and power, whose agendas and interests do not always coincide" (Hendon 1996:46). A household is where power relations and social differences are negotiated on a day-to-day basis. As an intimate domain in which myriad cultural practices are learned, it is a privileged arena for the enculturation of power relations and social differences. Social differences and power relations in broader domains form a fundamental part of household life.

Thus, ancient households were not ideal nuclear families tied together by affective relations and egalitarian relations in contrast to the rest of the society. Households were inextricably tied to more encompassing organizations and activities, and it is their place within a changing urban settlement that I focus on here. Early studies treated households as if they were homogeneous molecules of social organization, each with similar unilateral functional ties to broader sociopolitical institutions. Upon conducting household archaeology at Lukurmata, Bermann (1994, 1997) persuasively argued that this was not the case in the Bolivian altiplano. Not only were households at Lukurmata diverse and variable, changes in households did not correspond nicely with changes in Tiwanaku sociopolitical organization, indicating that relations between household, community, and state were complex. Changes in households, Bermann argued, indexed complex interactions between the community, which enjoyed a long history preceding Tiwanaku hegemony, and local productive and socioeconomic pressures that emerged in relation to changes at regional and state levels. In this chapter, which benefits from a large database at both Tiwanaku and Lukurmata, I take this argument a step further. Focusing primarily on Tiwanaku, I present a case in which urban residential groups maintained vibrant identities, social memories, and local bases of power, even though these were created and reproduced, for the most part, by drawing on the prominent values, symbols, and relations of Tiwanaku state culture.

Such a view encourages us to consider households as more than simply domestic groups (Ames 1995; Hendon 1996; Janusek 1999; Manzanilla 2002). Households are generally thought to be the locus of "domestic activities," and so household archaeology is considered the primary means of reconstructing past domestic life. However, in Tiwanaku and other major prehispanic centers in the Andes and elsewhere, the conventional divisions between domestic and other types of spaces and activities break down. Much of Tiwanaku was devoted to activities not explicitly domestic, and residential areas often were places for human burial, ritual practices, and craft specialization. Places where women and men slept, ate meals, and raised children often were the same places where they conducted ceremonies or plied a particular trade. This is in keeping with ethnohistoric and ethnographic research in the Andes, which pinpoints supra-household kin groups known as ayllus as the primary locus of communal ritual and specialized production.

The urban character of Tiwanaku also affected the process and interpretation of household archaeology. In any residential sector, repeated cycles of building, disposal, abandonment, and renewal had continuously disturbed previous archaeological contexts. Many excavation areas yielded little but refuse middens and pits, some of which measured several meters across and several meters deep. The sheer amount of continual post-depositional disturbance at Tiwanaku explains why earlier excavations revealed little of its chronology and social character. By the same token, the massive volumes of refuse and extensive areas devoted to depositing it highlight Tiwanaku's significance as a magnet center. Through time, household life was increasingly linked to the site's role as a place of ceremonial convergence.

The practical complications of doing household archaeology, in Tiwanaku, or any other complex society, invite a broader theoretical research focus. More often than repetitive household units, excavations consistently exposed segments of larger bounded compounds that incorporated the remains of a wide spectrum of life spanning domestic, specialized, and ritual activities. These, I argue, were fundamentally the activity areas of larger supra-household groupings similar to later ayllus (see M. Smith 1993 for a similar comparison in Central Mexico). Consequently, in this chapter I employ the more general term "residences" instead of "households." Rather than attempting to elucidate a partial and arbitrarily defined group of "domestic activities," I seek to illuminate the practical dimensions of daily life and offer a perspective on the social character of Tiwanaku. Considered in relation to changes in broader communities, changes in residential life illuminate some of the historical processes involved in the formation, consolidation, and collapse of the larger polity.

Power and Identity

Attention to residences in the history of a city invites a dynamic approach to power and identity that accounts for long continuities and rapid transformations and grounds history in the deep principles of day-to-day activities. First, according to commonly held notions about power, leaders, elite groups, and central governments are often considered primary loci of power (Weber 1947). Considered the property of certain privileged people or an essential condition of the roles they fill, power is thought to be much like an object or a commodity – transferred, exchanged, or appropriated (Barnes 1988). Inherent in practice theory is the alternative perspective that power is an intrinsic condition of society. As Michel Foucault observed (1980: 142) power is manifest in diverse cultural institutions and social relations, it is "co-extensive with the social body," no one is "outside of" power, for "there are no spaces of primal liberty between the meshes of its network." To the extent that humans participated in past social orders, engaging their specific cultural logics and practices, they were empowered. To the extent that they acted creatively, authoring ideas and actions in the face of novel circumstances, they actively – intentionally or not – transformed those contexts and their attendant social relations. In any social world and its ever-shifting webs of relations, "power relations are *always* two-way . . . however subordinate an actor may be in a social relationship, the very fact of involvement in that relationship gives him or her a certain amount of power over the other" (Giddens 1979:6, emphasis mine). To be sure, social hierarchies are reified by hegemonic ideologies in which power is considered the exclusive property (or essential nature) of authority figures or "superior beings." Nevertheless, systems of inequality inevitably produce "contradictory consciousness" (Gramsci 1971:333) – some alternative, countercultural attitudes of resistance that, while perhaps remaining subdominant for a time (as "hidden transcripts," see Scott 1990), may eventually foster more public, active measures.

A salient element of power relations is social identity. Grounded in shared memory, ancestry, place, occupation, rituals, gender, or cultural expressions, identity is all of the characterizations of "us" that a person or group will engage when moving from one social context to the next. As a potent medium through which humans apprehend, navigate, and transform social and cultural worlds, identity indexes multiple nested social scales and overlapping groups. At the local end of the continuum are groups with corporate roles, or shared political, economic, or ritual activities. These will range from households to clans or extended lineages, such as those that occupied the "apartment compounds" in the great ancient Central Mexican city of Teotihuacan. Implicit in the activities of such groups are economic production and social reproduction. At the "macro" end of the continuum are more inclusive and encompassing affiliations that form less intimate, more "imagined communities" (Anderson 1983). Including ethnic and "national" affiliations, such forms of identity, though often more tenuous, are almost always tethered to concrete events, places, and phenomena. Such a group may congregate periodically in major ceremonies or commemorations, its identity tied to a bounded territory, common ritual landscape, or productive regime. A sense of cultural coherence may be linked to distinctive styles of clothing, language, spatial or architectural order. Such material expressions form the symbolic capital of any form of identity, for they give concrete, often public expression to a group or community that lives "in the heart and mind" as much as, or more than, in face-to-face interaction.

Lending a particularly dynamic and diachronic dimension to the relation of power and identity is their expression in ideology and "practical hegemony" (Janusek 2004). Ideology is the "stated" cosmology of a group or society, as well as the views, actions, and styles that can be readily brought to consciousness. It is in such a discursive domain that kin-groups, factions, lineages, or even a gender, as sub-groups or social "categories" in a larger society or interaction network, consciously acknowledge and identify one another. While multiple ideologies may comprise any social formation or inhabit any landscape, those promoted by privileged or elite groups will usually be predominant. However, predominant conceptions of the world work in more mysterious ways, and potentially inhabit "all manifestations of individual and collective life" (Gramsci 1971:328). Practical hegemony refers to the patterned ideals and practices that come to be "taken for granted as the natural, universal, and true shape of the social being" (Comaroff and Comaroff 1992:28). It is the uncontested order of things, the "unstated" cosmology of a group, an underlying structure of symbols and actions that are presumed to be natural: the way things are and always have been.

Ideology and practical hegemony are interdependent modalities of cultural perception and practice, and their domains may shift through time. As that part of a predominant ideology that has been internalized and rendered natural, practical hegemony resides in accepted, even praised practices and institutions (e.g., educational systems, modern medicine, family values, and legal procedures). Even so, it is threatened by contradictory consciousness and "the vitality that remains in the forms of life it thwarts" (Comaroff and Comaroff 1991:25). That which was once uncontested can be brought to light, "reopened for debate," especially as "the con-tradictions between the world as represented and the world as experienced become ever more palpable, ever more insupportable" (Comaroff and Comaroff 1991:26). At certain historical junctures, perhaps in conjunction with profound environmen-tal, political, or ideological shifts or crises, and cumulative dissatisfaction with a hegemonic context, many will seek cultural coherence, social resolution, or survival through a variety of subtle, and perhaps ultimately not-so-subtle means. Cultural "resistance" or mobilization may well involve the revitalization of a volatile sense of identity among incorporated social groups and political factions. At these times a social and cultural order may transform violently, rapidly, and profoundly.

Urbanism, Ritual, and Identity

Considering power and identity from a practice perspective encourages nuanced perspectives of complexity that can be applied to its paradigmatic social-spatial phe-nomenon, the city. Most archaeologists concur that urbanism is a concrete expres-sion of social complexity and state organization. Yet, archaeological models of past cities mimic traditional approaches that treat cities as integrated and integrative institutions. Max Weber (1958) argued that the rise of "the city" required the dis-solution of kin, clan, ancestor cult, and other intimate "totemistic" ties to more impersonal territorial and political relations. V. Gordon Childe argued (1950:16), in a similar vein, that a city is a social community sui generis, held together by both "organic solidarity" or occupational specialization and "ideological devices" that mask the appropriation of "social surplus" by a "tiny ruling class." According to Childe, in functioning ancient cities there was simply "no room for skeptics and sectaries."

In contrast to such views, archaeological research in various world regions indi-cates that ethnicity, political factions, kin-groups, lineages, and other domains of social identity may be endemic features of a social order and its urban centers (Brumfiel 1994; Crumley 1987; McGuire 1983). In many contexts and time periods, social complexity and state formation were founded on lineage segments and rival factions. Ethnohistorical documentation and archaeological research for the Aztec and Inca states indicate that factionalism intensified with increasing political centralization, social hierarchy, and imperial expansion. In Tenochtitlan and Cuzco, the political, cultural, and religious centers of these polities, urban orga-nization reflected in spatial order the social differences among diverse groups and identities, calpullis and ayllus, respectively. Tenochtitlan and Cuzco, each a highly ordered built landscape crafted as a cosmogram, or an idealized reflection of its respective cosmos, were subdivided into spatially bounded compounds and neigh-borhoods or barrios. Each discrete sector housed residences, activity areas, and shrines associated with a particular group and its constituent households.

A paradigmatic example of such a city was Teotihuacan, arguably the most important political, economic, and ritual center of Mesoamerica in the Classic Period (A.D. 200–650). Extending over $20\,km^2$ at its greatest extent, the city incorporated some 2,000 walled residential compounds, collectively housing at least 125,000 people around massive monumental complexes that stretched along the city's primary axis, the "Avenue of the Dead." The city was a well-planned, highly ordered cosmogram; all structures followed a single alignment oriented to the pathways of celestial bodies and sacred terrestrial features such as mountains and caves (Manzanilla 1996; Millon 1994). Further, Teotihuacan ancestry was a powerful source of prestige for ruling dynasties in many Maya polities located far to the east. Nevertheless, Teotihuacan was not simply a royal or priestly city. Semi-autonomous kin groups, who claimed distinct ancestors, inhabited the compounds. Many compounds plied some specialized trade, and most clearly differed in social status (Spence 1981; Storey 1992). It may well be that each group formed the segment of more encompassing lineages distributed around the city, whose head groups – those "closest" to spiritually powerful apical ancestors – enjoyed elite status (Headrick 1996). Be that as it may, some compounds clearly were enclaves inhabited by "foreigners," some from Oaxaca and at least one from the Gulf Coast, and these groups maintained distinct identities as well as special ties with their homeland for many generations (Paddock 1983; Rattray 1990). Teotihuacan was a city and a ceremonial center, a representation of both state and society, in which distinct interests and multiple identities coexisted in the same densely populated place.

In the highland Andes in historically documented times, we find analogous patterns in an entirely distinct expression of "urbanism." Major centers, termed markas in Aymara and llacta in Quechua, were more than permanent population centers, they were also places of social, political, and ceremonial convergence. In part, they were cosmograms representing the social groups and spiritually imbued landscape around them, centered on public loci such as the central church and plaza, and surrounded by barrios bounded by adobe walls and streets, each associated with specific kin-based groups known as micro-ayllus (Abercrombie 1998; Rasnake 1988). In addition, markas were places that people periodically visited, promoting through concrete activity the coherence of social groupings. They were where significant political reunions were called, and where events and issues involving the entire macro-ayllu or polity were discussed. Most significantly, they were where major festivals culminated, hosted by ambitious individuals seeking political power in the community. In festival times, markas became centers of feasting and ceremonial activity. Such festivals were ritual eruptions in the practice of everyday life, times of reversal when otherwise sparsely populated towns were encompassed in ritual time. At these times a marka became a bustling, lively center that anchored the social identity of widely distributed imagined communities.

These perspectives illuminate the following examination of residential patterns over a thousand years in Tiwanaku, enabling us to see changing power relations and expressions of social identity throughout the history of one of the Andes' most evocative cities. The foregoing theoretical discussions prompt important questions: How was social diversity and identity expressed in Tiwanaku? Was Tiwanaku similar to other New World centers such as Teotihuacan? Was it, like later markas, also a center of feasting and ceremonial convergence? How was state formation manifested in residential patterns, and how were shifting power relations expressed in

such contexts? What types of materials or practices manifested a Tiwanaku dominant ideology, and in what ways did its expression change over time? What were
the causes of Tiwanaku state collapse, and does evidence implicate contradictory
consciousness, hierarchical power relations, or vibrant social identities? I address
these questions in a chronological narrative that examines Tiwanaku residence and
ritual from the site's Late Formative emergence, through the Middle Horizon
apogee (development and consolidation of the city and state), to the Tiwanaku collapse. For each of these phases I discuss Akapana East, followed by consideration
of other residential areas, built ritual places, and the region at large.

Emergence: Late Formative, 100 B.C.–A.D. 500

Excavations in Akapana East 1 revealed two superimposed occupations dating to
Late Formative 2 (A.D. 300–500) and Early Tiwanaku IV (A.D. 500–600).
However, "occupation" is not the best term to describe the contexts (Figure 10.1b).
Each consisted of two or three adobe buildings oriented eight degrees east of north,
set on an elaborately prepared floor. Interior and exterior space were sharply distinguished in soil color and texture. The floors inside of the buildings consisted of
yellow sand, while the floor outside of them consisted of red clay. The fine texture
of the floors distinguished them from other residential surfaces in Tiwanaku and
Lukurmata, indicating that the soils were specially selected and carefully mixed.
Floors inside of the structures contained shallow depressions in well-defined geo-
metrical shapes, and in the northeast corner of one was a banded prepared floor
with alternating yellow sand and red clay. Outside of the structures were several
shallow pits, each lined with a thin layer of finely pulverized bone. The bone was
encrusted in a green precipitate, indicating that powdered remains were deposited
with a liquid or vegetal substance. These pits undoubtedly represent some type of
sacrifice or offering. Most striking, the floors were impeccably clean. Unlike other
occupations at Tiwanaku, the floors both inside and outside of the buildings were
entirely free of ash, stains, artifacts, or any other domestic residue. In effect, they
were sterile. Nevertheless, just above the floor was the rim of a scalloped feline-
effigy incense burner, a ceramic type rare in contemporaneous domestic contexts.

  A tumulus covered the final surface, formed as the walls of the structures collapsed. The floor underneath was entirely free of domestic debris, and the structures appear to have been purposefully destroyed. A layer of charcoal covered the
tumulus, indicating that, just afterward, it was burnt, most likely as part of a ritual
interment for the complex. Most interestingly, at least three human bodies were
placed in the tumulus upon its ritual interment (Blom, Janusek, and Buikstra 2003).
Remains of a nearly complete infant 3 to 9 months old, and an incomplete, partially disarticulated adult (F.3, N7857 E5432) were placed near one another. A few
meters to the south were several bones of an incompletely represented adult. Most
unusually, this body had been defleshed. None of the interments occupied a visible
intrusive tomb, suggesting that the bodies were interred when the tumulus was
formed. Furthermore, the bones were deposited as secondary mummy bundles.

Before ritually burning the tumulus, it appears, the bundles were placed in the mound as offerings dedicated to the area's final interment.

Akapana East 1 during Late Formative 2 was clearly dedicated to unique ritual activities, whereas excavations in other areas of Tiwanaku revealed residential occupations. Much earlier in the 20th century, test units near the Kantataita, just northwest of Akapana East 1, revealed abundant ash deposits and domestic features, including a hearth (Bennett 1934). In Kk'araña, several hundred meters further northwest, recent excavations revealed superimposed residential occupations. In Late Formative 1 (100 B.C.–A.D. 300), the exposed segment of the occupation contained a rectangular building and an ovoid structure. By Late Formative 2, an extensive clay floor covered the early occupation, possibly forming part of a large structure or compound with adobe foundations. Both occupations yielded domestic artifacts, body adornments, and bone "hallucinogenic" implements. Ceramic assemblages here, as in other Late Formative residential contexts, consisted almost exclusively of undecorated bowls, cooking ollas, and jars.

In the 1950s Bolivian archaeologists excavated one other likely residential occupation under the Kalasasaya edifice, one of Tiwanaku's earliest major temples. Working under its sunken inner court, Carlos Ponce Sanginés and others revealed large rectangular wall foundations and paved surfaces associated with ash deposits and hearths (Ponce 1993). The occupation contained several offering pits and human burials that, together, yielded the caches of elaborate ceramic vessels Ponce used to define Kalasasaya ceramic style, diagnostic of Late Formative 1. Among other elaborate objects was a ceramic whistle crafted as a stylized dwelling or temple with a decorated frieze and T-shaped entrance. If this area was residential as Ponce suggests (1980, 1993), it included both "domestic" and ritual activities, and inhabitants enjoyed relatively high status.

Akapana East formed a unique ritual environment very different from such residential sectors and from the monumental ritual complexes that occupied the site core by the end of Late Formative 2. In Akapana East 1, as in many built ritual places cross-culturally, cleanliness was critical to the maintenance of ritual purity; domestic refuse was "dirt" in a real sense, "matter out of place" (Douglas 1966:36). Nevertheless, residential groups occupied many areas around this complex. Thus, it may have been a private shrine, in which one or more social groups, perhaps an entire local community, maintained the complex and conducted ritual activity there. In any case, it was a place for specific types of ritual activity, by all accounts relatively solemn and fastidious, that differed markedly from the types of ceremonies that were becoming more common in other areas.

Tiwanaku covered perhaps 20 ha in Late Formative 1, one of several relatively large settlements in the southern Titicaca Basin. Other major sites included Kala Uyuni on the Taraco Peninsula, Kallamarka in the Tiwanaku Valley, Lukurmata in the Katari Valley, and Khonkho Wankane in Machaca to the south. Recent excavations at Khonkho Wankane indicate that this site incorporated a large plaza and a series of ceremonial sunken courts, one attached to a residential compound housing a high-status group of, perhaps, religious specialists (Janusek, Ohnstad, and Roddick 2003). During the last part of the Late Formative, Tiwanaku expanded into a major center of over $1 \, km^2$, the most extensive in the Lake Titicaca Basin. Both sites had several large sandstone monoliths depicting deities, perhaps mythical ancestors, decorated with zoomorphic and anthropomorphic figures. By the end of Late Formative 2, however, the Kalasasaya was built, or at least initiated, and Khonkho Wankane may have been waning in influence. Tiwanaku's urban expansion, it appears, was tied to changing networks of interaction in a region where several centers, each the ritual and political center of a regional polity, coexisted, interacted, and competed for regional influence.

Development: Residential Patterns in Tiwanaku IV, A.D. 500–800 (Early Middle Horizon)

Extensive excavations conducted in Akapana East revealed a diverse range of activities dating to Tiwanaku IV (A.D. 500–800). Akapana East housed several extensive compounds, each consisting of a large perimeter wall enclosing one or more structures and various activity areas (Figure 10.1c). Built environments were uniformly ordered; all architecture followed the same general orientation of approximately eight degrees east of north. In Akapana East 1M and 2, dwellings had prepared surfaces and were associated with hearths, storage pits and bins, and outdoor patios and middens (Figures 10.1c and 10.1d). In Akapana East 1M a street covered with ash lenses and a central drainage ditch passed between two compounds. Represented in the compounds were activities associated with the social reproduction of the resident groups, such as food preparation, cooking, making tools, weaving clothing, and eating and drinking. Also represented in the compounds were activities associated with the ritual reproduction of resident groups. These included fetal camelids and, in one case, a human child buried under house floors and walls (it is interesting to note that in traditional Andean communities today, fetal camelids and human placentas are buried as offerings during the construction or rehabilitation of a house or residential compound, see Arnold 1992:51). In Akapana East 2, a burial cist containing three humans, two children and an adult male (35–45 years old), was located under an outdoor patio, and an elongated stone marked the location of the burial (Figure 10.1d). Patterns indicate that compounds formed bounded residential communities, each consisting of numerous dwellings and activity areas for domestic, ritual, and other activities (Janusek 1999, 2002, 2003b).

New ceramic assemblages in Akapana East mark a quantum leap in the significance and role of consumption at Tiwanaku. Most remarkable were red-slipped serving and ceremonial wares in a wide, if regulated, range of forms. These included flaring bowls (tazons) for drinking and eating, tall keros (beakers or goblets) for drinking, and small bottles used as pitchers. Most vessels depicted characteristic iconography including feline, avian, and geometric motifs and elements, following specific parameters that expressed, like the vessels themselves, a clear and distinctive Tiwanaku style. In complement to elaborate serving wares, assemblages also included high-volume cooking pots, or ollas, and a range of large jars (tinajas), with thick, durable, and impermeable walls – for storing liquids and fermenting drinks such as maize and quinoa-based alcoholic beverages (chicha). The relatively high quantities of such vessels in Akapana East indicate that elaborate serving and ceremonial wares and the activities of consumption associated with their use were widely distributed among sectors and groups throughout Tiwanaku.

Excavations throughout Akapana East, but in particular over the interred ritual sector in Akapana East 1, revealed a third significant pattern. Excavations in all areas revealed extensive refuse pits and middens associated with, and in many cases cutting into, earlier compounds and structures. Such secondary deposition contexts became increasingly ubiquitous and extensive after A.D. 600, in Late Tiwanaku IV (A.D. 600–800). In this phase Akapana East 1, once home to potent, if enigmatic, ritual offerings and activities, was dedicated in large part to depositing waste and refuse. Extensive sheet middens covered large areas, and numerous deep, amorphous pits filled with immense quantities of ash, camelid dung, and refuse, perforated the sector. These were "borrow pits" with two functions: to provide clay for the construction of adobe buildings and, afterward, to contain vast quantities of refuse. Several hearths, partial wall foundations, and a deep well suggest that the area served as something like a "backyard" for nearby residential groups. However, the enormous amounts of refuse deposited in the pits, middens, and even the well, represent more than the waste produced in what are generally considered typical domestic activities. They included immense quantities of splintered and butchered bones of camelids, guinea pigs, birds, and fish; broken lithic and ground stone tools; macro-botanical food remains including quinoa seeds, tuber fragments, and maize cobs and kernels; abundant ash and camelid dung, as fuel for hearths; and thousands of broken ollas, tinajas, serving and ceremonial vessels. The few superimposed strata in most pits indicate that in many cases ash and refuse were deposited quickly, as major dumping events. Such contexts were deposits, in part, for the "ritual meals," or major feasts, noted by early excavators at the site.

Many patterns in Akapana East also characterized other residential sectors in Tiwanaku. Excavations across the site revealed that Tiwanaku expanded from a site of approximately 1 km^2 to an urban center of over 6.5 km^2 by A.D. 700, some 300 years. Several other areas were occupied by residential compounds and neighborhoods similar to those recovered in Akapana East. Residential areas in Putuni in the monumental core, Mollo Kontu to the south, and La Karaña to the northeast, revealed compound walls similar to those in Akapana East. Ch'iji Jawira, a residential complex at the far eastern edge of the site was, in addition to a wall, bounded by a modified natural channel (Rivera 2003). Remnants of dwellings and residues of domestic activities were found in all of these areas, and the Lakaraña compound, bounded to the south by a masonry terrace wall, also incorporated a large circular storage building (Escalante 2003). As in Akapana East 2, burials and in some cases entire mortuary clusters were found in many residential areas, indicating that having the deceased close to home was common practice in Tiwanaku. In fact, it remains unclear whether there were truly discrete "cemeteries" at the site. Like Akapana East 1, much of Kk'arana became a residential midden in Tiwanaku IV, and Ch'iji Jawira was eventually converted into a midden in Tiwanaku V. The quantities and types of materials deposited in these areas, as well as their manner of disposal, leads me to hypothesize that they were generated in feasts as well as more typical domestic activities.

Other built environments, including several major ritual complexes, were dedicated to various flavors of ritual and pomp. In the urban core, the imposing Akapana, initiated in Early IV and possibly built over several successive stages, was built near Kalasasaya and the Sunken Temple (Kolata 1993; Manzanilla 1992). To the southwest was Pumapunku, an extensive complex of platforms and plazas that may have served as a "point of entry" into Tiwanaku for devout religious pilgrims (Vranich 1999). Meanwhile the Kalasasaya, home of the Ponce Monolith, was converted into a massive raised platform while the adjacent Sunken Temple, with stelae and tenoned heads now representing both previous and contemporary periods, encapsulated a Tiwanaku version of history and cultural patrimony.

It is significant that discrete ritual environments were built outside of Tiwanaku's urban core. In Akapana East 1, esoteric ritual activity continued through Early IV, and in Late IV, a terraced platform with a unique scalloped tip was built in Mollo Kontu, near local residential compounds and on a visual path between Akapana and Cerro Kimsachata, to the south (Couture 2003). Tiwanaku incorporated diverse ritual environments, including a core of discrete monumental complexes and several structures and areas located in the growing urban periphery. The latter were probably places created and tended by groups residing in local residential compounds and neighborhoods. The diverse character of monumental complexes in the core suggests that they, too, were "local" places, created and tended by distinct, perhaps competing elite factions or ruling dynasties.

Conformity, Ideology, and Practical Hegemony in Tiwanaku

Common patterns of spatial organization and material culture emphasize conformity with broader patterns of Tiwanaku urbanism and culture. All architecture, residential and ceremonial, replicated a common directional orientation approximately eight degrees east of north. First apparent in Late Formative 1, the orientation was reproduced across the expanding settlement, as new residential compounds and ritual complexes were built, as well as through time, in local cycles of construction, abandonment, and renewal. The orientation defines an urban plan that reified an ideal spatial cosmology, a master plan that extended to other major centers, including Lukurmata and Khonkho Wankane. The proximity of the orientation to cardinal directions suggests that it was grounded, in part, in the movement of astronomical bodies such as the sun and the rise and set points of stellar constellations. Most entrances to compounds and residential structures faced east or west, as did primary entrances to major temple complexes such as Kalasasaya, Akapana, and Pumapunku. Potentially, the primary east–west axis traced, in broad spatial terms, the daily path of the sun (Kolata 1993). In addition the orientation approximates visual pathways with major peaks, including Cerro Kimsachata to the south and the tip of Illimani to the east (Reinhard 1985a). Tied to primordial celestial and terrestrial elements, Tiwanaku spatial organization instantiated and simulated ideals linked to principles considered sacred, perhaps timeless, in Tiwanaku myth and ideology. Still, for most people Tiwanaku was to be experienced rather than abstractly conceived, and they walked through it day after day more than they beheld it from a distance (see discussion in Chapter 9, this volume). Recurring experience in this built landscape instilled a grand sense of spatial order extending far beyond the power, knowledge, and life of the subject, and approximating the inviolable cycles and patterns of sacred features and mythical protagonists.

Second, ceramic assemblages in compounds and complexes throughout Tiwanaku presented certain patterns similar to those from Akapana East, indicating that they were desirable for most people. In any residential compound or ritual offering, most ceramic vessels displayed elements of Tiwanaku style (Alconini 1995; Janusek 2003a). On the one hand, the ubiquity of elaborate serving wares indirectly points to an operating system of redistribution in which such valued goods were obtained in reciprocal compensation for participation in the emerging political economy. On the other hand, the ubiquity of such vessels marks the widespread distribution and acceptance of predominant Tiwanaku ideals and practices. Tiwanaku vessels, especially elaborate serving-ceremonial wares, manifested a clearly discernible style in regimens of production, form, and decoration, and they depicted significant iconographic themes, frozen and stylized "stills" of Tiwanaku mythic narratives and ritual practices.

As patently, the widespread use of such assemblages, as intricate technologies for preparing and serving food and drink, marks the increasing significance of rituals of consumption. The ubiquity of elaborate assemblages in Tiwanaku, other major centers, and even small rural settlements, indicates that feasting was not entirely co-opted by elites, but was a shared cultural practice. Feasting was evident in many other patterns consistently found in Tiwanaku residential areas, including vast pits and middens containing high quantities of vessels and other feasting refuse. As in the Andes today, feasting involved "commensal politics" (Dietler 1996, 2001), highly charged face-to-face contexts for the negotiation of status and identity among diverse groups. In part feasts – intimate events involving gestures of generosity – served to build or intensify status differences by creating social debt among those who consistently participated as guests. Thus, while establishing relations of reciprocity, feasts were prime arenas for building followings and enhancing prestige among those who successfully hosted them, the nascent elites of Tiwanaku.

Spatial order and valued goods instantiated and expressed themes, values, and practices central to Tiwanaku culture. They manifested elements of a predominant ideology that, through experience and repeated practice generation after generation, eventually was considered the "the natural . . . and true shape of the social being" (Comaroff and Comaroff 1992: 28). Through such material patterns, and the practices and myths that breathed life into them, Tiwanaku ideology was locally adopted and widely shared as part of a more general identification with the state. It eventually merged with popular consciousness as a commonsense understanding of the world, or practical hegemony, forming a key part of local realities.

Diversity in Tiwanaku: Status, Craft, and Social Identity

Nevertheless, profound diversity crosscut social conformity, and bounded compounds and neighborhoods formed the most salient unit of social differentiation. Identification with Tiwanaku state culture was but one of many more intimate dimensions of social affiliation for the groups inhabiting urban compounds. Some groups clearly differed in status. Excavations in Putuni revealed two superimposed Tiwanaku IV occupations, the second containing a structure dedicated to cooking and food preparation (Couture and Sampeck 2003). The latter existed among multi-room buildings faced with plaster and set on foundations incorporating ashlar masonry, elegant architectural elements that were rare elsewhere. The complex was served by an intricate subterranean drainage network, in which feeder canals drained waste and runoff into a massive canal consisting of well-carved stones. Adjacent to the residential areas was a bounded mortuary complex, with several burials, many looted in antiquity, containing fine sumptuary offerings including necklaces of turquoise beads, pectorals of gold sheets depicting ancestor or deity faces, bone trays for hallucinogenic snuff, and highly elaborate ceremonial vessels. Unlike other residential areas, ceramic assemblages included abundant elegantly wrought flaring-rim bowls (escudillas), ceremonial basins (fuentes), and modeled figurines depicting, among them, men carrying llamas on their backs. Keros and tazons, the most common serving types in other residential areas, comprised smaller proportions of assemblages.

Some groups clearly engaged in specialized craft production (Janusek 1999; Rivera 2002). Excavations in Ch'iji Jawira indicate that residents produced certain types of ceramic vessels, including tinajas and tazons, for non-elite consumers. Firing practices were expedient, consisting of open enclosures and pit-kilns, surrounded by ceramic wasters and partially baked clay lumps, and immense quantities of ash. Implements and by-products of ceramic manufacture, absent in other excavated areas of Tiwanaku, were found, along with pieces of plaster molds, ceramic and stone burnishing implements, and ground pigments in a variety of colors. Archaeobotanical analysis revealed that camelid dung and hardy grasses, fuels preferred by ceramic producers in Andean communities today, were denser in Ch'iji Jawira than they were anywhere else in Tiwanaku (Wright, Hastorf, and Lennstrom 2003). Collective evidence indicates that the production of ceramic vessels was organized and managed locally, as the enterprise of a local residential neighborhood occupied relatively late in Tiwanaku.

Status and specialization clearly distinguished certain residential compounds, but alongside status and economic differences, usually considered hallmarks of "complexity," were forms with somewhat different dimensions. While some compounds differed in status and occupation, all manifested other aspects of social identity. First, within any compound, serving-ceremonial wares maintained remarkable continuity over time, while between them, assemblages varied significantly (Janusek 2002, 2003b). These were the wares on display in various types of feasting events. In Akapana East 1M serving assemblages formed a fairly orthodox

local expression of Tiwanaku styles; serving wares adhered relatively strictly to standardized canons of Tiwanaku form and iconography. In Akapana East 2 serving
assemblages differed in subtle, but significant, ways. Some 20 percent of serving
wares comprised styles not found in Akapana East 1M, including tazons with volute
motifs, a style quite common at Lukurmata, and non-local vessels representing
contemporaneous cultures in warmer valleys southeast of the Titicaca Basin.
Ceramic assemblages varied from compound to compound, to varying degrees and
in varied manners, but assemblages in Ch'iji Jawira were most unusual. Certain
common serving forms were uncommon or altogether absent, and llama motifs,
rare in Akapana East and other known areas, were relatively common. More significant, non-local vessels from the eastern valleys were common, as well as high
quantities of wares (approximately 18 percent of serving wares) of a distinct
Tiwanaku regional style associated with the Cochabamba region 200 km to the
southeast. The high percentages of this hybrid style point to strong affiliations with
this region. Potentially, inhabitants settled in Tiwanaku as an urban colony, analogous to the ethnic colonies that inhabited the Oaxaca and Merchant compounds
in Teotihuacan.

In addition to distinct assemblages of feasting vessels, compound groups also
maintained distinct diets. Through archaeobotanical analysis, Melanie Wright and
colleagues (2003) determined that proportions of crop remains such as tubers,
chenopodium, and maize varied significantly among compounds. Overall,
chenopodium (quinoa) seeds were most frequent and best distributed, followed by
tubers and maize. The distribution of maize, however, was anomalous. We expected
greater quantities in high-status residential areas such as the Putuni. Maize, which
does not grow well in the altiplano, was highly valued in the highlands. In Tiwanaku
maize was most frequent in Akapana East 2 and best distributed in Ch'iji Jawira,
compounds with consistent proportions of non-local wares associated with the
valleys where maize grows well. This important pattern indicates that, in some cases,
social characteristics other than status fostered the acquisition of valued goods and
the maintenance of long-distance ties. These characteristics, it appears, included
social affiliations to the regions from which compound groups emigrated, or at least
to which specific Tiwanaku groups maintained kin-based or more widely cast
ethnic-like social and economic relations.

In this light the presence of burials and mortuary clusters in or near living spaces
becomes most significant. Local mortuary rituals and the ideal of keeping certain
deceased close to home were important elements of life for Tiwanaku residential
groups. The desire to inter individuals near intimate living areas may represent
ancestor veneration, in which groups periodically made offerings to deceased individuals claimed to be lineage or group progenitors. This proposition requires extensive mortuary analysis and a larger sample of human remains. That burials appeared
under living spaces, in at least one case with a prominent landmark, indicates that
certain deceased, adults as well as children, were periodically remembered and
bestowed offerings. Their perceived relation to living families and compound groups
is unclear, but they clearly played an important role in the creation and, potentially,
periodic reanimation of group memory and identity. In relation to other patterns

of local activity and identity, evidence for local burials and mortuary rituals emphasizes the central place of social memory for local groups in Tiwanaku.

Consolidation: New Urban Patterns in Tiwanaku V, A.D. 800–1000 (Late Middle Horizon)

Substantial transformations characterized Akapana East beginning around A.D. 800, reflecting among other things an elevated role for rituals of consumption in the urban core. In Akapana East 1M, a new compound wall was built almost directly over the last, but the renewed compound incorporated an internal spatial order and activity distribution very distinct from those in earlier occupations. Excavations revealed a structure with a series of large rooms (none of which clearly was a dwelling), all associated with a large outdoor patio. Features and artifacts indicate that activities were similar to those found in the preceding occupation: food preparation, cooking, weaving, tool-making, and consuming food and drink. However, large ollas for cooking foods in great quantities were more common, and tinajas for storing and preparing drink increased from 29 to 35 percent of assemblages. At the same time serving-ceremonial assemblages consisted almost entirely of quickly decorated forms as the more elaborate wares present in Tiwanaku IV assemblages became uncommon. All in all, serving assemblages reflect an increasing emphasis on mass production.

More extensive excavations in Akapana East 1, just to the east, revealed major segments of two compounds, shedding further light on the nature of changes in the area. The first compound, to the south, rested directly over the refuse-filled quarry pits and dense middens of Late Tiwanaku IV that covered the more ancient ritual tumulus (Figure 10.1e). It incorporated a series of small structures associated with an extensive outdoor area, one large kitchen, a corridor, at least one dwelling, and a mortuary sector. The structures were distinctly vernacular and unlike those of higher-status residential complexes; architecture consisted of cobblestone and earth foundations, with superstructures consisting of organic sod, and areas were not leveled before construction, so that living surfaces followed the contours of the earlier tumulus. The kitchen structure was most unusual. It contained a well and 12 hearths, scattered around which were thousands of sherds of cooking vessels, including high proportions of large ollas and a unique roasting bowl not found elsewhere. Also among the sherds were thousands of splintered and butchered faunal remains, largely camelid bones but also smaller quantities of guinea pig and bird remains. Other areas, including the corridor and outdoor area, contained high quantities of tinajas for storing and fermenting liquids. As in Akapana East 1M, serving-ceremonial assemblages were redundant and most vessels quickly decorated, reflecting relatively expedient production techniques.

Few areas in Tiwanaku could have been as different from the south compound as was the compound to the north. In the compound was an extensive edifice that incorporated one or more sunken courtyards. Reminiscent of Putuni constructions, construction techniques and materials contrasted sharply with those in the south compound. Walls consisted of clean, finely selected red clay standing on ashlar foundations, and the sunken surfaces consisted of prepared floors with a gravel aggregate base. Further, artifacts from interior floors included high proportions of exotic and sumptuary goods, including vessel sherds in a variety of non-local styles, a copper ornament, and a three-footed bowl exquisitely carved of volcanic basalt. Nevertheless, they included consumption residues similar to those found in nearby residential areas, including butchered camelid bones and sherds of cooking and serving-ceremonial wares. In fact, the area between the compound wall and the edifice, consisting of hearths, refuse pits, and ash deposits, appears to have been a corridor for preparing food and drink.

The north compound, it appears, was the locus of public ceremonial activities associated in part with relatively high-status groups. The south compound, it would appear, much like the compound in Akapana East 1M, was dedicated to the production of food and drink for feasts and ceremonies conducted in nearby sunken courtyards. Excavations on the other side of the north compound revealed patterns similar to those in the south compound, supporting the idea that the north compound was surrounded on all sides by compounds dedicated, at least in part, to the "specialized production" of feasts for the rituals of consumption conducted there. Such a scenario explains predominant archaeobotanical patterns in the south compound, where quinoa and maize were present in high proportions, but in addition, kernel-to-cob ratios of maize were far higher than in any other excavated area (Wright, Hastorf, and Lennstrom 2003). Quinoa and maize were most likely roasted in special bowls like those found in and around the kitchen, and maize itself, grown in warmer valleys far from Tiwanaku, entered the compound as already-shelled kernels, possibly provisioned by high-status groups which sponsored some of the feasts conducted in the north compound. Such a scenario also helps explain the new importance of structures that served not as dwellings but as ancillary structures with ephemeral, temporary occupations. In contemporary Andean towns, ancillary buildings accommodate guests and visiting family members who help prepare food and drink for the festival. Thus, it appears that Akapana East, in a massive project of urban renewal, was converted into an extensive urban sector dedicated to producing and conducting the rituals of consumption that were apparently becoming more significant and perhaps more frequent in Tiwanaku. Commensal politics were becoming increasingly significant.

While residential life further out in the Tiwanaku urban periphery, in areas such as Akapana East 2 and Ch'iji Jawira, continued much as it had in Tiwanaku IV, other sectors of Tiwanaku changed in significant ways. The apex of the Akapana, the center of which may have held a sunken court, now included an architectural complex consisting of a series of rooms surrounding an extensive paved patio. With foundations of impeccably carved ashlars, this was a residential area occupied by an elite group and quite possibly some of Tiwanaku's most powerful priests. As in Akapana East, ceramic assemblages included high proportions of large cooking ollas and tinajas, as well as elaborate serving-ceremonial wares (Alconini 1995). Also, some of the inhabitants were buried under the patio, and burial arrangements marked important differences among the interred individuals. One burial, apparently of the principal person, was set apart from the rest. His burial included elaborate objects, including a bone snuff spoon and a feline effigy incensario (Kolata 1993; Manzanilla 1992). This person may have been a high-status priest and quite possibly an important ancestor for later inhabitants.

Substantial changes also characterized the Putuni area. Around A.D. 800, the Late Tiwanaku IV residential complex was razed, leveled, and ritually interred (Couture and Sampeck 2003; Janusek 2004). An elaborate floor was laid over the early occupation, and, like renewal events in other residential areas, this involved buried offerings of camelids and humans. One offering was an adult female who had a copper disk mirror, a lead flask, and a hammered gold pectoral depicting an impassive deity mask. The Putuni complex was built on this floor. It was an elaborate monumental ensemble consisting of a platform surrounding a spacious inner courtyard, attached to paved corridors and plazas and an elite residence or "Palace." Set into a recessed section of the Putuni platform, the Palace was set on carved ashlar foundations, like other elite residential areas, but the adobe walls of its five rooms were painted in a variety of brilliant colors. Scattered on the floor and secluded in corners of its rooms were sumptuary goods: lapis and sodalite necklaces, copper pins and labrettes, carved shell ornaments, hammered gold sheets, and a silver tube filled with blue pigment. In sum, a high-status residential complex was re-created as monumental space, indexing a transition from relatively high rank to markedly distinct, institutionalized status. Together with evidence from Akapana, this transition marks the emergence of an elite class and the crystallization of a rigidly defined social hierarchy. Quite possibly we see both the emergence of a Tiwanaku royal dynasty and elite castes of priests. In any case, Tiwanaku now housed a number of elite groups and lineages that may well have formed distinct, competing factions.

In Tiwanaku IV, evidence for vibrant social identities, in the context of an urban landscape with predominant symbols and practices fostering identification with the state, attests to a simultaneous invigoration of local and state avenues to power by A.D. 800. Somewhat paradoxically, state power resided in the widespread acceptance and internalization of Tiwanaku state culture, which in turn fortified local group identity and power. After A.D. 800, entire urban sectors of the core were covered, interred, and restructured as areas dedicated to activities more closely tied to elite residence and ceremony. New complexes in Akapana and Putuni housed some of the elite groups whose "presence" was now felt throughout the urban core and, as we will see, elsewhere. Meanwhile, ceremonial feasting became an increasingly important arena for interaction among elite and non-elite groups. Like Andean markas but on a much larger scale, Tiwanaku was becoming more significant as a center of social and ceremonial convergence, and thus for the continual reinvigoration of a potent, inclusive Tiwanaku cultural identity.

State Incorporation and Transformation in the Katari Valley and Beyond

Research in various sites and regions outside of Tiwanaku helps us more fully understand the trajectory of these changes, and their ultimate effects on Tiwanaku state and society. In the Katari Valley, just north of Tiwanaku, local settlement networks transformed significantly, and urban density at Lukurmata, arguably Tiwanaku's "second city" in Tiwanaku IV, decreased precipitously (Bermann 1994; Janusek 2004). The decline of Lukurmata would have dramatically shifted the sociopolitical balance of the Tiwanaku core, which consisted of the Tiwanaku and Katari valleys. Lukurmata was an important center with a long history preceding Tiwanaku hegemony. During the Late Formative, it was the center of a multi-community polity that interacted and most likely competed with Tiwanaku for religious prestige and trade networks. Throughout Tiwanaku IV, Lukurmata, intimately tied to Tiwanaku as a regional center of state power and culture, expanded into an urban cluster of $2 km^2$. Residential groups, nevertheless, maintained a coherent social identity distinct from that of groups at Tiwanaku, as manifested in local styles of serving wares, an "annular" form of cranial modification, and specific burial patterns and mortuary rituals (Blom 1999; Janusek 2002, 2004). Significantly, local identity was expressed, in great part, in the context of Tiwanaku state material culture, manifested as local "twists" on predominant styles and practices. In the context of regional settlement patterns, Lukurmata and the Katari region formed a semi-autonomous political unit within the ambit of Tiwanaku hegemony, in which local identity and power thrived, in part, on some collective memory of its pre-Tiwanaku history.

Local identity and power also thrived on the Katari Valley's great productive potential, which included both lacustrine and agricultural resources, a situation that helps clarify the causes of major changes here. Research in fossil raised field systems in Katari, which generated 35 radiocarbon measurements, indicates that settlement changes corresponded with an intensification of agricultural production in Tiwanaku V (Janusek and Kolata 2003). The Katari floodplain is low and prone to seasonal lake flooding, and so, as indicated by extensive agro-archaeological research in the region, is better suited to intensive raised field production than many nearby valleys, including Tiwanaku (Binford and Kolata 1996; Kolata 1986, 1991; Kolata and Ortloff 1996; Ortloff and Kolata 1989). Assuming dates from raised field beds reflect phases of construction and use, 24 percent were built during Tiwanaku IV, 64 percent during Tiwanaku V, and the remainder in post-Tiwanaku phases. Thus, urban deflation at Lukurmata, located at the far edge of these systems and better positioned for a productive strategy balancing lake and farming, was most likely related to a demographic shift to sites nearer raised fields. To support raised field farming, clusters of small sites in the floodplain were occupied by mobile tent-like structures that housed rotating field guardians, known today as kamani. Thus, the Katari Valley, whose inhabitants had formed a coherent, wealthy, and powerful ethnic-like group, was transformed into a state-managed agricultural estate. Such a transformation, and most importantly Lukurmata's decline, would have shifted the focus of power in the Tiwanaku core, once distributed between the two regions, to Tiwanaku itself.

Further evidence with powerful implications for understanding changes in the core comes from far regions incorporated into Tiwanaku's political sphere. Research on the Island of the Sun, in the southern part of Lake Titicaca, indicates that in Tiwanaku V the island witnessed a "total reorganization of settlement," most clearly at the major site of Chucaripupata (Seddon 1998: 367). In Tiwanaku V, a local site dedicated to domestic residence and ceremonial feasting was converted into a major center with a platform temple enclosed by a large retaining wall and domestic areas with high quantities of Tiwanaku-style ceramic wares and sumptuary goods. Farther from the Titicaca Basin, the entire Moquegua middle valley, a warmer region in southern Peru, transformed from an early Tiwanaku colony into an integrated province dedicated to producing and processing maize (Goldstein 1989, 1993). Most important was Chen Chen, a massive site with seasonally occupied buildings, as many as 10,000 storage cists, and interred populations with dental and isotope signatures indicative of diets focused on maize (Blom 1999; Tomczak 2001). Tiwanaku-affiliated populations practiced a "flattened" style of cranial modification entirely distinct from the annular style so common in the Katari Valley. Maize grown in Moquegua was processed in Chen Chen and shipped to the altiplano, at least in part to fund rituals of consumption at Tiwanaku. Such a scenario explains the high kernel-to-cob ratios for maize in Akapana East 1, where feasting was sponsored, at least in part, by emergent elites. Viewed in this light, intensified farming in the Katari Valley, where tubers and quinoa were grown on extensive raised fields, also supported elite-sponsored rituals of consumption.

It is thus significant that Tiwanaku leaders developed a range of transformative strategies of productive and sociopolitical organization just as high-status groups crystallized into elite-led factions, and as the state political economy increasingly became a feasting economy. Feasts had been important since Early Tiwanaku IV as significant tournaments for the negotiation of status and identity among groups living in and affiliated with Tiwanaku. In Tiwanaku V, it appears, feasting became increasingly important as an arena for commensal politics, as tournaments for the negotiation of identity, status, and followings, among elite groups (Dietler 1996, 2001). Feasting also was critical for maintaining relations of reciprocal obligation between elite and non-elite groups just as the character and power of Tiwanaku hegemony intensified. Elite-sponsored feasting such as that which took place in Akapana East 1 was most likely motivated in part by the desire to curry support among non-elites. Gestures of generosity by feast-givers would have established relations of obligation among feast-takers, solidifying relations of inequality just as ruling strategies were pushing to unprecedented limits the etiquette of accepted social and economic relations, and perhaps in the face of increasing competition among elite factions.

Collapse: Late Tiwanaku V, A.D. 1000–1150 (Late Intermediate Period)

Transformations in Akapana East occurred once again sometime around A.D. 1000, at the beginning of a volatile phase of cultural transformation I term Late Tiwanaku V. In Akapana East 1M, a final residential occupation consisted of a relatively small domestic structure of vernacular construction. Its foundation followed the same directional orientation that had characterized Tiwanaku's urban plan for centuries, and in and around the structure were Tiwanaku-style material culture and residues of typical Tiwanaku domestic activities. However, the structure incorporated several cut stone blocks, indicating that to build it, some monumental edifice or elite-associated structure had been cannibalized. To the east, the feasting complexes of Akapana East 1 were at some point abandoned, the only evidence for later occupation consisting of a few localized middens, refuse pits, and hearths. By all accounts, the area housed a far more ephemeral, temporary occupation of people who were quarrying once significant buildings. It appears that the sector was abandoned gradually, or perhaps abandoned by earlier occupants and then reoccupied by smaller, more mobile groups. No post-Tiwanaku, Pacajes-affiliated occupations were located in Akapana East. Rather, by A.D. 1150 the site had shifted to a slight bluff at the west of the old city, covering an area of, at most, 3 percent of its prior extent.

The Late Tiwanaku V occupation in Akapana East occurred in a dynamic phase of volatile cultural and political transformations. Large-scale monumental construction at Tiwanaku had apparently ceased by the beginning of the phase, and one elite residential sector – that associated with Putuni – had been razed to the ground (Couture and Sampeck 2003). Possible evidence for violence at this time comes from remnant stone monoliths found across Tiwanaku, many of which had been defaced or destroyed (Janusek 2004). It remains unclear when this happened, and it is plausible that it occurred long after the Tiwanaku state collapsed. However, many monoliths had been defaced or "decapitated" in highly patterned modes of destruction, suggesting that they had been ritually "killed" to neutralize their meaning and power. To the extent that monoliths represented Tiwanaku deities or the ancestors of its ruling lineages, defacing them effaced the power of those groups and the ideological foundations of their status and identities. Ritualized hostility was directed at specific elite groups, and perhaps in a more abstract sense, the Tiwanaku state.

Most recent models of Tiwanaku state collapse attribute partial cause to a long-term drought that began in the 11th century A.D. and lasted several hundred years (Binford et al. 1997; Kolata and Ortloff 1996; cf. Erickson 1999). Evidence for decreasing precipitation in this region, which comes from both ice cores at the Quel-ccaya glacier and sediment cores in Lake Wiñaymarka, points to a severe, long-term drop in rainfall that lasted several hundred years. Drought conditions such as those represented in mutually supportive cores would have caused the lake edge to recede and water tables to drop dramatically in low, flat agricultural basins like the Koani Pampa, stranding inland raised field systems and other agricultural features, including sunken basins (qochas).

Evidence from Tiwanaku and other centers, as discussed above, indicates that drought conditions exacerbated an already fragmented sociopolitical landscape. This scenario is supported by regional evidence from the southern Titicaca Basin and other regions. Mounting evidence suggests that "the seeds of Tiwanaku's collapse were sown during [its] apogee" (Mathews 1997: 259). Settlement patterns in the Tiwanaku Valley in Early Tiwanaku V reveal a significant increase in the size of secondary villages and the number of smaller hamlets, a situation that may have encouraged decentralized control of local productive systems and the increasing power of local corporate groups (Albarracín-Jordán 1996). In the Moquegua Valley, and facing environmental deterioration, groups heretofore closely affiliated with Tiwanaku appear to have asserted local autonomy to control local productive systems (Williams 2002).

Supporting a scenario of sociopolitical fragmentation and environmental deterioration are most of the changes that amounted to a new cultural complex known locally as Pacajes in the Late Intermediate Period. First, settlement patterns throughout the southern Lake Titicaca Basin demonstrated a radical shift to a highly dispersed settlement system (Albarracín-Jordán and Mathews 1990; Bandy 2001; Janusek and Kolata 2003; Stanish 2003). In any region, numerous hamlets and villages clustered around slightly larger centers, forming the kin-based ayllus and central markas known from the colonial period onward. Second, evidence for critical demographic decline in the old Tiwanaku core correlated with a demographic and political shift to the south, drier areas that had always favored pastoralism. Not surprisingly, many Late Tiwanaku V and Pacajes occupations were ephemeral, characteristic of pastoral societies. Third, change in the archaeological parameters of domestic life occurred in objects and contexts that had been highly charged domains for the expression of social identity and memory in Tiwanaku culture. These included, most notably, entirely new ceramic serving wares and mortuary practices emphasizing highly visible, above-ground burial chambers. Serving wares and mortuary patterns were socially contested objects and practices that, once the state came to be viewed as a burdensome, exploitative source of misery, were transformed strategically as a symbolic negation of Tiwanaku culture and power. Groups erased their affiliations with Tiwanaku in the process of crafting new social identities, cultural affiliations, and political alliances. Eventually, perhaps over a few generations, Tiwanaku was no longer a significant part of their "living" social memories.

Evidence suggests that conflict at this time developed out of old tensions and followed deep social rifts with histories dating to and perhaps pre-dating Tiwanaku hegemony. Tiwanaku was diverse, and its long-term stability was, in part, a function of its ability to promote an attractive vision of the cosmos and society, an ideology that groups adopted, reformulated, and internalized as practical hegemony, living tradition, and "the way things have always been." Political unity was grounded in incorporative strategies, a dominant ideology emphasizing reciprocal obligation, a prestigious state culture, a desirable cultural affiliation, and general well-being. Incorporation in Tiwanaku's hegemonic web had to remain attractive in order for its increasingly hierarchical sociopolitical structure to remain appealing. It appears that in Tiwanaku V, as rulers implemented transformative strategies of control and appropriation, contradictory consciousness – a clear disparity of "the world as experienced and the world as represented" – must have increasingly inspired a cynical interpretation of Tiwanaku as burdensome and exploitative. Aggravated by the onset of a long-term drought, such a situation would have incited many to erase their affiliations with the state and to seek out new political alliances, productive enterprises, and social identities.

Conclusions

Tiwanaku was a bustling prehispanic city, the first to arise in the south-central Andes. Like a cultural and political center in any pristine civilization, Tiwanaku was not simply a dense nucleation of populations. It was also an intense concentration of the ideals and practical realities of those populations: elite, non-elite, and non-local. On the one hand, certain elements of Tiwanaku – including its singular orientation – indicates, as Kolata suggests (1993, 2002), that Tiwanaku was a cosmogram, a built representation of the cosmic order narrated in predominant myths and enacted in ritual events, and a symbol of the macro-community with which its diverse groups affiliated. Most important, Tiwanaku was an exciting experience. As a place of ceremonial convergence for those affiliated with Tiwanaku, including pilgrims, this concrete symbol became the living anchor of political unity, religious affiliation, and cultural identity. Tiwanaku was also, in part, a center of elite cultural values and activities. At various times and in slightly different manners, the Sunken Temple, Kalasasaya, Akapana, and Pumapunku each comprised a monumental complex in which the predominant ideology of Tiwanaku, or more specifically that which was purveyed by a given ruler or dynasty, was breathed into life and recharged in elite-sponsored pomp and ritual.

Nevertheless, Tiwanaku was more than an elegant symbol and an elite center. It was also the place where groups of diverse statuses, backgrounds, socioeconomic networks, and kin relations resided and visited. Even if all who resided in Tiwanaku were closely related to elite groups, or played some direct role in the temples or urban economy, as Kolata suggests, these groups clearly maintained certain distinct patterns of material culture, reverence to local ancestors, and local identities. As such, Tiwanaku was where social identities co-resided and commingled, where power relations were expressed and redressed on a day-to-day basis, and where social hierarchies were constructed, refashioned, and deconstructed. It is significant, Deborah Blom notes (1999), that like styles of ceramic wares, two entirely distinct styles of cranial modification – one characteristic of the Katari Valley, and one of the Moquegua region – were both represented in Tiwanaku in the IV and V phases. Co-residence among groups with distinct, culturally modified bodily forms highlights the patterns presented in some residential compounds: Tiwanaku was, in part, a cosmopolitan place. Groups with non-local backgrounds and foreign affiliations settled in Tiwanaku, plying their own trades and maintaining, it appears, ties to their distinct homelands. All such groups affiliated with Tiwanaku and subscribed, to some degree, to its prestigious cosmology and ideological principles, for status and social identities were largely expressed in Tiwanaku-style valued goods and typical domestic and ritual practices. Still, not only did local urban groups maintain local values and practices, some of these values and practices shaped Tiwanaku's predominant ideology as it shifted through time.

Social identity remained alive at local scales, most likely among elite groups and political factions just as it did among non-elites. I argue that social tensions attendant on such social differentiation fostered state disintegration in the face of increasing state appropriation and environmental deterioration. The long-term history of Tiwanaku residential life, as represented specifically in Akapana East, recounts a narrative of prestigious ritual activity, vibrant social identities, and shifting power relations. In the Formative Period, Tiwanaku emerged as one of many competing and interacting political and ceremonial settlements, the center of a relatively small multi-community polity and a site of diverse ritual practice and local religious experience. In the Early Middle Horizon Tiwanaku developed into the center of a multi-regional state grounded in incorporative political strategies; its internal social diversity, monumental constructions, and high-status residences reflected such characteristics. By the Late Middle Horizon incorporative strategies were becoming transformative, grounded in tighter control over social groups and productive enterprises, and the conversion of regions into integrated provinces and elite-managed estates. In Tiwanaku we see the crystallization of an elite class, and a greater role for the rituals of consumption that legitimized, or at least rendered "liveable," their privileged status, wealth, and social power. In deteriorating climatic conditions which effectively removed an elite fund of power (massive rituals of consumption and their attendant politics), collapse was probably inevitable. Over the centuries Tiwanaku ideology had been adopted and internalized as a critical part and parcel of the traditions, practices, and identities of local groups; much was for the most part beyond contestation, the world as it was and always had been. This constructed world, this practical hegemony with its centralized political system and reified social hierarchy, suffered a shakedown toward the end of the Late Middle Horizon. In the Late Intermediate Period, perhaps over three or four generations, it was negated and forgotten in the face of new climatic conditions, political alliances, interaction networks, and cultural affiliations.

The archaeology of households, or more accurately residential patterns and activities, provides a unique and dynamic perspective to our current understanding of the Tiwanaku city as it does of other major centers of prehispanic civilizations in the Americas. The search for repeating household units in Tiwanaku was successful, but more significantly it led to the identification of more encompassing compound groups, local specialized and ritual activities, and associated nearby ritual complexes. Many prehispanic residences were, as many scholars point out, domains not just for what we typically think of as domestic activity but a host of other social activities as well. As important, households were not in any strict sense fundamental or homogenous social units. They were primary in the sense that the most intensive enculturation, and many of the most intimate social activities in Tiwanaku society, took place there. Nevertheless, households were integrated with large corporate groups in Tiwanaku, as well as the urban community at large, participating in wider domains of identity formation, gender relations, social differentiation, and productive activity that must have varied significantly across society and through time. An understanding of past residences enriches an understanding of the Tiwanaku city, and also fosters an understanding of the broader social contexts and built environments in which they thrived.

ACKNOWLEDGMENTS

The National Science Foundation (BNS# 9021098) and Fulbright-Hays funded research in Akapana East. Vanderbilt University and the Curtiss T. and Mary G. Brennan Foundation funded research in Khonkho Wankane. I thank many colleagues and friends who were closely involved with this research, including Chris Begley, Nicole Couture, Deborah Blom, Martin Giesso, Claudia Rivera, and especially Alan Kolata, director of Proyecto Wila Jawira.

11

Late Prehispanic Sociopolitical Complexity

Christina A. Conlee, Jalh Dulanto,
Carol J. Mackey, and Charles Stanish

Introduction

By definition the Late Intermediate Period (henceforth, LIP; ca. A.D. 1000–1470) is the time between empires and, as such, offers the opportunity to examine the various reconfigurations of Andean lifeways in the space created by the political collapse of the Wari and Tiwanaku Empires while providing the fundamental cultural patterns that were reworked by the Incas in their rapid consolidation in the following period of time known as the Late Horizon (LH). The LIP was a time of major transformations in the Central Andes. On the north coast the great Chimú Empire rose, as well as the spectacular Lambayeque polity that it conquered. In addition, there was a third polity on the north coast, Casma, in the southern area. This Casma polity has been overshadowed in archaeological fieldwork and the literature because of the political cohesion, monumentality of architecture, and brilliance of crafts in the previous two; though Casma is still relatively unknown, further study could reveal the existence of another key political power on the north coast. On the central coast at least four polities are known from the ethnohistorical sources. The best known of these polities is Ychsma, whose principal center was Pachacamac, the preeminent pan-Andean shrine and pilgrimage center during Inca times. On the south coast each valley had an independent and varying political configuration, from the apparently centralized realm of the Chincha to less powerful iterations. In the Titicaca Basin the demise of the millennial Tiwanaku Empire was succeeded by the ethnohistorically known "Lake Kingdoms," whose vast wealth in animal stock (camelids) so impressed the Spaniards when they arrived in the area. This chapter treats the major ancient societies of the Late Intermediate Period because they are the best documented and may be meaningfully compared.

Figure 11.1. Aerial view of the core of the Chimú capital city of Chan Chan, showing several of the ciudadelas (royal palaces) as well as the dense urban occupation surrounding them

The North Coast Polities

The geopolitical landscape of the north coast underwent major transformations during the LIP as several polities jockeyed for political power. The north coast includes some 700 km, and is composed of the valleys from Casma in the south to the modern Peru–Ecuador border in the north (Mackey and Klymyshyn 1990). During the LIP, three major polities controlled the north coast, each with their own method of governance. The two best-known polities, Lambayeque (A.D. 800–1350) and Chimú (A.D. 900–1470), were heirs of the Moche north coast tradition. One feature inherited from the Moche was the sociopolitical schism that divided the north coast into two sub-areas, with a border north of the Chicama River (Castillo 2001; Donnan 1988). During the LIP, the area north of the Chicama became the Lambayeque core region, while the Chimú heartland lay to the south of this divide.

Lambayeque can best be described as a complex non-state society composed of dispersed ceremonial centers. It displayed its power through ideology and control over the manufacture and distribution of ritual objects. The Chimú, or the Kingdom of Chimor, centralized political and economic power at Chan Chan, their capital, to become on the eve of the Inca conquest, ca. A.D. 1470, the largest polity to challenge the Inca. At the same time, Casma, a third polity, flourished south of the Chimú heartland (ca. A.D. 800/900–1300) and ruled from its purported capital of El Purgatorio in the Casma Valley (Collier 1962; Mackey and Klymyshyn 1990; Tello 1956; Wilson 1995). Indications of its influence, based on the spread of "Casma Incised" ceramics, cover a territory encompassing several north coast valleys from Huarmey to Chao (Mackey and Klymyshyn 1990). This evidence suggests that it, too, wielded power, but the nature of its political organization and the extent of its influence are largely undocumented archaeologically.

While the origins of the Casma, Lambayeque, and Chimú polities can be traced to the preceding Middle Horizon, they all developed their distinctive cultural traits during the LIP. Although the territorial consolidation of the burgeoning Chimú state has been well recognized, the fact that the three polities coexisted for almost 300 years is equally important and intriguing. Chimú consolidation came late in their rule. By the time of the Inca conquest (ca. A.D. 1470), the political map of the north coast reflected only Chimú hegemony.

While it is important to mention the Casma polity, the focus of this section is on Lambayeque and Chimú. Architectural patterns, found at major sites constructed by these polities, are viewed as manifestations of social, political, and ideological control and provide the primary line of evidence for their disparate paths to power.

The Lambayeque polity

Lambayeque arose on the north coast during the Middle Horizon, a time of social, political, and ideological change. Initially, both highland and coastal traits influ-

:ed Lambayeque, but its roots were coastal and relied heavily on Moche (Bennett 1939; Shimada 1995). From ca. A.D. 850 to 1350 Lambayeque held sway over the Leche, Lambayeque, Reque, and Zaña Valleys. It also pushed its influence north to Piura (Shimada 1990) and south into Jequetepeque (Donnan and Cock 1997) and the Chicama Valley (Shimada 1995).

Large-scale scientific excavations of a Lambayeque center began some 20 years ago at the Sican Precinct, an archaeological site located within the larger archaeological zone of Batan Grande. Directed by Izumi Shimada, this project identified three chronological phases for Lambayeque culture; the phases were named after the small Sican Precinct: Early Sican, A.D. 750–900; Middle Sican, A.D. 900–1100; and Late Sican, A.D. 1100–1350 (Shimada 1981). The materials excavated at the Sican Precinct date to the Middle phase. Clusters of a dozen or more truncated pyramids (called huacas) characterize Lambayeque ceremonial centers. Smaller centers of varying sizes, such as Chotuna in the Lambayeque Valley (Donnan 1990a, 1990b) and single mound sites, often with painted murals such as Urupe (Alva and Alva 1983), may have served as local temples or shrines.

Sican (A.D. 900–1050/1100)

The Sican Precinct contains the remains of at least 12 pyramids ranging in height from 10 to 40 m (Shimada 1995). Their chamber and fill construction technique (rectangular adobe chambers filled with rubble) is typical of northern north coast edifices and differs from the solid brick structures found in the Chimú heartland (Shimada 1997). The preeminence of pyramid construction, the temples atop the pyramid's summit, the lack of residential architecture (either elite or commoner), and the funerary evidence from looted and extant tombs suggest that Sican's function was ceremonial not administrative (Shimada 1995). Grave goods from more than 20 excavated tombs provided data on the political economy and the social hierarchy. The occupants of the tombs represented at least four social classes based on the presence or absence of exotic goods (Shimada 1995). For example, burials excavated at the base of Sican's Huaca Loro included precious metal – silver and gold. Precious metal ores are scarce on the north coast and were procured from great distances: the Cajamarca area of the northern highlands, or the Marañon region east of the Lambayeque core. Quantities of shells, especially *Spondylus princeps* and *Conus fergusoni*, from the warm waters of modern Ecuador, were interred whole in the tombs or made into beads. Other imported materials were cinnabar (mercuric sulfide) found in Peru and Ecuador and emeralds from modern Colombia (Burger and Matos Mendieta 2002; Shimada 1995, 2000). The imported raw materials demonstrated that ancient trade networks were much more complex and far-reaching than previously thought. Metalworking tools found near the Sican huacas and other metal workshops on the precinct's periphery suggest that artisans' workshops were directly associated with the temples (Shimada 1995).

Sican's elite commissioned objects decorated with symbolic imagery. The features of Lambayeque's main deity – a square face, upturned, comma-shaped eyes, and square or pointed ears – are represented in various forms and media.

Representations of the deity continued into Late Sican times, though less frequently (Heyerdahl, Sandweiss, and Narvaez 1995). In contrast with the earlier Moche period, renowned for the variety of its supernatural images, the Lambayeque pantheon is restricted to a few deities and anthropomorphic forms (Cordy-Collins 1996; Mackey 2001; Shimada 1990).

Tucume (A.D. 1050–1350/1400)

Just prior to the devastating El Niño of A.D. 1100, purposeful fires destroyed the temples atop the pyramids at Sican and a new center, Tucume, was established 15 km to the west. The 26 truncated pyramids resemble those of Sican in form, construction techniques, access patterns, and summit structures. Unlike Sican, however, the bases of some of Tucume's pyramids are flanked by enclosures, such as the one at Huaca 1 (Heyerdahl, Sandweiss, and Narvaez 1995:116). Although these enclosures contain rooms and patios, the general lack of residential architecture (both elite and commoner) prompts archaeologists to argue that Tucume was primarily a ceremonial center. Though the majority of pyramids are dated to Late Sican, architectural and artifactual comparisons with coeval centers are difficult since the Lambayeque temples were destroyed during the later rebuilding by the Chimú and Inca Empires (Heyerdahl, Sandweiss, and Narvaez 1995). Fragments of precious metals and *Spondylus princeps* found in the Lambayeque levels indicate that Tucume's elite continued to have access to exotic resources and manufactured goods (Heyerdahl, Sandweiss, and Narvaez 1995).

Pacatnamu (A.D. 1100–1200/1300)

Situated at the mouth of the Jequetepeque River on high bluffs overlooking the Pacific, the 1 km^2 site of Pacatnamu is located 100 km south of Tucume. Pacatnamu flourished from approximately A.D. 1100 until its conquest by the Chimú between A.D. 1200 and 1300 (Donnan and Cock 1986; Keatinge and Conrad 1983). Traditionally, scholars have interpreted the progression of Lambayeque culture as linear, with Sican (Middle Sican phase) as the first known center, followed by the contemporaneous Tucume and Pacatnamu centers (Late Sican phase) (Heyerdahl, Sandweiss, and Narvaez 1995; Shimada 1990). It now appears, however, that the Jequetepeque Valley had a longer Lambayeque occupation than previously imagined. Recent radiocarbon assays from a tomb at San José de Moro (Nelson et al. 2000), ceramics excavated by Ubbelohde-Doering from Pacatnamu (Hecker and Hecker 1995), and ceramics from other sites such as Farfan (Mackey and Jaúregui 2002) and Cabur (Sapp 2002) indicate a Middle Sican (A.D. 900–1100) occupation in the Jequetepeque Valley.

The center at Pacatnamu echoes the Lambayeque architectural tradition: clusters of truncated pyramids with rooms on their summits. The 37 truncated adobe mounds that Donnan (Donnan and Cock 1986) calls Huaca Complexes show major architectural changes. These complexes contain small pyramids surrounded by walls, adjacent enclosures with rooms and patios, U-shaped rooms known as concillios, and areas with restricted access. It is difficult to pinpoint the origin of these architectural changes since walled enclosures are the hallmark of the coeval Chimú state. Archaeologists have not yet located large, elite tombs at Pacatnamu to rival those of Sican. On the other hand, weaving implements and iconography found on textiles excavated in Huaca 1 suggest that weaving specialists were attached to the huacas (Donnan and Cock 1986:114). The emphasis on the truncated temple-pyramid and the associated luxury goods reiterate the primarily ceremonial nature of the Lambayeque centers. It appears that these major centers were never politically centralized, but instead formed a loose confederation united by kinship ties (Heyerdahl, Sandweiss, and Narvaez 1995; Kosok 1965). Nevertheless, there is a strong cultural and artistic tradition that unites the Lambayeque core.

Chimor

Most scholars concur that Chimor, known archaeologically as the Chimú, emerged at the end of the Middle Horizon (i.e., A.D. 900–1000), later than Lambayeque (Kolata 1990; Mackey 2001). Chimú's cultural roots lie on the north coast. Non-native elements, such as the seated burial position, reflect highland influence but were probably incorporated via Lambayeque in the north, or from the pilgrimage center of Pachacamac to the south (Mackey 2001). The Chimú core area was the Moche Valley, home to its capital of Chan Chan. According to the Spanish chronicles the empire spread some 1,000 km along the coast, from Tumbez in the north to Carabayllo in the south (J. Rowe 1948). However, archaeological survey and excavation shows that actual Chimú settlements occupied a smaller region of the coast – the contiguous valleys from Motupe in the north to the Casma Valley in the south (Mackey and Klymyshyn 1990). This acquisition of territory was gradual and took place over a 200-year period (Mackey and Klymyshyn 1990; Shimada 2000; T. Topic 1990). The Chimú period has been divided into three chronological phases, with the Early phase still poorly understood (Donnan and Mackey 1978; Kolata 1990; J. Topic and Moseley 1983): Early Chimú, A.D. 900/1000–1200; Middle Chimú, A.D. 1200–1300; and Late Chimú, A.D. 1300–1470 (Kolata 1990). Several authors refer to the Middle and Late phases as Imperial Chimú (e.g., Conrad 1990).

The Chimor capital of Chan Chan, A.D. 900/1000–1470

Chan Chan was the political and religious center of Chimor, and contained the residences and final resting place of its god-kings. Located close to the Pacific on the north side of the Moche Valley, the capital's 6 km^2 core contains repetitive architectural components. Five pyramids continue the north coast tradition of freestanding monuments, with the tallest one, located on the margins of the city core, rising 20 m (Day 1982). The city's architectural signature, however, is its high-walled adobe enclosures (ciudadelas) classified on the basis of size, height of exterior walls, and internal architectural traits. Ten of the largest ciudadelas functioned as the palaces of the Chimú kings while the smaller ones housed the nobility. Finally, cane-walled structures scattered in and around the city core served as artisans' residences and workshops. While Shimada analyzed the contents of Sican's tombs to identify Lambayeque's social hierarchy, the archaeologists at Chan Chan used architectural variables to differentiate two social classes: nobles and artisans (Day 1982; Moseley 1975c; Moseley and Mackey 1973; J. Topic 1982). Using variables such as construction details, floor plan and associated artifacts, these classes were internally differentiated into at least four ranks of nobility and two of artisan class (Klymyshyn 1987; J. Topic 1990).

The ten monumental enclosures or palaces, surrounded by walls 9 m high, were multifunctional in nature. The spatial organization of the rooms within the palaces, combined with tortuous access patterns between rooms and sectors, are crucial to understanding the function of the palaces (Day 1982; Moore 1996). During their lifetimes, Chimú kings and nobility resided in roofed, U-shaped structures known as audiencias. Seen as the architectural symbol of Chimú authority, each palace had an average of ten audiencias (Klymyshyn 1987), many decorated with adobe friezes depicting sacred iconography (Pillsbury 1993).

On his death, the Chimú king was buried in a multi-tiered burial platform within the palace. Constructed of large blocks of tamped adobe, or tapia, that ranged in height from 3.5 to 12 m, the king's tomb was located in the center of the burial platform, surrounded by smaller, cell-like tombs as well as an attached platform annex presumably for royal lineage members (Conrad 1982). Each palace also contained several enclosed plazas that served as the setting for feasts and ceremonies (Morris and Thompson 1985). A wooden architectural model of a Chimú-style plaza, excavated in a tomb outside of Chan Chan (Uceda 1997), may represent a ritual commemorating the ancestors buried there. The scene includes miniature wooden figures in attendance, some playing musical instruments and others tipping jars as if they are pouring liquid into cups. Palaces are also distinguished by undecorated, cell-like storerooms that occupy more floor space than any other architectural feature in the compounds (Klymyshyn 1987). The majority of the goods warehoused in the storerooms were probably used in the plaza ceremonies, either as food, drink, or gifts for guests, or included as offerings to the god-king and his retainers buried in the royal burial platform. The link between stored goods and plaza ceremonies played a vital part in the redistribution system practiced by ancient Andean polities.

Chan Chan's smaller elite compounds share several of the palace's architectural features. Using architectural function as well as the presence or absence of particular features, Klymyshyn (1987) differentiated at least three ranks of non-royalty. The elite compounds had fewer audiencias and considerably fewer storerooms. They did not contain burial platforms or large plazas, suggesting once again that these features were reserved for royalty.

The cane-walled residences of the artisans contrast with the high, adobe walls of the royal compounds. The artisans, who worked in their homes rather than in separate workshops, made up the bulk of Chan Chan's population, which at its peak is estimated to have reached 30,000 people (J. Topic 1982). Higher-status artisans were attached to the royal compounds, while others lived in houses surrounding the city core. Households did not specialize, but rather several crafts were produced in the same house (J. Topic 1990).

The objects crafted in the artisan barrios transmitted the sacred images of Chimú religious art. As in Lambayeque, the Chimú pantheon had few deities. Chief among these is the ubiquitous front-facing figure whose stance and apparel recall those seen in Lambayeque representations. The secular transition of the front-facing deity is complete in Chimú religious art as the deity's face is more human than its Lambayeque counterpart. The main deity shared the pantheon with a goddess who, as her associated imagery suggests, performed multiple duties (Mackey 2001). The nobility's ownership of these national treasures was legitimized by north coast myths that recognized separate creation for the elite class (Moore 1996; Netherly 1977).

Chimú expansion

Chimú settlement patterns, in the regions subjugated outside of the Moche Valley, reveal the four-tiered hierarchy characteristic of ancient states (Mackey 1987). Architecturally the lower-level administrative centers recall Chan Chan's elite compounds (Mackey and Klymyshyn 1990) and their strategic locations afforded them control over agricultural fields and irrigation systems (Keatinge 1974). The first wave of Chimú expansion absorbed the valleys peripheral to the Lambayeque and Casma polities, leaving the core of these rival polities intact while the second and third waves incorporated their core areas and they ceased to exist as political entities.

Judging by the number of new settlements founded in the Jequetepeque Valley, as well as their size and labor investment, the Chimú obviously viewed this valley as strategic to their political and economic interests. Though the fertile farmlands of this region may have been an impetus for conquest (A. von Hagen and Morris 1998), of equal import was access to the resources held by Lambayeque. Jequetepeque provided a gateway to Cajamarca in the highlands, an area that had previously provided metal ores to Lambayeque's metal smiths. It was possible, however, for Lambayeque to continue to procure ores from the Marañon region, possibly via Olmos.

During the Middle to Late Chimú phases (A.D. 1250 to the 1400s), the Chimú constructed large Chan Chan-like enclosures, creating the provincial center of Farfan. The architectural features within these enclosures blended features characteristic of both royal and elite architecture. Though the compounds contain few audiencias and storerooms, they do have large plazas and burial platforms (Keatinge and Conrad 1983; Mackey and Zavelata 2000). The lack of a large resident population and artisans' workshops suggests that Farfan's compounds functioned as a series of royal residences that legitimized the state's presence and provided a venue for state ceremonies. The task of administration fell to the lower-level centers within the valley such as Talambo (Keatinge and Conrad 1983) and Algarrobal de Moro (Castillo, Mackey, and Nelson 1997) that were staffed by lower-level Chimú nobles. Finally, sites such as Cabur, the seat of local Jequetepeque lords, ranked lowest in the settlement hierarchy. These lords continued to control an area in the southern part of the valley, enjoying considerable autonomy (Sapp 2002).

During Late Chimú, after the establishment of Farfan, the Chimú initiated their second wave of expansion, beginning south of the Santa Valley. It appears that the Casma polity was still in control of the area at the time of the Chimú conquest. The Chimú constructed a new provincial center, called Manchan, which they located at the southern end of the valley (Mackey and Klymyshyn 1990).

Manchan's plan and spatial organization contrast markedly with those of Chan Chan and Farfan. At Manchan the compounds are organized into two groups: freestanding adobe compounds that resemble Chan Chan's elite enclosures and rectangular agglutinated enclosures that follow local, not Chimú, canons of architecture (Mackey and Klymyshyn 1990). Taken as a whole, the site is a metaphor for a different political strategy that emphasized joint rule by the Chimú and the local lords. The freestanding compounds deviate even further from Chimú tradition, since some functioned as residences and others contained only subter-ranean tombs. Unlike Farfan, Manchan did have a resident population of part-time craftsmen who manufactured utilitarian goods, such as copper tweezers, and great quantities of chicha (corn beer) the main beverage consumed in ceremonies (Moore 1981, 1989). The sharing of power with the local lords is also reflected in the Casma Valley, where few Chimú centers were constructed and local lords continued to rule from their ancestral homes (Mackey and Klymyshyn 1990).

According to Shimada (2000), the conquest of the Lambayeque area north of the Jequetepeque Valley occurred ca. A.D. 1350 to 1400. In the take-over of the Lambayeque center of Tucume, the Chimú deviated from their past strategy and did not build an intrusive center. Instead, they constructed a compound for their administrator, who shared power with the lords of Tucume who continued to dwell in Tucume (Heyerdahl, Sandweiss, and Narvaez 1995). This resident noble was probably of royal rank, since the Chimú constructed a small burial platform; however, the audiencia has not been located. After so many years of détente with this northern north coast region, the Chimú may have placated local rulers at Tucume by not using overt political symbols – a strategy later employed by the Inca on the north coast.

The Central Coast Polities

The central coast of Peru extends from the Fortaleza Valley in the north to the Cañete Valley in the south, and from the Pacific Ocean on the west to the coun-terforts of the Andes on the east. The central coast is about 400 km long and 40 km wide, and covers, from north to south, the lower and middle sections of at least a dozen coastal valleys: Fortaleza, Pativilca, Supe, Huaura, Chancay, Chillón, Rimac, Lurín, Chilca, Mala, Asia, and Cañete. Ethnohistorical and archaeological research indicates that during the LIP and the LH these valleys were not controlled by one single polity but by several polities of a similar level of complexity. At least four polities are known from the ethnohistorical sources. This section focuses on one of these polities, the Ychsma polity or Señorío de Ychsma, a polity that appears to have grouped the populations of the Rimac and Lurín Valleys in late prehispanic times. The reason for focusing on the Ychsma polity is simple: it is the only polity of the central coast for which there is ethnohistorical and archaeological information that allows us to make some inferences about central coast social and political complexity.

Ethnohistory

Archaeological investigations of the late prehispanic occupation of the central coast are greatly aided by the work of the great Peruvian ethnohistorian María Rostworowski. Her research has contributed enormously to our understanding of the economic, social, and political organization of the central coast during late prehispanic and early colonial times. The description below is a result of a critical evaluation of her analyses of early colonial documents (e.g., Rostworowski 1972, 1977a, 1978, 1978–80, 1989, 1992, 1993, 1999a).

The documents describe the populations of the central coast as populations organized in "parcialidades." These parcialidades were groups of people subordinated to one or more lords. Under the direction of these lords they were involved in different kinds of activities, but the documents usually describe them as undertaking almost only economic activities. After all, these were the kind of activities that especially interested the colonial administration. The parcialidades are described as groups of persons occupying a territory, exploiting certain natural resources, producing certain kinds of goods, exchanging certain products, and building and maintaining certain public buildings. The "lords," on the other hand, are essentially described as those responsible for mobilizing the labour force of the parcialidades for the fulfillment of these activities. Theoretical and empirical reasons tell us that the parcialidades and the lords described in the documents are, in reality, "economized" representations of more complex actors.

The parcialidades and the lords are also described as subordinated to one another in what seems to have been a complex network of political relationships. It is not unusual to find references to parcialidades and lords who benefited from labour force and goods coming from other parcialidades and lords. It is mainly from the description of these relationships of subordination between parcialidades and lords that we infer different sorts of political entities: "señoríos," "states," and even "empires." The reconstruction of the social and political reality of the central coast populations in prehispanic times, then, depends greatly on our capacity and disposition: first, to define as relevant social and political actors the parcialidades and lords who are described in the early colonial documents mainly as economic actors; and, second, to contrast them with the social and political actors that we may be able to define based on late prehispanic archaeological evidence.

Maria Rostworowski's studies allow us to take the first of these steps. According to her, the central coast populations were not subordinated to one lord. Several lords controlled the valleys that cross-cut the central coast. Rostworowski identifies these higher-rank lords with political units and calls these political units señorios. The documents inform us of at least four señorios that controlled one or more valleys: the Señorío de Huaura (between the Pativilca and Chancay valleys), the Señorío de Collique (in the Chillón Valley), the Señorío de Ychsma (in the Rimac and Lurín valleys and probably several small valleys to the south up to the Mala Valley) and the Señorío de Guarco (in the Cañete Valley and probably other small valleys to the north and to the south). Of these four, the Señorío de Ychsma is the best known and, therefore, the one that allows us to formulate some general ideas about the social and political complexity of the central coast.

The Señorío de Ychsma seems to have been organized in at least three levels of social and political aggregation. Rostworowski calls the units of these levels ayllus, minor señorios, and major señorios. An ayllu is essentially a parcialidad; several ayllus or parcialidades form a minor señorío; and several minor señorios form a major señorio. In this frame, the Señorío de Ychsma seems to have been a major señorio that grouped at least 12 minor señorios that were subordinated to the lord of the minor señorío of Pachacamac. Eight of these minor señorios occupied territories in the Rimac Valley (i.e., the minor señorios of Lati, Sulco, Guatca, Lima, Amancaes, Maranga, Guala, and Callao) and four in the Lurín Valley (i.e., the minor señorios of Pachacamac, Manchay, Caringa, and Quilcay). For at least one of these minor señorios, the Señorío de Sulco, we also know the names of some of the ayllus that were part of it (the ayllus of Calla, Ydcay, Centaulli, and Cuncham).

Some references in the documents allow us to formulate some ideas about the principles on the basis of which these units where articulated. According to Rostworowski several references suggest that the minor señorios occupied territories along main irrigation canals while the ayllus occupied territories along secondary irrigation canals. Other references suggest that these units were organized in groups of two, four, and even eight units and that in several cases one half of the units had a higher rank than the other. Thus, two of the principles that organized the aggregation of lower-level units into higher-level ones (ayllus into minor señorios, and minor señorios into major señorios) were the territorial location of the unit in relation to the hydraulic systems and its place within a system of dual organization. If this is true, the Señorío de Ychsma could have been organized in a way very similar to that proposed by Patricia Netherly (1976, 1984, 1990) for the north coast polities – that is, on the basis of principles of hierarchy and duality. Up to what point these particular units and the principles upon which they were articulated could be extrapolated to prehispanic periods is a problem that we still need to solve on a case-by-case basis. Archaeology may substantially contribute to solving this problem.

Archaeology

Archaeological work on the central coast has produced impressive amounts of information that can be useful to understand the social and political reality of the region during the LIP and the LH. However, since most of these studies have not been conducted within research projects of regional focus and scale, systematic comparison of the information they have produced is difficult, and proper evaluation of the social and political organization of the central coast almost impossible at the moment.

Fortunately, there exists a very specific type of monumental building in the Rimac and Lurín Valleys, known as "pyramids with ramps," whose analysis may allow us to evaluate the way the Señorío de Ychsma was organized. The following description and interpretation of the patterns that characterize these structures is based on the critical evaluation of the evidence and interpretations presented by several investigators (Bazán 1990; Bueno 1974–75, 1977, 1982; Dolorier 1999; Dulanto 1998; Eeckhout 1995, 1999, 2000; Franco 1998; Jiménez Borja 1985; Jiménez Borja and Bueno 1970; Paredes Botoni 1990; Paredes Botoni and Franco 1988; Shimada 1991).

The pyramids with ramps are public monumental buildings. They are a sort of rectangular platform with one or more terraced levels. These platforms usually have an open patio in the front, a roofed room on the top, and several rectangular rooms to the sides and behind. A straight ramp centrally placed on the frontal side of the platform connects the open patio in the front with the roofed room on the top. The whole complex is usually surrounded by a perimetric wall and has a restricted access at the front or at one of the sides.

There are at least two hypotheses about the function of the pyramids with ramps. Some scholars interpret these structures as provincial temples that consecrated the relationship of different groups with the Pachacamac ceremonial center (e.g., Bueno 1974–75, 1982; Jiménez Borja 1985; Jiménez Borja and Bueno 1970; Paredes Botoni 1990); for other scholars they were the palaces and tombs of the lords of the Señorío de Ychsma (Eeckhout 1999, 2000). If our objective is to understand the organization principles of the groups that built and used the pyramids with ramps, then it is enough to know that they were public buildings and to suppose that, in some way, they represented the identity of these groups.

At least 40 of these monumental buildings have been recorded in the Rimac and Lurín valleys and, thus far, only in these two valleys. Therefore, they could indicate some sort or degree of interaction between the groups that built and used them. We cannot yet determine if such interaction included the political unification of these groups. However, certain structural patterns such as design, location, orientation, and size allow us to investigate in this direction.

The pyramids with ramps are not identical in design. They all have a terraced platform with a central ramp, but they differ considerably in the number and kind of rooms surrounding the platform, in the location and horizontal and vertical distribution of these rooms, and in the access systems connecting them. The fact that they are not identical in design is usually considered an indicator that the groups involved in the building of each structure were different and at least in some degree autonomous. This alone, however, is not an indicator of the principles on the basis of which these groups were articulated with each other or the aggregation levels to which they belonged.

The location of the pyramids with ramps within the Rimac and Lurín valleys, and within the sites where they occur, allow us to formulate some ideas in this regard. For instance, the structures' location within the valleys suggests that one of their articulation principles was their territorial position in relation to the hydraulic system. All the known pyramids with ramps are found in the lower valleys, in sites located at, or very near, the upper limit of the hydraulic system (i.e., Huaquerones and Monterrey in the Rimac Valley and Pampa de Flores and Tijerales in the Lurín Valley), or very near their lower limit (i.e., Maranga in the Rimac Valley and Pachacamac in the Lurín Valley). Bazán (1990) and Eeckhout (1999) consider as pyramids with ramps a platform with a central ramp at the top of Huaca de Tres Palos and another within a set of rooms in Huaycán of Cieneguilla. Several differences in the design of these structures permit us to exclude them from the group of structures analysed for this study.

In addition, with the remarkable exception of the pyramids with ramps of Pachacamac, all the structures, besides being near the river, are located on the south side of the valley, which is the side with a greater area of irrigated land. The location of these same structures within the sites where they occur suggests that another of the principles around which these groups were organized was their belonging to one or the other half within a dual organization system. At least in the case of Pachacamac and Pampa de Flores the pyramids with ramps are clearly organized in four and two sectors respectively, which are clearly delimited by streets that cross the width and length of the site.

The orientation of the pyramids with ramps seems to strengthen these ideas. The pyramids with ramps at sites located near the upper limit of the hydraulic system are all oriented to the intakes of the main canals irrigating the south sides of both valleys (i.e., Huaquerones and Monterrey in the Rimac Valley, and Pampa de Flores and Tijerales in the Lurín Valley). Within the site, the structures show a consistent orientation: either they are oriented more or less in the same direction (i.e., Huaquerones and Monterrey in the Rimac Valley), or they are oriented more or less in one of two directions that differ from one from another in around 90 degrees (i.e., Maranga in the Rimac Valley and Pachacamac, Pampa de Flores and Tijerales in the Lurín Valley). In all of these cases the orientation is defined by the orientation of the main ramps at the front of the pyramids with ramps.

The size of the pyramids with ramps suggests some ideas about the way in which these two principles could have been operating in the articulation of the groups that built and used these structures. If we compare the area of the pyramids with ramps we discover two facts: first, that the Pachacamac structures have an average area and a variation of the areas significantly greater than the structures of the other sites, and, second, that the structures of the other sites do not significantly differ from one another, either in their average area or in the variations of their areas. Even if we assume that the pyramids with ramps were built and maintained by different groups and that the size of the structures was a good indicator of the group's rank, there are several possible views resulting from this. A possible view is that Pachacamac has the greatest structures because it was the center of the higher-rank groups, and the greater variation in the structures' size is because it was also the center of a greater unit formed by groups of different rank that were subordinated to the higher-rank groups. This view is consistent with the idea of a political unit organized in more and more inclusive aggregation levels. Clearly, much more fieldwork (adding the all-important dimension of habitation sites) and analysis of diagnostic material (especially pottery and textiles) remain to be done in order to resolve issues of identity, allegiance, and prestige on the central coast that are raised by the pattern of pyramids with ramps and the ethnohistoric documentation of señoríos.

The South Coast Polities

The south coast of Peru encompasses the area from the Chincha Valley in the north to the Yauca Valley in the south. However, the limits of this cultural area are not always so easy to define. The Cañete Valley to the north of Chincha, and the Atiquipa and Chala valleys south of Yauca, also were a part of the south coast cultural sphere at different periods during prehistory.

Throughout prehispanic times there was significant interaction among the different valleys of the south coast and they shared a common cultural development. Following the collapse of the Wari Empire in the Middle Horizon (A.D. 750–1000) there was reorganization on the south coast with the emergence of a new cultural tradition that loosely tied the valley-based regional groups together. During the LIP the Cañete Valley was the home of two independent and powerful polities – Lunahuaná in the upper valley and Guarco in the lower valley (Hyslop 1985; Marcus 1987; Rostworowski 1978–80), and they may have helped connect societies farther south into a larger economic and cultural system based on the central coast of Peru. However, the south coast valleys with the most similar cultural traditions during the LIP were Chincha, Pisco, Ica, Nazca, and Acarí.

Chincha

Scholars seem to agree that there was a major polity in the Chincha Valley, and some argue that the many valleys of the south coast were part of this polity (i.e., Engel 1981). A relatively homogeneous material culture is described in many of the valleys, and this has supported the argument for political unity. This interpretation of south coast political organization is based primarily on historical documents and the absence of archaeological data outside of Chincha. Both historical documents and archaeological evidence indicate that the Chincha Valley was the home of the most powerful and sociopolitically complex group in the region. But the territorial extent of Chincha's power remains to be determined because a closer examination of the archaeological record reveals that there were distinctions in the ceramic styles and differences in site types, construction material, and settlement size in each valley. This evidence suggests that, while the valleys shared many cultural attributes, each was an independent political entity during the LIP.

Descriptions from historical documents have formed many of the conclusions about Chincha in late prehispanic times. This information depicts the valley, and its leader, as very powerful and important both before and during Inca rule. The Chincha lord accompanied Atahualpa during the Inca's fateful encounter with Pizarro in Cajamarca, indicating he held a privileged position under this emperor. The origins of Chincha's power in the LIP are unknown, but historical sources suggest they gained prominence through warfare and raiding (Cieza 1976; Menzel and Rowe 1966). The Chincha are said to have come from elsewhere and then conquered the valley that would become their home (this is a pervasive mythology cross-culturally). After this conquest, the population of the area grew and neighboring valleys tried to ally themselves with the Chinchas. According to Menzel and Rowe (1966:64), Fray Cristóbal de Castro (who worked at the first Dominican mission in the valley) reported in 1558 that according to local tradition the valleys of Cañete, Chincha, and Ica were each independent and the Chinchas engaged in constant warfare.

Besides depicting the Chincha as powerful in warfare, the historical documents also portray the valley as a center of economic activity. Rostworowski (1970, 1977b, 1978–80, 1989) has done extensive research on late prehispanic and early colonial societies in coastal Peru and concludes that significant differences existed between coastal and highland groups. In late prehispanic times the economy of the highlands was based on ecological complementarity ("verticality") while the coastal economy was based on specialization and commercial exchange. Rostworowski (1970:248–250) found that a large population of occupational specialists lived in Chincha; the most numerous were merchants, fishermen, and farmers, and others included miners, makers of fine cloth, potters, and carpenters. She also concludes that many of these specialists were full-time, in contrast to the highlands, where most specialists were part-time (Rostworowski 1999b:163). Sandweiss (1992) evaluated the information concerning specialization from the historical documents by excavating at the Late Horizon Chincha fishing village of Lo Demás. He concluded that a local fishing lord (or lords) lived here with attached specialists. Sandweiss also suggests that specialized fishing settlements similar to Lo Demás likely predate the Inca.

Merchants from Chincha are well documented in the historical records and Rostworowski states that they traveled as far as Ecuador in order to obtain Spondylus shells for trade. From her readings of historical information in the *Aviso*, Rostworowski (1970:171) reports that the Chincha merchants in the LH were so well developed that they used money, the only place in the Inca Empire where this was the case. According to this account, the Chincha used different metals in their monetary system; copper had a fixed value, and gold had a fixed exchange rate with silver. Moseley (1992:247), however, suggests the Chimú were the primary controllers of the Spondylus trade until the Inca conquered them and gave over the trade to the Chincha. Very little Spondylus shell has been found in archaeological contexts in the region (Morris 1988:134; Sandweiss 1992:23), indicating that long-distance trade in this artifact by Chincha merchants may have been overstated. Craig Morris proposes that Chincha had a role as an intermediary in exchange between the Inca and other groups during the LH (Morris 1988:138). If the Inca did favor the Chincha and helped them to prosper in the LH, this impression may have influenced the authors of some of the ethnohistorical sources in their descriptions of local society before the Inca. It is evident that there are discrepancies between the historical and archaeological record, and possibly much of the historical record describes Chincha after the Inca conquest when the valley may have been given special status and underwent reorganization. This is an issue that future archaeological investigations will hopefully address.

Archaeological evidence, especially the presence of many large mound sites, supports the historical description of high levels of sociopolitical organization and integration in Chincha. The largest late prehispanic sites in the Chincha Valley include Lurín Chincha, San Pedro, La Cumbe, Tambo de Mora, and La Centinela (Menzel 1959; Uhle 1924a; Wallace 1959); they were all constructed primarily of tapia (poured adobe). La Centinela and Tambo de Mora are the largest and most prominent sites in the valley, and both include large mounds and extensive town-like settlements around them. Max Uhle was the first to conduct extensive archaeological research in the region and he concluded that Tambo de Mora was the home of the principal chief of the valley before the Inca conquest (Uhle 1924a:66). La Centinela is, however, the largest and arguably the most important settlement in the valley, and it was here that the Inca built their administrative center. Later surveys by Dwight Wallace (1970a, 1970b, 1971) located 30 to 40 mounds in diverse areas of the valley dating to the LIP. He found five concentrations of ten or more mounds and defined them each as small urban centers. During this time there was continued dense occupation of the lower valley and an expansion of population into the upper valley where new sites were established. Wallace (1991) also identified a road system in Chincha that radiates out from the center of La Centinela to other settlements in the valley. A coastal road originates from here and leads to the lower Pisco Valley and to the base of the Paracas Bay. From the end of the road in Pisco there are roads that branch off to the middle Ica Valley and south to Nazca. Another road out of Chincha leads to where the Pisco Valley heads up into the mountains, and here it probably joins a major road into the highlands that was used by the Inca. Wallace believes the Chincha road system had both religious and economical uses within the region, and because the roads were connected to the major south and east routes in the Andes, they were also likely used for trading goods over long distances.

Pisco

South of Chincha is the Pisco Valley where the Inca established two administrative sites at Lima La Vieja and Tambo Colorado, neither of which was associated with local centers. Menzel (1959) proposes that the Inca administered the Pisco Valley in two separate units, indicating a lack of centralized administration in the LIP and therefore causing the Incas to develop additional infrastructure in order to rule the valley efficiently. Little is known about local society in Pisco during the LIP or the LH. From his survey in Pisco, Wallace (1971) found a concentration of large tapia mounds in the lower valley on the north side of the river. In contrast, sites in the central and upper valley are smaller and do not have any ceremonial architecture. Wallace thinks the site distribution is the result of Chincha's control of the Pisco Valley since large mound sites are found in the area most accessible to the Chincha Valley. The presence of straight roads that run out of these sites and their connection with a road to Chincha adds support to this argument. Menzel and Rowe (1966:66) also suggest that Pisco was ruled (possibly directly) by Chincha during the LIP based on the presence of imported Chincha pottery in the Pisco Valley. However, Wallace (1970b:22) observed that the ceramic style of Pisco is more similar to that of Ica than it is to Chincha. In later writings, Menzel (1977) concluded that Pisco was independent and not a part of the Chincha polity.

Ica

Archaeological and historical information from Ica suggests that, while this valley was less powerful politically and economically than Chincha, it was the center of production of a prestigious and widespread ceramic style, indicating that the valley was an important cultural or religious center (Lumbreras 1974a:195; Menzel 1959, 1976). Uhle's remark that the "Ica valley contains no important ruins, but ancient remains are extraordinarily abundant" (Uhle 1924b:122) probably first led to the image of the area as not very developed politically. It is true that in contrast to the many large mound sites in Chincha, only one large mound site (Ica Vieja) has been identified in Ica. The site of Ica Vieja (also called Tajaraca) is located just to the south of the modern city of Ica and was the LIP capital of the valley. This center contains several adobe brick ceremonial mounds, habitation refuse, and many large cemeteries. Unfortunately little is known about the region around the capital because the town of Ica and modern industrial agriculture have obscured or destroyed settlements in this area. It has been noted that much of the valley around the capital during the LIP probably consisted of dispersed hamlets (Menzel 1959, 1976). Cook (1992b) has conducted a survey in the lower Ica Valley and found large LIP sites in that area.

At Ica Vieja, Uhle excavated a series of noble and commoner graves that provide excellent information on prehispanic social relations in the valley. A more detailed analysis of this material, along with some additional material collected by John Rowe and his students, was later undertaken by Dorothy Menzel (1976, 1977). According to Menzel, Ica society was stratified with a class of nobles who lived in elaborate adobe structures. The noble tombs at Ica Vieja were large, deep, and contained up to 12 individuals (Menzel 1977:9). They also often had carved wooden grave markers and entry steps that made the chamber easier to enter. Entry into the tombs was important because secondary burial was common for elites. A year after nobles were buried there was a special ceremony in which the bones were painted red and then placed into urns. Inside the urns were gold, silver, pottery, various ornaments, and face masks (Menzel 1977:12). For commoners the traditional method of burial was also in urns; however, their tombs were shallow, unstructured, and without any means of re-entry. In other aspects of material culture there was not a great difference between nobles and commoners. The same type of well-made, fancy Ica pottery was used by everyone and indicates that the quality of life was often similar between the different social groups (Menzel 1976:233). During Inca times, however, there were larger differences between the commoners and the different ranks of nobles in terms of pottery styles and access to precious metals. These changes reflect a greater amount of social division that appears to have been the result of Inca rule.

Ica was the origin of a widespread ceramic style found on the south coast during the LIP. The Ica style was imported widely, north to the Ancón and Rimac valleys and even reportedly to the highlands west of Cuzco at Huancarama (Menzel and Rowe 1966:65). South of Ica, imports and imitations of the Ica style are common and extend to the Acarí and Yauca valleys. The broad distribution and influence of the Ica ceramic styles suggest that Ica had some prominence in a large area of the south coast or at least possessed a popular and often imitated ceramic style. The Ica ceramic style is similar in some design aspects to that of the ceramic style of the Chincha Valley. This similarity has often led researchers to conclude that the two areas were unified during the LIP. Analysis of the two ceramic styles by Menzel (1966) has identified each as separate traditions. During the early part of the LIP the Chincha style borrowed from the Ica style, but after this Ica influence diminished and the Chincha pottery style had more in common with styles of the central coast. Chincha influence was found in Ica ceramics right before the Inca conquest. However, this is not seen as evidence of direct Chincha rule because the influence consisted primarily of imitations and not direct imports; instead, it is seen as an indication of a shift in prestige relationships (Menzel and Rowe 1966:66). Menzel (1977:8) concluded that during the LIP the Ica Valley was, similar to the Pisco Valley, an independent polity and not controlled by Chincha.

Nazca

In comparison to Ica and Chincha, the Río Grande de Nazca region is generally perceived as uncentralized and peripheral during the LIP (Clarkson 1990:126; Engel 1981; Menzel 1959, 1976). Nazca is thought to have had little political centralization, primarily because there are no LIP sites with monumental architecture and Ica-style pottery is found at many settlements in the drainage. In addition, ethnohistorical accounts tell of little resistance to the Inca, implying a lack of regional integration and political power. In her study of the Inca occupation of the south coast, Menzel (1959) points out that it was necessary for the Inca to established two administrative centers in the Río Grande de Nazca drainage because local centers were absent; this is comparable to the situation she reported in the Pisco Valley. Menzel argues that the Inca adopted this strategy when they encountered a region with a poorly developed infrastructure and without elites to aid in local administration. However, archaeological data collected from survey and excavation, and an analysis of the LIP and LH Nazca ceramic tradition, indicate the drainage was the home of an integrated regional polity that was politically independent from Ica and Chincha.

Although Robinson (1957) explicitly identified pervasive, local, late prehispanic styles in the Río Grande de Nazca drainage, some researchers argue that the ceramic tradition of Nazca is the same as that found in the Ica and Chincha valleys. The ceramics found at late prehispanic sites in the drainage have been called Ica/Chincha despite the fact that the Ica style is an entirely different style from that of Chincha (Menzel 1966). In addition, analysis of ceramics from excavations at the small village of Pajonal Alto reveals that, although elements of the Ica style were used in Nazca, the local style is independent (Conlee 2000, 2002). Also there are few aspects of the Chincha style in the Nazca LIP or LH ceramic tradition so the designation Ica/Chincha is misleading and should not be employed. The Ica ceramic style appears to have been the most prestigious and widespread during late prehispanic times, but it did not stylistically unify the south coast (Conlee 2000, 2002; Menzel 1977; J. Rowe 1956). There appear to have been more similarities in the ceramic styles early in the period, and John Rowe (1956) notes that the styles of the south coast continued to diverge throughout the LIP and LH, lending further support to the argument that the valleys were independent.

Another misconception about the Río Grande de Nazca drainage is that after the Wari collapse the region never returned to a complex level of sociopolitical organization. This is due to the decline in the quality of ceramics and textiles and, again, the lack of monumental architecture. However, archaeological surveys in both the northern and southern drainage reveal that there was an increase in the number and size of sites in the LIP (Browne 1992; Browne and Baraybar 1988; Carmichael 1991; Engel 1981; Proulx 1998; Reindel and Isla 1998; Robinson 1957; Schreiber 1999; Schreiber and Lancho 1995; H. Silverman 1993, 1994). Population during this time was at its highest and there was more aggregation than during any previous period. The main settlement types were large agglutinated villages and towns that contained many internal divisions, although smaller sites including hamlets were also found in the region (Browne 1992; Schreiber and Lancho 1995). In the coastal areas, the first permanent settlements appear to have been established in the LIP and LH, possibly by people specialized in obtaining marine resources (Carmichael 1991:24).

The Río Grande de Nazca drainage is composed of a northern group of valleys (the Santa Cruz, Grande, Viscas, Palpa, Ingenio) and a southern group (Aja, Tierras Blancas, Taruga, Las Trancas). In the north, sites were generally located away from the most fertile and widest part of the valley in defensible positions (Browne 1992:80). One of the largest LIP sites in the northern drainage is Huayurí in the Santa Cruz Valley. There are conflicting reports on the size of the site, from 7 ha (Ojeda 1981) to an estimate of 1 km long and 30–50 m in width (Alfaro de Lanzone 1978). There is a great deal of internal differentiation in architecture at the town and it was probably an important political capital. The settlement is also called

Ciudad Perdida because it is hidden between two hills, and the defensive location of this site may be due to its location in the northernmost part of the drainage on the edge of the pampa that divides the Ica and Nazca drainages. The defensive nature of this site and others in the northern drainage may have stemmed from conflict within the drainage, or it may be a result of a threat from the Ica Valley. The latter contrasts with previous views that attribute the Ica influence found in Nazca during the LIP to Ica's prestige in the region and the desire of other areas to emulate the Ica art style.

In the southern drainage fewer sites are found in defensible locations. Settlement data show a hierarchy of site sizes and a variety of site types indicating the presence of a complex settlement and sociopolitical system (Schreiber 1999; Schreiber and Lancho 1995). The largest documented site in the drainage during the LIP was the town of La Tiza (28 ha) located along the Aja branch of the Nazca Valley (Conlee and Rodríguez 2002). La Tiza was probably the political capital of the southern drainage and it is at least twice as big as the next-largest sites, which are located in the smaller Taruga and Las Trancas valleys, and which may have been secondary centers. The town of La Tiza contains a great diversity of domestic architecture, and this may reflect a complex sociopolitical hierarchy and/or the existence of distinct ethnic groups. The settlement also contains a variety of nondomestic architecture, including ridgetop lookout/ceremonial structures, plazas, cemeteries, and defensive terraces with piles of sling-stones.

Investigations at the small village of Pajonal Alto in the Taruga Valley in the southern drainage revealed that many changes occurred in village life during the LIP (Conlee 2000, 2003). At this village there is a mound and associated plaza that is much smaller than both previous mounds in the region and contemporary ones in Chincha and Ica, reflecting a move away from large regional ritual practices to smaller community- or elite-based practices. There was also evidence of a shift in economic activities, and it appears that communities and households were less self-sufficient than in earlier times with a greater focus on the production of utilitarian items. The identification of elites at this small village was important because little social differentiation was present at earlier village sites in the region. Overall, the evidence from settlement patterns, excavations at Pajonal Alto, and investigations at the large center of La Tiza indicate that a lack of monumental architecture and fine iconography in the late prehispanic period did not coincide with a lack of sociopolitical complexity. Population was at its highest in the region, domestic sites were larger, the likely political center of the drainage had an unprecedented variety of domestic architecture, economic activities flourished, and there appears to have been a more extensive hierarchy of elites.

Acarí

In the 1950s Dorothy Menzel and Francis A. Riddell conducted a survey and excavations in the Acarí and Chala valleys with the express purpose of defining the late period pottery style with a particular focus on the LH (J. Rowe 1956; Menzel and

Riddell 1986). Menzel and Riddell (1986:103) concluded that the Acarí style was on the receiving end of influence that went south from Ica to Nazca to Acarí. Similar to the situation in Nazca, there is no evidence of late prehispanic monumental architecture, but there are some relatively large habitation sites (Menzel 1959). Riddell and colleagues conducted surveys and excavations beginning in the 1980s. They have identified additional late prehispanic sites and have found that during this period there was the largest number of sites in the valley.

The South Central Andean Polities

The late prehispanic period in the south central Andes corresponds to the time after the collapse of the Tiwanaku state around the turn of the first millennium A.D. Tiwanaku was the first and only indigenous state to develop in the Andes south of Cuzco. It began as regional political power around A.D. 600, peaked around A.D. 900, and had collapsed by A.D. 1000. Following its collapse, a number of new political groups emerged. Some of these groups maintained moderately complex chiefly political organizations. They developed distinctive canons on pottery and textiles that were derived from Tiwanaku, and they established regional economic systems that most likely were modifications of Tiwanaku patterns. Other groups were less complex, ranging from egalitarian village societies in economically peripheral areas to simple chiefly societies in much of the region.

Around A.D. 1450, and possibly a generation or so earlier, the Inca Empire advanced into the Titicaca Basin. By A.D. 1500, most of the south-central Andes was under Inca control, or at the very least, posed no strategic threat to Inca hegemony. The Inca state was a great empire controlling over 1 million km^2 in western South America. As with all empires, there was considerable political and economic variation within their provinces. This section, however, will focus largely on the pre-Inca, post-Tiwanaku periods, leaving the region under the Inca to be understood as a territory of an imperial state.

In cultural terms, the south-central Andes is defined as the area of the maximum extent of the influence of the Tiwanaku state at its height. This area generally conforms to the 16th-century distribution of archaic Aymara and Pukina languages. Today, Aymara flourishes as one of the great indigenous languages of Peru and Bolivia. Pukina, on the other hand, is now extinct. Quechua and related languages dominated the central and north-central Andean highlands, with Muchik languages found on the north coast of Peru. In short, at the time of the Spanish conquest and well before, the Central Andes had three separate linguistic areas – the south-central Andes, the north and central highlands, and the coast. Each of these areas had distinctive cultural histories, histories that were submerged into "national" cultures during the periods of Inca and early Spanish political and cultural hegemony.

The demographic and cultural center of the south-central Andes was the Titicaca Basin, located at 3,800 m above sea level in the high Andes on the border between modern Peru and Bolivia. The Titicaca Basin is defined as the hydrological boundary of the lake drainage. Given that it is a high-altitude desert, the limits of water availability largely define the areas of human settlement. Surrounding the Titicaca Basin to the east and the west are two mountain ranges, where human settlement is sparse. To the north is the high mountain pass of La Raya that divides the Titicaca region from the Cuzco area. There is no stark geographical boundary to the south, but there is also very little settlement south of the lake environment away from the rivers. In the far south Titicaca Basin, human settlement is very sparse and rainfall is meager. Therefore, the hydrological limits of the Titicaca Basin generally correspond to the cultural limits of the heartland of the south-central Andes.

The Titicaca Basin covers approximately 50,000 km². In total, the south-central Andes is substantially larger, about 400,000 km². This is about the size of the modern US state of California. In short, the south-central Andes is a huge region that encompasses desert coast, dry mountains, extensive highland grasslands, and tropical forests. A substantial portion of two of the four quarters of the Inca state were located in this area – Collasuyu, located in the southeastern portion of the empire, and Contisuyu, the dry, coastal areas to the southwest Pacific watershed. The south-central Andes can be divided into several cultural-geographical subregions: the immediate Titicaca Basin itself, the Pacific drainages located to the west of the lake, the lowlands located to the east of the lake, the rich agricultural and pasture lands to the north of the lake between the mountains up to La Raya, and the high plains or altiplano located south of the lake basin.

In practice, the Late Intermediate Period, as a chronological marker, is used somewhat differently by most archaeologists working in the south-central Andes than it is used in the rest of the Central Andes. It is defined as the time after the collapse of Tiwanaku and the beginning of Inca influence in the region around A.D. 1450, or possibly earlier. If one uses this definition, the dates of the LIP vary by as much as two centuries. This is because the actual emergence of autonomous polities out of the Tiwanaku collapse was an uneven process, beginning as early as A.D. 900 in the Pacific drainages and not starting until A.D. 1000 or 1100 in the Tiwanaku heartland proper. Likewise, the control of the region by the Inca was a generations-long process. Therefore, defined as the period between the florescence of two states, the dates for the LIP vary by as much as two centuries across the region.

The Titicaca Basin proper

The most complex late prehispanic polities in the entire south-central Andes developed in the Titicaca Basin proper. A number of Aymara "kingdoms" or "señoríos" surrounded the lake. These included the Lupaqa in the west, the Colla to the north, and Pacajes in south. Other smaller groups existed in the east in the Omasuyus area. Good evidence for the nature of that political organization was assumed to be available in historical documents prepared by Spanish Crown officials in the generation or so after the conquest. In 1567, the Spanish authority Garci Diez de San Miguel conducted a tax assessment or "visita" in the Lupaqa region. Lupaqa was a political-ethnic term denoting the groups living on the western and southwestern shores of the lake who recognized the authority of a dual political leadership centered in their capital at Chucuito. Chucuito was located in the western lake edge.

The evidence in the visita of 1567, plus the writings of Cieza de Leon, indicate that a state-level society existed among the Lupaqa in the 16th century, albeit one incorporated into the Spanish and earlier Inca imperial systems. Likewise, in Cieza's *Crónica*, we are told that immediately prior to or during the reign of Viracocha Inca, the Lupaqa and their rivals to the north, the Colla, were fighting each other. Fearing an Inca–Lupaqa alliance, the Colla initiated an attack against the Lupaqa. In the plains of Paucarcolla, between Puno and Juliaca, 150,000 troops were assembled for a great battle between the two great Aymara kingdoms. At this battle, Cieza says that 30,000 died, including the Colla king, and it was a decisive victory for the Lupaqa. Viracocha Inca was very disappointed in being unable to take advantage of the conflict and the battle permitted the Lupaqa to become a major political power in the Titicaca Basin (Cieza 1976:219). While the number of troops is almost certainly an exaggeration, the essence of the account is most likely accurate.

In these accounts, there are a number of suggestions that the Lupaqa and Colla were very powerful kingdoms with state levels of organization. For instance, following the battle, the king of the Lupaqa, known as Cari, returned to Chucuito. Cieza's account of what followed next is most intriguing. He says that Cari graciously received the Inca Viracocha at Chucuito, where they both drank from a golden goblet. The Inca offered a daughter to Cari and an alliance was sealed. What is significant here is that this is an extremely rare occasion in the chronicles that actually suggested an equal power relationship between the Inca and a major rival. In fact, in one reading of Cieza's account, the Inca lost the battle and Inca Viracocha had to settle for an equitable alliance between his young empire and the Lupaqa. In this account, we get a sense that the Lupaqa were as great as the Inca in power and authority in this early period of Inca expansion. They were a power that the Inca had to reckon with and a power that may have even stopped the advance of the Inca Empire until the ascension of Viracocha's son, Pachacuti.

That the Aymara kingdoms during the pre-Inca periods were state societies was the accepted model of Lupaqa political structure for years (e.g., Murra 1968; Pease 1973). However, more recent archaeological research and a reinterpretation of the documents does not support this model (Frye 1994; Stanish 1989a, 2003). These new data suggest that the pre-Inca polities were not integrated at a state-level society, and that the political structure suggested in Garci Diez de San Miguel's visita was largely the creation of the Inca state perpetuated by the Lupaqa elite in order to enhance their legal position in the Spanish courts (Stanish 2000). Apart from the massive labor used to build the large fortresses, or pukaras, that dot the landscape, there is no evidence for a complex political organization of the pre-Inca Lupaqa beyond that of either segmentary chiefdoms or complex chiefly societies. Unlike the earlier Tiwanaku state and the later Inca one, the Lupaqa produced none of the markers of state organization characteristic of other Andean polities.

Settlement pattern analysis indicates no substantial site size hierarchy, with the exception of the large pukaras, and these were not permanently occupied. The lack of elite ceramics and typical nucleated settlement patterns (seen in the pre-Tiwanaku and Tiwanaku periods) all further suggest that the LIP Lupaqa was not a state-level society. Above-ground chullpa tombs, traditionally interpreted to be indications of elite organization, are in fact quite common and are best interpreted as the common funerary mode for ayllu and/or other social groups. The large, truly rare and elite chullpa tombs are, in fact, almost all post-LIP in date.

The archaeological data therefore support the argument that the 16th-century Lupaqa state organization was a result of Inca reorganization, and not a pre-Inca, autochthonous development. Fieldwork by Kirk Frye near the Lupaqa capital of Chucuito also supports this argument. According to Frye, the LIP Lupaqa were "small-scale political groups most likely organized at the level of what evolutionary anthropologists have referred to as simple chiefdoms" (Frye 1997:137).

The conclusions for the pre-Inca Lupaqa also appear to hold for the Colla, the other powerful polity in the Titicaca Basin. Research in the southern areas of the Titicaca Basin, known as the Pacajes, also supports this model of the "Altiplano Period" political organization. In other words, the prevailing model of pre-Inca, post-Tiwanaku political economic complexity is one of smaller, autonomous societies organized around major pukaras and/or other fortified settlement clusters. They were not state-level societies; rather, they were only moderately ranked societies with little evidence of elite groups or socio-economic differentiation.

The Pacific watershed polities

The limits of Tiwanaku influence in the coastal drainages reach to approximately the Majes River in the north, and to the San Pedro de Atacama oasis in northern Chile. Human occupation in this area is as old as almost anywhere in the Andes, going back well into the Palaeo-Indian or Lithic period. There was considerable diversity in political organization during the later prehistory of the Pacific watersheds. The most complex societies developed in the Arequipa (upper Majes) area, the Moquegua coast and northern Chile in Azapa. Without exception, each of these complex polities shows direct relationships to the earlier Tiwanaku cultures in iconography and settlement continuities.

The principal Tiwanaku-derived cultures of the Pacific watershed include the Churajon complex in the Arequipa area, the Chiribaya in the Moquegua valley, and the San Miguel/Gentilar cultures of northern Chile. By far, the best-known of these is Chiribaya. Chiribaya is a coastal-focused polity. The main sites of Algarrobal and Chiribaya Alta are found near the coast along the river (Owen 1993). However, Chiribaya sites are found throughout the Moquegua drainage as high as the Otora Valley at 3,200 m above sea level. A major Chiribaya settlement is located at around 1,000 m at the site of Yaral. Likewise, a number of Chiribaya materials have been discovered in the modern town of Moquegua, located at 1,500 m in the richest part of the valley. In particular, the site of Maria Cupina contained a number of Chiribaya materials. Rescue work conducted at the site suggests a settlement a bit smaller than, but roughly the same site size rank as, the largest Chiribaya sites on the coast.

In short, the Chiribaya polity incorporated almost all of the ecological zones in the valley, from the coast to the sierra.

The Chiribaya peoples created a chiefly society with centers on the coast and in the mid-valley area near Moquegua. They established settlements up and down the valley. This pattern permitted access to goods ranging from marine products to highland goods. Exchange was most certainly brisk between these settlements, conducted via social mechanisms of reciprocity and redistribution. For well over three centuries, probably more, Chiribaya groups successfully lived in and exploited this large region with a political organization less complex than a state.

Given our present data, the Chiribaya pattern is the best model for the other valleys in the Pacific watershed. Arequipa remains poorly known. We do know that some substantial sites are found in the region. In particular, the site of Churajon represents a large settlement with substantial stone architecture. Churajon pottery styles also fit within the Tricolor del Sur tradition, although the links to Tiwanaku are less than in Chiribaya. Churajon appears to be a Chiribaya-type pattern on a larger scale, reflecting the much larger resource base in the Arequipa area. At the present time, we conclude that Chiribaya was a chiefly society of great extent that existed throughout the lower and upper Majes drainage.

Stretching across the mid-sierras from the Tambo River in the north to the Locumba River in the south was a partially contemporary culture known as Estuquiña. Estuquiña sites developed around A.D. 900–1000 and continued up to the Inca conquest around A.D. 1450. Estuquiña culture is less complex than Chiribaya. Settlements are uniformly located on hilltops and are fortified. Complex pottery styles are virtually nonexistent, although a vigorous domestic pottery production continued. Estuquiña sites are strikingly similar in size. There is a clear catchment distribution with sites located in geographically discrete areas of high resources. There is, therefore, no site size hierarchy at all. Likewise, there is no evidence of any corporate architecture. Exchange was brisk with both the coast and the altiplano (Stanish 1985). Like Chiribaya, it most likely mediated through social mechanisms of redistribution and reciprocity. Evidence of feasting includes large quantities of grinding stones and serving vessels on Estuquiña sites. Our best model to date suggests that Estuquiña peoples were organized as simple chiefly or very moderately ranked societies with minimal political hierarchies.

The eastern lowlands

The eastern slopes of the south-central Andes actually lie in the Amazonian drainage. This is a virtually unknown area archaeologically, with the exception of a few reports and some brief reconnaissances (e.g. Neira 1962, 1967). One reasonably published site is known as Iskanwaya, located in the Larecaja region in Bolivia. This site is exceptionally well preserved. Two-story structures cover an area of at least several hectares. There are some open areas on the site that could have functioned as walled public plazas. Likewise, there are possibly some undressed stone stelae. The pottery of the region, known as Mollo, is executed in Tiwanaku-derived styles. Other sites of such size and complexity are found throughout the region, obscured by the vegetation. We simply have too little evidence to propose any reasonable models of the political organization of this area. However, the absence of any large sites at the present, plus the absence of any polychrome pottery style substantially distinct from the derived Tiwanaku types that are found in the west, argue against the existence of any complex, state society in the region at this time. Rather, a model of complex chiefly organization would be the best model that we can propose at this time.

In the Carabaya area to the northeast corner of the south-central Andes, reconnaissance by Larry Coben and Charles Stanish (in press) indicates that there is a huge number of post-Tiwanaku settlements along the major river drainages. These sites follow a road into the forest. Many of these sites are quite extensive. They are all hillside terraces sites, but there is no evidence of corporate architecture. Pottery styles are exclusively domestic, and they are linked to the northern Titicaca Basin, suggesting that there was a brisk exchange from the lowland to the altiplano. Apart from these data, there is little information that we can use to define the political organization of the eastern slopes of this period. However, there is nothing to suggest a political organization more complex than chiefdoms.

Northern Titicaca Basin

There has been little research in the northern Titicaca Basin until recently. The historical documents refer to groups of people known as the Canas and Canchis that lived between the Collas to the south and the Cuzco area peoples north of the La Raya pass. We know that there are abundant pukaras or fortresses throughout the region that most likely date to the LIP. Recent work by Elizabeth Arkush has identified several dozen of these fortified sites throughout the north. Likewise, systematic research in the region indicates a huge LIP and LH occupation in the north.

Pacajes to the south

The people of the southern Pacajes region during the LIP were known as the Pacajes. This term refers to different ethnic groups that inhabited the region. Archaeological research is sparse, except for the Tiwanaku valley. The work and informal reconnaissance projects indicate that there are far fewer pukaras or fortified sites in this area. The chullpa burial tower tradition, in contrast, is very strong, with scores of sites with numerous burial towers from the LIP and Inca periods. Populations were very dense in the Tiwanaku valley during the LIP. There were equally high population densities along the lake edge. To the southeast of the lake, pastoral economies flourished in the LIP. Settlements were much less dense in the regions away from the lake, unlike other areas of the Titicaca Basin.

Conclusions

Both the Lambayeque and Chimú polities dominated the landscape of the north coast during the LIP. Each had a unique political organization and each polity emphasized different aspects of its political and ideological agenda. Yet they coexisted for several hundred years, possibly because of economic interdependence and a shared cultural heritage that can be traced to the last phases of Moche. It does not appear that Lambayeque was ever a centralized state, nor did it have a four-tiered settlement hierarchy. The Lambayeque centers emphasized the sacred and ceremonial and manifested these concepts in their monumental temple/pyramids. The sacred centers scattered throughout the Lambayeque core area seem to conform to the pilgrimage/shrine model analogous to Pachacamac (Burger 1988; Keatinge 1977). Unlike Pachacamac, however, the Lambayeque ceremonial centers were underwritten by a strong economic foundation since they held a monopoly on the access to materials and the production of objects that were deemed essential, especially by the rival Chimú.

The Chimú achieved the first north coast centralized state and the architecture of their central place underscored the power of the monarchs. Although the monumental enclosures appear more secular than the pyramids of Lambayeque, it should not be assumed that religion was unimportant since it probably played a major role in the legitimization of the king and the expansion of the state. The Chimú capital, in comparison with the Lambayeque centers, demonstrated greater complexity in social hierarchy and occupational groups, but certainly less than found during the subsequent Inca period. A key element of the Chimú power base was the centralization and accumulation of wealth at the capital. Their economic system was built upon the accumulation of goods to be used in a redistribution system that was crucial in establishing and cementing political relationships. Like other archaic states, the Chimú maintained their power by employing great flexibility in their governing strategy, choosing joint rule in some areas but not in others depending upon the area conquered and native resources. The north coast, during the LIP, offers a great potential to view complex polities exercising alternative modes of power.

On the central coast, the analysis of the variation in design, location, orientation and size of the pyramids with ramps at Pachacamac and other sites allows us to suggest that the groups that built and used these structures could have been organized in a very similar way to the early colonial parcialidades of the central coast and north coast. Several lines of evidence allow us to suggest that two of the principles that governed the lower-level units' aggregation into higher-level units were probably the territorial location of these units in relation to the hydraulic systems and the belonging of the unit to one or other half within a dual organization system. However, the way in which these principles governed not only the progressive aggregation of the lower-level units into higher-level units but also their progressive hierarchical distinction needs to be clarified ethnohistorically and archaeologically.

Research into the late prehispanic societies of the south coast has often focused on the Chincha and Ica valleys and has been heavily guided by historical accounts. While this emphasis has provided important and interesting information about prehispanic life in the region, more recent archaeological projects have begun to present a new and more complex perspective of the region during this time.

The situation in the south-central Andes was extremely complex in the LIP. In the Titicaca Basin there were a number of independent societies of varying sociopolitical complexity and organization. Of particular importance is the revision to traditional understanding of the LIP Lupaqa, who now appear to have been organized as segmentary chiefdoms or complex chiefly societies.

Although various scholars have written synthetically of the cultural movements underwriting the great Andean horizon manifestations (Chavín, Wari, Tiwanaku, Inca), comparative syntheses of the intermediate periods, early or late, are rare in the literature. Even this brief overview of the better-known LIP polities reveals a tremendous range of sociopolitical organization and its spatial correlates. Such a view makes the subsequent Inca achievement of rapid areal integration all the more noteworthy.

12

Knowing the Inca Past

Juha Hiltunen and Gordon F. McEwan

Introduction

Throughout the past decade Andean research has been in a state of "fermentation" and a major paradigm shift is currently underway. The integrated use of a number of new techniques generated by archaeology, archaeoastronomy, palaeolinguistics, genetics, climatology, and chemistry has greatly increased our understanding of the Andean prehistoric past. In addition, many structural-functionalist concepts prevalent during the second half of the 20th century are being challenged, and the historicist strategy expounded by scholars such as Philip A. Means, John H. Rowe, and Burr C. Brundage, which prevailed in Andean studies half a century ago, is being reconsidered under a so-called neo-historicist viewpoint that draws on new perspectives in archaeology and ethnohistory to contend that ancient oral traditions contain much useful historical information. The neo-historicist research strategy seeks to locate correspondences between the structural-functionalist and historicist viewpoints.

The ongoing paradigm shift in Andean studies also may be due to the influence of research results and models from Mesoamerican studies. Mesoamerican ethnohistoric research has always been more extensive than Andeanist, a fact which is directly related to the quantity and nature of basic research source material. There is much more surviving written material in colonial and, notably, precolumbian documents and texts in Mesoamerica than in the Andes. There was no true writing system in the Andes prior to the arrival of the Spanish, notwithstanding recent interpretations of the quipu (see Quilter and Urton 2002) and the tocapu pictograms. And in the Andes almost all surviving ethnohistories were written in Spanish chronicles relatively late after the conquest, when the processes of acculturation and colonial efforts at eliminating ancient traditions were well under way. Most of these stories were based on oral traditions, as elsewhere in the Americas.

The achievements of Mesoamerican research highlight the need to pursue more multiform research strategies in the field of Andean studies. In the course of this process broad new approaches to ethnohistory and the exploitation of mythohis-torical narratives can be taken. Moreover, auxiliary disciplines, such as linguistics and archaeology, allow us to test ancient sources with promising new results.

Catherine Julien (2000) has recently proposed a number of interesting questions concerning new interpretations of Inca history from the ethnohistoric perspective. She has made an analysis of the content of all principal chronicles of Inca history, and concludes that their content reflects to a great extent the historical tradition of the Incas in the way that they themselves wanted to narrate and express it. Her interpretation contradicts the structuralist viewpoint which claims that the histori-cal narratives recorded in the Spanish chronicles were strongly influenced by European concepts and propaganda. According to structuralist thinking, the native Andean peoples did not have a concept and idea of history in the European sense.

Before making a new attempt at understanding the Inca past, it is necessary to present the prevailing ideas of Inca dynastic structure. During the last half of the 20th century, with the rise of structuralist thinking, dualist (e.g., Zuidema 1964 inter alia) and triadist (e.g., Pärssinen 1992) models have gained ground, and almost completely replaced the traditional unilineal dynastic model. However, a group of scholars has turned anew toward the latter, historicist viewpoint. As Julien has pointed out, the structuralist models markedly contradict traditional ideas that overwhelmingly predominate in the written records comprising ethnohistorical documents and chronicles.

History as the Incas Presented It

On the eve of the Spanish conquest, 1532, the Incas believed that they dominated the entire world. Certainly they dominated the western part of the South Ameri-can continent (the world as they knew it) and, from a global perspective, this empire was the second or third largest in the world at that time. More important than the actual extent of their empire was the Inca ideology of world dominion, which was a common concept and doctrine of many historic conquest states. The Incas presented themselves as "Children of Sun," to whom the solar deity gave a mandate to govern other peoples of the world. This doctrine was taught in the royal school (yachaywasi) in Cuzco to young noble students of both the provinces and metro-politan area with the intention that the graduates of this program would promote it in their future leadership positions. A single canonic official form of Inca history was adopted for the empire. Interestingly, this canonic history appears in two basic versions in the Spanish written sources: one in which the cave of Pacariqtambo appears as the Inca place of origin, and another, in which the Inca origin location is Lake Titicaca. These stories were compiled by the Spanish conquerors based on interviews conducted with surviving Incas.

Most accounts stated that the first Inca emperor was created by the Sun God and emerged with his brothers and sisters from the three caves called Tambo Tocco near a place called Pacariqtambo close to Cuzco. After a series of adventures the first Inca, Manco Capac, led his followers into the valley of Cuzco, conquered the local inhabitants, and set up the Inca state. The gist of this origin story is that the Incas were basically supermen specially created and chosen by the Sun God to rule the earth. They essentially invented Andean culture and civilized the barbarian tribes that had existed until then. All of the marvelous things that the Spanish encountered were attributed to the Incas. In Spanish colonial times a small town about 26 km south of Cuzco became identified as Pacariqtambo, the official origin place of the Inca dynasty. Recent scholarship has shown that this identification came about largely because of political jockeying among surviving Incas in the colonial period (Urton 1990).

The second version of the Inca origin story states that the Incas were created by the Sun God on an island in Lake Titicaca. The Incas migrated northward to Cuzco and conquered the locals they found there in order to set up their state. At least the Inca elite knew that in the region of sacred Lake Titicaca an earlier civilization had existed. This was the ancient dominion of Tiwanaku, source of a number of contributions to Inca statecraft. In certain versions of this Inca origin legend the name Tiwanaku is actually mentioned. In other sources, the myth of Pacariqtambo and the Titicaca origin legend were intertwined, a fact that could reflect the original canonization of the story by the Incas. Before taking a closer look at how the stories possibly served official Inca historical thinking and political propaganda, we must present one more version of the Inca origin story. In this case only one major source for the story has survived, the chronicle of the Spanish cleric Fernando de Montesinos.

The Story of the Ancient Kings

Fernando de Montesinos was a Spaniard who apparently belonged to the Jesuit Order. He spent 15 years in Peru, acting as a secretary, judge, inspector, and cleric. While there he engaged in intensive historical research that resulted, in 1642, in a three-volume work, entitled *Ophir de España* or *Memorias Antiguas Historiales y Políticas del Perú* (as the second volume in particular has been known).

The story of the Incas told by Montesinos differs significantly from the other major Spanish chronicles, especially in its narrative of preceding dynasties who ruled Peru before the Incas. Another peculiarity of this story is its references to ancient writing skills of the Peruvians, and finally Montesinos' view of the historical context, which was interlocked with the Bible and the notion of descent of the Peruvian dynasties from Ophir, the great-grandson of Noah. Because of these peculiarities, ever since its first publication in 1840 most scholars have neglected the value of Montesinos' chronicle as a historical source. Hiltunen's recent work (1999) is the first volume on Montesinos – his works and historiography – to appear in book form during the entire 150 years of Montesinian research. His study is the first large-scale document analysis to comprehensively use ethnography, archaeology, and palaeolinguistics. Hiltunen suggests that there may be considerable historical validity to Montesinos' account. Especially interesting are new data from the archaeological site of Chokepukio, in the Cuzco Valley, which lend support to Montesinos' account. Before entering into a discussion of the evidence from excavations at Chokepukio and how the data correspond with the story told by Montesinos, it is necessary to present an overall idea of Montesinos' Inca and pre-Inca history.

According to Montesinos the Incas were dynastic latecomers who settled in Cuzco and took their ideas of government from earlier cultures. In this story, their first ruler, Inca Roca, actually descended from the last king of a preceding dynasty referred to by Montesinos as the Tampu Tocco dynasty. Before the Tampu Tocco dynasty there was an earlier line of kings called amautas, because of their wisdom (amauta means "wise man" in Quechua). The "Golden Age" of the empire of these amautas occurred long ago and extended far and wide. Their rule collapsed in a furious attack from the south (i.e., present-day Bolivia). The survivors of the amauta elite took refuge in a place called Tampu Tocco, and little by little succeeded in revitalizing their rule locally in the Cuzco region as the Tampu Tocco dynasty. Finally this revived government also collapsed, and after a relatively short interregnum the Incas appeared on the historical stage. The Tampu Tocco dynasty has a key role in connecting ethnohistory to archaeological data and is the topic of this chapter.

The Dynasty of Tampu Tocco and Chokepukio

The names and sites of Tampu Tocco, Pacariqtambo, and Tampu have often been used interchangeably in Andean research and chronicles. All are related to Inca origins. The site of Tampu Tocco occurs in Montesinos' chronicle as a seat of decadent amauta rulers, but without exact reference to its location, except its nearness to Cuzco. Nevertheless, some scholars have attempted to locate the site of Montesinos' Tampu Tocco. Perhaps the best-known attempts were made by Hiram Bingham (1915, 1922) and Luis Pardo (1946, 1957). Bingham proposed that Tampu Tocco was Machu Picchu, while Pardo concluded that the site was located around the ruins of Maucallacta, in the modern province of Paruro.

Recent excavations carried out by Gordon McEwan and his colleagues Arminda Gibaja and Melissa Chatfield (1995, 2000, 2002) in the Lucre Basin of the Cuzco Valley have suggested interesting new possibilities for locating the site of Tampu Tocco. It now appears that the site of Chokepukio is a likely candidate. Here we argue that the story narrated by Montesinos is informative for understanding Chokepukio and vice versa.

According to Montesinos' text, after an epic battle at the Vilcanota pass, in which the last emperor of the amautas proper, Titu Yupanqui Pachacuti VI, was killed, the amauta empire collapsed. Provinces rose in rebellion and invaders poured into its southern parts. A few members of the amauta elite were able to escape to a place called Tampu Tocco, and there a very young heir of the last emperor was installed as king and founded the new dynasty of Tampu Tocco. During the first reigns of this new dynasty, the territory all around Tampu Tocco was in political turmoil, until a king called Tupac Cauri came to rule. He seems to have been a usurper from an outside group who inserted himself into the Tampu Tocco dynasty. He and his successors were able to gain ground and establish a regional hegemony. Eventually, however, the reign of the Tampu Tocco kings came to an end and their rule collapsed. This collapse seems to have been precipitated by the invasion of yet another outside group. These people probably are the Pinaguas and the Moynas mentioned in the Spanish chronicles.

After an interval of warfare and confusion, a hero of the next historical act appeared on the scene. His name was Inca Roca. His equally courageous and influential mother, Mama Siuacu, was no less than a daughter of the last ruler in the Tampu Tocco dynasty. By using the still existing prestige of the previous dynasty as a political springboard, the mother and son together re-created the basis of an ancient regime, and eventually oversaw the birth of a new one which became the empire of the Incas. The account in the narrative explicitly states that the idea of statecraft was inherited by the Incas from their dynastic predecessors.

We can calculate the approximate absolute chronology of some of these events by examining the king lists given by Montesinos (and see J. Rowe 1945). The number of kings in the Tampu Tocco dynasty is given as 26–28 (a slight difference occurs between the surviving copies of the manuscript). Hiltunen (1993, 1999) has noticed that dynasties of 13 to 35 successions contain an average span of 16.5 years, while in multiple macro-dynasties this reduces to 14.8 years. Therefore the duration of Tampu Tocco rule could be calculated to be 445 (27 × 16.5) years.

If we accept Montesinos' account as historical, then using these figures we can calculate the time of the usurpation resulting in Tupac Cauri's reign and place it within an absolute chronology. According to Montesinos, Tupac Cauri was the fourteenth or sixteenth king of the dynasty; we can use the fifteenth king as a reference point. Further calculations require a relatively well-founded fixed date on which we can base time measurements. Modern scholarship has long accepted the dates given by Cabello de Balboa (1951[1586]) as the most plausible ones in building up a regnal span chronology for the imperial period Incas (i.e., A.D. 1438–1532, the reigns of Pachacuti through Huascar). Dynastic chronology antedating Inca Pachacutec has been a more complicated issue, but at least a few preceding reigns could be calculated with reasonable probability by using available references from the chronicles. All sources agree that the immediate predecessor of Pachacuti, Inca Viracocha, had an exceptionally long reign. Many sources refer to 50 years or more (including Cabello). Montesinos has given 45 years for the length of this reign. Brundage (1967) instead has accepted A.D. 1400 as the most plausible accession date for this ruler (allowing only 38 years). We assume that the beginnings of Inca Viracocha's reign very likely occurred somewhere between A.D. 1390 and 1400, based on information in Cabello and Montesinos.

We may use our ethnohistorical references as a basis of building up a relative regnal span chronology. Hiltunen (1981, 1993, 1999) has made and revised these calculations in his studies to suggest the most likely regnal spans for Inca Roca, Yahuar Huacac, and Inca Viracocha. Of these, the early sources agree that both Viracocha and Inca Roca had long reigns, but Yahuar Huacac's rule was relatively short. We are presently inclined to accept Montesinos' figure of 45 years for Viracocha's rule, which according to the generally accepted termination date of his reign (A.D. 1438) sets his accession around A.D. 1393. Yahuar Huacac's length of reign has been calculated at 15–20 years and Inca Roca's at 25–30 years. The result, therefore, is the dynastic beginnings of the Hanan-Cuzcos (Late Inca kings) around A.D. 1350. There is also an interesting reference in Montesinos' chronicle that could provide confirmation for this date. According to him, two remarkable comets appeared in the sky during the reign of Inca Capac Yupanqui (predecessor of Inca Roca) and in fact, two significant comets were seen in the year 1337.

Some sources and scholars tend to interpret the dynastic change between the Hurin/Early and Hanan/Late kings as a violent incident, and consequently Inca Roca as a usurper. We share this view.

The beginning of the reign of Inca Roca and Hanan-Cuzco rule apparently occurred around A.D. 1350. The end of the previous Tampu Tocco dynasty was not much earlier according to Montesinos' history. According to Montesinos the inter-regnum between the end of Tampu Tocco rule and the emergence of Inca Roca was about one hundred years. Hiltunen's study of Montesinos has indicated that Montesinos' chronology has a tendency to double the lengths of some time periods. This was also noticed by Markham (1920) and Means (1920). The "doubled" 100 years therefore could be around 50 years in reality. It is also significant that clima-tological studies indicate that at about this same time, A.D. 1245–1310, the Central Andes suffered a severe drought (Kolata 1993). No doubt this was a major factor in political changes and migrations of people. The end of Tampu Tocco rule most likely occurred at that time and when the Pinagua-Muynas appeared on the scene.

During this period the Lady Mama Siuacu, descendant of the last Tampu-Tocco ruler, gave birth to Inca Roca, and raised him to adulthood. Interestingly, the story indicates only that the mother of Inca Roca was a descendant of the previous lineage, leaving open the question of who his father was. It is therefore possible that the father of Inca Roca came from another ethnic group or dynasty, possibly the Pinagua-Muyna. From the foregoing it may be assumed that the end of the Tampu Tocco dynasty occurred around A.D. 1300, a date that can be used as a chrono-logical fixed point in further calculations.

The duration of the Tampu Tocco rule according to our calculations is around 445 years. By counting backwards from A.D. 1300 its beginnings should be placed around A.D. 855. From the latter, a count of 15 (×16.5 years) reigns sets the begin-nings of Tupac Cauri's reign around A.D. 1102.

In summary then, we interpret Montesinos narrative to indicate that three sig-nificant regime changes occurred at Tampu Tocco during the centuries preceding the accession of Inca Roca. The first of these occurred around A.D. 855 with the establishment of the Tampu Tocco dynasty. The second occurred around A.D. 1102 when Tupac Cauri usurped the throne. The third occurred around A.D. 1300 with the end of the Tampu Tocco dynasty and an assumption of power by the Pinagua-Muyna. Interestingly, archaeological data have revealed that profound changes occurred at Chokepukio at these same times.

Archaeological Evidence in the Cuzco Valley

In terms of the archaeology of the Cuzco region it is clear that the Incas did not just suddenly appear out of nowhere. It is now evident that around A.D. 600 the

Wari Empire conquered the Cuzco area and built there the two largest Wari imperial settlements (other than their capital in Ayacucho): these are the Pikillacta complex in the Lucre Basin of the Cuzco Valley and the Huaro complex which is 15 km further east in the Vilcanota Valley (McEwan 1991, 1994, 1996, 1998; Glowacki and McEwan 2002).

The Wari Empire occupied the Cuzco Valley and region for several hundred years and had a tremendous cultural impact. Importantly, during this time there is very little evidence of any interaction between Cuzco and the Titicaca Basin which was the homeland of the Tiwanaku state. Very few classic Tiwanaku ceramics have been found in the Cuzco area. This may be due to a hostile relationship between the Wari and Tiwanaku states.

The end of the Wari occupation at Chokepukio is marked by the burial of some Wari temples and the complete razing of a number of very large buildings on the site. These were dismantled leaving only their foundations. On the surface above these foundations, new structures were built that seem to have functioned as halls for ancestor worship. The first building phase of these large niched halls can be radiocarbon dated to have begun between A.D. 1045 and 1105. These buildings contain elaborate hydraulic works and small sunken courts, rows of large niches, and in the walls of some of the buildings are human burials. Many of these burials are secondary, representing the interment of skeletal remains rather than fleshed bodies. Preliminary mitochondrial DNA analysis of human remains in the wall tombs indicates that some share a common ancestor and thus may represent a lineage. Even more significant is the fact that DNA studies show that some of these human remains are related to the Aymara ethnic group of Bolivia.

A second building phase at Chokepukio is radiocarbon dated to have begun in the early 1300s and continued into the 1400s. This phase continued the tradition of large niched temples but seems to add new spaces through agglutination. These spaces possibly served as elite residences. They give a more defensive character to the site and entrances in the architecture of this new phase were protected by lookouts in the walls.

After the end of Wari influence in Cuzco, somewhere between A.D. 850 and 1100, there is evidence of a vigorous new group of people. They built large temples at Chokepukio, which was a major center until about A.D. 1450 when it probably was abandoned with the founding of the Inca Empire. Associated with this new construction and all of the subsequent buildings of the Late Intermediate Period are two ceramic styles that archaeologists have named the Lucre and K'illke styles. The Lucre style seems to predominate among the ceremonial and feasting ceramics but K'illke is also well represented. The Lucre style shows some clear affinities with the preceding Wari styles in vessel form and polychrome decoration. Head ornaments painted on Lucre face-neck vessels, however, show similarities to the ornaments peculiar to Collasuyu (the southern Inca province including the Titicaca Basin) that are depicted in the drawings of Guaman Poma (1980).

The K'illke style does not seem to show much if any influence from the Wari or other outside groups. It appears to develop out of the local regional Middle Horizon ceramic style called Qotacalli that may be related to the pre-Wari Huarpa style of the Wari heartland in Ayacucho.

A particular type of drinking tumbler with distinctive handle forms also appears at Chokepukio at this time. This tumbler is almost identical to tumblers of the Late Intermediate Period Mollo culture at the site of Iskanwaya in northern Bolivia (Arellano Lopez 1985). This form has no local antecedents and appears to be intrusive at Chokepukio.

At present it is unclear what the Lucre and K'illke styles represent in social terms. They possibly reflect two different ethnicities but could also represent some other phenomenon such as two centers of ceramic production serving a widespread number of ethnic groups or political units. We presently have a large spectrum of material culture that we can associate with the Lucre style, including architecture, metal work, lithics, lapidary and bone work. None of these artifact classes is uniquely associated with pure K'illke contexts in the Cuzco Valley. Settlement pattern information is also lacking that could distinguish these two styles as belonging to separate cultures. Regional survey of the western part of the Cuzco Valley may help to resolve some of these questions (e.g., Bauer and Covey 2002). But due to the historical peculiarities of Inca, Spanish, and modern urban renewal of that region of Cuzco what is needed most is an intensive excavation sampling strategy combined with an integrated multi-disciplinary approach to data interpretation. This will facilitate discrimination of the remains of the Lucre and K'illke occupations as well as several other ethnic groups mentioned by the chronicles as occupying the region during the Late Intermediate Period. Technologically, at least, it can be said that the Lucre and K'illke styles represent two different potting traditions (Chatfield 1998).

One other major change that occurred in the Cuzco region during the Late Intermediate Period was mortuary in nature: the introduction of burying certain individuals in chullpas or burial towers. There are over 45 chullpas known in the Lucre Basin with a number of these occurring on the site of Chokepukio. Chullpas are unknown for the Wari culture so these structures appear to be a post-Middle Horizon introduction. A few have been dated by radiocarbon to the Late Intermediate Period. Stylistically the chullpas closely resemble those found in southern Peru and Bolivia.

Who were the Incas in terms of the preceding scenario? Were they locals who were influenced by outside empires (i.e., Wari and Tiwanaku) from whom they learned statecraft? Were they remnants of the collapsed Wari Empire? Or were they a group that migrated northward from the seat of the Tiwanaku Empire in Bolivia when it collapsed around A.D. 1100?

The manuscript by Montesinos suggests that some migration occurred north toward Cuzco from the Tiwanaku area after the collapse of Montesinos' amauta empire. Elsewhere, Hiltunen (1999) has argued that the amauta dynasty most likely represents the rulers of the Wari Empire and that their survivors established the first dynasty at Tampu Tocco. It is possible that later a new lineage moved north from the Titicaca Basin in Bolivia and usurped power by inserting itself into the Tampu Tocco dynasty with the accession of the king, Tupac Cauri. At Chokepukio there is an influx of new elites, presumably rulers, who can be radiocarbon dated to around A.D. 1000–1100. These people brought with them elements of foreign ceramic styles, new burial architecture (chullpas), and possibly the remains of their royal ancestors which were buried in the niched walls of newly constructed temples. Monumental architecture continued to be constructed through at least two major building phases until around A.D. 1400–1450, at which time we begin to see imperial Inca buildings and artifacts at the site. The data seem to indicate that the group at Chokepukio eventually joined with their immediate neighbors at the northwestern end of the Cuzco Valley to become one of the two moiety divisions (Hanan-Hurin) of the royal Inca line (Chatfield 1998; McEwan, Chatfield and Gibaja 2002; McEwan, Gibaja and Chatfield 1995). If this is true, then the Incas (or at least a large and important part of them) did in fact come from Lake Titicaca to the south just as the legend suggests, and not from the traditional origin place of Pacariqtambo. It also may turn out to be the case, as suggested, that Tampu Tocco is Chokepukio. In the Quechua language Tampu Tocco refers to caves, but in the Aymara language, spoken by the peoples around Lake Titicaca, it can refer to niches. When the Incas said that they came out of Tampu Tocco they may have referred to the fact that the ancestors from whom they sprang were physically in the walls of the temples of Tampu Tocco (Chokepukio).

By the time of the Inca Empire, from approximately A.D. 1450 onward, the site of Chokepukio again undergoes a profound change. The end of the last pre-Inca occupation at Chokepukio is marked by the closure of several huacas through ceremonial acts. The huacas were provided with offerings of foodstuffs in the form of sacrificed camelids and guinea pigs, and beverages (likely chicha) that were placed in jars sealed with gypsum plaster. The huacas were then buried and a feast apparently was held on the surface above them. This feasting activity resulted in the breakage of quantities of polychrome ceramics (tumblers and serving bowls). Many of the large niched temples and associated structures appear to have been abandoned and the roofs were burned. A radiocarbon date from the burned roofs suggests that this abandonment probably took place no later than A.D. 1460. Those structures not destroyed were converted to other uses by the Incas. Evidence from excavation suggests that the site was no longer a center of religious and political power. The Incas built a village on the site that housed people engaged in at least two manufacturing functions: making ceramics and textiles. Their buildings were comparatively small, with shallow foundations suggesting that they were erected hastily and without much care. Although the Inca population was substantial, no monumental buildings were erected and there are no signs of elite-status residences. Finally, the Inca occupation is also marked by the introduction of a new imperial ceramic style that Chatfield's (1998) work has shown is the result of a blending of the Lucre and K'illke ceramic technologies.

In sum, the results of excavation show that a constellation of new cultural features appeared at the site of Chokepukio immediately following the Wari collapse. These features include new ceramic influences, new architectural forms, and a new elite burial pattern. Some of these features seem to point to southern influence emanating from the Titicaca Basin. Many of the burials found in the niched halls appear to be secondary, indicating that the bodies of these ancestors had been curated for some period at a location different from their final resting place. DNA studies show that some of these people were biologically related to the Aymara ethnicity of Bolivia. All of these data taken together seem to indicate the intrusion of a foreign group perhaps coming from the Titicaca Basin. This group may have, without causing a wholesale culture change, usurped the local leadership, bringing with them their own ancestors' remains and installing them in the new temples that were built. Chokepukio reached its greatest florescence during the Late Intermediate Period, just prior to the rise of the Incas.

Linguistic Evidence about Inca Origins

The lexical comparative analysis of the names occurring in the long list of kings in Montesinos' account is also interesting (Hiltunen 1999). The names on the list are predominantly Quechua, but a significant portion of these names are clearly Aymara and some Puquina seems to be present as well. Most interestingly, the dynasty of Tampu Tocco has a significantly higher percentage of words (45 percent) that indicate a blending of Quechua and Aymara.

The most active king and conqueror in the Tampu Tocco line was Tupac Cauri, who was also hailed as Pachacuti VII. His name indicates an Aymara origin. Equally, the name of his successor, Arantial, appears foreign. Among his successors are four kings having an appellative Roca in their names. Guinaldo Vasquez (1930) has called Tupac Cauri and his successors a "dynasty of conquerors." We think they presumably represented a new Aymara-speaking dynasty that usurped or replaced the previous rule at Tampu Tocco/Chokepukio. The rulers of the replaced dynasty were most likely the last kings of the Wari polity or at least its southern sphere.

Emergence of the Incas

A number of powerful competitive polities existed in the Cuzco region before the emergence of the imperial Incas. Early sources refer frequently to such groups as the Ayarmacas, Pinaguas, and Muynas among others. The Incas had a rival relationship with these polities: diplomatic at best and warring at worst. The Pinagua-Muyna polity seems to have been the most powerful in the region before the reign of Inca Viracocha. These two groups jointly occupied the Lucre Basin and were likely the two moieties of a combined political unit.

We think that our data identify Chokepukio as the seat of the ethnohistorical Pinagua-Moyna polity. This site controlled the access to the strategic Lucre Basin and passage to the south (to the altiplano). Together with the Pinagua–Moyna alliance, the important settlements of Andahuaylillas, Huaro, and Urcos probably formed a powerful confederate mini-state, which was long able to prevent the Inca extension toward the east and Collao (Titicaca) region. It is noteworthy that these sites all contain the archaeological remains of major Wari occupations. This mini-state is very likely a fragment of the old Wari imperial structure.

A third group of importance in the Cuzco region was the Ayarmacas. This confederation, which was centered in the region northward from Cuzco, controlled the northwestern part of the Cuzco Valley in those times. The Ayarmacas also were said to be connected with the Pinaguas, which might have meant that all three groups mentioned were ethnically related. According to the chronicles, the Ayarmacas were able to contest power with the Incas during the reign of Inca Roca. The Inca–Ayarmaca alliance was formed during the next reign, when Yahuar Huacac married a daughter of Tocay Capac, the Ayarmaca ruler. In some sources the Ayarmacas and Pinaguas have been connected politically. According to Martín de Murua (1946[1590]), the realm of Ayarmacas and Pinaguas extended from Vilcanota to Angares in the west. Brundage (1967) has suggested that the Muynas subjugated the Ayarmacas and the Incas temporarily during the reign of the weak Inca Lloque Yupanqui. Hence, one may suggest that in Murua's account we have a reference to the greatest extension of the Muyna polity. The duration of this "temporary subjugation" may in fact have included most of the Hurin-Cuzco rule until the time of Inca Roca.

As mentioned above, archaeological data and radiocarbon dates indicate two Late Intermediate Period building phases at Chokepukio. The first begins around A.D. 1000–1100 and the second begins more or less around A.D. 1300. The first date suggests the establishment of the immigrant Aymara dynasty (king Tupac Cauri) at the site. According to Montesinos' narrative and our chronological framework, this dynasty came to an end around A.D. 1300. Therefore a new ruling group must have taken over – those who started the second building phase. We suppose that they were the Pinaguas-Muynas, but not much can be said about their origins.

After the fall of the Tampu Tocco dynasty there was a possible power vacuum in the Cuzco region. Migrating groups may have entered from many directions. Presumably one of them was powerful enough to give a final blow to Tampu Tocco rule and gain hegemony in the area. This new power presumably took Chokepukio as its seat. Ethnohistorically speaking they were the Pinagua–Muyna alliance, arch enemies of the first Incas.

Inca Roca was the first king of the Hanan-Cuzco line as indicated by the sources. Some modern scholars have held the opinion that he possibly acquired the upper hand at Cuzco from the previous Hurin-Cuzco line by force (Rostworowski 1953). He was the first who adopted the title Inca, the first to build a palace for himself, and was possibly the creator of the yachaywasi institution. One source, Martín Murua, informs us that this Inca was involved in the assassination of his predecessor, Capac Yupanqui.

Zuidema (1964) has presented a model in which the relationship between the Hanan-Cuzcos and Hurin-Cuzcos was that of conquerors to conquered. He bases this argument on Gutiérrez de Santa Clara (1963[1595–1603]), whose text states that a new city, Hanan Cuzco, was built over old Cuzco by the conquering Incas and that the king of old Cuzco was pursued and killed by the Inca ruler. Zuidema concludes, "the rulers of Hanan-Cuzco were the real Inca and the conquerors of the town and . . . the rulers of Hurin-Cuzco were classed as pre-Inca populations." This argument of "conquerors" and "conquered" is also based on an old Andean concept and tradition, in which the original inhabitants of a region were conceived of as peasants with metaphorical feminine attributes, and the latecomers – usually conquerors – as pastoralists with masculine attributes. The first were called "huari" and the latter "llacuaz" (Duviols 1973). They were the lower (Hurin) and upper (Hanan) sayas of the common moiety division (Duviols 1973; Urteaga 1931). Furthermore, the Hanan-Saya people were often associated with a migrant warrior class accustomed to bloodshed and sacrifice through their pastoral intimacy with animal slaughter. Their mobility and mastery of the use of bolas and slings made them fearsome and able warriors (Sullivan 1996). They preferably worshipped celestial gods, such as Sun (Inti), Thunder (Illapa), and stars, while the huaris adored terrestrial objects, such as ancestral mummies and huacas (Ossio 1978).

The traditional number of reigns in the Hurin-Cuzco line is five, but if the ancestral founder, Manco Capac, is considered as a mythical character (as many scholars believe), there were possibly four actual rulers. If the emergence of Inca Roca and the Hanan-Cuzcos occurred around A.D. 1350, then the Hurin-Cuzcos were in place shortly before A.D. 1300. If the Pinagua-Muyna truly subjugated Cuzco and the Ayarmacas at the time of Lloque Yupanqui, this could have happened around A.D. 1300 or shortly thereafter. Consequently, the date of the fall of Tampu Tocco's old dynasty and the emergence of Pinagua-Muyna hegemony were contemporary events.

The first ruler of the Hurin line (if the mythical founder is excluded) was Sinchi Roca. It is very likely that the old sources and chronicles often confused and mixed the names, persons, and deeds of Sinchi Roca and Inca Roca. Nonetheless, it seems that both individuals existed, and founded their lineages in Cuzco. This confusion could also partly explain the attempts to make their lineages coexistent and configure diarchal models for the Inca dynasty.

The Hanan-Cuzcos apparently were the Incas proper, as suggested above. Whence did they come? Montesinos has given us a plausible clue. Inca Roca may have been a descendant of the preceding Tampu Tocco royal (Aymara) house. Montesinos makes this connection through a female relative, princess or queen, Mama Siuacu, who was said to be the mother of Inca Roca. Considering the temporal gap of some 50 years since the fall of the Tampu Tocco line, Mama Siuacu could well have been a daughter of its last ruler. Let us suppose that this "queen" really existed. Her husband could have belonged to the new Pinagua-Muyna lineage. Possibly she, with her son Roca, wanted to overthrow the Muyna rule and restore their ancient line and power base. In this scenario we may see Roca as a kind of exiled "King Arthur" waiting for an opportunity to restore his rightful royal heritage, or perhaps like Netzahualcoyotl of Mexico who, with the aid of the Aztecs, rose against Tepanec tyranny and brought back his ancestral kingdom.

We suggest that Inca Roca and the followers of his cause allied themselves with the Hurin-Cuzcos, who thereafter gained independence from Pinagua-Muyna. Sarmiento de Gamboa's account probably exaggerates in stating that Inca Roca, in the beginning of his reign, "conquered the territories of Muyna and Pinagua with great violence and cruelty." The basis for this historical distortion was possibly as much the Inca's own official mythography as Toledan propaganda. Pinagua-Muyna apparently held its independence and power until the reign of Inca Viracocha.

During this interlude the political arena shifted toward a kind of equilibrium, in which both states warred on each other, but expanded in opposite directions. Finally Inca Viracocha, in the beginning of his reign (around A.D. 1400), attacked Pinagua-Muyna successfully and subjugated it. Thereafter the conquest road toward the south was open.

The story of the rise and fall of Pinagua-Muyna has an epilogue, however. In the closing years of reign of Inca Viracocha a general uprising threatened the Inca state. The Chancas threatened from the north, and in the Cuzco Valley the Ayarmacas and Pinagua-Muynas rebelled. Only through heroic acts of a new ruler, Cusi Yupanqui Pachacuti (Inca Pachacuti), were the opponents, one after another, eventually subjugated. One of the hardest blows of revenge was aimed at Pinagua-Muyna. Pachacuti had their principal site destroyed. This could have occurred around A.D. 1450. Chokepukio shows evidence of being burned at this time.

Inca Pachacuti and the Canonic History of the Incas

Pachacuti found it necessary to make a complete reform of many basic institutions and policies of the Inca state. Hard experiences with the policy of his predecessors had taught that internal strife must be settled before an overall imperial expansion could begin. One fundamental problem was the proper settlement of the statuses between the Hurin-Cuzcos and Hanan-Cuzcos. The "conquered" Hurin-Cuzcos apparently had opposed the overlordship of the Hanan-Cuzcos since the beginning of Inca Roca's reign. As told by Cieza de Leon, the most dramatic incident in this respect was the assassination of Inca Yahuar Huacac by the Cuntisuyu (one of the four quarters of the empire) faction in Cuzco who belonged to the Hurin-Cuzcos.

The historical position of the Hurin-Cuzco "Incas" has always been a mystery. They had no true palaces in Cuzco (at least in the Cuzco which Pachacuti rebuilt). Apparently the far-sighted political genius Pachacuti chose to use compromises and compensation in handling potential troubles with the Hurin-Cuzcos which otherwise might be catastrophic for the state, especially when this threat had its seat in the very center of the empire. One of Pachacuti's first acts was to grant the Hurin-Cuzcos full acknowledgment as Incas. Thenceforth their lineages were artificially linked with the Hanan-Cuzcos by "genealogical ties." Inca history was then written anew: an unbroken lineage extended from the mythic founder through the Hurin and Hanan lines. As a "living" visible testimony, Pachacuti ordered mummy bundles to be made of ancestral Hurin-lineage "Incas."

Inca Roca apparently dreamed of restoring his ancestors' rule. According to Montesinos, at the beginning of his reign he commanded that a meeting of amautas and quipucamayocs (record keepers) be held so that they would teach him about the deeds of his ancestors, what provinces were subject to the ancient kings, and the character of their inhabitants. He also inquired what fortresses they had, what manner of fighting, and which provinces had been loyal to the crown and which had not.

Inca Roca founded the yachayhuasi at Cuzco according to some sources. Montesinos tells us that a similar school already had been founded at Tampu Tocco by Tupac Cauri Pachacuti VII. It is reasonable to assume that Inca Roca founded his school as an imitation of this older institution which once existed in Tampu Tocco. Founding of such a school at a turning point of dynastic rule almost certainly did not occur by chance. If our idea of Tupac Cauri and his dynasty as Aymara-descent usurpers is correct, the founding of the school by him fits fairly well into the picture. We also know that one of the first acts of Inca Pachacuti as a new emperor was a full-scale restoration and enlargement of the yachayhuasi in Cuzco. Without any doubt one of the most important functions of these schools was indoctrination and proper presentation of Inca history as the Incas wanted it to be told. Historical usurpers and usurping dynasties must always maintain careful vigilance over how their ideas may better be spread and accepted once they have appeared violently on the scene.

It is likely that Inca Roca wanted to keep records and preserve the intellectual heritage of his ancestors. There were possibly old amautas alive who were acting as teachers in his new school. Presumably the title of the sage – amauta – was then adopted to honor the kings' ancient wisdom. It is possible that at least part of the records of this ancient kingship were memorized and kept "on file" (by means of quipu) during the succeeding reigns. But all was changed after the great rebellion and overall destruction of Pinagua-Muyna and accession of Inca Pachacuti.

The fury and hatred that the Incas expressed toward the foreign Pinagua-Muynas is exceptional and exaggerated. There is some ambivalent frustration in their ultimate acts which led to total destruction of their political center. The rule of the Pinagua-Muynas as an independent polity probably lasted some 100 years (A.D. 1300–1400), with a period of supremacy at the first half of this epoch. By the time of the final destruction of the Pinagua-Muyna by Inca Pachacuti, some 150 years had elapsed since Chokepukio was dominated by ancestors of Roca and the "true" Incas.

Inca Pachacuti had a very complicated political-historical problem to resolve. He had to create a canonic history that would satisfy the needs of both major political factions: the Hanan-Cuzcos and the Hurin-Cuzcos. That history had to function well as a vehicle of imperialistic propaganda. The principal challenge was how to spin a good story of Inca origins in which traditions of Hurin and Hanan lineages were merged. We have already identified the origins of the Hanan-Cuzcos (or Incas proper) at Tampu Tocco (Chokepukio), as an Aymara-descended elite group which presumably migrated there from the Lake Titicaca region around A.D. 1000–1100. The Hurin-Cuzcos occupied the site of Cuzco before them, and we may suppose that the myth of Pacariqtambo originally belonged to their tradition. Thus, there were two origin stories: the myth of the origin at Titicaca (originating from the Hanan-Cuzcos) and the creation story at Pacariqtambo (pertaining to the Hurin-Cuzcos). The clever mythographers and amautas of the yachayhuasi apparently solved the problem by merging the stories into a hybrid tradition in which the creation occurred in Titicaca and the Inca emerged at Pacariqtambo.

Another problem was the ancient dynastic heritage itself. Should the narrative and deeds of ancient kings be included in Inca history? In the official doctrine and origin myth the Incas were the first and rightful rulers on earth who created all the institutions and taught these to barbarian tribes all around. Inclusion of earlier kings and their deeds would considerably diminish the credibility and justification of Inca conquests. This could also cause more jealousy from the Hurin faction if the ancient dynastic ties that, in fact, belonged to the Hanan-Cuzco tradition were emphasized. Besides, the site of this tradition was contaminated for more than a hundred years by the hated foreign intruders and arch enemies of the Incas, the Pinagua-Muynas. It would be politically hazardous to keep any connection with this site: the Incas were obliged to emphasize the origin seat of Hurin tradition instead – Pacariq-tambo. There could have been still another reason for this historical amnesia. Inca Pachacuti was a usurper, who took the throne from his brother Urcon. Like many usurpers in history, he seems to have had a megalomaniac need to express justification of his rule. This was closely related to personal vanity fed by a series of military successes in the beginning of his reign. He adopted the title Pachacuti, which signifies "cataclysm" or "reformer of the world." This was probably his only public concession to the ancient tradition, since he certainly was aware that this title was used by the former kings of significance. Pachacuti, "the super-king," had a pressing need to reform and conquer the world. Consequently, in the new propagandistic view of Inca history the Incas were responsible for all the achievements of importance and Pachacuti took credit for himself as much as possible.

Pachacuti had Inca history written anew. In this process many of the ancient traditions were deleted. Shortly before the Spanish conquest, Inca Atahuallpa ordered the quipu archives of Cuzco, which belonged to his brother Huascar, to be destroyed. We assume that all was not destroyed in this process because a total erasure of history does not serve the new order best, especially if it wants to benefit from the lessons and knowledge preserved in records of predecessors. Therefore, copies of the most important documents probably were kept in caches of Inca archives to be used by trusted amautas and the emperor himself in learning statecraft, for instance. In public and officially, however, all the past was forgotten; before the Incas there was nothing but barbarism.

The Legacy of Ancient Kings

Hundreds of years before the Incas the great empires of Wari and Tiwanaku flourished in the highlands and the Chimú Empire arose on the north coast. From all of them, directly or indirectly, the Incas inherited many of their institutions, government infrastructure, and statecraft, no matter what their canonic history wanted to express for posterity.

Recently a growing number of scholars have accepted the idea that a principal source of statecraft used by the Incas was the legacy of the Wari and Tiwanaku civilizations. In the present chapter we have set forth evidence to indicate that the ancient site of Chokepukio likely played a key role in transmitting this heritage to the Incas. Most interestingly, at this site both sources of this political-cultural heritage met. After a long period of occupation by the Wari Empire, Chokepukio was occupied by peoples from the Titicaca Basin who brought with them influences from Tiwanaku.

We think that the amauta dynasty proper in Montesinos' narrative most likely were the kings of the Wari Empire. The fall of the Wari Empire presumably occurred sometime not too long after A.D. 850 based on the archaeological evidence from the imperial capital in Ayacucho. There is some evidence that Wari rule probably continued locally in southern Peru and the Cuzco region until around A.D. 1000–1100. Thereafter a polity centered at Chokepukio (rather than Pikillacta) rose to predominance. Most likely Chokepukio was the kingdom of Tampu Tocco mentioned in Fernando de Montesinos' chronicle. Shortly before the rise of the Incas this important site was also seat of power for their rivals, the Pinaguas and Muynas.

The chronology of ancient kings as told by Montesinos fits well with the current archaeological data, particularly for the period A.D. 800–1300 (Figure 12.1). The end of the amauta empire and Wari Empire can both be fixed at around A.D. 850 in this chronology. Montesinos relates a vivid and plausible story about the end of the amauta empire. It culminated in a great battle at the Vilcanota pass, where the intruding troops from the south were victorious. From this direction the only polity powerful enough to challenge the Wari would have been the Tiwanaku state. Although there are scant archaeological data that reveal the relationship between these major polities, it is likely that they often had conflicting interests and hostile relations (Moseley 1992). The Inca tradition esteemed Tiwanaku and its heritage, but their perception of the Wari legacy is not as well known. According to our view, the latter had an equal importance, but for political reasons the Inca chose to give more precedence to Tiwanaku.

Conclusions: Knowing the Inca Past

Diachronic penetration of the Andean ethnohistorical past is a complicated matter. One has to deal with a number of historical turning points at which the information was seriously distorted. These consist of major political-historical phases, each with a distinct ideological interest in filtering and manipulating the historical information. The latest of these phases was the Spanish colonial world and particularly the period when the major chronicles, our primary sources, were written. Antedating this phase was the imperial period of the Incas and probably others before them. The pre-Inca ethnohistorical fragments that have survived through these later thresholds have a special value.

When the Spanish conquest of Peru eventually ended with the defeat of the Vilcabamba state and execution of last Inca ruler, Tupac Amaru, in 1571, the victorious Viceroy Francisco Toledo decided to adopt a policy in which Inca historical heritage was presented as illegitimate. Part of this project was an investigation and gathering of a "true history of the Incas" and "nature of their rule." A selected

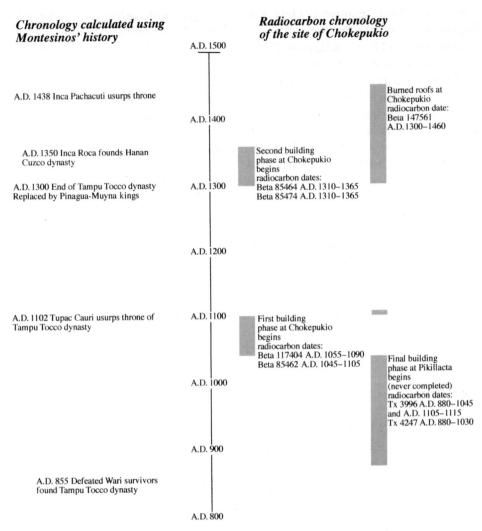

Chronology calculated using Montesinos' history

Radiocarbon chronology of the site of Chokepukio

A.D. 1500

A.D. 1438 Inca Pachacuti usurps throne

Burned roofs at Chokepukio radiocarbon date: Beta 147561 A.D. 1300–1460

A.D. 1400

A.D. 1350 Inca Roca founds Hanan Cuzco dynasty

Second building phase at Chokepukio begins radiocarbon dates:

A.D. 1300 End of Tampu Tocco dynasty Replaced by Pinagua-Muyna kings

A.D. 1300

Beta 85464 A.D. 1310–1365 Beta 85474 A.D. 1310–1365

A.D. 1200

A.D. 1102 Tupac Cauri usurps throne of Tampu Tocco dynasty

A.D. 1100

First building phase at Chokepukio begins radiocarbon dates: Beta 117404 A.D. 1055–1090 Beta 85462 A.D. 1045–1105

Final building phase at Pikillacta begins (never completed) radiocarbon dates: Tx 3996 A.D. 880–1045 and A.D. 1105–1115 Tx 4247 A.D. 880–1030

A.D. 1000

A.D. 900

A.D. 855 Defeated Wari survivors found Tampu Tocco dynasty

A.D. 800

Figure 12.1. Comparison of dates from archaeologically recovered radiocarbon samples with dates postulated for Montesinos' dynasties. The radiocarbon dates are expressed at the second sigma (95 percent) confidence level

number of elderly members of the Inca caste were chosen as principal informants for this "history." They were obliged to answer suggestive questions, which led to an overall negative view of Inca rule. One result of this study was the chronicle of Sarmiento de Gamboa. These reports revealed the Incas as cruel tyrants, whose empire was a relatively recent construction, but without any civilized predecessor. The political message was used to justify the Spanish conquest, and propagate the idea to the common people that the Spanish government was benign. Any tradition that could refer to an ancient "Golden Age" of sagacious kings certainly did not fit the propaganda of the Spaniards. Therefore, very little information of pre-Inca kings or dynasties could ever have passed through this threshold.

We already have treated the possible impacts of Inca dynastic propaganda on this tradition. Their reaction to antecedent tradition was not unlike that of many other conquest empires in universal history. The Inca state certainly was one of the greatest political constructions in world history, both in geographic extent and in its complicated infrastructure. At the height of their power, even though few generations had elapsed since their humble tribal emergence, most Andean subject people almost certainly firmly believed that all the civilized achievements of this world were created by the Incas. This illusion probably influenced the Spaniards as well. Much later, in the chronicle by the mestizo author Garcilaso de la Vega (1966[1609]), Inca rule was presented in a most flattering manner. This became one of the most popular accounts of the Inca state and culture, spreading this illusion worldwide. Inca society was thenceforth idealized by writers of the Enlightenment, Romanticism, and Marxism. Learning to know the Inca past is a very challenging and interesting study. Fortunately current research has opened useful new paths to understand their world. Obstacles in the quest for the Inca past will always remain, but our understanding and ability to see beyond these obstacles is constantly improving.

ACKNOWLEDGMENTS

The ethnohistoric study of the Montesinos manuscript was initially carried out as the dissertation research of Juha Hiltunen. Archaeological studies at Chokepukio were co-directed by Gordon McEwan and Arminda Gibaja, assisted by Melissa Chatfield, Sheldon Baker, Valerie Andrushko, Alana Cordy-Collins, Froilan Iturriaga, and the men and women of the village of Huacarpay, Cuzco, Peru. Advice and assistance were provided by Alfredo Valencia and Luis Barreda. The DNA analyses were carried out by Andrew Merriwether. Archaeological research at the Chokepukio site in Cuzco, Peru has been made possible by the generous support of the Bernard Selz Foundation, supplemented by the Curtiss T. and Mary G. Brennan Foundation, the National Science Foundation, the National Geographic Society, and numerous small donations.

13

Andean Empires

Terence N. D'Altroy and
Katharina Schreiber

Introduction

Commentators from the conquistadores onward have commonly used the Inka realm as a prism through which to view earlier states and simpler societies. Even for cultures two thousand years removed from Francisco Pizarro's invasion, Inka-era features are often taken as an interpretive starting point, whether for the duality and kinship central to political relations, or the mutuality and collective resource ownership ingrained in economics. For late prehistory, there are certainly justifiable reasons for adopting this approach, notably the lack of a native Andean writing system that we have been able to recognize and decipher. Early Spanish documents, based on interviews with native Andeans, provide rationales for action along with details of history and daily life that would otherwise be inaccessible. Moreover, the Inkas were willing to acknowledge other great Andean polities to the extent of adopting key elements into their statecraft, for example, the earlier Wari system of roads linking provincial centers, along with Chimor's artistic expertise and perhaps some of its organizational features.

Even so, we run a risk of finding only Inka-analogous designs if we project Tawantinsuyu (the name the Inkas gave to their empire, literally, "The Four Parts Together") too vigorously into Andean antiquity. In a sense, the relationship between the Inkas and their predecessors was reciprocal. Creating a new collective memory for Andean peoples, which would later be passed along to the Spaniards, was an essential part of Inka dominion. The Inkas' transfiguration of early statecraft, coupled with a political vision in which long-dead ancestors played a vigorous role, meant that a living Andean past was integral to the Inka present. Conversely, the Inkas grounded elements of their present in the mists of Andean history to legitimize their dominion, for example linking their dynasty's emergence and structure to the world's origins and claiming the preeminence of sun worship practically at the inception of time.

This interplay between power and history means that understanding the relationship between Tawantinsuyu and antecedent states is a layered task. In recent years, archaeologists have been assessing the rise of Andean imperialism without relying so heavily on an Inka model, and have begun to study the emergence of the Inkas as a preimperial power through fieldwork in the Cuzco region. From the standpoint of historiography, scholars have become more finely attuned to the multiple layers of meaning embedded in the colonial sources, recognizing that many voices were represented (e.g., C. Julien 2000; Pease 1995). The documents' contents, often drawn from competing native interests, were shaped in the first analysis by their authors, the context of inquiry, the choice of witnesses, the questions asked, and the mediating work of translators and scribes. Historians have also drawn attention to the contrasting Andean and European notions of the nature of the past (e.g., cyclical or linear), and its appropriate uses (e.g., legitimizing power relations, relating secular to religious phenomena), and how those differences shaped the information that is available to us now or excluded from written memory. At a deeper level, Inka and Spanish conventions of remembering were dissonant. The balance between oral and recorded memory; the relative weight given to event sequence, space, or hierarchy in composing accounts; and the role of public performance in validating narratives have all contributed to the differing, surviving visions of the Andean past.

This situation means that we need to be aware of the partial messages found in different sources of information. By extension, a joint analysis of archaeological and historical sources, where available, will be more profitable than one that privileges one source over the other. The dilemma, of course, is that we have access to both sources only for the Inkas and their contemporaries and not for earlier polities. Some of the information that we have from native Andean contexts was recorded on knotted cords called khipu, which have been found in deposits dating as early as Wari, that is, to the mid-first millennium. The Inkas also used tapestries, painted panels, and decorated poles as memory aids. In Tawantinsuyu, these media recorded information that was recounted by knot-record masters (khipu kamayuq) and court savants (amauta) (Ascher and Ascher 1981; Salomon 2001; Urton 1995). Julien (2000) observes that there may have been distinct genres of Inka narrative, such as genealogies and life histories, which were not well distinguished by Spanish authors. The conflicting stories told to the Spaniards, for example about the exploits and legitimacy of different members of the royal families, illustrate the uses to which the Inkas put a flexible past in their personal and imperial interests.

In the built environment, which constitutes much of what we analyze archaeologically, the Inkas expressed their power through performance and visual cues in an infrastructure of massive plazas, ceremonial platforms, and modular architecture. Access to portable media, especially multihued textiles, conferred more nuanced messages of status within the realm (C. Morris 1991, 1995). It may be surprising that statuary, reliefs, inscriptions extolling grand deeds, and other representations of individual rulers were not part of the Inka visual vocabulary. The extreme lack of human representation could not have contrasted more starkly with the narratives told to the Spaniards, in which heroic kings personally fashioned the realm out of anarchy. Together, these practices imply that the built environment, portable objects, the practice of power, and performance complemented one another in Inka statecraft, rather than repeating precisely the same message (D'Altroy, in press). Although we cannot yet prove that precisely analogous relationships held for earlier Andean states, we need to be consciously aware of the partial messages recoverable from the archaeological record.

In this chapter, we would like to offer a view of Andean empires through a summary analysis of the available information on the first and last of them – Wari, with its origins in the Ayacucho region of southern Peru, and Tawantinsuyu, with its heartland in the Cuzco region. Wari, unlike the Inka Empire, is accessible only through archaeological sources and the challenges of interpretation are thus different. There were, of course, other polities in the Andes that have been treated as empires, most notably Tiwanaku, in the southern Lake Titicaca Basin, and Chimor along the north Peruvian coast. We will make passing reference to both of the latter polities in this chapter, but will restrict most of our commentary to Wari and the Inkas. Before doing so, however, we would like to consider some more general aspects of the nature of empires, to set the stage for our review of the Inkas and Wari.

Empires and Andean Imperialism

An initial question, which resonates especially among scholars from the Andean region, is whether the European-derived concepts of *empire* and *imperialism* can legitimately be applied to any of the native South American states (e.g., Rostworowski 1999b). Some worry that, in employing the concepts, we may make the mistake of assuming non-existent aspects of Andean society, resulting in inaccurate portrayals. While a debate over terminology runs the risk of quickly turning sterile, there is a history to this problem. The Spaniards immediately recognized certain structural similarities between the Inka realm and the Roman Empire, their prime historical example. As a result, they misinterpreted some aspects of Inka culture, such as equating the aqllakuna ("chosen women") with vestal virgins (see MacCormack 2001). Similarly, the earliest writers used the term "mosque" for the Inkas' heathen temples, that being the closest referent they had at hand for their compatriots at home. Some of the chroniclers also struggled to make sense of Andean self-images, ideology, and history through a Classical/Christian lens (e.g. Cabello Valboa 1951[1586]). From the modern perspective of concerned scholars, the term *empire* and its initial conception derive explicitly from the Roman experience, and there is no reason that linguistic or temporal precedence should create a standard against which to compare all other complex polities. Neither should we expect the relationships among the various media that express identity, power, and history to translate neatly from one place to another. It seems especially problematic to some scholars to transpose Classical models to other societies where intellectual life was maintained orally or represented in ways other than documents, as was the Andean case (D'Altroy, in press).

While we acknowledge that there can be problems in applying concepts cross-culturally, we use the term *empire* in our work in part because comparative analysis would not be possible without a shared conceptual vocabulary, and in part because the essential features of empires are clearly present in the Andes. The ideal is to find terms that are precise and broad enough to be applicable cross-culturally, so it will be useful to clarify what we mean when we apply this term to particular Andean polities. For this discussion, we will adopt what Barfield (2001:29–33) calls *primary empires* as our working definition. Barfield defines these polities as societies that are large in geographic extent – continental or subcontinental in size – with populations numbering in the millions or tens of millions. Typically established through military conquest, they feature a unified, centralized administrative system, and are supported through the extraction of tribute or taxes from the conquered populace. They maintain a large, permanent military force in order to preserve internal order and protect the marked frontiers of the empire. In the case of the Inkas, for which we have written documentation, this definition works well. For those pre-Inka societies for which we have no written documents, however, we must carefully evaluate the evidence for each element, especially military conquest and the use of permanent armies to control and defend the empire. Moreover, population sizes are difficult to compute, even in the Inka case where we have some tabulated census data. We would prefer not to put any lower limits on the size of a population of empires, except to say that they are typically far more populous than other political forms.

Empires share a number of internal characteristics, the first being that they are organized to administer and exploit diversity (Barfield 2001:29–30). We put particular emphasis on this point, arguing that it is the diversity of empires that distinguishes them from other forms of states. Imperial diversity may be seen in two general contexts. First, empires control regions with varied ecological conditions and economic systems. The extreme environmental heterogeneity of the Andes, where the climate may range from arctic to tropical on a single mountainside, created special challenges for Andean empires. The Inkas were perhaps the ultimate masters of geographic diversity, controlling as they did the dry southern Andean highlands, the wetter central highlands, the high páramo grasslands of the north, the humid and densely vegetated eastern slopes, and the hyperarid Pacific coastal regions. The Wari Empire also controlled territories and populations in the highlands and on the desert coast, but it fell short of the diversity found in Tawantinsuyu. Second, empires control diverse societies, with different forms of political organization and socioeconomic practices. They establish political dominion incorporating or eliminating aspects of local political hierarchies, and establish a political economy that requires the partial reorganization of local patterns of production and consumption. Subject societies typically include a variety of different ethnic groups and languages, with distinct religions, rituals, and cosmologies that must be considered in imperial strategies of control.

For all their trappings, empires are grounded in power, which is exerted in a variety of domains. By power we mean the ability of one person or group to cause another person or group to take actions that they would not otherwise take, through the use or threat of sanctions (Haas 1982:157). Power can take one or another of several forms: social, political, economic, military, and ideological (see Mann 1986). The internal diversity of empires implies that no single strategy of control can be applied successfully to all situations; rather, each circumstance necessitates a specific, tailor-made approach, balancing among the differing forms of power. Frequently, what the leadership hopes to achieve are provinces comprising a relatively large region and population, pacified and controlled from a single administrative node, from which tribute or taxes are routinely and smoothly collected (Schreiber 1992:17). The administrative node will typically sit at the top of a hierarchically organized series of settlements and subordinate rulers. In some cases the highest levels of provincial administration will be left in the hands of cooperative local rulers, while at other times the central leaders may need to impose their own personnel, and rule the province more directly.

Historians frequently distinguish between two types of empires on this basis: *territorial empires*, employing direct imperial control of conquered regions, and *hegemonic empires*, which rely on indirect rule (sometime called home rule) through local officials (Hassig 1985; Luttwak 1976; cf. Doyle 1986). In our work, we have found that imperial strategies are much more complex than this simple dichotomy would imply, and that rulers frequently employ elements of both strategies in a single region. Thus direct and indirect forms of control are two ends of a continuum, and most imperial strategies of control lie somewhere in between (D'Altroy 1992:19–24; Schreiber 1992:14–17). Moreover, imperial strategies are not set in stone once established, and may change as imperial goals or local conditions change. For example, a region that required more direct control upon initial conquest may come to acquiesce and gradually increase its level of cooperation with the empire; in such a case imperial rulers may be replaced with local collaborators. Conversely, a group that initially cooperated with imperial occupation may become rebellious and require more direct occupation. We will see both instances in play in the Inka case.

We can usefully contrast an empire's need for centralized and hierarchically organized political control with the diversity of political forms encountered in conquered regions (see Schreiber 1992:17–27). The correspondence or disparity between necessary forms of imperial control and extant local regimes provides us with a general picture of possible imperial strategies, and the need to invest in various aspects of administrative infrastructure in each region. In some cases, an empire may conquer a region with preexisting centralization, and will be able to leave the extant local control hierarchy intact. Local rulers may be allowed to continue to maintain some level of power, thus entailing minimal costs on the part of the empire, or conversely the empire may choose to place its own operatives in the highest positions of control. In regions lacking sufficient levels of local political hierarchy and centralized control, we expect to find an increased level of investment in the region in order to create centralized authority, and subsume a larger number of people under a single node of control. In more complex regions, such as other states, the empire may perceive a level of threat to its own control and proceed to take over or even dismantle the state apparatus.

Collectively, these circumstances mean that we must be wary of treating imperial states as single, monolithic entities, rather than a complex systems with multiple, and even competing, agendas (Schreiber, in press). Both historical and archaeological data can provide evidence of such multiple agendas, even within a single region, as different motivations shaped the actions of the expanding state's leadership in different cultural and geographic settings. Moreover, indigenous groups conquered or otherwise, drawn into an empire cannot be assumed to have been non-reactive and passive, simply receiving and accepting the control of the dominant society. We must keep in mind that indigenous societies were active participants in the process and contributed materially to a negotiated outcome. It is unlikely that any host society welcomes control by a foreign empire, but its willingness to cooperate or ability to resist varies from place to place, or even within different segments of a single society. Local individuals may find it to their political and economic advantage to cooperate with the colonists (see Robinson 1972), or may mount overt resistance. The less empowered may find their options limited to more subtle forms of resistance that in some cases may give the appearance of cooperation. Local agency may be difficult to discern archaeologically, but explanation of changes in local society during colonial encounters should consider the active role of the host society. The final result of the expansion of control of the empire and the establishment of administrative hierarchies in host societies is thus a negotiated and continually metamorphosing product, the result of the interdigitation of multiple imperial agendas with multiple local agendas (Schreiber, in press).

This constantly changing complexity implies that archaeologists face significant challenges in their pursuit of prehistoric empires. Sinopoli (1996:4) identifies four interrelated issues that we must confront. First, because empires exist on a very large geographic and demographic scale, archaeologists must study regions that may be far-flung in extent, and that may also fall within different modern countries, each with its own set of challenges. In the case of the Inka empire, we must work in Ecuador, Peru, Bolivia, Chile, and Argentina. Second, the breadth and scope of the data that must be considered are immense, including not only archaeological data, but textual and spatial information as well. Third, because empires are characterized by high levels of internal variability and diversity in their political consolidation strategies, economic exploitation, and ideological forms of control of conquered territories, multiple lines of evidence must be considered simultaneously on both the grand and fine-grained scale. And fourth, empires expand and collapse at a relatively rapid pace, one that is often difficult to discern using archaeological techniques.

These challenges are substantial in the case of the Inka empire, where we have the advantage of Spanish colonial written descriptions, but are especially significant in earlier cases, such as the Wari. When we rely on purely archaeological remains to reconstruct an empire, we are faced with the totality of remains left by that empire – the end result of its efforts. Easily lost are the more dynamic aspects of imperial control, from initial conquest to the establishment of political control, to extending that control to economic extraction, and the ultimate establishment of ideological dominion, and the changes in identification of conquered people to members of the imperial society.

No single archaeologist can ever hope to completely study every region and facet of an empire, but he or she can focus on specific areas, and thus contribute to an overall understanding of an imperial society. Archaeologists and historians have taken many different approaches to the study of Andean empires that, when considered together, give us some sense of the richness and diversity of these polities. We will discuss these further below, in the specific archaeological cases of the Inkas and Wari. While it may seem odd that we begin our discussion with the Inkas, after cautioning about applying Inka models to polities a millennium earlier, the fact remains that Tawantinsuyu is by far the best documented and best understood of all Andean empires and it will be useful to begin where our evidence is the best.

Tawantinsuyu: The Inka Empire

The emergence of the Inka polity

In a recent publication, one of us bemoaned the paucity of information on the pre-imperial Inkas (D'Altroy 2002:48). It will probably always be the case that much of early Inka history will lie beyond our reach, because the imperial building programs largely wiped out the Killke (pre-imperial) settlements of the Cuzco basin. Fortunately now, however, archaeological research in the heartland is providing details on the formation of the Inka state that can be set against the mytho-history found in the early documents. Refinement of the regional chronology and settlement fieldwork have together begun to fill in crucial parts of the puzzle (see, especially, Bauer and Covey 2002). These studies show that the rise of Inkas to power was a far more gradual, longer-term affair than the legendary Inka narratives would have us believe. Coupled with evidence that the powerful pre-Inka states of the Andean highlands declined somewhat later than has long been thought, the hiatus between the fall of Wari and Tiwanaku and Inka designs on creating a new power may not be nearly as long as the half-millennium interregnum conventionally assumed.

Following the decline of Wari and Tiwanaku in the late first millennium A.D. (see below), the Inkas were one of several societies embroiled in a regional contest for power in the southern Peruvian highlands. By the early 15th century A.D., they had achieved dominance in the region and began their imperial exploits, but the circumstances leading to their emergence have long been obscure, at least from an archaeological perspective. The narratives of the early Inka era portray it as a volatile time, when ancestral heroes created order from sociopolitical chaos. The conventional genealogies began with the deified Manqo Qhapaq and continue through 12 rulers (D'Altroy 2002: table 1.1). Most accounts attributed the empire's creation to Pachakuti, the ninth monarch on the list, although the narratives tended to ascribe imperial designs to his father, Wiraqocha Inka (e.g., Betanzos 1996; Cobo 1979; Sarmiento 1960[1572]). The Spaniards met only the last ruler who

Table 13.1. The conventional Inka king list of the prehispanic era

Name as ruler	Gloss	Royal moiety
1 Manqo Qhapaq	Powerful [Ancestor]	Lower (Hurin) Cuzco
2 Zinchi Roq'a	Warlord Roq'a	Lower (Hurin) Cuzco
3 Lloq'e Yupanki	Honored Left-handed	Lower (Hurin) Cuzco
4 Mayta Qhapaq	Royal Mayta	Lower (Hurin) Cuzco
5 Qhapaq Yupanki	Powerful Honored	Lower (Hurin) Cuzco
6 Inka Roq'a	Inka Roq'a	Upper (Hanan) Cuzco
7 Yawar Waqaq	He Who Cries Bloody Tears	Upper (Hanan) Cuzco
8 Wiraqocha Inka	Creator God Inka	Upper (Hanan) Cuzco
9 Pachakuti Inka Yupanki	Cataclysm Honored Inka	Upper (Hanan) Cuzco
10 Thupa Inka Yupanki	Royal Honored Inka	Upper (Hanan) Cuzco
11 Wayna Qhapaq	Powerful Youth	Upper (Hanan) Cuzco
12 Waskhar Inka	Golden Chain Ruler	Upper (Hanan) Cuzco
13 Atawallpa	–	Upper (Hanan) Cuzco

Source: Based on D'Altroy 2002: table 1.1.

had been enthroned in Cuzco, Waskhar (the twelfth ruler), and his half-brother Atawallpa, who deposed him in a bloody war that closed just as the Spaniards arrived in 1532.

According to most narratives, Pachakuti took power when his father fled Cuzco in the face of an attack by a neighboring ethnic group from Andahuaylas, the Chankas. Following his military victory, Pachakuti usurped the throne and began a sequence of conquests that expanded Inka control from the Lake Titicaca Basin to central Ecuador. He initially sent armies northward through the Central Andes, onto the Peruvian coast, and into the Bolivian altiplano. Sometime during his reign, Pachakuti turned over the reins of the military to his son Thupa Inka Yupanki, who led campaigns into the eastern Andean slopes, into Ecuador, and into the southern Andes. This son later succeeded him and continued to expand the empire to its virtually complete extent (Figure 13.1). The third imperial ruler, Wayna Qhapaq, was more concerned with organizational affairs than his predecessors, but still extended Inka rule in the far north.

The conventional chronology for this sequence is taken from the chronicle written by the cleric Miguel Cabello Valboa (1951[1586]). According to the priest's calculations, Pachakuti assumed power about A.D. 1438, turned over the military to his son in 1463, and died in 1471. Thupa Inka Yupanki ruled until his death in 1493 and Wayna Qhapaq then held the throne until 1526. His death, from an epidemic of hemorrhagic smallpox that preceded the physical Spanish invasion, set off a dynastic war between Waskhar, the ruler enthroned in Cuzco, and Atawallpa, who commanded the experienced armies of the northern Andes. Atawallpa prevailed in the contest, but was captured in Cajamarca by Pizarro's small contingent of 158 horsemen and foot soldiers in a surprise attack, when the victorious prince prepared to meet his brutish visitors in the town center. Over the next eight months, Pizarro extracted a ransom in gold and silver (estimated in today's money at $50

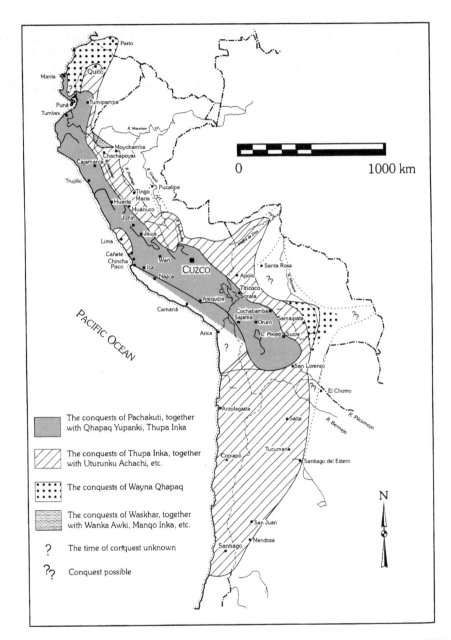

Figure 13.1. Hypothetical reconstruction of the expansion of the Inka Empire (from D'Altroy 2002: fig. 4.1)

million), but then executed his prisoner under pressure from newly arrived Spanish reinforcements.

The lightning rise of the Inkas from a small-scale regional polity to an imperial state told in this story has been the standard view of Inka history for almost 500 years. It is most obviously paralleled by the well-documented achievements of

Alexander the Great, so the celerity of the Inka rise to power is not reason enough in itself to discount the narratives. However, combined radiocarbon dates and survey evidence for the immediately pre-imperial Killke era now indicate that the Inkas were developing a powerful regional polity over a period of as long as four centuries before the great expansion (Adamska and Michczyski 1996; Bauer 1992), much like Phillip of Macedon did in unknowing anticipation of his son's deeds. Bauer and Covey (2002) have used large-scale survey (recording over 2,000 sites) to document the gradual development of regional settlement hierarchies and a complex series of political relationships between the Inkas and their neighbors in the greater Cuzco region. They suggest that the political vacuum created after A.D. 1000 by the fall of Wari (see below) set the stage for an intense regional competition for supremacy. During the Late Intermediate Period (ca. A.D. 1000–1400), Cuzco developed as a major settlement (up to 50 ha), which became the center of an emerging state (Figure 13.2).

Drawing on both archaeology and the written sources, Bauer and Covey suggest that the Inkas used a combination of military conquest, intimidation, marital and political alliance, and economic relationships to slowly bring their neighbors under Cuzco's sway (see also D'Altroy 2002:48–61). As they expanded their power, the Inkas transformed the regional landscape politically and economically, to provide a stable foundation for what would later become the state at the heart of the empire. By the end of the 14th century, the Inkas had established themselves as the region's dominant polity, setting the stage for the rapid expansion that would occur in the next century. This scenario does not substantially increase the length of the imperial era over the conventional historical reading, but it does have important implications for the nature of the Inka polity at the inception of the imperial era and its preparation for expansion. Rather than being essentially just another local polity, the Inkas seem to have developed an organizational and military capacity that prepared them for grander designs. Despite their differences, the archaeological and historical evidence both suggest that the empire emerged in the first half of the 15th century and lasted just a few generations. The archaeological record further indicates that there was a roughly contemporaneous extension of Inka material culture across the Andes, which we might expect from a polity that was rapidly expanding.

Imperial rule

Inka rule was organized primarily by kinship, class, and ethnic groupings. The final form of imperial government was a patrilineal monarchy, fleshed out by a complex array of royal and aristocratic families. At the apex stood the emperor and his immediate family, below whom were two classes of aristocratic Inka kin and one class of honorary Inka nobility. At the time of the Spanish conquest, the most powerful aristocrats were ten royal kin groups (panaqa), who were paired with ten non-royal kindreds. Conventionally, each panaqa was created at the death of a ruler in a custom called split inheritance (see Conrad 1981), in which the throne was inherited by the "most able" son of the deceased ruler. His other descendants formed a

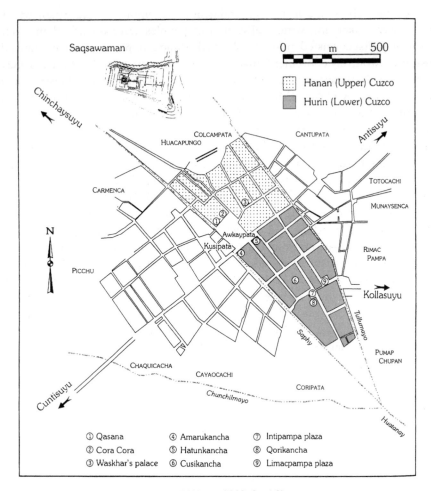

Figure 13.2. Plan of Inka Cuzco (from D'Altroy 2002: fig. 6.2)

corporate group that inherited his properties, usually under the leadership of one of his brothers. A panaqa's principal formal duties consisted of venerating its ancestor's mummy and perpetually caring for his properties, which not so incidentally kept the descendants richly endowed. In practice, the panaqa also served as an aristocratic council that played a crucial role in determining the choice of imperial successor. In this system, long-dead rulers thus continued to play a role in the affairs of state through an elaborate system of ancestor worship.

The Inkas sought to rule the 10–12 million people ultimately drawn into the empire through a combination of generosity on the grand scale, intimidation, application of a few standardized policies, and a massive program of resettlement. They attempted to ease acceptance of their rule by cloaking exploitation in the idiom of mutual obligations that already existed among local societies. Their goal was to mask the arrangement as a benevolent extension of traditional, familiar relationships

(Murra 1980). To judge from later indigenous testimony to the Spaniards, few subjects were taken in. Structurally, subject peoples were organized into about 80 provinces that consisted more of reshuffled ethnic groups, arranged into units that were administratively convenient, than a bureaucratic structure (C. Morris 1982). A province ideally consisted of 20,000 or 30,000 households, presided over by a governor appointed by Cuzco. Ethnic Inkas usually filled the upper levels of provincial government, but the Inkas relied heavily on the services of the provincial lords (kuraka) to govern their own people. An evolving hierarchy of state officials drawn from both ethnic Inkas and local lords thus tied the state and local levels together.

Several standardized policies were enacted over time in an effort to unify the administrative apparatus. Most importantly, a decimal hierarchy of officials organized able-bodied heads of household into units of 10, 50, 100, 500, 1,000, 5,000, and 10,000. The Inkas used the hierarchy to tabulate labor for both civil duties, including farming, herding, and artisanry, as well as portage, guard duty, and war service. In order to keep tabs on the population, a periodic census was established, which allowed the Inkas to mobilize workers for duties as required. Second, the Inkas established the Cuzco dialect of Quechua as a lingua franca for conducting affairs of state. Sometime early in their rule, they also began to move subjects about as colonists (mitmaqkuna), in a program that ultimately resulted in the resettlement of a quarter to a third of the populace. The colonists were set to work as soldiers, craft specialists, and farmers, among their many specialized duties.

The Inka economy

As they annexed new people and territories, the Inkas set about creating an economy that would allow them to exploit the vast human and natural resources of the Andes. According to many early observers, the Inkas divided the lands and herds of new subjects among the state, the official church, and the communities. In addition, the Inkas claimed all the raw resources of the empire, including minerals and forest products. In principle, each state institution was supported by its own resources so that none of the products derived from community resources could be appropriated. Cobo and Polo, among others, recognized that the divisions were not equal, but estimates of the precise allocation of resources are still beyond us, although we have details about particular locations. For example, Wayna Qhapaq dedicated the entire western valley of Cochabamba, Bolivia (Wachtel 1982) to growing crops for the state, and the province of Chuquicache may have been given over entirely to the Sun.

The state apportioned farming and grazing land back to the communities in exchange for rotating corvée service, called mit'a. In practice, communities kept many of their ancestral resources, but did yield farmlands, pastures, and other resources. In addition, prime lands near Cuzco and in the provinces were set aside as private estates for the royalty and aristocracy. Pastoralism also had institutional and private dimensions, despite blanket statements in the early sources that the Inkas owned all flocks in the empire. Similarly, craft production, exchange, and access to many kinds of raw materials and finished products were only partially subject to state supervision, Inka claims to the contrary notwithstanding. When we take into account that the coastal economies were more specialized and integrated than those of their mountain neighbors (see, e.g., Rostworowksi 1977a), it is apparent that a simple tripartite division of the economy misses the complexities of Andean practice under the Inkas.

The Inkas built upon existing structures to mobilize the labor that they needed to make the economy run. In local highland communities, which served as the Inkas' model, households nested within a corporate kin group called an ayllu gained access to farmlands, pastures, and other resources as an outgrowth of their membership in the group. The ayllu often tried to disperse their populations across ecozones in an effort to be as self-sufficient as possible (Murra 1972). Local lords had rights to farm and pastoral labor, personal service, and some craft products, in return for their ceremonial, political, and military leadership, and for sponsoring festive events.

General lists of the labor rendered by taxpayers enumerated over 40 kinds of tasks (Falcón 1946[1567]) that correspond fairly well to reports taken down in Spanish provincial inspections. In Peru's Huánuco region, for example, witnesses reported that they had carried out 31 different duties for the state, ranging from farming and herding, to masonry, military service or guard duty, mining, portage, and artisanry (Helmer 1955–56[1549]; Ortiz de Zúñiga 1967[1562], 1972[1562]). Each assignment was allocated according to the population of the region, as assessed by a periodic census, taking into account the resources that could be exploited. In return for their efforts, the laborers were entitled to be supported with food and chicha while carrying out state directives. Some of the most important state institutions were special labor groups, among which the mitmaqkuna (see above), yanakuna (lifelong servants), and aqllakuna (see above) stand out (see J. Rowe 1982).

A key element of the Inka economy consisted of specialized production, often of standardized crafts. The Inkas set skilled artisans to mass-producing textiles and ceramics, to crafting works of beauty and veneration in cloth and metals, and to making all manner of other objects that the state required. The Inkas, like other Andean peoples, used craft goods to make statements about their place in the cultural landscape – about their mythic history, ethnicity, class, status, gender, occupation, ritual, and relations with the supernatural. For the Inkas in particular, this kind of visual information was an essential part of statecraft because subject people spoke so many different languages and had no common symbolic system. Textiles were the most highly valued medium for such expression (see Chapter 7, this volume), but items executed in metals, ceramics, and other media also met the dual ends of symbol and practical use.

The ideological dimension

In this volume we can only make a few comments about the role of ideology in Inka statecraft, but a few comments are essential. A first, key point is that the Inkas attempted to create a new collective memory for Andean peoples by claiming Andean history as their own. They did this by reinventing a history that linked living rulers to the genesis of humanity, a mere 12 generations earlier. In this mytho-history, the Inka rulers were elevated to the status of gods on earth, scions of the sun itself. Worship of the sun was the centerpiece of the official state religion, but the Inka approach to religion was catholic, in the sense that it was willing to recognize and accommodate the various ancestors, multifarious local spirits, gods, and oracles of the peoples brought under their dominion. The Inkas themselves venerated a wide variety of animate beings, whose association with specific locales helped to create an immensely complicated sacred landscape around Cuzco. In the practice of state religion, subjects were required to venerate the sun and pay homage to the deified Inka ruler and his ancestors. Grand rituals, such as the qhapaq ucha which celebrated the life, death, or other major event in an emperor's existence, were elaborated to such an extent that the entire empire could be involved. The ritual caches and human sacrifice of high elevation sites in the south Andes, for example, are probably the direct product of the qhapaq ucha. Together, these practices and beliefs allowed the Inkas to claim a right to dominate the peoples of the Andes. The limited success of their efforts is attested to by the rapid demise of sun worship, the solar calendar, and maintenance of Inka temples, fields, and flocks following the collapse of Cuzco's power. The disappearance of these elements among all but the Inkas of Cuzco shortly after 1532 is testimony to the fact that, outside Cuzco, Inka ideology was more an instrument of policy than a creed shared by imperial subjects.

The infrastructure

Perhaps the most celebrated – and certainly the most visible – physical aspect of Inka rule is the remarkable array of provincial centers that were built throughout the empire, joined by the 40,000 km-long road systems. The centers ranged from Huánuco Pampa, the grandest of them all (see, e.g., Morris and Thompson 1985), to small way stations positioned every 20 km or so along the roads. North of Cuzco were Vilcaswaman, Hatun Xauxa, Pumpu, Huánuco Pampa, Cajamarca, Tumipampa, and Quito. South of Cuzco lay Hatunqolla (C. Julien 1983), Chucuito, Chuquiabo (La Paz), Paria, and Charkas. Along Peru's south-central coast, Inkawasi (Hyslop 1985) and Tambo Colorado stand out as planned installations. No important tampu were built on the populous north coast of Peru and only a couple of military sites south of central Bolivia exceeded about 35 ha. The centers were simultaneously seats of provincial administration, the location of state ritual and hospitality, and symbols of state power. They provided residence for temporary workers discharging their labor duties to the state and for more permanent occupants, such as the women's religious orders. Each center, ranging from the smallest to the greatest, boasted storehouses that maintained stocks of all the supplies that state personnel might need. The largest storage facilities, such as Cotapachi and Hatun Xauxa, could hold as many as 2,500 buildings.

The Inka royal highway that joined the provincial centers unified the empire physically and conceptually (Hyslop 1984). The network was based on two north–south highways, linked by more than 20 routes that crossed the western mountains, while other roads ran over the eastern cordillera into the montaña and lowlands. Along the east, a few roads ran well beyond the last significant state sites into the jungles or plains, where they seem to have been used to aid military expeditions or ties to people beyond Inka control. To build their highway, the Inkas claimed exclusive rights over numerous traditional routes, including some that had been built centuries earlier. Some ran right through Wari centers such as Pikillaqta and Azángaro, leaving no doubt as to their original cultural associations (Schreiber 1987a, 1992).

The varied strategies of provincial rule

As we described earlier, despite the disproportionate power wielded by the Inkas, and their attempts to standardize rule, the social diversity of the Andes dictated that the Inkas adapt their policies to local situations. The provinces in Peru's central highlands were the most intensively integrated into the empire. They typically shared all of the characteristics outlined above and formed the heart of the empire. Peru's north coast presented a different kind of challenge, for this region had already seen 1,500 years of state society. Chimú resistance to the Inka advances was stout and the Inkas distrusted most of the coastal populace. A key Inka goal was therefore to eliminate resistance orchestrated by native elites. To that end, they held the Chimú king hostage in Cuzco, while dividing control among local lords who each headed up a territory roughly corresponding to a valley (J. Rowe 1948). For the most part, the Inkas governed the dense coastal populace from installations at least partway into the highlands. Sites built according to Inka canons are virtually absent along the north coast. The Inkas built no major centers there and, in fact, their most elaborate construction was probably the tapia-walled desert road (Hyslop 1984:37–55). The intensive rule on Peru's south coast contrasted starkly with these policies. The Chincha, for example, were so esteemed that their foremost lord fell at Atawallpa's side in Cajamarca's plaza. Physical evidence of Inka rule in Chincha is concentrated at La Centinela, in the Chincha Valley, where a small Inka sector was erected in the center of the pre-Inka center. It seems to have been intended for the ceremonial and political activities that legitimized both Inka rule and the privileges enjoyed by the valley's aristocrats (Morris 1998:296–297). In the adjacent Pisco valley, the Inkas built two new centers, called Lima La Vieja and Tambo Colorado.

The Lake Titicaca region held abundant attractions for the Inkas. While the lake lay at the center of the Inkas' genesis myths, the altiplano's wealth made it an early target for Cuzco's aspirations. In 1532, the peoples living in the Titicaca Basin had been reorganized into 13 provinces, among whom the Lupaqa enjoyed a privileged position (C. Julien 1993). Much of the populace was resettled, as some of the rebellious Qolla were sent to Ecuador, while seven altiplano groups south of the lake provided 14,000 workers for Wayna Qhapaq's farms at Cochabamba, Bolivia (Wachtel 1982). The most variegated pocket of colonists lay at Copacabana, where members of 42 ethnic groups were resettled from all over the empire (Ramos Gavilán 1976:43). The most prominent centers in the northwest basin were Hatunqolla and Chucuito, both of which were newly founded provincial capitals.

The southern Andes were less intensively occupied than the rest of Tawantinsuyu, but the general lack of documentary information on the region belies the extensiveness of the archaeological record. Regional surveys have now recorded close to 400 Inka sites or sectors in south Bolivia, Chile, and Argentina (e.g., Raffino 1983). In stark contrast to the Central Andes, there is no known evidence for the installation of the decimal administration in this vast region. Instead the Inkas appear to have relied heavily on the colonists to carry out their designs. The archaeological evidence indicates that the Inkas intensified mining, farming, herding, and artisanry in and around pockets of strategically situated state centers, such as Samaipata and Shinkal. They also improved security by building fortresses along the upper edges of the eastern and western Andean slopes, well above other Inka settlements and farms that were situated to take advantage of warmer valley farmlands. Finally, the Inkas claimed the sacred landscape by constructing many shrines on the highest peaks (Reinhard 1985b). In addition to their ritual purposes, the shrines served a political end by interjecting the state between the indigenous peoples and their founding ancestors, who were thought to have descended from the peaks.

In the far north, the Inkas combined indirect rule through local chiefs and construction of their second capital at Tumipampa (Salomon 1986:172–186). The Ecuadorian polities resisted Inka rule for decades, but occupied desirable temperate uplands and traded outside Inka-controlled territory for Spondylus shell, gold, feathers, and other materials that the Inkas wanted. Salomon suggests that the Inkas shifted over time from ruling through a paramount chief toward a policy of social and political integration. Small versions of the state tribute and political systems were also set up within the chiefdoms, but the decimal hierarchy was found largely among the colonists, not the native populace. The resettlement program altered the ethnic composition of the south Ecuadorian highlands as much as any part of the empire, as the entire landscape around Tumipampa was reformed. Although there are notable Inka sites in Ecuador, the recorded archaeological remains are less numerous than the intensity of rule might lead us to expect. Tumipampa and Quito were the most important centers, but both unfortunately lie under modern cities. Ingapirca is more spectacular. Situated about 40 km north of Tumipampa, this site consists of an Inka ceremonial and residential complex built over an important Kañari settlement (Hatun Cañar) that had been occupied for several hundred years (Alcina Franch 1978). There is also a notable concentration of fortress complexes north and east of Tumipampa and Quito, while other sites were dedicated to transportation and communication, ceremony, and royal residence. Overall, however, Inka settlements related to agricultural and craft production, herding, colonies, and residential sites with imperial ceramics are largely missing from Ecuador's archaeological register.

Wari

The Wari Empire of prehistoric Peru expanded from its capital in the central Andean highlands at approximately A.D. 750. It controlled territory presently located throughout most of the highlands and the coastal desert of Peru, and collapsed sometime before A.D. 1000. Like the Inkas, Wari was an aliterate society and produced no written documents (although it did keep numerical records on knotted strings, khipu). Unlike the Inkas we have no eyewitness accounts of Wari, because it collapsed and disappeared long before the European invasion of the New World. Thus Wari presents the challenge of studying an empire based purely on archaeological data.

The Wari Empire is so named because Wari is the modern name of the archaeological capital city. The name means "honored ancestor." But, of course, we do not know what the ancient people called themselves or their capital. The name of the capital city at the time of the Spanish conquest was Viñaque. Legends recorded in the 16th century about two Wari sites, Wari and Jinkamocco, report that the installations were built by a people called viracochas, but this word can refer to any foreigner and does not necessarily indicate the prehistoric name of the empire.

The existence of a pre-Inka empire was first suspected in the early 20th century when the widespread distribution of a very distinctive iconography was noted by a variety of researchers (Kroeber 1944; Larco 1948; Uhle 1903). This iconography formed the basis for the definition of what came to be called the Middle Horizon. Initially thought to have originated from the highland site of Tiwanaku in Bolivia, it quickly became apparent that the Horizon style fell into two spatially and stylistically discrete groups. The southern style, restricted mostly to the circum-Titicaca region and a few points south did indeed pertain to the Bolivian site of Tiwanaku and represents its influence. However, the northern styles, stretching some 1,300 km through most of the Peruvian sierra, were thought to be the result of the spread of either a religious movement or the expansion of an empire based at the Peruvian site of Wari.

The archaeological investigation of Wari can be divided into several levels of analysis, ranging from the individual artifacts and iconography, to distinct architectural forms, to the excavation of particular sites, to the archaeological survey of large regions. We also find that data from the imperial core – that is, the area around Wari (which we call the Huamanga region) – and data from the conquered provinces outside this core, provide different but complementary sources of information about the empire and its effects on conquered peoples.

Detailed study of Wari ceramics enabled Dorothy Menzel to define a series of styles pertaining to the empire, and to develop a chronology of Wari expansion and collapse (Menzel 1964, 1968). She divided the Middle Horizon (MH) into four phases, numbered 1 through 4, with phases 1 and 2 being subdivided into two epochs each, named a and b. Several offering deposits she felt pertained to MH1a, while the great expansion of the empire began in epoch 1b. Changes in Wari styles led her to suggest that the empire underwent a major reorganization at the beginning of epoch 2a; the empire collapsed at the end of epoch 2b. Phases 3 and 4, based mostly on ceramics from the south coast of Peru, seemed to her to be a period analogous to the European Dark Ages that followed the collapse of Rome. Subsequent work by Wari scholars such as Anita Cook (1994) and Patricia Knobloch (1983) has refined the sequence developed by Menzel, and Cook has used Wari imagery to understand aspects of Wari imperialism, leadership, and religious practices (Cook 1992a, 1994, 2001).

Archaeological research in the Huamanga region, the Wari core, began in the late 19th century, but until excavations were begun there by Julio C. Tello in the 1930s, Wari was not recognized as a major center and the point of dispersal of the Wari styles. Wari is one of the largest sites known in the Andes (González Carré 1981; Isbell and Schreiber 1978; Lumbreras 1960, 1975, 1980). Its architectural core, characterized by densely spaced structures, many of them monumental in size, covers about 250 ha. The greater extent of the site, including areas of habitation with less durable structures and trash disposal, covers up to 15 km^2 (Isbell, Brewster-Wray, and Spickard 1991:24). The architecture of the site core is of the distinctive planned cellular forms characteristic of all Wari imperial sites. Although the site had a long earlier occupation, all of the standing buildings in the core date exclusively to the Middle Horizon, indicating a complete remodeling of the site and a huge investment of labor. The core comprises areas of great rectangular enclosures, most at least two stories tall, along with areas set aside for special purposes.

In the 1960s, a major project was undertaken in the Huamanga region that combined survey with excavation, under the direction of Richard S. MacNeish. Although he was interested primarily in sites of much earlier times, several archaeologists undertook excavations at Wari; unfortunately the results of these excavations have never been published. In the late 1970s William H. Isbell undertook several seasons of excavations at Wari, focused on an area of typical rectangular architecture (Isbell, Brewster-Wray, and Spickard 1991). Unfortunately, terrorist activity in the early 1980s brought his project to a sudden close.

Recent work by Peruvian archaeologists has revealed the construction of a religious precinct, and a major D-shaped temple (González Carré et al. 1996). Additional small D-shaped temples were built around the precinct, oriented to cardinal directions (see Cook 2001) and D-shaped temples are located throughout the core of the site, as well as at some Wari-related sites in the provinces. Adjacent to the religious precinct is an area of extensive subterranean stone-lined galleries, currently undergoing excavation. Nearby is an area with cut stone chambers that may have served as royal tombs (Benavides 1991); unfortunately these chambers were completely looted, probably in prehispanic times, so their exact content may never be known.

In addition to excavations at Wari, several Wari-related sites in the wider Huamanga region have been excavated, ranging from local centers and villages (Ñawimpuquio and Aqo Wayqo, see Ochatoma 1989), to Wari towns with offering deposits (Conchopata) to large Wari installations devoted, perhaps, to agricultural intensification (Azángaro, see Anders 1991).

Despite these efforts, we know relatively little about the organization of Wari or the activities carried out there and in its urban hinterland. Artifact assemblages from these sites could provide a baseline for comparison with assemblages from provincial sites, but most are yet unpublished. Although Wari sites, both in the core and in the provinces, exhibit a unique architectural style, no detailed studies of this style have yet been undertaken at Wari or other sites in the core; indeed, the style is better known from provincial sites. Although some tombs have been identified at Wari, as discussed above, these are very few in number, and more typical burial patterns at Wari and within its core society are yet little known. Also deserving of future study are features such as agricultural terracing and irrigation, and road networks.

Based on MacNeish's survey of the region (as published by Benavides 1978), we do have a sense of the urban settlement network, and relations between Wari and its immediate hinterland. Although this survey was more extensive and less intensive than we might hope, it did locate most of the major settlements in the region. Numerous habitation sites were located throughout the immediate hinterland during MH1, but in MH2 there was a marked drop in the number of sites, while Wari grew to enormous proportions (see Schreiber 1992:88–92). Like the area around Teotihuacan in Mexico, it appears that over time the countryside was nearly depopulated, and the majority of the populace moved to the city. At the end of MH2 Wari was completely abandoned, the population of the region dropped dramatically, and the empire collapsed.

As we move from the core out into the provinces, certain aspects of Wari culture and society become clearer. But first we must ask, why did Wari expand out of the Huamanga region? How fast did it expand? Why did it cease its expansion when and where it did? These are very difficult questions to address when one must base one's interpretations purely on archaeological data.

We cannot know either the general or proximate cause of Wari expansion. In other cases, such as Rome, or the Inkas, we can attribute the initial expansion to conflict with and defeat of a traditional enemy as the proximate cause. In the case of Wari all we see is increased "interaction" with the Nasca culture of the Peruvian south coast, as seen in the adoption of designs and ceramic technology from Nasca in the pre-imperial Huarpa ceramic style (Knobloch 1976; Menzel 1964). We cannot know at this time if this is related to the Wari expansion. Likewise, we do not know how quickly the empire expanded. Archaeological dating techniques are simply not sufficient to separate events that took place within a century or two. Radiocarbon dates from provincial sites indicate that all were built in a period ranging from about A.D. 750 to 900 (Williams 2001), but the speed of expansion, and even the order of the expansion, cannot be gleaned from these data.

The geographic extent of Wari control can be best estimated from the distribution of its built infrastructure: an extensive series of administrative centers or military garrisons, and a network of roads (Schreiber 1987b). Wari administrative architecture is very distinctive (Schreiber 1978; Spickard 1983). A typical site comprises a large rectangular enclosure, regularly subdivided into square or rectangular cells; the individual cells include one or more open patios, surrounded by long, narrow galleries. This architectural style is unique, unmistakable, and clearly associated with Wari. Many of the sites are, in turn, associated with prehistoric roads, some of which were later incorporated into the Inka system of royal highways (Schreiber 1984, 1991a), as noted above. Most known sites are found in the sierra, but current research in coastal drainages continues to discover previously unknown Wari sites in the Pacific watershed (see Figure 13.3 for major Middle Horizon sites).

Based on the distribution of Wari sites and other features, it appears that the empire extended no farther north than the Cajamarca region of northern Peru, and that it stopped short of the Titicaca Basin in southern Peru. The presence of the Tiwanaku polity in the south may explain the southern boundary, some 500 km from Wari. In the north it is possible that the infrastructure and communications abilities of the fledgling empire were overextended in this region, 800 km distant from the capital, or local resistance may have prevented it from establishing control there. Wari installations in Cajamarca, and in the Huamachuco region just to the south, all appear to be unfinished and never occupied (see J. Topic 1991). The northernmost Wari sites that were completed and occupied all lie in north-central Peru, in a valley called the Callejón de Huaylas (see Schreiber 2001).

Archaeological research at individual sites and certain regions of the Wari provinces provides important evidence not only on the diversity of societies that fell under Wari control, but also differences in Wari strategies of conquest and incorporation of conquered groups. Thus the research agenda in the provinces is somewhat different than it is in the core. In provincial regions we are dealing with Wari as an intrusive, foreign element, and the relationship between it and the existing cultures within these regions. At the analytical level of the artifact we need to define local chronological sequences, as well as identify intrusive Wari styles or local copies of Wari styles; these then need to be correlated with the core sequences in order to date the phases in which Wari or Wari "influence" was present.

At the level of specific Wari cultural features, we have seen a good deal of research in the provinces. The Wari architectural style was defined first on the basis of the provincial sites (J. Rowe, Collier, and Willey 1950; Schreiber 1978; Spickard, 1983). The existence of Wari road networks is probably seen more clearly in the provinces than in the core. Intrusive tomb forms and changes in local burial patterns correlated with the Wari expansion can be seen clearly in the provinces, and recent work by Anita Cook (2001) has also demonstrated that the D-shaped temple has a wide distribution in the provinces, as well as at Wari. Introduction of agricultural terracing in various regions has also been correlated with the Wari presence (Schreiber 1987b).

At the level of the site, as in the case of artifacts, provincial research is dealing with two cultures: local and foreign. To date most provincial sites excavated have been Wari provincial centers such as Pikillaqta (McEwan 1987, 1991), Viracochapampa (J. Topic 1991), Jinkamocco (Schreiber 1991b, 1992), Honco Pampa (Isbell 1989), and others. Long thought to be empty storehouses, or even jails, it is now clear that these sites were occupied by large numbers of people, both foreigners from Wari and local peoples. Portions of some sites were set aside for storage, but their primary function seems to have been political: these were imperial capitals of

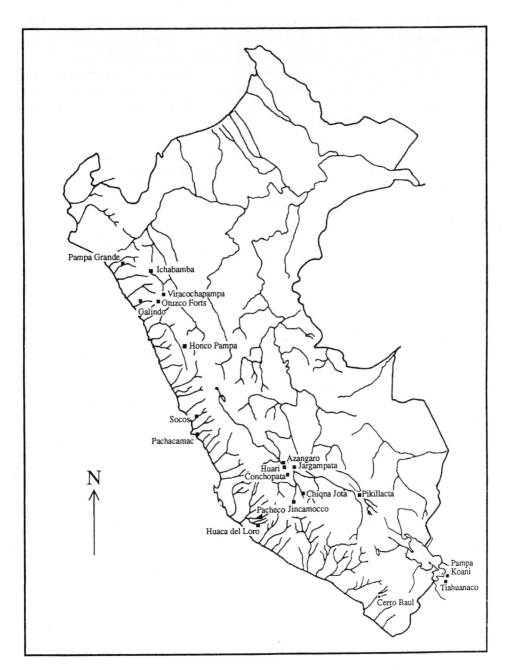

Figure 13.3. Major sites of the Middle Horizon (from Isbell and McEwan 1991: fig. 1)

conquered provinces. However, we are still lacking the reciprocal portion of this level of analysis in virtually every region: excavations of local Middle Horizon sites that will enable us to gauge the impact of Wari on conquered settlements.

Finally, intensive regional surveys have now taken place in several regions within the Wari sphere. These studies, which focus on the region as the level of analysis, provide data on local organization prior to the arrival of Wari, and changes in that organization during the Wari occupation. Only by viewing Wari remains in the local context can we begin to understand what Wari was, and why it expanded. In other words, by looking at its effects, we can get a sense of its motivations. Further, by looking at changes in the Wari occupation within the Middle Horizon, we can better understand changes in Wari strategies and motivations.

While many, if not most, valleys of the Peruvian highlands have yet to be surveyed intensively, it is the case that Wari sites are not found everywhere, certainly not in every region with a substantial population. The lack of Wari sites has led some investigators to argue that there was no Wari presence in those regions. This may be true. However, the existence of imperial control does not in every case mean that imperial installations were necessarily established in every region under its control. While the presence of imperial infrastructure is a good indication of imperial control, or at least some sort of intent on the part of Wari, the reverse is not always true. Various writers have dealt with the issues of direct versus indirect control on the part of empires (D'Altroy 1992; Sinopoli 1996) and the broad range of different forms of control intermediate between those extremes (Schreiber 1992). Dealing with purely archaeological remains we can make the assumption that in places where the empire established its own infrastructure – that is, it built administrative centers, roads, etc. – the existing infrastructure was insufficient for its needs. This in turn implies that the particular region was not politically centralized, that there existed no controlling authority that had established the infrastructure necessary for political control of the region. The study of settlement patterns in the region can also indicate an absence of central places, or only weakly developed centralization.

However, in those areas with an existing centralized political system, and hence an existing infrastructure, an empire does not need to go to the expense of establishing a completely new infrastructure. The study of settlement patterns again can reveal the presence of central places, levels of control hierarchy, and the extent of a region controlled by a local polity. It is therefore ironic that, when dealing with purely archaeological data, and in the absence of written records, we are most certain of imperial occupations only in regions in which the empire invested heavily in building the infrastructure. Some of the most important occupations, those involving the conquest of groups that were already complex and centralized, may be the ones least visible to the archaeologist.

Finally we consider the dynamics of the Wari expansion not in terms of absolute dates of particular conquests, but rather in terms of changes in Wari strategies and occupations over time. The archaeological remains of a Wari occupation are not simply a snapshot of an instant in time. They are the remains of several generations, if not centuries, of activity. It is unlikely that an empire, upon initial conquest of a region, could foresee its needs much farther down the line. As noted above, some sites were planned and construction begun, but were never finished. Other sites, such as Pikillaqta, were planned, partially finished and occupied, but never fully completed. Clearly, what Wari planned when it laid out the outlines of the site had changed before it could be completed. There is abundant evidence that Wari priorities changed over time, from political motivation (control of people), to economic motivation (control of production and distribution of agricultural products). For example, in the Sondondo Valley, about 4–5 days' travel south of Wari, a substantial administrative center, Jinkamocco, was built in MH1. The site measured about 3.5 ha, and formed a single large rectangular unit of typical Wari architecture. In MH2 that site nearly tripled in size, to at least 15 ha, and at least three additional Wari sites, all of them less than a hectare in extent, were constructed in other parts of the valley. During the Wari occupation, local villages located at the boundary between the tuber and herding zones (3,600–3,800 m above sea level) were moved downward to 3,300 m or lower in order to exploit the lower maize-producing zone. Extensive tracts of agricultural terraces, necessary for maize cultivation at such high altitudes, were built below 3,300 m. The labor investment in this project was extremely high, and certainly beyond the capacity of the small local population, which numbered fewer than 1,000 people. The enlargement of Jinkamocco may have been due to the need to provide quarters for imported laborers, as well as storage areas for the increased volumes of produce. Thus, in this region agricultural production was greatly increased at the behest of the empire in MH2.

A third example of increased economic control comes from Nazca. The site of Pacheco was established in MH1, and may have served as a political capital of this conquered province. In MH2, a second Wari site, one much smaller, was established in the upper Nazca Valley. This site, Pataraya, is located adjacent to a tract of agricultural fields probably used for the production of coca (Schreiber 1999). Earlier sites dating to the Nasca culture were abandoned, and new sites occupied by highland people were established in the Middle Horizon. This evidence suggests that Wari co-opted this coca-growing zone for its own use, moved out the local people, and moved in its own allies.

In sum, Wari appears to have emerged in Middle Horizon epoch 1b as an enormous urban center in its core region, and to have expanded its political control to a vast geographic area during that same epoch. The initial construction of sites such as Jinkamocco in the mid-eighth century A.D. gives us a good approximation of the timing of the expansion. The focus of the expansion seems to have been primarily political at the beginning, moving into and taking over or establishing hegemony with local cultures.

In MH2 the empire's political control may have been somewhat reduced. Various imperial centers built in MH1 were abandoned, especially those at the northern and southern extremes of the empire, suggesting a reduction in the overall size of the empire. At the same time, in the remaining provinces of the empire, economic control took on much greater importance. Efforts were made to bring new regions and environmental zones under production, and control over maize and coca cultivation was given high priority. And new installations may have been built on the now established borders of the empire.

At the end of MH2 the empire collapsed, for reasons yet unknown. Data from Jinkamocco suggest that the site was abandoned gradually in MH2, with sections of it falling into disuse and used for trash disposal. Dating collapse is a complicated task for the archaeologist, as chronometric techniques tend to date construction and occupation, not abandonment. We can probably assume the empire lasted no more than two or three centuries.

Archaeologists have made tremendous progress in understanding Wari over the last 50 years. Research efforts have moved beyond the study of artifacts and the building of inter-regional chronological sequences, and have begun to address more interpretive models. If one considers various explanations of the distribution of Wari cultural features, they can be divided generally into three classes: (1) models of political control (control of people); (2) models of economic interaction (simple commerce between regions, or some measure of control over resource exploitation and production of goods); and (3) religious movements.

The presence of Wari artifacts in a region can support any of the models. On the other hand, a system of roads might support either the political or economic models. The presence of features such as D-shaped temples, Wari tombs, or changes in burial patterns, and the offering deposits indicate a strong element of religion and ideology in the Wari expansion. Construction of agricultural terraces can support both political and economic models. The presence of large administrative structures, with resident populations and a variety of functions, is most supportive of a model that emphasizes control of people – a political model. Finally, changes in local settlement patterns provide another line of evidence. The relocation of local population so as to create a centralized political hierarchy supports the political end of the spectrum, while the relocation of people to new resource zones supports both political and economic models.

To conclude, all the evidence we have at present indicates a strong political element to the Wari expansion, coupled with increased economic control, and also including a strong element of the ideological. It is clear that Wari was not simply a religious movement. Nor can the presence of Wari cultural elements throughout the Central Andes, and the changes in local culture associated with the Wari presence, be explained as the result of simple trade. Wari was a political expansion that included elements of both the economic and religious spheres, and incorporated a large portion of the Central Andes, including a wide diversity of peoples and places. We therefore feel justified in calling it an empire.

Conclusions

Our intent in this chapter has been twofold: to frame the problem of studying indigenous Andean empires in a comparative, theoretical context, and to outline key features of the earliest and latest of those empires. Although the discussion has been brief, we have tried to highlight issues that illustrate how the analysis of these polities can fruitfully be brought into the larger field of empire studies. A defining feature, for example, is the core imperial society's ability to exercise extensive political and economic control over other polities, often through rapid military conquest that may not include a contiguous territory. Similarly, Wari and Tawantinsuyu shared the cultural richness and administrative headaches characteristic of multi-ethnic polities seen elsewhere, for example, in the Roman and Achaemenid empires. For the Inka case, we know that the ethnic groups of the heartland at least initially regarded conquered peoples as foreign and that the rulers, in turn, were regarded as foreign by those whom Cuzco dominated; there is some suggestion along the same lines in the residential sectors of Wari provincial settlements. Even so, there is also evidence in both cases for the exportation of a homogenizing imperial agenda, recognizable in standardized residential, administrative, and temple architecture and in the artifacts of ceremony. Similarly, the rulers of both empires exhibited an interest in developing an integrating infrastructure (e.g., roads, storage, provincial facilities) and tools of statecraft (e.g., khipu).

There is good historical reason for relatively easy comparison between the Wari and Inka empires since, as we noted at the outset, the Inkas appropriated both concepts of rule and a physical infrastructure from Wari and other predecessor states, such as Chimor and Tiwanaku. Moreover, the temporal lag between the Wari and Inkas seems to be considerably less than imagined not too long ago. As we also observed, however, we need to take care not to extrapolate the full array of the Inkas' statecraft onto their ancestors, despite the obvious links. The first and last of the Andean empires arose in markedly different historical contexts and drew from cultural matrices that were only partially overlapping. To put this point another way, if we assume that the visible parallels imply that we can apply the written record on the Inkas to all aspects of Wari, then all we will ever see is an earlier version of the Inkas. The challenge to us and other scholars is to find more creative ways of exploring the nature of these and other empires, using archaeological data both on its own and in conjunction with history.

Cumulative Bibliography

Abercrombie, N., S. Hill, and B. S. Turner, 1980 The Dominant Ideology Thesis. London: G. Allen & Unwin.

Abercrombie, Thomas A., 1998 Pathways of Memory and Power: Ethnography and History Among an Andean People. Madison: University of Wisconsin Press.

Acosta, José de, 1880 The Natural and Moral History of the Indies. Reprinted from the English edition of Edward Grimson [1604], vols. 1–2 (1588–90). London: Hakluyt Society.

Adamska, Anna, and Adam Michczyski, 1996 Towards radiocarbon chronology of the Inca state. Andes. Boletín de la Misión Arqueológica Andina 1:35–58. Warsaw.

Albarracín-Jordán, Juan V., 1996 Tiwanaku settlement system: The integration of nested hierarchies in the lower Tiwanaku Valley. Latin American Antiquity 7(3):183–210.

Albarracín-Jordán, Juan V., and James E. Mathews, 1990 Asentamientos Prehispánicos del Valle de Tiwanaku, vol. 1. La Paz: CIMA.

Alcina Franch, José, 1978 Ingapirca: Arquitectura y áreas de asentamiento. Revista Española de Antropología Americana 127–146.

Alconini Mujica, Sonia, 1995 Rito, Símbolo e Historia en la Pirámide de Akapana, Tiwanaku: Un Análisis de Cerámica Ceremonial Prehispánica. La Paz: Editorial Acción.

Aldenderfer, Mark, 1998 Montane Foragers: Asana and the South-Central Andean Archaic. Iowa City: University of Iowa Press.

Alfaro de Lanzone, Lidia C., 1978 Informe Final al Proyecto Huayurí. Report submitted to the Instituto Nacional de Cultura. Lima, Peru.

Allen, Catherine J., 2002 The Hold Life Has: Coca and Cultural Identity in an Andean Community. Washington, DC: Smithsonian Institution Press.

Allen, John, Doreen Massey, and Allan Cochrane, 1998 Rethinking the Region. Routledge: New York.

Allison, P. M., ed., 1999 The Archaeology of Household Activities. London: Routledge.

Alva, Walter, 2001 The royal tombs of Sipán: Art and power in Moche society. In Moche Art and Archaeology in Ancient Peru. Joanne Pillsbury, ed. pp. 223–245. Washington, DC and New Haven: National Gallery of Art and Yale University Press.

Alva, Walter, and Susana Meneses de Alva, 1983 Los murales de Ucupe en el valle de Zaña, norte del Peru. Beitrage zur Allgemeinen und Vergleichenden Archäologie, no. 5, pp. 335–360. Bonn: Deutsches Archäologisches Institut.

Alva, Walter, and Christopher B. Donnan, 1993 Royal Tombs of Sipán. Los Angeles: Fowler Museum of Cultural History, University of California, Los Angeles.

Amano, Yoshitaro, 1961 Huacos Precolombinos del Perú. Tokyo: Bijutsu Shuppan-Sha.

Amat Olazábal, Hernán, ed., 1997 Julio C. Tello: Forjador del Perú Auténtico. Lima: Centro de Estudios Histórico-Militares de Perú.

Ames, Kenneth M., 1995 Chiefly power and household production on the Northwest Coast. *In* Foundations of Social Inequality. T. Douglas Price and Gary M. Feinman, eds. pp. 155–187. New York: Plenum Press.

Anders, Martha, 1986 Dual Organization and Calendars Inferred from the Planned Site of Azangaro – Wari Administrative Strategies. Ph.D. dissertation, Department of Anthropology, Cornell University.

——1991 Structure and function at the planned site of Azangaro: Cautionary notes for the model of Huari as a centralized secular state. *In* Huari Administrative Structure: Prehistoric Monumental Architecture and State Government. William H. Isbell and Gordon F. McEwan, eds. pp. 165–197. Washington, DC: Dumbarton Oaks.

Anderson, Benedict, 1983 Imagined Communities. London: Verso.

Andronicos, Manolis, 1993 Delphi. Athens: Ekdotike Athenon SA.

Angeles, Rommel, and Denise Pozzi-Escot, 2000 Textiles del Horizonte Medio: Las evidencias de Huaca Malena, valle de Asia. *In* Huari y Tiwanaku: Modelos vs. Evidencias. Peter Kaulicke and William H. Isbell, eds. pp. 401–424. Boletín de Arqueología PUCP, vol. 4. Lima: Departamento de Humanidades, Especialidad de Arqueología, Pontificia Universidad Católica del Perú.

Arellano Lopez, Jorge, 1985 Mollo: Investigaciones Arqueológicas. La Paz: Imprenta Nacional.

Arnold, Denise Y., 1992 La casa de adobes y piedras del Inka: Género, memoria y cosmos en Qaqachaka. *In* Hacia un Orden Andino de las Cosas, pp. 31–108. La Paz: Hisbol/ILCA.

Arriaza, Bernardo T., 1995 Beyond Death: The Chinchorro Mummies of Ancient Chile. Washington, DC: Smithsonian Institution Press.

Ascher, Marcia, and Robert Ascher, 1981 Code of the Quipu. Ann Arbor: University of Michigan Press.

Ashmore, Wendy, and Richard R. Wilk, eds., 1988 Household and Community in the Mesoamerican Past. Albuquerque: University of New Mexico Press.

Aveni, Anthony F., ed., 1990 The Lines of Nazca. Philadelphia: The American Philosophical Society.

Bandelier, Adolph, 1911 The ruins of Tiahuanaco. Proceedings of the American Antiquarian Society 21:218–265.

Bandy, Matthew S., 2001 Population and History in the Ancient Titicaca Basin. Ph.D. dissertation, Department of Anthropology, University of California, Berkeley.

Bankmann, Ulf, 1979 Moche und Recuay. Baessler-Archiv, nf vol. 27:253–271.

Baraybar, José Pablo, 1987 Cabezas trofeo Nasca: Nuevas evidencias. Gaceta Arqueológica Andina 15:6–10.

Barber, Wayland Elizabeth, 1994 Women's Work: The First 20,000 Years. New York: Norton.

Barfield, Thomas J., 2001 The shadow empires: Imperial state formation along the Chinese-nomad frontier. *In* Empires: Perspectives from Archaeology and History. Susan A. Alcock, Terence N. D'Altroy, Kathleen D. Morrison, and Carla M. Sinopoli, eds. pp. 10–41. Cambridge: Cambridge University Press.

Barnes, Barry, 1988 The Nature of Power. Urbana: University of Illinois Press.

Bastien, Joseph W., 1995 The mountain/body metaphor expressed in a Kataan funeral. *In* Tombs for the Living: Andean Mortuary Practices. Tom D. Dillehay, ed. pp. 355–378. Washington, DC: Dumbarton Oaks.

Bauer, Brian, 1991 Pacariqtambo and the mythical origins of the Inca. Latin American Antiquity 2(1):7–26.

—— 1992 The Development of the Inca State. Austin: University of Texas Press.

—— 1998 The Sacred Landscape of the Inca. Austin: University of Texas Press.

—— 2003 Early Intermediate and Middle Horizon ceramic styles of the Cuzco Valley. Fieldiana, Anthropology new series 34. Field Museum of Natural History, Chicago.

Bauer, Brian, and R. Alan Covey, 2002 Processes of state formation in the Inca heartland (Cuzco, Peru). American Anthropologist 104(3):846–864.

Bawden, Garth, 1977 Galindo and the Nature of the Middle Horizon on the North Coast of Peru. Ph.D. dissertation, Department of Anthropology, Harvard University, Cambridge.

—— 1982a Galindo: A study in cultural transition during the Middle Horizon. In Chan Chan: Andean Desert City. Michael E. Moseley and Kent C. Day, eds. pp. 285–320. Albuquerque: University of New Mexico.

—— 1982b Community organization reflected by the household: A study of Pre-Columbian social dynamics. Journal of Field Archaeology 9:165–183.

—— 1990 Domestic space and social structure in Pre-Columbian northern Peru. In Domestic Architecture and the Use of Space: An Interdisciplinary Cross-Cultural Study. Susan Kent, ed. pp. 153–171. Cambridge: Cambridge University Press.

—— 1995 The structural paradox: Moche culture as political ideology. Latin American Archaeology 6(3):255–273.

—— 1996 The Moche. Oxford: Blackwell.

—— 2001 The symbols of Late Moche social transformation. In Moche Art and Archaeology in Ancient Peru. Joanne Pillsbury, ed. pp. 285–305. Washington, DC and New Haven: National Gallery of Art and Yale University Press.

Bazán, Francisco, 1990 Arqueología y Etnohistoria de los Reynos Prehispánicos Tardíos de la Costa Central del Perú. Tesis de Licenciatura. Escuela Académico Profesional de Arqueología. Universidad Nacional Mayor de San Marcos, Lima.

Bean, S. Susan, 1998 Reviews. Journal of Material Culture 3(1):115–120.

Benavides C., Mario, 1978 Yacimientos arqueológicos en Ayacucho. Ayacucho: Universidad Nacional de San Cristóbal de Huamanga.

—— 1991 Cheqo Wasi, Huari. In Huari Administrative Structure: Prehistoric Monumental Architecture and State Government. William H. Isbell and Gordon F. McEwan, eds. pp. 55–69. Washington, DC: Dumbarton Oaks.

Benfer, Robert A., 1989 The Preceramic Period site of Paloma, Peru: Bioindications of improving adaptation to sedentism. Latin American Antiquity 1:284–318.

Bennett, Wendell C., 1934 Excavations at Tiahuanaco. Anthropological Papers of the American Museum of Natural History 34:359–494.

—— 1939 Archaeology of the north coast of Peru. Anthropological Papers of the American Museum of Natural History 37(1).

—— 1944 The north highlands of Peru: Excavations in the Callejón de Huaylas and at Chavín de Huántar. Anthropological Papers of the American Museum of Natural History 39(1).

—— 1946 Archaeology of the Central Andes. In Handbook of South American Indians, vol. 2. The Andean Civilizations. Julian H. Steward, ed. pp. 61–149. Bulletin 143, Bureau of American Ethnology. Washington, DC: Smithsonian Institution.

—— 1948a The Peruvian co-tradition. In A Reappraisal of Peruvian Archaeology. Wendell C. Bennett, ed. Memoirs, 4. Society for American Archaeology.

—— ed., 1948b A Reappraisal of Peruvian Archaeology. Memoirs, 4. Society for American Archaeology.

—— 1950 The Gallinazo Group, Virú Valley, Peru. Yale University Publications in Anthropology, 43. New Haven.

—— 1953 Excavations at Wari, Ayacucho, Peru. Yale University Publications in Anthropology, 49–50. New Haven.

Bennett, Wendell C., and Junius B. Bird, 1964[1949] Andean Culture History. Garden City: The Natural History Press.

Benson, Elizabeth, P., ed., 1972 Cult of the Feline. Washington, DC: Dumbarton Oaks.

Berezkin, Yuri E., 1983 Mochika. Leningrad: USSR Academy of Sciences.

Bermann, Marc P., 1994 Lukurmata: Household Archaeology in Prehispanic Bolivia. Princeton: Princeton University Press.

—— 1997 Domestic life and vertical integration in the Tiwanaku heartland. Latin American Antiquity 8(2):93–112.

Berthon, P. A. A., 1911 Étude sur le précolombien du bas-Pérou. Paris: Impr. Nationale.

Betanzos, Juan de, 1996[1550s] Narrative of the Incas. 1st edition. Roland Hamilton and Dana Buchanan, eds. Austin: University of Texas Press.

Billman, Brian R., 2001 Understanding the timing and tempo of the evolution of political centralization on the Central Andean coastline and beyond. In From Leaders to Rulers. Jonathan Haas, ed. pp. 177–199. New York: Kluwer Academic/Plenum Publishers.

—— 2002 Irrigation and the origins of the southern Moche state on the north coast of Peru. Latin American Antiquity 13(4):371–400.

Binford, Lewis, 1971 Mortuary practices: Their study and their potential. In Approaches to the Social Dimensions of Mortuary Practices. James A. Brown, ed. pp. 2–29. Memoirs, 25. Society for American Archaeology.

Binford, Michael W., and Alan L. Kolata, 1996 The natural and human setting. In Tiwanaku and its Hinterland: Archaeology and Paleoecology of an Andean Civilization, vol. 1. Alan L. Kolata, ed. pp. 23–56. Washington, DC: Smithsonian Institution Press.

Binford, Michael W., Alan L. Kolata, Mark Brenner, John W. Janusek, Matthew T. Seddon, Mark Abbott, and Jason H. Curtis, 1997 Climate variation and the rise and fall of an Andean civilization. Quaternary Research 47:235–248.

Bingham, Hiram, 1915 The story of Machu Picchu. National Geographic Magazine (February):172–217.

—— 1922 Inca Land: Explorations in the Highlands of Peru. Boston and New York: Houghton Mifflin.

Bird, Junius B., 1943 Excavations in northern Chile. Anthropological Papers of the American Museum of Natural History 38(4).

—— 1948 Preceramic cultures in Chicama and Virú. American Antiquity 4(2):21–28.

—— 1963 Technology and art in Peruvian textiles. New York Museum of Primitive Art Lecture Series 3:45–77.

—— 1964 Shaped tapestry bags from the Nazca-Ica area of Peru. Textile Museum Journal 1(3):2–7.

Bird, Junius B., and Louisa Bellinger, 1954 Paracas Fabrics and Nazca Needlework, 3rd Century B.C.–3rd Century A.D. Catalogue raisonnée. Washington, DC: National Publishing Company.

Bird, Junius B., John Hyslop, and Milca Skinner, 1985 The preceramic excavations at the Huaca Prieta, Chicama Valley, Peru. Anthropological Papers of the American Museum of Natural History 62(1):1–294.

Bird, Robert McK., 1990 What are the chances of finding maize in Peru dating before 1000 B.C.? Reply to Bonavia and Grobman. American Antiquity 55:828–840.

Blasco, María C., and Luis J. Ramos, 1980 Cerámica Nazca. Valladolid: Seminario Americanista de la Universidad de Valladolid.

————1991 Catálogo de la Cerámica Nazca del Museo de América. 2 vols. Madrid: Ministerio de Cultura.

Bloch, Maurice, and Jonathan Parry, 1982 Introduction: Death and the regeneration of life. In Death and the Regeneration of Life. Maurice Bloch and Jonathan Parry, eds. pp. 1–44. Cambridge: Cambridge University Press.

Blom, Deborah E., 1999 Tiwanaku Regional Interaction and Social Identity: A Bioarchaeological Approach. Ph.D. dissertation, Department of Anthropology, University of Chicago.

Blom, Deborah E., John W. Janusek, and Jane E. Buikstra, 2003 A re-evaluation of human remains from Tiwanaku. In Tiwanaku and its Hinterland: Archaeological and Paleoecological Investigations of an Andean Civilization, vol. 2. Alan L. Kolata, ed. Washington, DC: Smithsonian Institution Press.

Bonavia, Duccio, 1978 El origen del maíz andino. In Estudios Americanistas 1. R. Hartman and U. Oberem, eds. pp. 82–91. St. Agustin.

————1982 Los Gavilanes. Mar, Desierto y Oasis en la Historia del Hombre. Lima: COFIDE and Instituto Arqueológico Alemán.

————1991 Perú, Hombre e Historia. De los Orígenes al Siglo XV. Lima: Ediciones Edubanco.

————1996a De la caza-recolección a la agricultura: Una perspectiva local. Boletín del Instituto Francés de Estudios Andinos 25(2):169–186. Lima.

————1996b Los Camélidos Sudamericanos: Una Introducción a su Estudio. Lima: Instituto Francés de Estudios Andinos and Universidad Peruana Cayetano Heredia, Conservación Internacional.

————1997[1993–95] La domesticación de las plantas y los orígenes de la agricultura en los Andes Centrales. Revista Histórica 37:77–107. Lima.

————1998 Bases marítimas o desarollo agrícolas? In 50 Years of Americanist Studies at the University of Bonn, pp. 45–62. BAS 30. Markt Schwaben: Verlag Anton Saurwein.

Bonavia, Duccio, and Alexander Grobman, 1989a Preceramic maize in the Central Andes: A necessary clarification. American Antiquity 54:836–840.

————1989b Andean maize: Its origins and domestication. In Foraging and Farming: The Evolution of Plant Exploitation. D. R. Harris and G. C. Hillman, eds. pp. 456–470. London: Unwin Hyman.

————2000 Revisión de las pruebas de la existencia de maiz precerámico de los Andes Centrales. In El Período Arcaico en el Perú: Hacia una Definición de los Orígenes. Peter Kaulicke, ed. pp. 239–262. Boletín de Arquelogía PUCP, vol. 3. Lima: Departamento de Humanidades, Especialidad de Arqueología, Pontificia Universidad Católica del Perú.

Bonavia, Duccio, Laura Johnson, Elizabeth Reitz, Elizabeth S. Wing, and Glendon Weir, 1993 Un sitio precerámico de Huarmey (PV35–6) antes de la introducción del maíz. Boletín del Instituto Francés de Estudios Andinos 22(2):409–442.

Bonavia, Duccio, Laura Johnson-Kelly, Elizabeth Reitz, and Elizabeth S. Wing, 2001 El precerámico medio de Huarmey: Historia de un sitio (PV35–106). Bulletin de l'Institut Français Études Andines 30(2):265–333. Lima.

Bonnier, Elisabeth, 1997 Preceramic architecture in the Andes: The Mito Tradition. In Archaeológica Peruana 2. Elisabeth Bonnier and Henning Bischof, eds. pp. 120–144. Mannheim: Sociedad Arqueológica Peruano-Alemana, Reiss Museum.

Bourget, Steve, 2001 Children and ancestors: Ritual practices at the Moche site of Huaca de la Luna, north coast of Peru. In Ritual Sacrifice in Ancient Peru: New Discoveries and Interpretations. Elizabeth P. Benson and Anita G. Cook, eds. pp. 93–118. Austin: University of Texas Press.

Bowman, Sheridan, 1990 Radiocarbon Dating. Berkeley: University of California Press.

—— 1994 Using radiocarbon: An update. Antiquity 68:838–843.

Boytner, Ran, 1998a The Pacatnamu Textiles: A Study of Identity and Function. Ph.D. dissertation, Department of Anthropology, University of California, Los Angeles.

—— 1998b Textiles from the lower Osmore Valley, southern Peru: A cultural interpretation. Andean Past 5:325–356.

—— 2002 Preferencias culturales: Un punto de vista desde la investigación sobre los tintes de los textiles andinos. *In* Actas de la II Jornada Internacional Sobre Textiles Precolombinos. Victoria Demestre Solanilla, ed. Barcelona: Servicio de Publicación de la Universidad Autónoma de Barcelona.

—— In press. Class, control and power: The anthropology of textile dyes at Pacatnamu. *In* South American Textile Traditions. Margaret Young-Sanchez, ed. Denver: Denver Art Museum.

Bragayrac Davila, Enrique, 1991 Archaeological excavations in the Vegachayoq Moqo sector of Huari. *In* Huari Administrative Structure: Prehistoric Monumental Architecture and State Government. William H. Isbell and Gordon F. McEwan, eds. pp. 71–80. Washington, DC: Dumbarton Oaks.

Brewster-Wray, Christine C., 1990 Moraduchayuq: An Administrative Compound at the Site of Huari, Peru. Ph.D. dissertation, Department of Anthropology, State University of New York, Binghamton.

Briceño, Jesús, 1999 Quebrada Santa María: Las puntas en cola de pescado y la antigüedad del hombre en Sudamérica. *In* El Período Arcaico en el Perú: Hacia una Definición de los Orígenes. Peter Kaulicke, ed. pp. 19–30. Boletín de Arqueología PUCP, vol. 3. Lima: Departamento de Humanidades, Especialidad de Arqueología, Pontificia Universidad Católica del Perú.

Browman, David L., 1981 New light on Andean Tiwanaku. American Scientist 69(4): 408–419.

—— 1985 Cultural primacy of Tiwanaku in the development of later Peruvian states. Dialogo Andino 4:59–71.

Brown, Charles B., 1924 Detailed Description of Implements from El Estero, N. W. Peru. MS, Museum of Archaeology and Ethnology, Cambridge.

Brown, Kathryn, 2001 New trips through the back alleys of agriculture. Science 292:631–633.

Browne, David M., 1992 Further archaeological reconnaissance in the province of Palpa, Department of Ica, Peru. *In* Ancient America: Contributions to New World Archaeology. Nicholas J. Saunders, ed. pp. 17–116. Oxbow Monograph 24. Oxford: Oxbow Books.

Browne, David M., and José Pablo Baraybar, 1988 An archaeological reconnaissance in the province of Palpa, Department of Ica, Peru. *In* Recent Studies in Pre-Columbian Archaeology. Nicholas J. Saunders and Oliver de Montmollin, eds. pp. 299–325. Oxford: British Archaeological Reports, International Series, 421(ii).

Browne, David M., Helaine Silverman, and Rubén García Soto, 1993 A cache of forty-eight Nasca trophy heads from Cerro Carapo, Peru. Latin American Antiquity 4(3):274–294.

Bruce, Susan Lee, 1986 Textile miniatures from Pacatnamu, Peru. *In* The Junius B. Bird Conference on Andean Textiles: April 7th and 8th, 1984. Ann Pollard Rowe, ed. pp. 183–204. Washington, DC: The Textile Museum.

Brumfiel, Elizabeth M., 1991 Weaving and cooking: Women's production in Aztec Mexico. *In* Engendering Archaeology: Women and Prehistory. Joan M. Gero and Margaret W. Conkey, eds. pp. 224–251. London: Blackwell.

——1994 Ethnic groups and political development in ancient Mexico. *In* Factional Competition and Political Development in the New World. Elizabeth M. Brumfiel and John W. Fox, eds. pp. 89–102. Cambridge: Cambridge University Press.

Brundage, Burr C., 1967 Lords of Cuzco: A History and Description of the Inca People in their Final Days. Norman: University of Oklahoma Press.

Bryan, Alan L., ed., 1986 New Evidence for the Pleistocene Peopling of the Americas. Orono: Center for the Study of Early Man, University of Maine.

Bueno, Alberto, 1974–75 Cajamarquilla y Pachacamac: Dos ciudades de la costa central del Perú. Boletín Bibliográfico de Antropología Americana 37(46):171–211.

——1977 El Señorio de Ichimay. Revista Espacio 2:66–71.

——1982 El Antiguo Valle de Pachacamac: Espacio, Tiempo y Cultura. Lima: Editorial Los Pinos.

Bueno, Alberto, and Terence Grieder, 1988 The geography of the Tablachaca Canyon. *In* La Galgada, Peru: A Preceramic Culture in Transition, pp. 4–18. Austin: University of Texas Press.

Buikstra, Jane, 1995 Tombs for the living or for the dead: The Osmore ancestors. *In* Tombs for the Living: Andean Mortuary Practices. Tom D. Dillehay, ed. pp. 229–280. Washington, DC: Dumbarton Oaks.

Burger, Richard L., 1981 The radiocarbon evidence for the temporal priority of Chavín de Huántar. American Antiquity 46:592–602.

——1984a Archaeological areas and prehistoric frontiers: The case of Formative Peru and Ecuador. *In* Social and Economic Organization in the Prehispanic Andes. David L. Browman, Richard L. Burger, and Mario A. Rivera, eds. pp. 33–71. Oxford: British Archaeological Reports, International Series, 194.

——1984b The Prehistoric Occupation of Chavín de Huántar, Peru. University of California Publications, Anthropology, 14. Berkeley: University of California Press.

——1985 Concluding remarks. *In* Early Ceremonial Architecture in the Andes. Christopher B. Donnan, ed. pp. 269–289. Washington, DC.: Dumbarton Oaks.

——1988 Unity and heterogeneity within the Chavín Horizon. *In* Peruvian Prehistory. Richard W. Keatinge, ed. pp. 99–144. New York: Cambridge University Press.

——1992 Chavín and the Origins of Andean Civilization. New York: Thames & Hudson.

Burger, Richard L., and Robert B. Gordon, 1998 Early Central Andean metalworking from Mina Perdida, Peru. Science 282:1108–1111.

Burger, Richard L., and Ramiro Matos Mendieta, 2002 Atalla: A center on the periphery of the Chavín Horizon. Latin American Antiquity 13(2):153–177.

Burger, Richard L., and Lucy Salazar-Burger, 1980 Ritual and religion at Huaricoto. Archaeology 33(6):26–32.

———1985 The early ceremonial center of Huaricoto. *In* Early Ceremonial Architecture in the Andes. Christopher B. Donnan, ed. pp. 111–138. Washington, DC: Dumbarton Oaks.

———1986 Early organizational diversity in the Peruvian highlands: Huaricoto and Kotosh. *In* Andean Archaeology: Papers in Memory of Clifford Evans. Roberto Matos, Solveig Turpin, and Herbert Eling, Jr., eds. pp. 65–82. Monograph XXVII, Institute of Archaeology, University of California, Los Angeles.

———1991 The second season of investigations at the Initial Period center of Cardal, Peru. Journal of Field Archaeology 18(3):275–296.

Burger, Richard L., and Nicholas van der Merwe, 1990 Maize and the origin of highland Chavín civilization: An isotopic perspective. American Anthropologist 92(1):85–95.

Bushnell, G. H. S., 1963 Perú. New York: Frederick A. Praeger.

Cabello de Balboa [Valboa], Miguel, 1951[1586] Miscelánea Antártica: Una Historia del Perú Antiguo. Lima: Universidad Nacional Mayor de San Marcos.

Calhoun, Craig J., 1980 The authority of ancestors. Man 15:304–319.

Callen, Eric O., and Thomas W. Cameron, 1955 The diet and parasite of prehistoric Huaca Prieta Indians as determined by dried coprolites. Royal Society of Canada (Proceedings) 5:51–52. Ottawa.

Canziani, José, 1987 Análisis del complejo urbano Maranga Chayavilca. Gaceta Arqueológica Andina 14:10–17.

——1992 Arquitectura y urbanismo del período Paracas en el valle de Chincha. Gaceta Arqueológica Andina 6:87–117.

——2002 Estado y ciudad: Revisión de la teoría sobre la sociedad Moche. In Moche: Hacia el Final del Milenio. Santiago Uceda and Elias Mujica, eds. pp. 789–813. Trujillo: Universidad Nacional de la Libertad.

Cárdenas Martin, Mercedes, 1999 Tablada de Lurín, Excavaciones, 1958–1989. Lima: Pontificia Universidad Católica del Perú, Instituto Riva Agüero, Dirección Académica de Investigación.

Cardich, Augusto, 1964 Lauricocha. Fundamentos para una prehistoria de los Andes Centrales. Studia Praehistorica, 3. Buenos Aires: Centro Argentino de Estudios Prehistóricos.

——1978 Recent excavations at Lauricocha and Los Toldos. In New Evidence for the Pleistocene Peopling of the Americas. Alan L. Bryan, ed. pp. 296–302. Orono: Center for the Study of Early Man, University of Maine.

Carmichael, Patrick H., 1988 Nasca Mortuary Customs: Death and Ancient Society on the South Coast of Peru. Ph.D. dissertation, Department of Archaeology, University of Calgary.

——1991 Prehistoric Settlement of the Ica-Grande Littoral, Southern Peru. Research Report to the Social Sciences and Humanities Research Council of Canada.

——1995 Nasca burial patterns: Social structure and mortuary ideology. In Tombs for the Living: Andean Mortuary Practices. Tom D. Dillehay, ed. pp. 161–188. Washington, DC: Dumbarton Oaks.

Carr, Christopher, and Jill E. Neitzel, eds., 1995 Style, Society and Person: Archaeological and Ethnological Perspectives. New York: Plenum Press.

Carrión, Lucénida, 1998 Excavaciones en San Jacinto, templo en U en el valle de Chancay. In Perspectivas Regionales del Período Formativo en el Perú. Peter Kaulicke, ed. pp. 239–250. Boletín de Arqueología PUCP, vol. 2. Lima: Departamento de Humanidades, Especialidad de Arqueología, Pontificia Universidad Católica del Perú.

Carrión Cachot, Rebeca, 1949 Paracas Cultural Elements. Lima: Corporación Nacional de Turismo.

——1955 El culto al agua en el antiguo Perú: La paccha, elemento cultural pan-andino. Revista del Museo Nacional de Antropología y Arqueología 2(2):50–140.

——1959 La Religión en el Antiguo Perú. Lima: Tipografía Peruana.

Cassman, Vicki, 1997 A Reconsideration of Prehistoric Ethnicity and Status in Northern Chile: The Textile Evidence. Ph.D. dissertation, Department of Anthropology, Arizona State University, Tempe.

——2000 Prehistoric Andean ethnicity and status: The textile evidence. In Beyond Cloth and Cordage: Archaeological Textile Research in the Americas. B. Penelope Drooker and Laurie D. Webster, eds. pp. 253–267. Salt Lake City: University of Utah Press.

Castillo, Luis Jaime, 1989 Personajes Míticos, Escenas, y Narraciones en la Iconografía Mochica. Lima: Pontificia Universidad Católica del Perú, Fondo Editorial.

——1993 Prácticas funerarias, poder e ideología en la sociedad Moche Tardía. Gaceta Arqueológica Andina 7:67–82.

——1995 Los Mochica del norte y los Mochica del sur. *In* Vicús. Krzysztof Makowski et al., eds. pp. 143–176. Lima: Banco de Crédito del Perú.

——1997 La Tumba de la Sacerdotisa de San José de Moro. La Libertad: Instituto Nacional de Cultura.

——2001 The last of the Mochicas: A view from the Jequetepeque Valley. *In* Moche Art and Archaeology in Ancient Peru. Joanne Pillsbury, ed. pp. 307–332. Washington, DC and New Haven: National Gallery of Art and Yale University Press.

Castillo, Luis Jaime, and Christopher B. Donnan, 1994 La ocupación Moche de San José de Moro, Jequetepeque. *In* Moche: Propuestas y Perspectivas. Santiago Uceda and Elias Mujica, eds. pp. 93–146. Trujillo: Universidad Nacional de la Libertad.

Castillo, Luis Jaime, Carol Mackey, and Andrew Nelson, 1997 Informe Preliminar: Campaña 1996 del Proyecto Complejo Arqueológico de Moro. Lima: Instituto Nacional de Cultura.

Champion, T. C., ed., 1989 Centre and Periphery. Comparative Studies in Archaeology. London: Unwin Hyman.

Chapdelaine, Claude, 2000 Struggling for survival: The urban class of the Moche site, north coast of Peru. *In* Environmental Disaster and the Archaeology of Human Response. Garth Bawden and Richard M. Reycraft, eds. pp. 121–143. Anthropological Papers, 7. Maxwell Museum of Anthropology, University of New Mexico, Albuquerque.

——2002 La ciudad de Moche: Urbanismo y estado. *In* Moche: Hacia el Final del Milenio. Santiago Uceda and Elias Mujica, eds. pp. 749–787. Trujillo: Universidad Nacional de la Libertad.

Chatfield, Melissa, 1998 Ceramics from the Site of Chokepukio, Cuzco, Peru. Paper delivered at the 63rd Annual Meeting of the Society for American Archaeology.

Chauchat, Claude, Elizabeth S. Wing, Jean-Paul Lacombe, Pierre-Yves Demars, Santiago Evaristo Uceda Castillo, and Carlos Deza, 1992 Préhistoire de la côte nord du Pérou: Le Paijanien de Cupisnique. Cahiers du Quaternaire, 18. Paris: Centre Régional de Publications de Bordeaux, Éditions CNRS.

Chávez, Karen Mohr, 1988 The significance of Chiripa in Lake Titicaca Basin developments. Expedition 30(3):17–26.

——2002 Local differences and regional similarities in pottery of the Yaya-Mama Religious Tradition. Paper presented at the 67th Annual Meeting of the Society for American Archaeology.

Chávez, Sergio J., 2002 Excavation of a new temple site belonging to the Yaya-Mama Religious Tradition: Preliminary results. Paper presented at the 67th Annual Meeting of the Society for American Archaeology.

Childe, V. Gordon, 1950 The urban revolution. Town Planning Review 21(1):3–17.

Choy, Emilio, 1960 La revolución neolítica en los orígenes de la civilización americana. *In* Antiguo Perú: Espacio y Tiempo, pp. 149–198. Lima: Librería Editorial Juan Mejía Baca.

Church, Warren B., 1996 Prehistoric Cultural Development and Interregional Interaction in the Tropical Montane Forests of Peru. Ph.D. dissertation, Department of Anthropology, Yale University, New Haven.

Cieza de León, Pedro de, 1922 Crónica del Perú. Madrid: Imprenta Calpe.

——1976[1553 (pt. 1); 1554 (pt. 2)] The Incas of Pedro Cieza de León. Harriet de Onís, trans. Victor W. von Hagen, ed. Norman: University of Oklahoma Press.

——n.d. La Crónica del Perú. *In* Crónicas de la Conquista del Perú. J. Riverend, ed. pp. 125–497. Mexico DF: Editorial Nueva España.

——1986 Crónica del Perú. Segunda Parte. 2nd edition, corrected. Lima: Pontificia Universidad Católica del Perú.

Clapperton, Claude M., 1993 Quaternary Geology and Geomorphology of South America. Amsterdam: Elsevier.

Clark, Niki, 1990 Textiles arqueológicos y su contexto socio-cultural. *In* Trabajos Arqueológicos en Moquegua, Perú. Luis Watanabe, Michael E. Moseley, and Fernando Cabieses, eds. pp. 123–137. Ilo: Programa Contisuyu.

Clarkson, Persis B. 1990 The archaeology of the Nazca Pampa: Environmental and cultural parameters. *In* The Lines of Nazca. Anthony F. Aveni, ed. pp. 117–172. Philadelphia: The American Philosophical Society.

Classen, Constance, 1993 Inca Cosmology and the Human Body. Salt Lake City: University of Utah Press.

Coben, Lawrence, and Charles Stanish, In press. Archaeological reconnaissance in the Carabaya region, Peru. *In* Advances in the Archaeology of the Titicaca Basin, 1. Charles Stanish, Amanda B. Cohen, and Mark S. Aldenderfer, eds. Los Angeles: Cotsen Institute of Archeology, UCLA.

Cobo, Bernabé, 1979[1653] History of the Inca Empire: An Account of the Indians' Customs and their Origin, Together with a Treatise on Inca Legends, History, and Social Institutions. Roland Hamilton, trans. Austin: University of Texas Press.

——1990[1653] Inca Religion and Custom. Austin: University of Texas Press.

Cohen, Abner, 1979 Political symbolism. Annual Review of Anthropology 8:87–113.

Collier, Donald, 1955 Cultural Chronology and Change as Reflected in the Ceramics of the Virú Valley, Peru. Fieldiana: Anthropology, 43. Chicago: Field Museum of Natural History.

——1961 Agriculture and civilization on the coast of Peru. The Evolution of Horticultural Systems in Native South America: Causes and Consequences. A Symposium. Anthropological Supplement Publication, 2. Johannes Wilbert, ed. pp. 101–109. Sociedad de Ciencias Naturales, La Salle. Caracas: Editorial Sucre.

——1962 Archaeological investigations in the Casma Valley, Peru. Akten des 34. Internationalen Amerikanistenkongress, Wien, 1960, pp. 411–417.

Comaroff, Jean, and John Comaroff, 1991 Of Revelation and Revolution: Christianity, Colonialism, and Consciousness in South Africa. Chicago: University of Chicago Press.

——1992 Ethnography and the Historical Imagination. Boulder: Westview Press.

Conkey, Margaret, 1990 Experimenting with style in archaeology: Some historical and theoretical issues. *In* The Uses of Style in Archaeology. Margaret Conkey and Christine Hastorf, eds. pp. 5–17. New York: Cambridge University Press.

Conkey, Margaret, and Christine Hastorf, eds., 1990 The Use of Style in Archaeology. New York: Cambridge University Press.

Conklin, J. William, 1970 Textile fragment from the beginning of the Middle Horizon. Textile Museum Journal 3(1):15–24. Washington, DC.

——1971 Chavín textiles and the origin of Peruvian weaving. Textile Museum Journal 3(2):13–19.

——1983 Pucara and Tiahuanaco tapestry: Time and style in sierra weaving traditions. Ñawpa Pacha 21:1–44.

——1985 The architecture of Huaca Los Reyes. *In* Early Ceremonial Architecture in the Andes. Christopher B. Donnan, ed. pp. 139–164. Washington, DC: Dumbarton Oaks.

——1986 The mythic geometry of the ancient southern sierra. *In* The Junius B. Bird Conference on Andean Textiles: April 7th and 8th, 1984. Ann Pollard Rowe, ed. Washington, DC: The Textile Museum.

Conlee, Christina A., 2000 Late Prehispanic Occupation of Pajonal Alto, Nasca, Peru: Implications for Imperial Collapse and Societal Reformation. Ph.D. dissertation, Department of Anthropology, University of California, Santa Barbara.

——2002 Regional autonomy in the late prehispanic period: An analysis of ceramics from the Nasca Drainage. Andean Past 7.

——2003 Local elites and the reformation of Late Intermediate Period sociopolitical and economic organization in Nasca, Peru. Latin American Antiquity 14(1):47–65.

Conlee, Christina A., and Aurelio Rodríguez Rodríguez, 2002 Informe del Proyecto La Tiza 2002. Unpublished report submitted to the Instituto Nacional de Cultural, Lima, Peru.

Conrad, Geoffrey W., 1981 Cultural materialism, split inheritance, and the expansion of ancient Peruvian empires. American Antiquity 46:3–26.

——1982 The burial platforms of Chan Chan: Some social and political implications. In Chan Chan: Andean Desert City. Michael E. Moseley and Kent C. Day, eds. pp. 87–114. Albuquerque: University of New Mexico Press.

——1990 Farfán, General Pacatnamu, and the dynastic history of Chimor. In The Northern Dynasties: Kingship and Statecraft in Chimor. Michael Moseley and Alana Cordy-Collins, eds. pp. 227–242. Washington, DC: Dumbarton Oaks.

Cook, Anita, 1983 Aspects of state ideology in Huari and Tiwanaku iconography: The Central Deity and Sacrificer. In Investigations of the Andean Past: Papers from the First Annual Northeast Conference on Andean Archaeology and Ethnohistory. Daniel H. Sandweiss, ed. pp. 161–185. Ithaca: Cornell University Latin American Studies Program.

——1987 The Middle Horizon ceramic offerings from Conchopata. Ñawpa Pacha 22–23:49–90, 1984–1985.

——1992a The stone ancestors: idioms of imperial attire and rank among Huari figurines. Latin American Antiquity 3:341–364.

——1992b Investigaciones de Reconocimiento Arqueológico en la Parte Baja del Valle de Ica. Informe final 1988–1990. Instituto Nacional de Cultura, Lima.

——1994 Wari y Tiwanaku: Entre el Estilo y la Imágen. Lima: Fondo Editorial, Pontificia Universidad Católica del Perú.

——1996 The emperor's new clothes: Symbols of royalty, hierarchy and identity. Journal of the Steward Anthropological Society 24(1–2):85–120. Department of Anthropology, University of Illinois at Urbana-Champaign.

——1997a Identity and Gender Ambiguity in Wari Imagery. Paper presented at the 49th International Congress of Americanists, Quito.

——1997b Identity and gender ambiguity in Wari imagery. Paper presented in a session co-organized by Anita Cook and Joan Gero entitled Configuring Identities in Prehistory: Ethnicity, Class, Gender and Occupation, at the 49th International Congress of Americanists, Quito, Ecuador July 7–12, 1997.

——1999 Asentamientos Paracas en el valle bajo de Ica, Perú. Gaceta Arqueológica Andina 25:61–90.

——2000 Conspicuous Consumption: The Making of an Elite Wari Assemblage. Paper presented at the 65th Annual Meeting of the Society for American Archaeology.

——2001 Huari D-shaped structures, sacrificial offerings, and divine rulership. In Ritual Sacrifice in Ancient America. Elizabeth P. Benson and Anita G. Cook, eds. pp. 137–163. Austin: University of Texas Press.

Cook, Anita, and Nancy Benco, 2000 Vasijas para la fiesta y la fama: Producción artesanal en un centro urbano Huari. In Huari y Tiwanaku: Modelos vs. Evidencias. Peter Kaulicke and William H. Isbell, eds. pp. 489–504. Boletín de Arqueología PUCP, vol. 4. Lima: Departamento de Humanidades, Especialidad de Arqueología, Pontificia Universidad Católica del Perú.

Cook, Anita, and M. Glowacki, 2003 Pots, politics, and power: Wari ceramic assemblages and imperial administration. In The Archaeology and Politics of Food and Feasting in Early States and Empires. Tamara Bray, ed. New York: Kluwer Academic/Plenum Publishers.

Cordy-Collins, Alana, 1977 Chavín art: Its shamanic/hallucinogenic origins. In Pre-

Columbian Art History. Alana Cordy-Collins and Jean Stern, eds. pp. 353–362. Palo Alto: Peek Publications.

——1992 Archaism or tradition? The Decapitation Theme in Cupisnique and Moche iconography. Latin American Antiquity 3(3):206–220.

——1996 Lambayeque. *In* Andean Art at Dumbarton Oaks. Elizabeth H. Boone, ed. Washington, DC: Dumbarton Oaks.

——2001 Decapitation in Cupisnique and Early Moche societies. *In* Ritual Sacrifice in Ancient Peru: New Discoveries and Interpretations. Elizabeth P. Benson and Anita G. Cook, eds. pp. 21–34. Austin: University of Texas Press.

Correal, Gonzalo, and Thomas van der Hammen, 1977 Investigaciones Arqueológicas en los Abrigos Rocosos del Tequendama. Bogatá: Banco Popular.

Costin, Cathy L., 1993 Textiles, women and political economy in late prehispanic Peru. Research in Economic Anthropology 14:3–28.

——1998 Housewives, chosen women, skilled men: Cloth production and social identity in the late prehispanic Andes. *In* Craft and Social Identity. Cathy L. Costin and Rita P. Wright, eds. pp. 123–141. Archaeological Papers of the American Anthropological Association, 8. Washington, DC: American Anthropological Association.

Couture, Nicole, 2002 Construction of Power: Monumental Space and Elite Residence at Tiwanaku. Ph.D. dissertation, Department of Anthropology, University of Chicago.

——2003 Ritual, monumentalism, and residence at Mollo Kontu, Tiwanaku. *In* Tiwanaku and its Hinterland: Archaeological and Paleoecological Investigations of an Andean Civilization, vol. 2. Alan L. Kolata, ed. Washington, DC: Smithsonian Institution Press.

Couture, Nicole, and Kathryn Sampeck, 2003 Putuni: A history of palace architecture in Tiwanaku. *In* Tiwanaku and its Hinterland: Archaeology and Paleoecology of an Andean Civilization, vol. 2. Alan L. Kolata, ed. Washington, DC: Smithsonian Institution Press.

Craig, Alan K., and Norbert Psuty, 1968 The Paracas Papers. Studies in Marine Desert Ecology 1, Reconnaissance Report. Occasional Publication, 1. Department of Geography, Florida Atlantic University, Boca Raton.

Créque-Monfort, Count G. de, 1906 Fouilles de la mission scientifique française a Tiahuanaco. Ses recherches archéologiques et ethnographices en Bolivie, au Chili et dans la République Argentine. Internationaler Amerikanisten-Kongress. Vierzehnte Tagung Stuttgart, 1904, pt. 2:531–555.

Crumley, Carole, 1987 A dialectical critique of hierarchy. *In* Power Relations and State Formation. Thomas C. Patterson and Christine W. Gailey, eds. pp. 155–159. Washington, DC: American Anthropological Association.

Crumley, Carole, and William Marquadt, 1990 Landscape: A unifying concept in regional analysis. *In* Interpreting Space: GIS and Archaeology. Kathleen M. S. Allen, Stanton W. Green, and Ezra B. W. Zubrow, eds. pp. 73–79. London: Taylor & Francis.

Daggett, Richard, 1991 Paracas: Discovery and controversy. *In* Paracas Art and Architecture: Object and Context in South Coastal Peru. Anne Paul, ed. pp. 35–60. Iowa City: University of Iowa Press.

——1994 The Paracas mummy bundles of the great Necropolis of Wari Kayan: A history. Andean Past 4:53–76.

D'Altroy, Terence N., 1992 Provincial Power in the Inka Empire. Washington, DC: Smithsonian Institution Press.

——2002 The Incas. Oxford: Blackwell.

——In press. Remaking the social landscape: Colonization in the Inka empire. *In* The Archaeology of Colonies. Gil Stein, ed. Albuquerque: SAR Press.

Day, Kent C., 1982 Ciudadelas: Their form and function. *In* Chan Chan: Andean Desert

City. Michael E. Moseley and Kent C. Day, eds. pp. 55–66. Albuquerque: University of New Mexico Press.

DeBoer, Warren, 2002 *Review of* Formativo Sudamericano, Una Revaluación: Ponencias Presentadas en el Simposio Internacional de Arqueología Sudamericana, Cuenca-Ecuador. Homenaje a Alberto Rex González y Betty J. Meggers. Latin American Antiquity 113(1):121–122.

DeLeonardis, Lisa, 1991 Settlement History of the Lower Ica Valley, 5th–1st Centuries B.C. MA thesis, Department of Anthropology, Catholic University, Washington, DC.

——1997 Paracas Settlement in Callango, Lower Ica Valley, First Millennium, B.C. Peru. Department of Anthropology, Catholic University, Washington, DC.

——2000 The body context: Interpreting Nasca decapitated burials. Latin American Antiquity 11(4):363–386.

——2003 Early Paracas cultural contexts: New evidence from the west bank of Callango. Andean Past 7.

Demarest, Arthur Andrew, 1981 Viracocha: The Nature and Antiquity of the Andean High God. Monograph 6. Peabody Museum of Archaeology and Ethnology, Harvard University, Cambridge.

DeMarrais, Elizabeth Castillo, Luis Jaime Castillo, and Timothy Earle, 1996 Ideology, materialization, and power strategies. Current Anthropology 37:15–31.

Desrosiers, Sophie, 1992 ¿Las técnicas del tejido tienen un sentido? Una propuesta de lectura de los tejidos andinos y repuesta. Revista Andina 19(1):7–46.

Di Capua, Costanza, 1994 Valdivia figurines and puberty rituals: An hypothesis. Andean Past 4:229–279.

Dietler, Michael, 1996 Feasts and commensal politics in the political economy: Food, power, and status in prehistoric Europe. *In* Food and the Status Quest: An Interdisciplinary Perspective. Polly Wiessner and Wulf Schiefenhovel, eds. pp. 87–125. Oxford: Berghahn Books.

——2001 Theorizing the feast: rituals of consumption, commensal politics, and power in African contexts. *In* Feasts: Archaeological and Ethnographic Perspectives on Food, Politics, and Power. Michael Dietler and Brian Hayden, eds. pp. 65–114. Washington, DC: Smithsonian Institution Press.

Dietler, Michael, and Brian Hayden, eds., 2001 Feasts: Archaeological and Ethnographic Perspectives on Food, Politics, and Power. Smithsonian Institution Press, Washington, DC.

Dillehay, Tom D., 1979 Pre-Hispanic resource sharing in the Central Andes. Science 204(4388):24–31.

——1995 Mounds of social death: Araucanian funerary rites and political succession. *In* Tombs for the Living: Andean Mortuary Practices. Tom D. Dillehay, ed. pp. 281–313. Washington, DC: Dumbarton Oaks.

——2000 The Settlement of the Americas: A New Prehistory. New York: Perseus and Basic Books.

——2001 Town and country in Late Moche times: A view from two northern valleys. *In* Moche Art and Archaeology in Ancient Peru. Joanne Pillsbury, ed. pp. 259–283. Washington, DC and New Haven: National Gallery of Art and Yale University Press.

Dillehay, Tom D., Gerardo Politis, Gustavo Politis, and Maria C. Beltrao, 1992 Earliest hunters and gatherers of South America. Journal of World Prehistory 6:145–204.

Dillehay, Tom D., Jack Rossen, Greg Maggard, Kary Stackelback, and Patricia J. Netherly, 2003 Early localization and possible social aggregation in the Late Pleistocene and Early Holocene on the north coast of Peru. Quaternary International 109–10:3–12.

Dillehay, Tom D., Jack Rossen, and Patricia J. Netherly, 1997 The Nanchoc tradition: The beginnings of Andean civilization. American Scientist January–February: 46–55.

Disselhoff, Hans-Dietrich, 1956 Hand- und kopftrophäen in plastischen Darstellung der Recuay-keramik. Baessler Archiv, new series, 4:25–32.

Dobres, Marcia-Ann, 2000 Technology and Social Agency. Oxford: Blackwell.

——and John E. Robb, eds., 2000 Agency in Archaeology. London: Routledge.

Dolorier, Camilo, 1999 Pachacamac. Lima: Arkinka.

Donnan, Christopher B., 1972 Moche-Huari murals from northern Peru. Archaeology 25(2):85–95.

——1973 Moche Occupation of the Santa Valley, Peru. Los Angeles: UCLA Latin American Center Publications.

——1976 Moche Art and Iconography. Los Angeles: Latin American Studies Publications, UCLA.

——1978 Moche Art of Peru. Los Angeles: Fowler Museum of Culture History, UCLA.

——1986 An elaborate textile fragment from the Major Quadrangle. *In* The Pacatnamu Papers, vol. 1. Christopher B. Donnan and Guillermo Cock, eds. pp. 109–116. Los Angeles: Fowler Museum of Cultural History, UCLA.

——1988 Unraveling the mystery of the Warrior-Priest. National Geographic 174(4):551–555.

——1990a An assessment of the validity of the Naylamp dynasty. *In* The Northern Dynasties: Kingship and Statecraft in Chimor. Michael E. Moseley and Alana Cordy-Collins, eds. pp. 243–274. Washington, DC: Dumbarton Oaks.

——1990b The Chotuna friezes and the Chotuna-Dragon connection. *In* The Northern Dynasties: Kingship and Statecraft in Chimor. Michael E. Moseley and Alana Cordy-Collins, ed. pp. 275–296. Washington, DC: Dumbarton Oaks.

——1995 Moche funerary practice. *In* Tombs for the Living: Andean Mortuary Practices. Tom D. Dillehay, ed. pp. 111–160. Washington, DC: Dumbarton Oaks.

——2001a Moche ceramic portraits. *In* Moche Art and Archaeology in Ancient Peru. Joanne Pillsbury, ed. pp. 127–141. Washington, DC and New Haven: National Gallery of Art and Yale University Press.

——2001b Moche burials uncovered. National Geographic 199(3):58–73.

——2002 Tumbas con entierros en miniatura: Un nuevo tipo funerario Moche. *In* Moche: Hacia el Final del Milenio. Santiago Uceda and Elias Mujica, eds. pp. 55–90. Trujillo: Universidad Nacional de la Libertad.

Donnan, Christopher B., and Luis Jaime Castillo, 1992 Finding the Tomb of a Moche priestess. Archaeology 45:38–42.

——1994 Excavaciones de tumbas de sacerdotisas Moche en San José de Moro, Jequetepeque. *In* Moche: Propuestas y Perspectivas. Santiago Uceda and Luis Jaime Castillo, eds. pp. 415–424. Trujillo: Universidad Nacional de la Libertad.

Donnan, Christopher B., and Guillermo A. Cock, eds., 1986 The Pacatnamu Papers, vol. 1. Los Angeles: Fowler Museum of Cultural History, UCLA.

——eds., 1997 The Pacatnamu Papers, vol. 2. Los Angeles: Fowler Museum of Cultural History, UCLA.

Donnan, Christopher B., and Sharon G. Donnan, 1997 Moche textiles at Pacatnamu. *In* The Pacatnamu Papers, vol. 2. Christopher B. Donnan and Guillermo Cock, eds. pp. 215–242. Los Angeles: Fowler Museum of Cultural History, UCLA.

Donnan, Christopher B., and Carol J. Mackey, 1978 Ancient Burial Patterns of the Moche Valley, Peru. Austin: University of Texas Press.

Donnan, Christopher B., and Donna McClelland, 1979 The Burial Theme in Moche Iconography. Studies in Pre-Columbian Art and Archaeology, 21. Washington, DC: Dumbarton Oaks.

Douglas, Mary, 1966 Purity and Danger. London: Routledge.

Doyle, Mary E., 1988 The Ancestor Cult and Burial Ritual in Seventeenth and Eighteenth Century Central Peru. Ph.D. dissertation, Department of History, University of California, Los Angeles.

Doyle, Michael W., 1986 Empires. Ithaca, NY: Cornell University Press.

Dulanto, Jalh, 1998 Irrigated Landscapes and Sociopolitical Structures: The Regional Organization of the Ychsma Polity and the Ceremonial Center of Pachacamac. Paper read at the Center of Latin American Studies. University of Illinois at Urbana-Champaign.

——2001 Pampa Chica: Prácticas de culto a los ancestros en la costa central del Perú. Gaceta Arqueológica Andina 26:37–67.

Dumont, Louis, 1980 Homo Hierarchicus: The Caste System and its Implications. Chicago: University of Chicago Press.

——1986 Essays on Individualism: Modern Ideology in Anthropological Perspective. Chicago: University of Chicago Press.

Duviols, Pierre, 1973 Huari y llacuaz. Agricultores y pastores: Un dualismo prehispánico de oposición y complementaridad. Revista del Museo Nacional 39:153–1s87.

——1979 La dinastia de los Incas: Monarquia o diarquia? Journal de la Société de Américanistes 64:67–83.

Dwyer, Jane P., 1979 The chronology and iconography of Paracas-style textiles. In The Junius Bird Pre-Columbian Textile Conference. Ann P. Rowe, Elizabeth P. Benson, and Anne-Louise Schaffer, eds. pp. 105–128. Washington, DC: The Textile Museum and Dumbarton Oaks.

Dwyer, Jane P., and Edward B. Dwyer, 1975 The Paracas cemeteries: Mortuary patterns in a Peruvian south coastal tradition. In Death and the Afterlife in Pre-Columbian America: A Conference at Dumbarton Oaks, October 27, 1973. Elizabeth P. Benson, ed. pp. 145–161. Washington, DC: Dumbarton Oaks.

Earle, Timothy, 1972 Lurín Valley, Peru: Early Intermediate Period settlement development. American Antiquity 37:467–477.

Eeckhout, Peter, 1995 Pirámide con rampa No. 3, Pachacamac: Resultados preliminares de la primera temporada de excavaciones (zonas 1 y 2). Boletín del Instituto Francés de Estudios Andinos 24(1):65–106.

——1999 Pachacamac Durant l'Intermédiaire Recent: Étude d'un Site Monumental Préhispanique de la Côte Centrale du Pérou. Oxford: British Archaeological Reports, International Series, 747.

——2000 The palaces of the lords of Ychsma: An archaeological reappraisal of the function of pyramids with ramps at Pachacamac. Revista de Arqueología Americana 17–19: 217–254.

Eisleb, Dieter, 1987 Altperuanische Kulturen IV, Recuay. Berlin: Staatliche Museen Preussischer Kulturbesitz, Museum für Völkerkunde.

Engel, Fréderic, 1958 Algunos datos con referencia a los sitios precerámicos de la costa peruana. Arqueológicas 3:53–71. Lima.

——1963 A preceramic settlement on the central coast of Peru: Asia, Unit 1. Transactions of the American Philosophical Society, 53(3). Philadelphia.

——1966a Geografía Humana Prehistórica y Agricultura Precolombina de la Quebrada de Chilca. Lima: Universidad Agraria La Molina.

——1966b Le Complexe Précéramique d'El Paraiso, Pérou. Journal de la Société des Américanistes 46:67–155.

——1981 Prehistoric Andean Ecology: Man, Settlement and Environment in the Andes, the

Deep South, vol. 2. Papers of the Department of Anthropology, Hunter College of the City University of New York. New York: Humanities Press.

Erickson, Clark L., 1999 Neo-environmental determinism and agrarian "collapse" in Andean prehistory. Antiquity 73:634–642.

Escalante Moscoso, Javier F., 2003 Residential architecture in La Karaña, Tiwanaku. *In* Tiwanaku and its Hinterland: Archaeological and Paleoecological Investigations of an Andean Civilization, vol. 2. Alan L. Kolata, ed. Washington, DC: Smithsonian Institution Press.

Escobedo, Manuel, and Marco Goldhausen, 1999 Algunas consideraciones acerca de la iconografía Lima. Baessler-Archiv, new series, vol. 47:5–37.

Espejo Nuñez, Julio, 1957 Primeros indicios arqueológicos del estilo cultural Huaylas (Recuay) en la cuenca del Pukcha (Perú). Cuadernos Americanos 91:137–150.

Fabish, Joseph, 2003 The Origin and Evolution of Designs found in Huamachuco Blankets. Paper presented at the 43rd Annual Meeting of the Institute of Andean Studies, Berkeley.

Fagan, Brian, 1987 The Great Journey: The Peopling of Ancient America. New York: Thames & Hudson.

Falcón, Francisco, 1946[1567] Representación hecha por el Licenciado Falcón en Concilio Provincial sobre los Daños y Molestias que se hacen a los Indios. *In* Los Pequeños Grandes Libros de Historia Americana. Francisco A. Loayza, ed. Series 1, T. 10, pp. 121–164. Lima: D. Miranda.

Falcón Huayta, Victor E., 2000 Playa Grande: Entre la aldea y el santuario – ¿Un caso de interpretación arqueológica ambigua? Arqueológicas 24:53–61.

——2001 Copacabana: Un centro urbano de la cultura Lima en la costa central. *In* Los Trabajos del XII Congreso Peruano del Hombre y La Cultura Andina: "Luis G. Lumbreras," vol. 2. Ismael Perez, Walter Aguilar, and Medardo Purizaga, eds. pp. 126–139. Ayacucho: Universidad Nacional San Cristobal de Huamanga.

Feldman, Robert A., 1980 Aspero, Peru: Architecture, Subsistence Economy and Other Artifacts of a Preceramic Maritime Chiefdom. Ph.D. dissertation, Department of Anthropology, Harvard University, Cambridge.

——1983 From maritime chiefdom to agricultural state in Formative coastal Peru. *In* Civilization in the Ancient Americas. Richard M. Leventhal and Alan L. Kolata, eds. pp. 289–310. Albuquerque: University of New Mexico Press and Peabody Museum of Archaeology and Ethnology, Harvard University, Cambridge.

——1987 Architectural evidence for the development of nonegalitarian social systems in coastal Peru. *In* The Origins and Development of the Andean State. Jonathan Haas, Shelia Pozorski, and Thomas Pozorski, eds. pp. 9–14. New York: Cambridge University Press.

Fernández Sotomayor, José, 1960 El estilo Maranga. *In* Antiguo Perú: Espacio y Tiempo, pp. 241–250. Lima: Libería Editorial Juan Mejía Baca.

Flannery, Kent V., 1972 The cultural evolution of civilizations. Annual Review of Ecology and Systematics 3:399–425.

——ed., 1976 The Early Mesoamerican Village. New York: Academic Press.

Flores Espinoza, Isabel, 1981 Investigaciones arqueológicas en la Huaca Juliana. Boletín de Lima 13:65–70.

Fogel, Heidi, 1993 Settlements in Time: A Study of Social and Political Development During the Gallinazo Occupation of the North Coast of Peru. Ph.D. dissertation, Department of Anthropology, Yale University, New Haven.

Ford, James A., 1949 Cultural dating of prehistoric sites in Virú Valley, Peru. Anthropological Papers of the American Museum of Natural History, 43(1).

Fortes, Meyer, 1965 Some reflections on ancestor worship in Africa. *In* African Systems of Thought. Meyer Fortes and Germaine Dieterlen, eds. pp. 122–142. London: Oxford University Press.

Foucault, Michel, 1980 Power/Knowledge: Selected Interviews and Other Writings, 1972–1977. C. Gordon, ed. New York: Pantheon.

Frame, Mary, 1997–98 Chuquibamba: A highland textile style. Textile Museum Journal 36–37:3–48.

——1999 Nasca-Huari y otros textiles de la costa sur / Nasca-Huari and other south coast textiles. *In* Tejidos Milenarios del Perú / Ancient Peruvian Textiles. José Antonio de Lavalle and Rosario de Lavalle de Cárdenas, eds. pp. 311–352. Lima: Integra AFP.

——2001 Blood, fertility and transformation: Interwoven themes in the Paracas Necropolis embroideries. *In* Ritual Sacrifice in Ancient Peru. Elizabeth P. Benson and Anita G. Cook, eds. pp. 55–92. Austin: University of Texas Press.

Franco Jordán, Régulo, 1993 El centro ceremonial de Pachacamac: Nuevas evidencias en el Templo Viejo. Boletín de Lima 86:45–62.

——1998 La Pirámide con Rampa No. 2 de Pachacamac: Excavaciones y Nuevas Interpretaciones. Trujillo: Universidad Nacional de la Libertad.

Franco Jordán, Régulo, César Gálvez, and Segundo Vásquez, 1994 Arquitectura y decoración Mochica en la Huaca Cao Viejo, Complejo El Brujo: Resultados preliminares. *In* Moche: Propuestas y Perspectivas. Santiago Uceda and Elias Mujica, eds. pp. 147–180. Trujillo: Universidad Nacional de la Libertad.

Franquemont, Christine, 1986 Chinchero Pallays: An ethnic code. *In* The Junius B. Bird Conference on Andean Textiles: April 7th and 8th, 1984. Ann Pollard Rowe, ed. pp. 331–338. Washington, DC: The Textile Museum.

Franquemont, Christine, and Edward Franquemont, 1988 Learning to weave in Chinchero. Textile Museum Journal 26:55–78.

Frye, Kirk, 1994 Modelling the Process of Political Unification: The Lupaqa in the Titicaca Basin, Peru. MA thesis, Department of Anthropology, University of California, Santa Barbara.

——1997 Political centralization in the Altiplano Period in the southwestern Titicaca Basin. *In* Archaeological Survey in the Juli-Desaguadero Region of Lake Titicaca Basin, Southern Peru. Charles Stanish et al., eds. pp. 129–141. Fieldiana Anthropology. Chicago: Field Museum of Natural History.

Fung, Rosa, 1969 Las Aldas, su ubicación dentro del proceso histórico del Perú antiguo. Dédalo 5:9–10. São Paulo.

——1988 The Late Preceramic and Initial Period. Peruvian Prehistory. Richard Keatinge, ed. pp. 67–96. New York: Cambridge University Press.

Gálvez Mora, César and Jesús Briceño Rosario, 2001 The Moche in the Chicama Valley. *In* Moche Art and Archaeology in Ancient Peru. Joanne Pillsbury, ed. pp. 141–158. Washington, DC and New Haven: National Gallery of Art and Yale University Press.

García Soto, Rubén, n.d. Excavación de emergéncia en el sitio arqueológico de Cabezas Largas, Paracas, 1996. Manuscript on file, Museo Julio C. Tello de Sitio de Paracas, Peru.

Garcilaso de la Vega, Inca, 1966[1609] Royal Commentaries of the Incas and General History of Peru, pt. I. Harold V. Livermore, trans. Austin: University of Texas Press.

Gayton, Anna H., 1927 The Uhle collections from Nievería. University of California Publications in American Archaeology and Ethnology 21(8):305–329.

Gero, Joan M., 1990 Pottery, power, and . . . parties! Archaeology March/April: 52–56.

——1992 Feasts and females: Gender ideology and political meals in the Andes. Norwegian Archaeological Review 25(1):15–30.

——2001 Field knots and ceramic beaus: Interpreting gender in the Peruvian Early Intermediate Period. *In* Gender in Pre-Hispanic America. Cecilia Klein, ed. pp. 15–55. Washington, DC: Dumbarton Oaks.

Gero, Joan M., and Margaret W. Conkey, eds., 1991 Engendering Archaeology: Women and Prehistory. Oxford: Blackwell.

Giddens, Anthony, 1979 Central Problems in Social Theory: Action, Structure and Contradiction in Social Analysis. Berkeley: University of California Press.

Glassie, Henry, 1999 Material Culture. Bloomington: Indiana University Press.

Glowacki, Mary, 1996 The Wari Occupation of the Southern Highlands of Peru: A Ceramic Perspective from the Site of Pikillacta. Ph.D. dissertation, Department of Anthropology, Brandeis University, Waltham.

——2002 The Huaro archaeological site complex: Rethinking the Huari occupation of Cuzco. *In* Andean Archaeology I: Variations in Sociopolitical Organization. William H. Isbell and Helaine Silverman, eds. pp. 267–285. New York: Kluwer Academic/Plenum Publishers.

Glowacki, Mary, 1996 and Gordon McEwan, 2002 Pikillacta, Huaro, y la gran región del Cuzco: Nuevas interpretaciones de la ocupación Wari de la sierra del Sur. Boletín de Arqueología PUCP, vol. 5. Lima: Departamento de Humanidades, Especialidad de Arqueología, Pontificia Universidad Católica del Perú.

Godelier, Maurice, 1977 Perspectives in Marxist Anthropology. Cambridge: Cambridge University Press.

Goldhausen, Marco, 2001 Avances en el estudio de la iconografía Lima. Arqueológicas 25:223–263.

Goldstein, Paul S., 1989 Omo, a Tiwanaku Provincial Center in Moquegua, Peru. Ph.D. dissertation, Department of Anthropology, University of Chicago.

——1993 Tiwanaku temples and state expansion: A Tiwanaku sunken-court temple in Moquegua, Perú. Latin American Antiquity 4(1):22–47.

——2000 Communities without borders: The vertical archipelago and diaspora communities in the southern Andes. *In* The Archaeology of Communities. Marcello A. Canuto and Jason Yaeger, eds. pp. 182–209. London: Routledge.

González Carré, Enrique, Jorge Cosmopolis A., and Jorge Lévano P., 1981 La Ciudad Inca de Vilcashuaman. Ayacucho, Perú: Universidad Nacional de San Cristóbal de Huamanga.

González Carré, Enrique, E. Bragayraq Dávila, C. Vivanco Pomacanchari, V. Tiesler Blos, and M. Lopez Quispe, 1996 El Templo Mayor en la Ciudad de Wari: Estudios Arqueológicos en Vegachayoq Moqo – Ayacucho. Ayacucho: Laboratorio de Arqueología, Universidad Nacional San Cristóbal de Huamanga.

Gosden, Chris, 1997 The cultural biography of objects. World Archaeology 31(2):169–178.

Gose, Peter, 1994 Deathly Waters and Hungry Mountains: Agrarian Ritual and Class Formation in an Andean Town. Toronto: University of Toronto.

Gramsci, Antonio, 1971 Selections from the Prison Notebooks. Quintin Hoare and Geoffrey Nowell Smith, ed. and trans. New York: International Publishers.

Greenblat, Irwin M., 1968 A possible selective advantage of plant color at high altitude. Maize Genetics Cooperation Newsletter 42:144–145. Bloomington: Department of Botany, Indiana University.

Grieder, Terence, 1978 The Art and Archaeology of Pashash. Austin: University of Texas Press.

Grieder, Terence, and Alberto Bueno Mendoza, 1988 The history of La Galgada architecture. *In* La Galgada, Peru: A Preceramic Culture in Transition. Terence Grieder et al., eds. pp. 19–67. Austin: University of Texas Press.

Grieder, Terence, Alberto Bueno Mendoza, C. Earle Smith, Jr., and Robert Malina, 1988 La Galgada, Peru: A Preceramic Culture in Transition. Austin: University of Texas Press.

Grobman, Alexander, 1982 Maiz (Zea mays). *In* Precerámico Peruano. Los Gavilanes, Mar, Desierto y Oasis en la Historia del Hombre. Duccio Bonavia, ed. pp. 157–179. Lima: COFIDE and Instituto Arqueológico Alemán.

Grobman, Alexander, Wilfredo Salhuana, Ricardo Sevilla and Paul Mengelsdorf, 1961 Races of maize in Peru: Their origins, evolution and classification. National Academy of Sciences. National Research Council, Publication 915. Washington, DC.

Gruhn, Ruth, 1998 Linguistic evidence in support of the coastal route of earliest entry into the New World. Man 23:77–100.

Guaman Poma de Ayala, Felipe, 1978 Letter to a King. A Peruvian Chief's Account of Life Under the Incas and Under Spanish Rule. New York: E. P. Dutton.

——1980[ca. 1613–15] Nueva Corónica y Buen Gobierno. Critical edition by John V. Murra and Rolena Adorno; translations from the Quechua by Jorge L. Urioste. Mexico City: Siglo Veintiuno.

Guerrero Zevallos, Carlos D., and Jonathan B. Palacios Linares, 1994 El surgimiento del estilo Nievería en el valle de Rimac. Boletín de Lima 91–96:275–311.

Gundrum, Darrell, n.d. Reconsidering urbanization during the Late Paracas Period, south coastal Peru. Paper presented at the 64th Annual Meeting of the Society of American Archaeology.

Gutiérrez de Santa Clara, Pedro, 1963[ca. 1595–1603] Quinquenarios o Historia de las Guerras Civiles del Perú (1544–1548) y Otros Sucesos de las Indias. Madrid: Biblioteca de Autores Espanoles, vols. 165–166.

Haas, Jonathan, 1982 The Evolution of the Prehistoric State. New York: Columbia University Press.

——1985 Excavations on Huaca Grande: An initial view of the elite at Pampa Grande. Journal of Field Archaeology 12:391–409.

——2001a Cultural evolution and political centralization. *In* From Leaders to Rulers. Jonathan Haas, ed. pp. 3–18. New York: Kluwer Academic/Plenum Publishers.

——ed., 2001b From Leaders to Rulers. New York: Kluwer Academic/Plenum Publishers.

Haas, Jonathan, and Winifred Creamer, 2001 Amplifying importance of new research in Peru. Response. Science 294:1652–1653.

Haas, Jonathan, Winifred Creamer, and Alvaro Ruiz, 2002 Power and the emergence of complex polities in the Peruvian Preceramic. *In* Archaeological Papers of the American Anthropological Association/AP3A. [In press.]

————2003 Gourd Lord. Archaeology, May/June: 9.

Haas, Jonathan, Shelia Pozorski, and Thomas Pozorski, eds., 1987 The Origins and Development of the Andean State. Cambridge: Cambridge University Press.

Hardacre, Helen, 1987 Ancestor worship. *In* Encyclopedia of Religion. Mircea Eliade, ed. pp. 263–268. New York: Macmillan.

Hassig, Ross, 1985 Trade, Tribute, and Transportation: The Sixteenth-Century Political Economy of the Valley of Mexico. Norman: University of Oklahoma Press.

Hastings, Charles M., and Michael E. Moseley, 1975 The adobes of the Huaca del Sol and the Huaca de la Luna. American Antiquity 40:196–203.

Hastorf, Christine A., 1993 Agriculture and the Onset of Political Inequality Before the Inka. Cambridge: Cambridge University Press.

Hawkes, James, 1969 The Ecological Background of Plant Domestication: The Domestication and Exploitation of Plants and Animals. Peter J. Ucko and Gerald W. Dimbleby, eds. pp. 17–29. London: Gerald Duckworth.

Headrick, Annabeth, 1996 The Teotihuacan Trinity: UnMASKing the Political Structure. Ph.D. dissertation, Department of Art History, University of Texas, Austin.

Hecker, Giesela, and Wolfgang Hecker, 1995 Die Grabungen von Heinrich Ubbelohde-Doering in Pacatnamú, Nordperu: Untersuchungen an den Huacas 31 und 14 sowie Bestattungen und Fundobjekte. Berlin: Dietrich Reimer Verlag.

Hegmon, Michelle, 1992 Archaeological research on style. Annual Review of Anthropology 21:517–536.

Helmer, Marie, 1955–56[1549] La visitación de los Yndios Chupachos. Inka et encomendero 1549. Travaux de L'Institut Français d'Études Andines 5:3–50.

Helms, Mary W., 1998 Access to Origins: Affines, Ancestors, and Aristocrats. Austin: University of Texas Press.

Hendon, Julia A., 1996 Archaeological approaches to the organization of domestic labor: household practice and domestic relations. Annual Review of Anthropology 25:45–61.

Hernández Príncipe, Rodrigo, 1923 Mitología andina [1621–1622]. Inca. Revista Trimestral de Estudios Antropológicos 1:25–78.

Heyden, Doris, 1981 Caves, gods, and myths: World-view and planning at Teotihuacan. *In* Mesoamerican Sites and World-Views. Elizabeth P. Benson, ed. pp. 1–40. Washington, DC: Dumbarton Oaks.

Heyerdahl, Thor, Daniel H. Sandweiss, and Alfredo Narvaez, 1995 Pyramids of Tucume: The Quest for Peru's Forgotten City. New York: Thames & Hudson.

Hiltunen, Juha J., 1981 Inkahallitsijoiden historiallinen kronologia. Historiallinen Aikakauskirja 3:219–233. Helsinki.

——1993 Pyhitetyt valheet: Hallitsija, propaganda ja kronologia Mesoamerikassa. MA thesis, University of Helsinki.

——1999 Ancient Kings of Peru: The Reliability of the Chronicle of Fernando de Montesinos. Helsinki: SHS Bibliotheca Historica 45.

——2002 Strukturalistis-funktionalistisen diakronian problematiikka Andien alueen tutkimuksessa. Suomen Antropolgi 1:19–28.

Hirth, Kenneth G., 1993 The household as an analytical unit: Problems in method and theory. *In* Prehispanic Domestic Units in Western Mesoamerica: Studies of the Household, Compound, and Residence. Robert S. Santley and Kenneth G. Hirth, eds. pp. 21–36. Boca Raton: CRC Press.

Hocquenghem, Anne-Marie, 1987 Iconografía Mochica. Lima: Fondo Editorial, Pontificia Universidad Católica del Perú.

——1991 Frontera entre "areas culturales" nor y centroandinas en los valles y la costa del extremo norte peruano. Bulletin de l'Institut Français d'Études Andines 20(2):309–348.

Hocquenghem, Anne-Marie, and Patricia J. Lyon, 1980 A class of anthropomorphic supernatural females in Moche iconography. Ñawpa Pacha 18:27–48.

Hodder, Ian, ed., 1982a Symbolic and Structural Archaeology. Cambridge: Cambridge University Press.

——ed., 1982b Symbols in Action: Ethnoarchaeological Studies of Material Culture. Cambridge: Cambridge University Press.

Holdridge, Lawrence R., 1967 Life Zone Ecology. Tropical Sciences Center. San José, California.

Holguín, Diego González, 1989[1608] Vocabulario de la Lengua General De Todo El Perú Llamada Lengua Qquichua o del Inca. Edición facsimilar de la versión de 1952. Lima: Editorial de la Universidad Nacional Mayor de San Marcos.

Horié, Donna M., 1990–91 A family of Nasca figures. The Textile Museum Journal 29/30:77–92.

Horta, Helana, 1997 Estudios iconográfico de textiles arqueológicos del valle de Azapa, Arica. Chungará 29:81–108.

Hyslop, John, 1984 The Inka Road System. New York: Academic Press.

——1985 Inkawasi, the New Cuzco, Cañete, Lunahuaná, Peru. Oxford: British Archaeological Reports, International Series, 234.

Inokuchi, Kinya, 1998 La cerámica de Kuntur Wasi y el problem Chavín. In Perspectivas Regionales del Período Formativo en el Perú. Peter Kaulicke, ed. pp. 161–180. Boletín de Arqueología PUCP, vol. 2. Lima: Departamento de Humanidades, Especialidad de Arqueología, Pontificia Universidad Católica del Perú.

Isbell, William H., 1977 The Rural Foundations of Urbanism: Economic and Stylistic Interaction between Rural and Urban Communities in Eighth-Century Peru. Illinois Studies in Anthropology, 10. Urbana: University of Illinois Press.

——1987 Conchopata, ideological innovator in Middle Horizon 1A. Ñawpa Pacha 22–23:91–134.

——1989 Honcopampa: Was it a Huari administrative center? In The Nature of Wari: A Reappraisal of the Middle Horizon in Peru. R. M. Czwarno, ed. pp. 98–115. Oxford: British Archaeological Reports, International Series, 525.

——1991a Honcopampa: Monumental ruins in Peru's north highlands. Expedition Magazine 33(3):27–36.

——1991b Huari administration and the orthogonal cellular architecture horizon. In Huari Administrative Structure: Prehistoric Monumental Architecture and State Government. William H. Isbell and Gordon F. McEwan, eds. pp. 293–315. Washington, DC: Dumbarton Oaks.

——1997a Mummies and Mortuary Monuments. A postprocessual prehistory of Central Andean social organization. Austin: University of Texas Press.

——1997b Reconstructing Huari: A cultural chronology from the capital city. In Emergence and Change in Early Urban Societies. Linda Manzanilla, ed. pp. 181–227. New York and London: Plenum Press.

——2001a Huari: Crecimiento y desarrollo de la capital imperial. In Wari: Arte Precolumbino Peruano. L. Millones, M. Cabrera Romero, E. González Carré, W. H. Isbell, F. Meddens, C. Mesía Montenegro, J. Ochatoma Paravicino, D. Pozzi-Escot, and C. Williams León, eds. pp. 99–172. Sevilla: Fundación El Monte.

——2001b Huari, imperiumin pääkaupunki (Huari: An Imperial Capital). In Kultakruunu ja höyhenviitta: Inkat ja heidän edeltäjänsa – Peru kolme vuosituhatta (Gold crown and Feather Mantle: The Incas and their Predecessors – Three Millennia of Pre-Columbian Peru). A. Ilmonen and J. K. Talvitie, eds. pp. 158–174 (English text pp. 320–325). Tampere, Finland: Tampereen Taidemuseo (Tampere Art Museum).

——2001c[2000] Repensando el horizonte medio: El caso de Conchopata, Ayacucho, Perú. In Huari y Tiwanaku: Modelos vs. Evidencias. Peter Kaulicke and William H. Isbell, eds. pp. 9–60. Boletín de Arqueología PUCP, vol. 4. Lima: Departamento de Humanidades, Especialidad de Arqueología, Pontificia Universidad Católica del Perú.

——2002 Women, Men and Mythical Beings From Conchopata Peru. Paper presented at the 21st Annual Northeast Conference on Andean Archaeology and Ethnohistory, Pittsburgh.

——In press. Palaces and politics of Huari, Tiwanaku and the Middle Horizon. In Dumbarton Oaks Conference on New World Palaces. Susan Evans and Joanne Pillsbury, eds.. Washington, DC: Dumbarton Oaks.

Isbell, William H., Christine Brewster-Wray, and Lynda Spickard, 1991 Architecture and spatial organization at Huari. In Huari Administrative Structure: Prehistoric Monumental

Architecture and State Government. William H. Isbell and Gordon F. McEwan, eds. pp. 19–53. Washington, DC: Dumbarton Oaks.

Isbell, William H., and JoEllen Burkholder, 2002 Iwawi and Tiwanaku. *In* Andean Archaeology I: Variations in Sociopolitical Organization. William H. Isbell and Helaine Silverman, eds. pp. 199–241. New York and London: Kluwer Academic/Plenum Publishers.

Isbell, William H., JoEllen Burkholder, and Albaracin-Jordan Juan, 2002 Iwawi y Tiwanaku. Gaceta Arqueológica Andina 26:139–170.

Isbell, William H., and Anita G. Cook, 1987 Ideological Origins of an Andean Conquest State. Archaeology 40(4):26–33.

———2002 A new perspective on Conchopata and the Andean Middle Horizon. *In* Andean Archaeology II: Art, Landscape, and Society. Helaine Silverman and William H. Isbell, eds. pp. 249–305. New York: Kluwer Academic/Plenum Publishers.

Isbell, William H., and Gordon F. McEwan, eds., 1991 Wari Administrative Structure: Prehistoric Monumental Architecture and State Government. Washington, DC: Dumbarton Oaks.

Isbell, William H., and Katharina Schreiber, 1978 Was Wari a state? American Antiquity 48(3):372–389.

Isla Cuadrado, Johny, 2001 Una tumba Nasca en Puente Gentil, valle de Santa Cruz, Perú. Ein Grab der Nasca-Kultur in Puente Gentil, Santa Cruz-Tal, Peru. Beiträge zur Allgemeinen und Vergleichenden Archäologie 21:207–239.

Izumi, Seiichi, 1971 The development of the Formative Culture in the Ceja de Montaña: A viewpoint based on the materials from the Kotosh site. *In* Dumbarton Oaks Conference on Chavín. Elizabeth P. Benson, ed. pp. 49–72. Washington, DC: Dumbarton Oaks.

Izumi, Seiichi, P. Cuculiza, and C. Kano, 1972 Excavations at Shillacoto, Huánuco, Peru. The University Museum Bulletin, 3. University of Tokyo.

Izumi, Seiichi, and Toshihiko Sono, 1963 Andes 2. Excavations at Kotosh, Peru. University of Tokyo Expedition 1960. Tokyo: Kadokawa.

Izumi, Seiichi, and Kazuo Terada, 1972 Andes 4. Excavations at Kotosh, 1963 and 1966. Tokyo: University of Tokyo Press.

Jackson, Margaret Ann, 2000 Notation and Narrative in Moche Iconography, Cerro Mayal. Ph.D. dissertation, Department of Art History, University of California, Los Angeles.

———2002 Proto-writing in Moche pottery at Cerro Mayal, Peru. *In* Andean Archaeology II: Art, Landscape and Society. Helaine Silverman and William H. Isbell, eds. pp. 107–136. New York: Kluwer Academic/Plenum.

Jacquemin, Anne, 1999 Offrandes Monumentales A Delphes. Athens: Bibliothèque des Écoles Françaises d'Athènes et de Rome, École Française d'Athènes.

Janusek, John W., 1994 State and Local Power in a Prehispanic Andean Polity: Changing Patterns of Urban Residence in Tiwanaku and Lukurmata, Bolivia. Ph.D. dissertation, Department of Anthropology, University of Chicago.

———1999 Craft and local power: Embedded specialization in Tiwanaku cities. Latin American Antiquity 10(2):107–131.

———2002 Out of many, one: Style and social boundaries in Tiwanaku. Latin American Antiquity 13(1):35–61.

———2003a Vessels, time, and society: Toward a chronology of ceramic style in the Tiwanaku heartland. *In* Tiwanaku and its Hinterland: Archaeology and Paleoecology of an Andean Civilization, vol. 2. Alan L. Kolata, ed. Washington, DC: Smithsonian Institution Press.

———2003b The changing face of Tiwanaku residential life: State and social identity in an Andean city. *In* Tiwanaku and its Hinterland: Archaeological and Paleoecological

Investigations of an Andean Civilization, vol. 2. Alan L. Kolata, ed. Washington, DC: Smithsonian Institution Press.

——2004 Identity and Power in the Ancient Andes: Tiwanaku and Lukurmata. London: Routledge.

Janusek, John W., and Deborah E. Blom, 2003 Identifying Tiwanaku urban populations: Style, identity, and ceremony in Andean cities. *In* Population and Pre-Industrial Cities: A Cross-Cultural Perspective. G. Storey, ed. Tuscaloosa: University of Alabama Press.

Janusek, John W., and Alan L. Kolata, 2003 Prehispanic rural history in the Katari Valley. *In* Tiwanaku and its Hinterland: Archaeological and Paleoecological Investigations of an Andean Civilization, vol. 2. Alan L. Kolata, ed. Washington, DC: Smithsonian Institution Press.

Janusek, John W., Arik T. Ohnstad, and Andrew Roddick, 2003 Khonkho Wankane and the rise of Tiwanaku. Antiquity 77(296). Web publication: ⟨http://antiquity.ac.uk/ProjGall/janusek/janusek.html⟩.

Jijón y Caamaño, Jacinto, 1949 Maranga: Contribución al Conocimiento de los Aborígenes del Valle del Rimac, Perú. Quito: La Prensa Católica.

Jiménez Borja, Arturo, 1985 Pachacamac. Boletín de Lima 38:40–54.

Jiménez Borja, Arturo, and Alberto Bueno, 1970 Breves notas acerca de Pachacamac. Arqueología y Sociedad 4:13–25.

Jiménez Díaz, María Jesús, 2001 Los Tejidos Moche de Dos Cabezas (Valle de Jequetepeque): Hacia una Definición del Estilo Textil Mochica. Pacasmayo.

Jones, Julie, 1979 Mochica works of art in metal: A review. *In* Pre-Columbian Metallurgy of South America. Elizabeth P. Benson, ed. pp. 53–104. Washington, DC: Dumbarton Oaks.

——2001 Innovation and resplendence: Metalwork for Moche lords. *In* Moche Art and Archaeology in Ancient Peru. Joanne Pillsbury, ed. pp. 207–221. Washington, DC and New Haven: National Gallery of Art and Yale University Press.

Joyce, Rosemary A., 1993 Women's work: Images of production and reproduction in Pre-Hispanic southern Central America. Current Anthropology 34(3):255–274.

Julien, Catherine J., 1983 Hatunqolla: A View of Inca Rule from the Lake Titicaca Region. University of California Publications, Anthropology, 15. Berkeley: University of California Press.

——1993 Finding a fit: Archaeology and ethnohistory of the Incas. *In* Provincial Inca: Archaeological and Ethnohistorical Assessment of the Impact of the Inca State. Michael Malpass, ed. pp. 177–233. Iowa City: University of Iowa Press.

——2000 Reading Inca History. Iowa City: University of Iowa Press.

Julien, Daniel G., 1988 Ancient Cuismancu: Settlement and Cultural Dynamics in the Cajamarca Region of the North Highlands of Peru, 200 B.C.–A.D. 1532. Ph.D. dissertation, Department of Anthropology. University of Texas, Austin.

Kauffmann-Doig, Federico, Miriam Salazar, Daniel Morales, Iain Mackay, and Oscar Sacay, 1989 Andes amazónicos. Arqueológicas 20.

Kaulicke, Peter, 1978 Des Abri Uchkumachay und seine zeitliche Stellung innerhalb der Lithischen Perioden Perus. Allgemeine und Vergleichende Archaeologie-Beiträge 2. Bonn: Deutsches Archaeologisches Institut.

——1980 Beiträge zur Kenntnis der Lithischen Perioden in der Puna Junins. Ph.D. dissertation, University of Bonn, Germany.

——1991 El Período Intermedio Temprano en Alto Piura: Avances del Proyecto Arqueológico "Alto Piura (1987–1990)." Bulletin de l'Institut Français d'Études Andines 20(2):381–422.

——1992 Moche, Vicús Moche y el Mochica Temprano. Bulletin de l'Institut Français d'Études Andines 21(3):853–903.

——1994a Los orígenes de la civilización andina. Arqueología del Perú: Historia General del Perú, vol. 1. José Antonio del Busto, ed. Lima: Editorial Brasa.

——1994b La presencia Mochica en el Alto Piura: Problemática y propuestas. *In* Moche: Propuestas y Perspectivas. Santiago Uceda and Elias Mujica, eds. pp. 327–358. Trujillo: Universidad Nacional de la Libertad.

——1997 Contextos Funerarios de Ancón. Esbozo de una Síntesis Analítica. Lima: Fondo Editorial, Pontificia Universidad Católica del Perú.

Kaulicke, Peter, and Tom Dillehay, 1999 Introducción: Por qué estudiar el Período Arcaico en el Perú? *In* El Período Arcaico en el Perú: Hacia una Definición de los Orígenes. Peter Kaulicke, ed. pp. 9–17. Boletín de Arquelogía PUCP, vol. 3. Lima: Departamento de Humanidades, Especialidad de Arqueología, Pontificia Universidad Católica del Perú.

Keatinge, Richard W., 1974 Chimú rural administrative centers in the Moche Valley, Peru. World Archaeology 6(1):66–82.

——1977 Religious forms and secular functions: The expansion of state bureaucracies as reflected in prehistoric architecture on the Peruvian North coast. Annals of the New York Academy of Sciences 293:229–245.

Keatinge, Richard W., and Geoffrey Conrad, 1983 Imperialist expansion in Peruvian prehistory: Chimú administration of a conquered territory. Journal of Field Archaeology 10(3):255–283.

Keatinge, Richard W., et al., 1975 From the sacred to the secular: First report on the prehistoric architectural transition on the Peruvian north coast. Archaeology 28(2):128–129.

Keefer, D., Susan D. deFrance, Michael E. Moseley, James B. Richardson III, Dennis R. Satterlee, and Amy Day-Lewis, 1998 Early maritime economy and El Niño events at Quebrada Tacahuay, Peru. Science 281:1833–1835.

Kembel, Silvia Rodriguez, 2001 Architectural Sequence and Chronology at Chavín de Huántar, Perú. Ph.D. dissertation, Department of Anthropological Sciences, Stanford University.

King, Mary Elizabeth, 1965 Textiles and Basketry of the Paracas Period, Ica Valley. Ph.D. dissertation, Department of Anthropology, University of Arizona, Tucson.

Klymyshyn, A. Ulana, 1982 Elite compounds in Chan Chan. *In* Chan Chan: Andean Desert City. Michael E. Moseley and Kent C. Day, eds. pp. 119–143. Albuquerque: University of New Mexico Press.

——1987 The development of Chimú administration in Chan Chan. *In* The Origins and Development of the Andean State. Jonathan Haas, Shelia Pozorski, and Thomas Pozorski, eds. pp. 97–110. Cambridge: Cambridge University Press.

Knobloch, Patricia J., 1976 A Study of the Huarpa Ceramic Style of the Andean Early Intermediate Period. MA thesis, Department of Anthropology, State University of New York, Binghamton.

—— 1983 A Study of Andean Huari Ceramics from the Early Intermediate Period to the Middle Horizon Epoch 1. Ph.D. dissertation, Department of Anthropology, State University of New York, Binghamton.

Kolata, Alan L., 1986 The agricultural foundations of the Tiwanaku state: A view from the heartland. American Antiquity 51:748–762.

——1990 The urban concept of Chan Chan. *In* The Northern Dynasties: Kingship and Statecraft in Chimor. Michael E. Moseley and Alana Cordy-Collins, eds. pp. 107–144. Washington, DC: Dumbarton Oaks.

——1991 The technology and organization of agricultural production in the Tiwanaku state. Latin American Antiquity 2(2):99–125.

——1993 The Tiawanaku. Portrait of an Andean Civilization. Oxford: Blackwell.

——2003 Tiwanaku ceremonial architecture and urban organization. *In* Tiwanaku and its

Hinterland: Archaeological and Paleoecological Investigations of an Andean Civilization, vol. 2. Alan L. Kolata, ed. Washington, DC: Smithsonian Institution Press.

Kolata, Alan L., and Charles R. Ortloff, 1996 Agro-ecological perspectives on the decline of the Tiwanaku state. *In* Tiwanaku and its Hinterland: Archaeology and Paleoecology of an Andean Civilization, vol. 1. Alan L. Kolata, ed. pp. 181–202. Washington, DC: Smithsonian Institution Press.

Kosok, Paul, 1965 Life, Land and Water in Ancient Peru. New York: Long Island University Press.

Kroeber, Alfred Louis, 1925 The Uhle pottery collections from Moche. University of California Publications in American Archaeology and Ethnology 21(5):191–234.

——1926 The Uhle pottery collections from Chancay. University of California Publications in American Archaeology and Ethnology 21(7):265–303.

——1930 Archaeological Explorations in Peru, Part II: The Northern Coast. Anthropology, Memoirs, 2(2). Chicago: Field Museum of Natural History.

——1944 Peruvian Archaeology in 1942. Viking Fund Publications in Anthropology, 4. New York: The Viking Fund.

——1954 Proto-Lima: A middle period culture of Peru. Fieldiana: Anthropology, 44(1).

Kroeber, Alfred Louis, and Donald Collier, 1998 The Archaeology and Pottery of Nazca, Peru: Alfred L. Kroeber's 1926 Expedition. Patrick H. Carmichael, ed. Walnut Creek: Altamira Press.

Kubler, George, 1970 Period, style, and meaning in ancient American art. New Literary History 1(2):127–144.

——1975 The Art and Architecture of Ancient America. New York: Penguin Books.

——1985 Style and the historical representation of time. *In* Studies in Ancient American and European Art: The Collected Essays of George Kubler. Thomas F. Reese, ed. pp. 386–390. New Haven: Yale University Press. [1st pub. 1967 in Annals of the New York Academy of Sciences, vol. CXXXVIII, pp. 849–855]

Kus, Susan, 1982 Matters material and ideal. *In* Symbolic and Structural Archaeology. Ian Hodder, ed. pp. 47–62. Cambridge: Cambridge University Press.

Kutscher, Gerdt, 1954 Nordperuanische Keramic. Monumenta Americana, I. Berlin: Gebr Mann.

——1955 Ancient Art of the Peruvian North Coast. Berlin: Gebr Mann.

Kuznar, L. A., 1995 Awatimarka: The Ethnoarchaeology of an Andean Herding Community. Fort Worth: Harcourt Brace.

Lanning, Edward P., 1963 A preagricultural occupation on the central coast of Peru. American Antiquity 28:360–371.

——1967 Peru Before the Incas. Englewood Cliffs: Prentice-Hall.

Lapiner, Alan C., 1976 Pre-Columbian Art of South America. New York: Harry N. Abrams.

Larco Hoyle, Rafael, 1938 Los Mochicas, vol. 1. Lima: La Crónica y Variedades.

——1939 Los Mochicas, vol. 2. Rimac, Lima.

——1941 Los Cupisniques. Lima: La Crónica y Variedades.

——1944 La Cultura Salinar. Buenos Aires: Sociedad Geográfica Americana.

——1945 La Cultura Virú. Buenos Aires: Sociedad Geográfica Americana.

——1946 A culture sequence for the north coast of Peru. *In* Handbook of South American Indians, vol. 2, The Andean Civilizations. Julian H. Steward, ed. Bulletin 143, Bureau of American Ethnology. Washington, DC: Smithsonian Institution.

——1948 Cronología Arqueológica del Norte del Perú. Hacienda Chiclín, Trujillo. Buenos Aires.

——1965 La Cerámica Vicús. Lima: Santiago Valverde.

Lathrap, Donald W., 1956 An archaeological classification of culture contact situations. Seminars in Archaeology, 1955. Memoirs, 11. Society for American Archaeology.

Lau, George F., 2000 Espacio ceremonial Recuay. *In* Los Dioses del Antiguo Perú. Krzysztof Makowski, ed. pp. 178–197. Lima: Banco de Crédito.

——2001 The Ancient Community of Chinchawas: Economy and Ceremony in the North Highlands of Peru. Ph.D. dissertation, Department of Anthropology, Yale University, New Haven.

——2002 Feasting and ancestor veneration at Chinchawas, north highlands of Ancash, Peru. Latin American Antiquity 13:279–304.

Lavallée, Daniele, 2000 The First South Americans. The Peopling of a Continent from the Earliest Evidence to High Culture. Salt Lake City: University of Utah Press.

Lavallée, Daniele, Philippe Béarez, Alexandre Chevalier, Michele Julien, Pierre Usselmann, and Michel Fontugne, 1999 Paleoambiente y ocupación prehistórica del litoral extremo-sur del Perú: Las ocupaciones del arcaico en la Quebrada de los Burros y alrededores (Tacna, Perú). *In* El Período Arcaico en el Perú: Hacia una Definición de los Orígenes. Peter Kaulicke, ed. pp. 393–416. Boletín de Arqueología PUCP, vol. 3. Lima: Departamento de Humanidades, Especialidad de Arqueología, Pontificia Universidad Católica del Perú.

Lavallée, Daniele, Michele Julien, Jane Wheeler, and Claudine Karlin, 1995 Cazadores y Pastores Prehistóricos de los Andes. Lima: Instituto Francés de Estudios Andinos.

Lechtman, Heather, 1977 Style in technology: Some early thoughts. *In* Material Culture, Styles, Organization and Dynamics of Technology. Heather Lechtman and Robert S. Merrill, eds. pp. 3–20. 1975 Proceedings of the American Ethnological Society. St. Paul: West Publishing.

——1984 Andean value systems and the development of prehistoric metallurgy. Technology and Culture 25(1):1–36.

——1988 Traditions and styles in Central Andean metalworking. *In* The Beginning of the Use of Metals and Alloys. Robert Maddin, ed. pp. 344–378. Cambridge and London: MIT Press.

——1996 Cloth and metal: The culture of technology. *In* Andean Art at Dumbarton Oaks. Elizabeth Hill Boone, ed. pp. 33–43. Washington, DC: Dumbarton Oaks.

——1999 Afterword. *In* The Social Dynamics of Technology: Practice, Politics and World Views. Marcia Ann Dobres and C. R. Hoffman, eds. pp. 223–232. Washington, DC: Smithsonian Institution Press.

Lesure, Richard G., 2002 The goddess diffracted: Thinking about the figurines of early villages. Current Anthropology 43(4):587–610.

Lightfoot, Kent G., Antoinette Martinez, and Ann M. Schiff, 1998 Daily practice and material culture in pluralistic social settings: An archaeological study of culture change and persistence from Fort Ross, California. American Antiquity 63(2):199–222.

Llagostera, Augusto, 1979 9,700 years of maritime subsistence on the Pacific: An analysis by means of bioindicators in the north of Chile. American Antiquity 44:309–324.

Lorandi, Ana Maria, 1977 Arqueología y etnohistoria: Hacia una visión totalizadora del mundo andino. *In* Obra del Centenario del Museo de La Plata, vol. 2. Antropología, pp. 27–50. La Plata: Facultad de Ciencias Naturales y Museo, Universidad Nacional de La Plata.

Lothrop, Samuel K., and Joy Mahler, 1957 Late Nazca burials at Chaviña, Peru. Papers of the Peabody Museum of Archaeology and Ethnology 50(2):1–61. Cambridge: Harvard University.

Lovell, Nadia, 1998 Introduction: Belonging in need of emplacement? *In* Locality and Belonging. Nadia Lovell, ed. pp. 1–24. London: Routledge.

Lozada, María Cecilia Cerna, 1998 The Señorío of Chiribaya: A Bio-Archaeological Study in the Osmore Drainage of Southern Peru. Ph.D. dissertation, Department of Anthropology, University of Chicago.

Lumbreras, Luis G., 1960 La cultura de Wari. Etnología y Arqueología 1(1):130–227. Lima: Facultad de Letras, Universidad Nacional Mayor de San Marcos.

——1969 De los Pueblos, las Culturas y las Artes del Antiguo Peru. Lima: Moncloa-Compodonico.

——1970 Los Templos de Chavín. Lima: Corporación Peruana de Santa.

——1972 De los Orígenes del Estado en el Perú. Lima: Editorial Milla Batres.

——1974a The Peoples and Cultures of Ancient Peru. Washington, DC: Smithsonian Institution Press.

——1974b La Arqueología Como Ciencia Social. Lima: Ediciones Histar.

——1974c Los Orígenes de la Civilización en el Perú, 2nd edition. Lima: Editorial Milla Batres.

——1975 Las Fundaciones de Huamanga. Lima: El Club Huamanga. Editorial "Nueva Educación."

——1978 Arte Precolombino: Escultura y Diseño (segunda parte). Lima: Banco de Crédito.

——1980 El imperio Wari. Historia del Perú 2:11–91.

——1981 Arqueología de la América Andina. Lima: Editorial Milla Batres.

——1984 La cerámica como indicador de culturas. Gaceta Arqueológica Andina 12:3.

——1989 Chavín de Huántar en el Nacimiento de la Civilización Andina. Lima: Instituto Andino de Estudios Arqueológicos.

——1993 Chavín de Huántar. Excavaciones en la Galería de las Ofrendas. Materialien zur Allgemeinen und Vergleichenden Archäologie, vol. 51, Kommission für Allgemeine und Vergleichende Archäologie. Mainz am Rhein: Philipp von Zabern.

Lumbreras, Luis G., and Hernan Amat, 1968 Secuencia arqueológica del altiplano occidental del Titicca. Actas y Memorias del XXXVII Congreso Internacional de Americanistas 2:75–106.

Lumbreras, Luis G., Chacho González, and Bernard Lietaer, 1976 Acerca de la Función del Sistema Hidráulico de Chavín. Lima: Museo Nacional de Antropología y Arqueología.

Luttwak, Edward N., 1976 The Grand Strategy of the Roman Empire from the First Century A.D. to the Third. Baltimore: Johns Hopkins University Press.

Lynch, Thomas F., 1971 Preceramic transhumance in the Callejón de Huaylas, Peru. American Antiquity 36:139–148.

——1980 Guitarrero Cave. New York: Academic Press.

——1983 The Paleo Indians. Ancient South Americans. Jesse D. Jennings, ed. pp. 87–137. San Francisco: W. F. Freeman.

Lyon, Patricia J., 1978 Female supernaturals in ancient Peru. Ñawpa Pacha 16:95–140.

MacCormack, Sabine, 2001 Cuzco, another Rome? *In* Empires: Perspectives from Archaeology and History. Susan E. Alcock, Terence D'Altroy, Kathleen D. Morrison, and Carla M. Sinopoli, eds. pp. 419–435. New York: Cambridge University Press.

Mackey, Carol, 1987 Chimú administration in the provinces. *In* The Origins and Development of the Andean State. Jonathan Haas, Shelia Pozorski, and Thomas Pozorski, eds. pp. 121–129. Cambridge: Cambridge University Press.

——2001 Los dioses que perdieron los colmillos. *In* Los Dioses del Antiguo Perú, vol. 2. Lima: Banco de Crédito del Perú.

Mackey, Carol, and Charles M. Hastings, 1982 Moche murals from the Huaca de la Luna.

In Pre-Columbian Art History: Selected Readings. Alana Cordy-Collins, ed. pp. 293–312. Palo Alto: Peek Publications.

Mackey, Carol, and César Jaúregui, 2002 Informe Preliminar de Proyecto Arqueológico Farfán. Lima: Instituto Nacional de Cultura.

Mackey, Carol, and Alexandra Klymyshyn, 1990 The southern frontier of the Chimú Empire. *In* The Northern Dynasties: Kingship and Statecraft in Chimor. Michael E. Moseley and Alana Cordy-Collins, eds. pp. 195–226. Washington, DC: Dumbarton Oaks.

Mackey, Carol, and E. Zavelata 2000 Informe Preliminar de Proyecto Arqueológico Farfán. Lima: Instituto Nacional de Cultura.

MacNeish, Richard S., Thomas C. Patterson, and David L. Browman, 1975 The Central Peruvian Prehistoric Interaction Sphere. Papers of the Robert S. Peabody Foundation for Archaeology, 7. Andover: Robert S. Peabody Foundation for Archaeology.

MacNeish, Richard S., et al., 1980 Prehistory of the Ayacucho Basin, Peru, III: Nonceramic Artifacts. Ann Arbor: University of Michigan Press.

MacNeish, Richard S., Robert K. Vierra, Annette Nelken-Turner, and Carl J. Fagan, 1981 Prehistory of the Ayacucho Basin, Peru, II: Excavations and Chronology. Richard S. Mac-Neish, ed. Ann Arbor: University of Michigan Press.

Makowski, Krzysztof, 2001 Las civilizaciones prehispánicas en la costa central y sur. *In* Historia de la Cultura Peruana, pp. 163–244. Lima: Fondo Editorial del Congreso del Perú.

——2002 Power and social ranking at the end of the Formative Period: The lower Lurín cemeteries. *In* Andean Archaeology I: Variations in Sociopolitical Organization. William H. Isbell and Helaine Silverman, eds. pp. 89–120. New York: Plenum Publishers/Kluwer Academic.

Mann, Michael, 1986 The Sources of Social Power. Cambridge: Cambridge University Press.

Manzanilla, Linda, 1992 Akapana: Una Pirámide en el Central del Mundo. Mexico DF: Instituto de Investigaciones Antropológicas.

——1996 Corporate groups and domestic activities at Teotihuacan. Latin American Antiquity 7(3):228–246.

——2002 Living with the ancestors and offering to the gods. *In* Domestic Ritual in Ancient Mesoamerica. Patricia Plunket, ed. pp. 43–52. Los Angeles: Cotsen Institute of Archaeology, University of California.

Manzanilla, Linda, and Eric Woodward, 1990 Restos humanos asociados a la pirámide de Akapana: Tiwanaku, Bolivia. Latin American Antiquity 1(2):133–149.

Marcus, Joyce, 1987 Late Intermediate Period Occupation at Cerro Azul, Peru: A Preliminary Report. Technical Report, 20. Ann Arbor: Museum of Anthropology, University of Michigan.

——1998 Women's ritual in Formative Oaxaca: Figurine-making, divination, death and the ancestors. *In* Prehistory and Human Ecology of the Valley of Oaxaca, vol. 11. Kent V. Flannery and Joyce Marcus, eds. Memoirs, 33. Ann Arbor: Museum of Anthropology, University of Michigan.

Markham, Clements, 1920 Introduction. *In* Memorias Antiguas Historiales y Políticas del Perú by Fernando de Montesinos. Philip A. Means, ed. and trans. London: Hakluyt Society.

Massey, Sarah, 1986 Sociopolitical Change in the Upper Ica Valley: B.C. 400 to 400 A.D.: Regional States on the South Coast of Peru. Ph.D. dissertation, Department of Anthropology, University of California, Los Angeles.

——1991 Social and political leadership in the lower Ica Valley: Ocucaje phases 8 and 9. *In* Paracas Art and Architecture: Object and Context in South Coastal Peru. Anne Paul, ed. pp. 315–348. Iowa City: University of Iowa Press.

Mathews, James E., 1997 Population and agriculture in the emergence of complex society in the Bolivian altiplano: The case of Tiwanaku. *In* Emergence and Change in Early Urban Societies. Linda Manzanilla, ed. pp. 245–274. New York: Plenum Press.

Mayer, Enrique, 2001 The Articulated Peasant: Household Economies in the Andes. Boulder: Westview.

McAnany, Patricia A., 1995 Living with the Ancestors: Kinship and Kingship in Ancient Maya Society. Austin: University of Texas Press.

McCown, Theodore D., 1945 Pre-Incaic Huamachuco: Survey and Excavations in the Region of Huamachuco and Cajabamba. University of California Publications in American Archaeology and Ethnology 39(4):223–344.

McEwan, Gordon F., 1984 The Middle Horizon in the Valley of Cuzco, Peru: The Impact of the Wari Occupation of Pikillacta in the Lucre Basin. Ph.D. dissertation, Department of Anthropology, University of Texas, Austin.

——1987 The Middle Horizon in the Valley of Cuzco, Peru: The Impact of the Wari Occupation in the Lucre Basin. Oxford: British Archaeological Reports, International Series, 372.

——1990 Some formal correspondences between the imperial architecture of the Wari and Chimú cultures of ancient Peru. Latin American Antiquity 1:97–116.

——1991 Investigations at the Pikillacta site: A provincial Huari center in the Valley of Cuzco. *In* Huari Administrative Structure: Prehistoric Monumental Architecture and State Government. William H. Isbell and Gordon F. McEwan, eds. pp. 93–120. Washington, DC: Dumbarton Oaks.

——1992 El Horizonte Medio en el Cuzco y la sierra del sur peruano. *In* Estudios de Arqueología Peruana. Duccio Bonavia, ed. pp. 279–310. Lima: Fomciencias.

——1994 Pikillaqta: Ocupación Wari en el Cusco. Revista de Información Cultural 1(1):17–20. Cuzco: Instituto de Investigaciones Arqueológicas Marcavalle.

——1996 Archaeological investigations at Pikillacta, a Wari site in Peru. Journal of Field Archaeology 23(2):169–186.

——1998 The function of niched halls in Wari architecture. Latin American Antiquity 9(1):68–86.

——2002 The archaeology of Inca origins: Excavations at Chokepukio, Cuzco, Peru. *In* Andean Archaeology I: Variations in Sociopolitical Organization. William H. Isbell and Helaine Silverman, eds. pp. 287–301. New York: Kluwer Academic/Plenum Publishing.

McEwan, Gordon F., Arminda Gibaja, and Melissa Chatfield, 1995 Archaeology of the Chokepukio site: An investigation of the origin of the Inca civilization in the Valley of Cuzco, Peru. TAWANTINSUYU: International Journal of Inka Studies 1(1).

——————2000 Excavations at the Chokepukio site in the Valley of Cuzco: A summary report of the second and third field seasons, 1995 and 1996. TAWANTINSUYU: International Journal of Inka Studies 5(1).

McGuire, Randall H., 1983 Breaking down cultural complexity: inequality and heterogeneity. Advances in Archaeological Method and Theory 6:91–142.

Means, Philip A., 1920 Introduction. *In* Memorias Antiguas Historiales y Políticas del Perú by Fernando de Montesinos. Philip A. Means, ed. and trans. London: Hakluyt Society.

Meddens, Frank M., 1985 The Chicha/Soras Valley During the Middle Horizon: Provincial Aspects of Huari. Ph.D. dissertation, University of London.

Medlin, Mary Ann, 1986 Learning to weave in Calcha, Bolivia. *In* The Junius B. Bird Conference on Andean Textiles: April 7th and 8th, 1984. Ann Pollard Rowe, ed. pp. 275–388. Washington, DC: The Textile Museum.

——1991 Ethnic dress and Calcha festivals, Bolivia. *In* Textile Traditions of Mesoamerica and the Andes: An Anthology. B. Margot Schevill, Janet C. Berlo, and Edward B. Dwyer, eds. pp. 261–279. New York: Garland.

Mejía Xesspe, Toribio, 1941 Walun y Chinchawas: Dos nuevos sitios en la Cordillera Negra. Chaski 1(1):18–24. Lima.

——1957 Chullpas precolombinas en el área andina. Revista de la Universidad Nacional de La Plata 2:101–108.

Menzel, Dorothy, 1959 The Inca occupation of the south coast of Peru. Southwestern Journal of Anthropology 15(2):125–142.

——1960 Archaism and revival on the south coast of Peru. In Men and Cultures: Selected Papers of the Fifth International Congress of Anthropological and Ethnological Sciences. Anthony F. C. Wallace, ed. pp. 596–600. Philadelphia: University of Pennsylvania Press.

——1964 Style and time in the Middle Horizon. Ñawpa Pacha 2:1–105.

——1966 The pottery of Chincha. Ñawpa Pacha 4:77–144.

——1968 New data on the Wari Empire in Middle Horizon 2A. Ñawpa Pacha 6:47–114.

——1976 Pottery Style and Society in Ancient Peru: Art as a Mirror of History in the Ica Valley, 1350–1570. Berkeley: University of California Press.

——1977 The Archaeology of Ancient Peru and the Work of Max Uhle. Berkeley: R. H. Lowie Museum of Anthropology, University of California.

Menzel, Dorothy, and Francis A. Riddell, 1986 Archaeological Investigations at Tambo Viejo, Acarí Valley, Peru, 1954. Sacramento: California Institute for Peruvian Studies.

Menzel, Dorothy, and John H. Rowe, 1966 The role of Chincha in late pre-Spanish Peru. Ñawpa Pacha 4:63–76.

Menzel, Dorothy, John H. Rowe, and Lawrence E. Dawson, 1964 The Paracas Pottery of Ica: A Study in Style and Time. University of California Publications in American Archaeology and Ethnology, 50. Berkeley and Los Angeles: University of California Press.

Meskell, Lynn, 1999 Archaeologies of Social Life. Age, Sex, Class in Ancient Egypt. Oxford: Blackwell.

——2001 Archaeologies of identity. In Archaeological Theory Today. Ian Hodder, ed. pp. 187–213. Malden, MA: Blackwell.

——2002 The intersections of identity and politics in archaeology. Annual Review of Anthropology 31:279–301.

Millon, Rene, 1994 Urbanization at Teotihuacan, Mexico, vol. 1, The Teotihuacan Map: Parts One and Two. Austin: University of Texas Press.

Montesinos, Fernando de, 1869[1644] Memorias Antiguas Historiales y Políticas del Perú. La primera edición castellana y la transcripción fué brindada por Vicente Fidel López. Revista de Buenos Aires, 79 (Nov. 1869–Dic. 1870).

——1882[1644] Memorias Antiguas Historiales y Políticas del Perú. Cuidada por D. Marcos Jiménez de la Espada. Madrid: Imprenta de Miguel Ginesta.

——1920 Memorias Antiguas Historiales y Políticas del Perú. Philip A. Means, ed. and trans. London: Hakluyt Society.

Moore, Jerry D., 1981 Chimú socio-economic organization: Preliminary data from Manchan, Casma Valley, Peru. Ñawpa Pacha 19:115–128.

——1989 Prehispanic beer in coastal Peru: Technology and social context of prehistoric production. American Anthropologist 91:682–695.

——1992 Pattern and meaning in prehistoric architecture: The architecture of social control in the Chimú State. Latin American Antiquity 3(2):95–113.

——1996 Architecture and Power in the Ancient Andes. Cambridge: Cambridge University Press.

Morales, Daniel, 1998 Investigaciones arqueológicas en Pacopampa, Departamento de Cajamarca. In Perspectivas Regionales del Período Formativo en el Perú. Peter Kaulicke, ed. pp. 113–126. Boletín de Arqueología PUCP, vol. 2. Lima: Departamento de Humanidades, Especialidad de Arqueología, Pontificia Universidad Católica del Perú.

Morgan, Alexandra, 1988 "The master or mother of fishes": An interpretation of Nasca pottery figurines and their symbolism. *In* Recent Studies in Pre-Columbian Archaeology. Nicholas J. Saunders and Oliver de Montmollin, eds. pp. 327–360. Oxford: British Archaeological Reports, International Series, 421(ii).

Morris, Craig, 1972 State settlements in Tawantinsuyu: A strategy of compulsory urbanism. *In* Contemporary Archaeology: A Guide to Theory and Contributions. Mark Leone, ed. pp. 393–401. Carbondale: Southern Illinois University Press.

——1982 The infrastructure of Inka control in the Peruvian central highlands. *In* The Inca and Aztec states, 1400–1800: Anthropology and History. George A. Collier, Renato I. Rosaldo, and John D. Wirth, eds. pp. 153–171. New York: Academic Press.

——1988 Más allá de las fronteras de Chincha. *In* La Frontera del Estado Inca: Proceedings of the 45th Congreso Internacional de Americanistas. Tom D. Dillehay and Patricia Netherly, eds. pp. 131–140. Oxford: British Archaeological Reports, International Series, 442.

——1991 Signs of division, symbols of unity: Art in the Inka Empire. *In* Circa 1492: Art in the Age of Exploration. Jay A. Levenson, ed. pp. 521–528. Washington, DC: National Gallery of Art and Yale University Press.

——1995 Symbols to power: Styles and media in the Inka state. *In* Style, Society, and Person: Archaeological and Ethnological Perspectives. Christopher Carr and Jill E. Neitzel, eds. pp. 419–433. New York: Plenum Press.

——1998 Inka Strategies of Incorporation and Governance. *In* Archaic States, Gary M. Feinman and Joyce Marcus, eds. pp. 293–309. Santa Fe: School of American Research Press.

Morris, Craig, and Donald E. Thompson, 1985 Huánuco Pampa: An Inca City and its Hinterland. London: Thames & Hudson.

Morris, Ian, 1991 The archaeology of ancestors: The Saxe/Goldstein Hypothesis revisited. Cambridge Archaeological Journal 1:147–169.

Moseley, Michael E., 1975a The Maritime Foundations of Andean Civilization. Menlo Park: Cummings.

——1975b Prehistoric principles of labor organization in the Moche Valley, Peru. American Antiquity 40:191–196.

——1975c Chan Chan: Andean alternative of the preindustrial city. Science 187:219–225.

——1985 The exploration and explanation of early monumental architecture in the Andes. *In* Early Ceremonial Architecture in the Andes. Christopher B. Donnan, ed. pp. 29–58. Washington, DC: Dumbarton Oaks.

——1992 The Incas and their Ancestors. London: Thames & Hudson.

——2001 The Incas and their Ancestors, revised edition. London: Thames & Hudson.

Moseley, Michael E., and Kent C. Day, eds., 1982 Chan Chan: Andean Desert City. Albuquerque: University of New Mexico Press.

Moseley, Michael E., and Carol J. Mackey, 1972 Peruvian settlement pattern studies and small site methodology. American Antiquity 37:67–81.

————1973 Chan Chan, Peru's ancient city of kings. National Geographic, 143:319–345.

Mujica, Elias, 1985 Altiplano–coast relationships in the south-central Andes: From indirect to direct complementarity. *In* Andean Ecology and Civilization. Shozo Masuda, Izumi Shimada, and Craig Morris, eds. pp. 103–140. Tokyo: University of Tokyo Press.

Murra, John V., 1962 Cloth and its function in the Inca state. American Anthropologist 64:710–728.

——1968 An Aymara kingdom in 1567. Ethnohistory 15(2):115–151.

——1972 El control vertical de un máximo número de pisos ecológicos en la economía de las sociedades andinas. *In* Visita de la Provincia de León de Huánuco en 1562. Documentos por la Historia y Etnología de Huánuco y la Selva Central 2:427–476. Huánuco: Universidad Nacional Hermilio Valdizán.

——1975 Formaciones Económicas y Políticas en el Mundo Andino. Lima: Instituto de Estudios Peruanos.

——1980 The Economic Organization of the Inka State. Greenwich: JAI Press. [Ph.D. dissertation, Department of Anthropology, University of Chicago, originally written 1956]

——1985 The limits and limitations of the "vertical archipelago" in the Andes. *In* Andean Ecology and Civilization. Shozo Masuda, Izumi Shimada, and Craig Morris, eds. pp. 15–20. Tokyo: University of Tokyo Press.

——1989 Cloth and its function in the Inca state. *In* Cloth and Human Experience. Annette B. Wiener and Jane C. Schneider, eds. pp. 275–302. Washington, DC: Smithsonian Institution Press. [1st published 1962 in American Anthropologist 64:710–728]

Murua, Martín de, 1946[MS Loyola, ca. 1590–1609] Historia del Orígen y Genealogía real de los Reyes Incas del Perú, vol. 2. Constantino Bayle, ed. Madrid: Biblioteca "Missionalia Hispanica."

Muscutt, Keith, 1998 Warriors of the Clouds: A Lost Civilization in the Upper Amazon of Peru. Albuquerque: University of New Mexico Press.

Narváez, Alfredo, 1994 La Mina: Una tumba Moche I en el valle de Jequetepeque. *In* Moche: Propuestas y Perspectivas. Santiago Uceda and Elias Mujica, eds. pp. 59–92. Trujillo: Universidad Nacional de la Libertad.

Neira Avendaño, Máximo, 1962 Informe preliminar de la expedición arqueológica al altiplano. Kontisuyo, Boletín del Museo de Arqueología e Historia de la UNSA.

——1967 Informe preliminar de las investigaciones arqueológicas en el Departamento de Puno. Anales del Instituto de Estudios Socio Económicos 1(1). Puno: Universidad Técnica del Altiplano.

Nelson, Andrew, 1998 Wandering bones: Archaeology, forensic science, and Moche burial practices. International Journal of Osteology 8:192–212.

Nelson, Andrew, and Luis Jaime Castillo, 1997 Huesos a la deriva: Tafonomía y tratamiento funerario en entierros Mochica tardío de San José de Moro. *In* La Muerte en el Antiguo Perú: Contextos y Conceptos Funerarios. Peter Kaulicke, ed. pp. 137–163. Boletín de Arqueología PUCP, vol. 1. Lima: Departamento de Humanidades, Especialidad de Arqueología, Pontificia Universidad Católica del Perú.

Nelson, Andrew, C. S. Nelson, Luis Jaime Castillo, and Carol Mackey, 2000 Osteobiografía de una hilandera precolombina: La mujer detrás de la mascara. Iconos 4(2):30–43.

Netherly, Patricia, 1977 Local Level Lords on the North Coast of Peru. Ph.D. dissertation, Cornell University, New York.

——1984 The management of late Andean irrigation systems on the north coast of Peru. American Antiquity 49(2):227–254.

——1990 Out of many, one: The organization of rule in the north coast polities. *In* The Northern Dynasties: Kingship and Statecraft in Chimor. Michael E. Moseley and Alana Cordy-Collins, eds. pp. 461–485. Washington, DC: Dumbarton Oaks.

Newell, William H., 1976 Good and bad ancestors. *In* Ancestors. William H. Newell, ed. pp. 17–32. The Hague: Mouton.

Núñez, Lautaro and Calogero Santoro, 1990 Primeros poblamientos del cono sur de América (XII–IX Milenio A.P.). Revista Arqueología Americana 1:92–139.

Oakland, Amy, 1986 Tiahuanaco tapestry tunics and mantles from San Pedro de Atacama,

Chile. *In* The Junius B. Bird Conference on Andean Textiles. Ann Pollard Rowe, ed. pp. 101–121. Washington, DC: The Textile Museum. [*see also* Rodman, Amy Oakland]

Ochatoma Paravicino, José, 1989 Aqowayqo: Un Poblado Rural de la Epoca Wari. Lima: CONCYTEC.

Ochatoma Paravicino, José, and Martha Cabrera Romero, 2001a Ideología religiosa y organización militar en la iconografía de area ceremonial de Conchopata. *In* Wari: Arte Precolumbino Peruano. L. Millones, M. Cabrera Romero, E. González Carré, W. H. Isbell, F. Meddens, C. Mesía Montenegro, J. Ochatoma Paravicino, D. Pozzi-Escot, and C. Williams León, eds. pp. 173–211. Seville: Fundación El Monte.

———2001b Arquitectura y áreas de actividad en Conchopata. *In* Huari y Tiwanaku: Modelos vs. Evidencias. Peter Kaulicke and William H. Isbell, eds. pp. 449–488. Boletín de Arqueología PUCP, vol. 4. Lima: Departamento de Humanidades, Especialidad de Arqueología, Pontificia Universidad Católica del Perú.

———2001c Poblados Rurales Huari: Una Visión desde Aqo Wayqo. Lima: CANO Asociados SAC.

———2001d Descubrimiento del área ceremonial en Conchopata, Huari. *In* XII Congreso Peruano del Hombre y la Cultura Andina, vol. 2. I. Pérez, W. Aguilar, and M. Purizaga, eds. pp. 212–244. Ayacucho: Universidad Nacional de San Cristóbal de Huamanga.

———2002 Religious ideology and military organization in the iconography of a D-shaped ceremonial precinct at Conchopata. *In* Andean Archaeology II: Art, Landscape, and Society. Helaine Silverman and William H. Isbell, eds. pp. 225–247. New York: Kluwer Academic/Plenum Publishers.

Ojeda, Bernardino, 1981 La ciudad perdida de Huayuri. Boletín de Lima 16–18:78–82.

Onuki, Yoshio, 2000 El Período Arcaico en Huánuco y el concepto del Arcaico. *In* El Período Arcaico en el Perú: Hacia una Definición de los Orígenes. Peter Kaulicke, ed. pp. 325–334. Boletín de Arqueología PUCP, vol. 3. Lima: Departamento de Humanidades, Especialidad de Arqueología, Pontificia Universidad Católica del Perú.

Orefici, Giuseppe, 1992 Nasca: Archeologia per una Recostruzione Storica. Milano: Jaca Books.

Ortiz de Zúñiga, Iñigo, 1967[1562] Visita de la Provincia de León de Huánuco en 1562, Iñigo Ortiz de Zúñiga, Visitador, vol. 1. John V. Murra, ed. Huánuco: Universidad Nacional Hermilio Valdizán.

———1972[1562] Visita de la Provincia de León de Huánuco en 1562, Iñigo Ortiz de Zúñiga, Visitador, vol. 2. John V. Murra, ed. Huánuco: Universidad Nacional Hermilio Valdizán.

Ortloff, Charles R., 1996 Engineering aspects of Tiwanaku groundwater-controlled agriculture. *In* Tiwanaku and its Hinterland: Archaeology and Paleoecology of an Andean Civilization, vol. 1. Alan L. Kolata, ed. pp. 153–168. Washington, DC: Smithsonian Institution Press.

Ortloff, Charles R., and Alan L. Kolata, 1989 Hydraulic analysis of Tiwanaku aqueduct structures at Lukurmata and Pajchiri, Bolivia. Journal of Archaeological Science 16:513–535.

Osborn, Allan, 1977 Strandloopers, mermaids, and other fairy tales: Ecological determinants of marine resources utilization. The Peruvian case. *In* For Theory Building in Archaeology. Lewis Binford, ed. pp. 157–205. New York: Academic Press.

Ossio, Juan M., 1978 Las cinco edades del mundo según Felipe Guaman Poma de Ayala. Primera Jornada del Museo Nacional de Historia, Noviembre de 1976. Marcia Koth de Paredes and Amalia Castelli, eds. Lima: Museo Nacional de Historia.

Owen, Bruce, 1993 A Model of Multiethnicity: State Collapse, Competition, and Social Complexity from Tiwanaku to Chiribaya in the Osmore Valley, Perú. Ph.D. dissertation, Department of Anthropology, University of California, Los Angeles.

Paddock, John, 1983 The Oaxaca barrio at Teotihuacan. *In* The Cloud People: Divergent Evolution of the Zapotec and Mixtec Civilizations. Kent V. Flannery and Joyce Marcus, eds. pp. 170–175. New York: Academic Press.

Palka, Joel W., 1997 Reconstructing Classic Maya socioeconomic differentiation and the collapse at Dos Pilas, Peten, Guatemala. Ancient Mesoamerica 8(2):293–306.

Pardo, Luis A., 1946 La Metropoli de Pacaritampu. Revista de la Sección Arqueológica de la Universidad Nacional del Cuzco 2:3–46. Cuzco.

—— 1957 Historia y Arqueología del Cuzco, vols. 1–2. Cuzco.

Paredes Botoni, Ponciano, 1985 La Huaca Pintada o el Templo de Pachacamac. Boletín de Lima 41:70–77.

—— 1988 Pachacamac: Pirámide con Rampa No. 2. Boletín de Lima 55:41–58.

—— 1990 Pachacamac. Inca-Perú: 3000 Ans d'Histoire. Gent: Imschoot Uitgevers.

—— 1992 Cerro Culebras: nuevos aportes acerca de una ocupación de la cultura Lima (costa central del Perú). Gaceta Arqueológica Andina 22:51–62.

Paredes Botoni, Ponciano, and Régulo, Franco, 1986 Pachacamac: Las pirámides con rampa, cronología y función. Gaceta Arqueológica Andina 13:5–7.

Paredes Olivera, Juan, 1992 Cerro Culebras: nuevos aportes acerca de una ocupación de la cultura Lima (costa central del Perú). Gaceta Arqueológica Andina 22:51–62.

Parsons, Jeffrey R., 1968 An estimate of size and population for Middle Horizon Tiahuanaco, Bolivia. American Antiquity 33:243–245.

Pärssinen, Martti, 1992 Tawantinsuyo. The Inca State and its Political Organization. Studia Historica, 43. Helsinki: SHS.

Partida, Elena C., 2000 The Treasuries at Delphi: An Architectural Study. Jonsered: Paul Astroms.

Patterson, Thomas C., 1966 Pattern and Process in the Early Intermediate Period Pottery of the Central Coast of Peru. University of California Publications in Anthropology, 3. Berkeley: University of California Press.

—— 1971a Central Peru: Its population and economy. Archaeology 24(4):316–321.

—— 1971b Chavín: An interpretation of its spread and influence. *In* Dumbarton Oaks Conference on Chavín. Elizabeth P. Benson, ed. pp. 29–48. Washington, DC: Dumbarton Oaks.

—— 1986 Ideology, class formation and resistance in the Inca state. Critique of Anthropology 6(1):75–85.

Patterson, Thomas C., John P. McCarthy, and Robert A. Dunn, 1982 Polities in the Lurín Valley, Peru during the Early Intermediate period. Ñawpa Pacha 20:61–82.

Pauketat, Timothy R., 2001 Practice and history in archaeology. Anthropological Theory 1(1):73–98.

Paul, Anne, 1979 Paracas Textiles Selected from the Museum's Collections. Göteborgs: Etnografiska Museet.

—— 1990 Paracas Ritual Attire: Symbols of Authority in Ancient Peru. Norman: University of Oklahoma Press.

—— ed., 1991 Paracas Art and Architecture: Object and Context in South Coastal Peru. Iowa City: University of Iowa Press.

—— 1997 Color patterns on Paracas Necropolis weavings: A combinatorial language on ancient cloth. Techniques and Culture 29:113–153.

—— 2001 Bodiless human heads in Paracas Necropolis textile iconography. Andean Past 6:69–94.

Paul, Anne, and Solveig A. Turpin, 1986 The "Ecstatic Shaman" theme on Paracas textiles. Archaeology 39:20–27.

Paulsen, Allison C., 1983 Huaca del Loro revisited: The Nasca–Huarpa connection. *In* Investigations of the Andean Past. Daniel H. Sandweiss, ed. pp. 98–121. Ithaca: Cornell University Latin American Studies Program.

Pearsall, Deborah M., 1992 The origin of plant cultivation in South America. In The Origins of Agriculture: An International Perspective. C. W. Cowan and Patty Jo Watson, eds. pp. 173–205. Washington, DC: Smithsonian Institution Press.

Pearsall, Deborah M., and Dolores R. Piperno, 1990 Antiquity of maize cultivation in Ecuador: Summary and reevaluation of the evidence. American Antiquity 55(2):324–337.

——— 1998 The Origins of Agriculture in the Lowland Neotropics. New York: Academic Press.

Pease, G. Y., Franklin, 1973 Cambios en el reino Lupaqa (1567–1661). Historia y Cultura 7:89–105. Lima.

——— 1995 Las Crónicas y los Andes. Lima: Pontificia Universidad Católica del Perú.

Peregrine, Peter N., and Gary M. Feinman, eds., 1996 Pre-Columbian World Systems. Madison: Prehistory Press.

Pérez Calderón, Ismael, 1988 Monumentos arqueológicos de Santiago de Chuco, La Libertad. Boletín de Lima 60:33–44.

——— 1994 Monumentos arqueológicos de Santiago de Chuco, La Libertad. Boletín de Lima 91–96:225–274.

Peters, Ann H., 1987–88 Chongos: Sitio Paracas en el valle de Pisco. Gaceta Arqueológica Andina 4:30–34.

——— 1995 Paracas Cavernas, Paracas Necropolis, and Ocucaje: Looking at appropriation and identity with only material remains. In Contact, Crossover, Continuity: Proceedings of the Fourth Biennial Symposium of the Textile Society of America, 1994, pp. 305–317. Los Angeles: Textile Society of America.

——— 1997 Paracas, Topara, and Early Nazca: Ethnicity and Society on the South Central Andean Coast. Ph.D. dissertation, Department of Anthropology, Cornell University, Ithaca.

Pezzia Assereto, Alejandro, 1968 Ica y el Perú Precolombino: Arqueología de la Provincia de Ica, vol. 1. Ica: Ojeda.

——— 1972 Arqueología del Departamento de Ica: Panorama Prehistórico. Ica: Museo Regional de Ica.

Pillsbury, Joanne, 1993 Sculpted Friezes of the Empire of Chimor. Ph.D. dissertation, Columbia University, New York.

——— ed., 2001 Moche Art and Archaeology in Ancient Peru. Washington, DC and New Haven: National Gallery of Art and Yale University Press.

Piperno, Dolores R., 1990 Aboriginal agriculture and land usage in the Amazon Basin, Ecuador. Journal of Archeological Science 17:665–677.

——— 1993 Phytolith and charcoal records from deep lake cores in the American tropics. In Current Research in Phytolith Analysis: Applications in Archaeology and Paleoecology, MASCA Research Papers in Science and Archaeology 10:58–71. Philadelphia: University Museum of Archaeology and Anthropology.

Piperno, Dolores R., Thomas C. Andres, and Karen E. Stothert, 2000 Phytoliths in Cucurbita and other Neotropical Cucurbitaceae and their occurrence in early archaeological sites from the lowland American tropics. Journal of Archaeological Science 27:193–208.

Piperno, Dolores R., and Kent V. Flannery, 2001 The earliest archaeological maize (Zea mays L.) from highland Mexico: New accelerator mass spectrometry dates and their implication. Proceedings of the National Academy of Sciences 98(4):2101–2103.

Pires-Ferreira, Jane W., Eduardo Pires-Ferreira, and Peter Kaulicke, 1976 Prehistoric animal utilization in the Central Andes, Peru. Science 194:483–488.

Pires-Ferreira, Jane W., and Jane C. Wheeler, 1975 La fauna de Cuchimachay, Acomachay A, Acomachay B, Telarmachay, y Utco 1. Revista del Museo Nacional 41:120–127.

Platt, Tristan, 1986 Mirrors and maize: The concept of yanatin among the Macha of Bolivia. *In* Anthropological History of Andean Polities. John Murra, Jacques Revel, and Nathan Wachtel, eds. pp. 228–259. New York: Cambridge University Press.

Polo de Ondegardo, Juan, 1916[1571] Relacíon de los fundamentos acerca del notable daño que resulta de no guardar a los indios sus fueros. *In* Colección de Libros y Documentos Referentes a la Historia del Perú, vol. 3. Horacio H. Urteaga, ed. pp. 45–188. Lima.

Ponce Sanginés, Carlos, 1969 La ciudad Tiwanaku. Arte y Arqueología 1:5–32.

——1980 Panorama de la Arqueología Boliviana, 2nd edition. La Paz: Librería Editorial Juventud.

——1981 Tiwanaku: Espacio, Tiempo, y Cultura. La Paz: Los Amigos del Libro.

——1993 La cerámica de la época I (aldeana) de Tiwanaku. Pumapunku (nueva época) 4:48–89.

——2001 Tiwanaku y Su Facinante Desarollo Cultural: Ensayo de Sintesis Arqueológica. La Paz-Bolivia: Producciones CIMA.

Ponte Rosalino, Victor, 2000 Transformación social y política en el Callejón de Huaylas, siglos III–X DC. *In* Huari y Tiwanaku: Modelos vs. Evidencias. Peter Kaulicke and William H. Isbell, eds. pp. 219–251. Boletín de Arqueología PUCP, vol. 4. Lima: Departamento de Humanidades, Especialidad de Arqueología, Pontificia Universidad Católica del Perú.

Posnansky, Arthur, 1945 Tihuanaco: The Cradle of American Man (Tihuanacu: La Cuna del Hombre Americano), 2 vols. New York and La Paz: J. J. Augustin and Ministerio de Educación de Bolivia.

Pozorski, Shelia, and Thomas Pozorski, 1987 Early Settlement and Subsistence in the Casma Valley. Iowa City: University of Iowa Press.

——1990 Reexamining the critical Preceramic/Ceramic transition: New data from coastal Peru. American Anthropologist 92(2):481–491.

——1991 The impact of radiocarbon dates on the Maritime Hypothesis: Response to Quilter. American Anthropologist 93(2):454–455.

Pozorski, Thomas, 1971 Survey and Excavations of Burial Platforms at Chan Chan, Peru. BA thesis, Department of Anthropology, Harvard University, Cambridge.

——1980 The Early Horizon site of Huaca de Los Reyes: Societal implications. American Antiquity 45:100–110.

Pozorski, Thomas, and Shelia Pozorski, 1999 Una reevaluación del desarrollo de la sociedad compleja durante el precerámico tardío en base a los fechados radiocarbónicos y las investigaciones en el valle de Casma. *In* El Período Arcaico en el Perú: Hacia una Definición de los Orígenes. Peter Kaulicke, ed. pp. 171–186. Boletín de Arqueología PUCP, vol. 3. Lima: Especialidad de Arqueología, Departamento de Humanidades, Pontificia Universidad Católica del Perú.

Pozzi Escot, Denise B., 1991 Conchopata: A community of potters. *In* Wari Administrative Structure: Prehistoric Monumental Architecture and State Government. William H. Isbell and Gordon F. McEwan, eds. pp. 81–92. Washington, DC: Dumbarton Oaks.

Preucel, Robert W., and Ian Hodder, eds., 1996 Contemporary Archaeology in Theory: A Reader. London: Blackwell.

Protzen, Jean-Pierre, and Stella Nair, 1997 Who taught the Inca stonemasons their skills? Journal of the Society of Architectural Historians 56(2):146–167.

——2000 On reconstructing Tiwanaku architecture. Journal of the Society of Architectural Historians 59(3):358–371.

——2002 The gateways of Tiwanaku: symbols or passages? *In* Andean Archaeology II:

Art, Landscape, and Society. Helaine Silverman and William H. Isbell, eds. pp. 189–223. New York: Kluwer Academic/Plenum Publishers.

Proulx, Donald A., 1968 Local Differences and Time Differences in Nasca Pottery. University of California Publications in Anthropology, 5. Berkeley: University of California Press.

——1970 Nasca Gravelots in the Uhle Collection from the Ica Valley, Peru. Research Report 2. Amherst: Department of Anthropology, University of Massachusetts.

——1982 Territoriality in the Early Intermediate Period: The case of Moche and Recuay. Ñawpa Pacha 20:83–96.

——1985 An Analysis of the Early Cultural Sequence in the Nepeña Valley, Peru. Research Report 25. Amherst: Department of Anthropology, University of Massachusetts.

——1989 Nasca trophy heads: Victims of warfare or ritual sacrifice? In Cultures in Conflict: Current Archaeological Perspectives. Diana C. Tkaczuk and Brian C. Vivian, eds. pp. 73–85. Proceedings of the Twentieth Annual Chacmool Conference of the Archaeological Association of the University of Calgary, Calgary.

——1994 Stylistic variation in proliferous Nasca pottery. Andean Past 4:91–108.

——1996 Nasca. In Andean Art at Dumbarton Oaks. Elizabeth Hill Boone, ed. pp. 101–122. Washington, DC: Dumbarton Oaks.

——1998 Settlement Patterns and Society in South Coastal Peru. Unpublished report to the H. John Heinz III Charitable Fund.

——2001 Ritual uses of trophy heads in ancient Nasca society. In Ritual Sacrifice in Ancient Peru. Elizabeth P. Benson and Anita G. Cook, eds. pp. 119–136. Austin: University of Texas Press.

Quilter, Jeffrey, 1985 Architecture and chronology at El Paraíso, Peru. Journal of Field Archaeology 12:279–97.

——1989 Life and Death at Paloma: Society and Mortuary Practices in a Preceramic Peruvian Village. Iowa City: University of Iowa Press.

——1990 The Moche Revolt of the Objects. Latin American Antiquity 1:42–65.

——1991 Problems with the Late Preceramic of Peru. American Anthropologist 93(2):450–454.

——1997 The narrative approach to Moche iconography. Latin American Antiquity 8:113–133.

——2001 Moche mimesis: Continuity and change in public art in early Peru. In Moche Art and Archaeology in Ancient Peru. Joanne Pillsbury, ed. pp. 21–46. Washington, DC and New Haven: National Gallery of Art and Yale University Press.

Quilter, Jeffrey, Bernardino Ojeda, Deborah M. Pearsall, Daniel H. Sandweiss, John G. Jones, and Elisabeth S. Wing, 1991 Subsistence economy of El Paraiso, Peru. Science 251:277–283.

Quilter, Jeffrey, and Gary Urton, eds., 2002 Narrative Threads: Accounting and Recounting in Andean Khipu. Austin: University of Texas Press.

Raffino, Rodolfo, 1983 Los Inkas del Kollasuyu, 2nd edition. La Plata: Ramos Americana Editora.

Ramírez, Susan, 1996 The World Upside Down: Cross-Cultural Contact and Conflict in Sixteenth-Century Peru. Stanford: Stanford University Press.

Ramos Gavilán, Alonso 1976[1621] Historia de Nuestra Senora de Copacabana, 2nd edition. La Paz: Academía Boliviana de la Historia.

——1988[1621] Historia de Nuestra Señora de Copacabana. Rafael Sans, ed. La Paz: Imprenta de la Unión Católica.

Rasnake, Roger N., 1988 Domination and Cultural Resistance: Authority and Power Among an Andean People. Durham: Duke University Press.

Rattray, Evelyn C., 1990 The identification of ethnic affiliation at the Merchants' Barrio, Teotihuacan. *In* Etnoarqueología: Primer Coloquio Bosch-Gimpera. Y. Sugiura and M. C. Serra, eds. pp. 113–138. Mexico City: Universidad Nacional Autónoma de México.

Ravines, Rogger, 1981 Prácticas funerarias en Ancón (segunda parte). Revista del Museo Nacional 45:89–166.

——1995 La cerámica del sitio PV44–14G07, valle de Chancay, Lima. Boletín de Lima 100:57–76.

Ravines, Rogger, and William H. Isbell, 1976 Garagay: Sitio ceremonial temprano en el valle de Lima. Revista del Museo Nacional 41:253–275.

Raymond, J. Scott, 1982 The maritime foundations of Andean civilization: A reconsideration of the evidence. American Antiquity 46:806–821.

Reiche, Maria, 1974 Peruvian Ground Drawings. Munich: Kunstraum München.

Reichert, Raphael X., 1977 The Recuay Ceramic Style: A Reevaluation. Ph.D. dissertation, Department of Art History, University of California, Los Angeles.

——1989 Moche battle and the question of identity. *In* Cultures in Conflict: Current Archaeological Perspectives. Diana C. Tkaczuk and Brian C. Vivian, eds. pp. 86–89. Proceedings of the Twentieth Annual Chacmool Conference, University of Calgary, Calgary.

Reindel, Markus, and Johny Isla Cuadrado, 1998 Proyecto Arqueológico PALPA. Informe Final. Report submitted to the Peruvian Instituto Nacional de Cultura, Lima, Peru.

——————1999 Das Palpa-Tal: Ein Archiv der Vorgeschichte Perus. *In* Nasca: Geheimnisvolle Zeichen im Alten Peru. Judith Rickenbach, ed. pp. 177–198. Zurich: Museum Rietberg.

——————2001 Los Molinos und La Muña. Zwei Siedlungszentren der Nasca-Kultur in Palpa, Südperu. Los Molinos y La Muña. Dos centros administrativos de la cultura Nasca en Palpa, costa sur del Perú. Beiträge zur Allgemeinen und Vergleichenden Archäologie 21:241–319.

——————and Klaus Koschmieder, 1999 Vorspanische Siedlungen und Bodenzeichnungen in Palpa, Süd-Peru. Asentamientos prehispánicos y geoglifos en Palpa, costa sur del Perú. Beiträge zur Allgemeinen und Vergleichenden Archäologie 19:313–381.

Reinhard, Johan, 1985a Chavín and Tiahuanacu: A new look at two Andean ceremonial centers. National Geographic Research 1(3):395–422.

——1985b Sacred mountains: An ethno-archaeological study of high Andean ruins. Mountain Research and Development 5(4):299–317.

——1988 The Nazca Lines: A New Perspective on their Origin and Meaning. Lima: Editorial Los Pinos.

Reiss, Wilhelm, and Stübel, Alphons, 1880–87 The Necropolis of Ancon. London and Berlin: A. Ascher.

Rice, Don Stephen, ed., 1993 Latin American Horizons. Washington, DC: Dumbarton Oaks.

Richardson III, James, 1973 The Preceramic sequence and the Pleistocene and Post-Pleistocene climate of northwest Peru. *In* Human Variation. Donald W. Lathrap and Jody Douglas, eds. pp. 73–89. Urbana: University of Illinois Press.

——1978 Early man on the Peruvian coast: Early maritime exploitation and the Pleistocene and Holocene environment. *In* Early Man in the New World. Alan L. Bryan, ed. pp. 274–289. Orono: Center for the Study of Early Man, University of Maine.

——1992 Early man in America. Revista Arqueológica Americana 6:71.

Rick, John, 1980 Prehistoric Hunters of the High Andes. New York: Academic Press.

——1987 Dates as date: An examination of the Peruvian Preceramic radiocarbon record. American Antiquity 52(1):55–73.

——2002 The evolution of authority at Chavín de Huántar, Peru. Paper presented at the 101st Meeting of the American Anthropological Association, New Orleans.

Rick, John, Silvia Rodriguez Kembel, Rosa Mendoza Rick, and John A. Kembel, 1998 La arquitectura del complejo ceremonial de Chavín de Huántar: Documentación tridimensional y sus implicancias. *In* Perspectivas Regionales del Período Formativo en el Perú. Peter Kaulicke, ed. pp. 181–214. Boletín de Arqueología PUCP, vol. 2. Lima: Departamento de Humanidades, Especialidad de Arqueología, Pontificia Universidad Católica del Perú.

Rivera Casanovas, Claudia, 2003 Ch'iji Jawira: A case of ceramic specialization in the Tiwanaku urban periphery. *In* Tiwanaku and its Hinterland: Archaeological and Paleoecological Investigations of an Andean Civilization, vol. 2. Alan L. Kolata, ed. Washington, DC: Smithsonian Institution Press.

Robinson, David A., 1957 An Archaeological Survey of the Nasca Valley, Peru. MA thesis, Department of Anthropology, Stanford University.

Robinson, R. 1972 Non-European foundations of European imperialism: Sketch for a theory of collaboration. *In* Studies in the Theory of Imperialism. R. Owen and R. Sutcliffe, eds. pp. 117–40. London: Longman.

Rodman, Amy Oakland, 1992 Textiles and ethnicity: Tiwanaku in San Pedro de Atacama, north Chile. Latin American Antiquity 3(4):316–340.

Rodman, Amy Oakland, and Arabel Fernández, 2000 Los tejidos Wari y Tiwanaku: Comparaciones y contextos. *In* Huari y Tiwanaku: Modelos vs. Evidencias. Peter Kaulicke and William H. Isbell, eds. pp. 119–130. Boletín de Arqueología PUCP, vol. 4. Lima: Departamento de Humanidades, Especialidad de Arqueología, Pontificia Universidad Católica del Perú.

Roe, Peter G., 1974 A Further Exploration of the Rowe Chavín Seriation and its Implications for North Central Coast Chronology. Dumbarton Oaks Studies in Pre-Columbian Art and Archaeology, 13. Washington, DC: Dumbarton Oaks.

—— 1982 The Cosmic Zygote: Cosmology in the Amazon Basin. New Brunswick: Rutgers University Press.

Rosas, Hermilio, and Ruth Shady, 1974 Sobre el período formativo en la sierra del extremo norte del Perú. Arqueológicas 15:6–36. Lima: Museo Nacional de Antropología y Arqueología.

Rossen, Jack, 1991 Ecotones and Low-Risk Intensification: The Middle Preceramic Habitation of Nanchoc, Northern Peru. Ph.D. dissertation, Department of Anthropology, University of Kentucky, Lexington.

Rossen, Jack, Tom D. Dillehay, and Donald Ugent, 1996 Ancient cultigens or modern intrusions? Evaluating plant remains in an Andean case study. Journal of Archaeological Science 23:391–407.

Rostworowski de Diez Canseco, María, 1953 Pachacutec Inca Yupanqui. Lima: Editorial Torres Aguirre.

—— 1970 Mercaderes del valle de Chincha en la época prehispánica: Un documento y unos comentarios. Revista Española de Antropología Americana 5:135–178. Madrid: Departamento de Antropología y Etnología de América, Facultad de Filosofía y Letras, Universidad de Madrid.

—— 1972 Breve informe sobre el Señorío de Ichma o Ychima. Arqueología PUC 13:37–51. Lima: Pontificia Universidad Católica del Perú.

—— 1977a Etnía y Sociedad: Ensayos Sobre la Costa Central Prehispánica. Lima: Instituto de Estudios Peruanos.

—— 1977b Coastal fisherman, merchants, and artisans in pre-hispanic Peru. *In* The Sea in the Pre-Columbian World. Elizabeth P. Benson, ed. pp. 167–186. Washington, DC: Dumbarton Oaks.

——1978 Señoríos Indígenas de Lima y Canta. Lima: Instituto de Estudios Peruanos.

——1978–80 Guarco y Lunahuaná – dos señorios prehispánicos de la costa sur central del Perú. Revista del Museo Nacional 44:153–214.

——1989 Costa Peruana Prehispanica. Lima: Instituto de Estudios Peruanos.

——1992 Pachacamac y el Señor de los Milagros: Una Trayectoria Milenaria. Lima: Instituto de Estudios Peruanos.

——1993 Ensayos de Historia Andina I: Elites, Etnias y Recursos. Lima: Instituto de Estudios Peruanos.

——1998 Ensayos de Historia Andina II: Pampas de Nasca, Género, Hechicería. Lima: Instituto de Estudios Peruanos.

——1999a El Señorío de Pachacamac: El Informe de Rodrigo Cantos de Andrade de 1573. Lima: Instituto de Estudios Peruanos.

——1999b History of the Inca Realm. Harry B. Iceland, trans. Cambridge: Cambridge University Press.

Rowe, Ann P., 1979 Textiles from the Nasca Valley at the time of the fall of the Huari Empire. In The Junius B. Bird Pre-Columbian Textile Conference, 1973. Ann Pollard Rowe, Elizabeth P. Benson, and Anne-Louise Schaffer, eds. pp. 151–182. Washington, DC: Dumbarton Oaks and the Textile Museum.

——1980 Textiles from the burial platform of Las Avispas at Chan Chan. Ñawpa Pacha 18:81–164.

——1984 Costume and Featherwork of the Lords of Chimor: Textiles from Peru's North Coast. Washington, DC: The Textile Museum.

——1990–91 Nasca figurines and costume. The Textile Museum Journal 29/30:93–128.

Rowe, Ann P., and John Cohen, 2002 Hidden Threads of Peru: Q'ero Textiles. Washington, DC: The Textile Museum.

Rowe, Ann P., and Lynn Meisch, eds., 1998 Costume and Identity in Highland Ecuador. Washington, DC: The Textile Museum.

Rowe, John H., 1945 Absolute chronology in the Andean area. American Antiquity 3:265–284.

——1946 Inca culture at the time of the Spanish conquest. In Handbook of South American Indians, vol. 2. The Andean Civilizations. Julian H. Steward, ed. pp. 183–330. Bulletin 143. Bureau of American Ethnology. Washington, DC: Smithsonian Institution.

——1948 The kingdom of Chimor. Acta Americana 6:26–59.

——1954 Max Uhle, 1856–1974. A Memoir of the Father of Peruvian Archaeology. University of California Publications in American Archaeology and Ethnology 46(1):1–134.

——1956 Archaeological explorations in southern Peru, 1954–1955: Preliminary report of the Fourth University of California Archaeological Expedition to Peru. American Antiquity 22(2):135–151.

——1960 Cultural unity and diversification in Peruvian archaeology. In Men and Cultures: Selected Papers of the Fifth International Congress of Anthropological and Ethnological Sciences. Anthony F. C. Wallace, ed. pp. 627–631. Philadelphia: University of Pennsylvania Press.

——1962 Stages and periods in archaeological interpretation. Southwestern Journal of Anthropology 18(1):40–54.

——1967 Form and meaning in Chavín art. In Peruvian Archaeology: Selected Readings. John H. Rowe and Dorothy Menzel, eds. pp. 72–103. Palo Alto: Peek Publications.

——1982 Inca policies and institutions relating to the cultural unification of the empire. In

The Inca and Aztec States, 1400–1800: Anthropology and History. George A. Collier, Renato I. Rosaldo, and John D. Wirth, eds. pp. 93–118. New York: Academic Press.

——1986 Standardization in Inca tapestry tunics. *In* The Junius B. Bird Pre-Columbian Textile Conference: April 7th and 8th, 1984. Ann Pollard Rowe, ed. pp. 151–182. Washington, DC: The Textile Museum.

Rowe, John H., Donald Collier, and Gordon R. Willey, 1950 Reconnaissance notes on the site of Huari, near Ayacucho, Peru. American Antiquity 16(2):120–137.

Rowe, John H., and Dorothy Menzel, eds., 1967 Peruvian Archaeology. Selected Readings. Palo Alto: Peek Publications.

Ruiz, Alvaro, Jonathan Haas, Winifred Creamer, 2003 Informe Final Proyecto Arqueológico Norte Chico Etapa 1. Report submitted to Instituto Nacional de Cultura, Lima, Peru.

Russell, Glenn S., Leonard Banks, and Jesús Briceño, 1994 Cerro Mayal: Nuevos datos sobre producción de cerámica Moche en el valle de Chicama. *In* Moche: Propuestas y Perspectivas. Santiago Uceda and Elias Mujica, eds. pp. 181–206. Trujillo: Universidad Nacional de la Libertad.

Russell, Glenn S., and Margaret A. Jackson, 2001 Political economy and patronage at Cerro Mayal, Peru. *In* Moche Art and Archaeology in Ancient Peru. Joanne Pillsbury, ed. pp. 159–175. Washington, DC and New Haven: National Gallery of Art and Yale University Press.

Rydén, Stig, 1947 Archaeological Researches in the Highlands of Bolivia. Göteborg: Elanders Boktryckeri Aktiebolag.

Sackett, James, 1982 Approaches to style in lithic archaeology. Journal of Anthropological Archaeology 1:59–112.

Salomon, Frank, 1986 Native Lords of Quito in the Age of the Incas. Cambridge: Cambridge University Press.

——1991 Introduction. *In* The Huarochirí Manuscript. Frank Salomon and George Urioste, eds. pp. 1–38. Austin: University of Texas Press.

——1995 "The beautiful grandparents": Andean ancestor shrines and mortuary ritual as seen through Colonial records. *In* Tombs for the Living: Andean Mortuary Practices. Tom D. Dillehay, ed. pp. 315–353. Washington, DC: Dumbarton Oaks.

——2001 How an Andean "writing without words" works. Current Anthropology 42:1–27.

Salomon, Frank, and George Urioste, eds., 1991 The Huarochirí Manuscript. Austin: University of Texas Press.

Samaniego, Lorenzo, Enrique Vergara, and Henning Bischof, 1985 New evidence on Cerro Sechin, Casma Valley, Peru. *In* Early Ceremonial Architecture in the Andes. Christopher B. Donnan, ed. pp. 165–190. Washington, DC: Dumbarton Oaks.

Sandweiss, Daniel H., 1992 The Archaeology of Chincha Fisherman: Specialization and Status in Inka Peru. Bulletin 29. Pittsburgh: Carnegie Museum of Natural History.

Sandweiss, Daniel H., Kirk A. Maasch, Richard L. Burger, James B. Richardson III, Harold B. Rollins, and Amy Clement, 2001 Variations in Holocene El Niño frequencies: Climate records and cultural consequences in ancient Peru. Geology 29 (7):603–606.

Sandweiss, Daniel H., Heather McInnis, Richard L. Burger, Asunción Cano, Bernardino Ojeda, Rolando Paredes, María del Carmen Sandweiss, and Michael Glascock, 1998 Quebrada Jaguay: Early South American maritime adaptations. Science 281:1830–1832.

Sandweiss, Daniel H., J. B. Richardson III, E. J. Reitz, H. B. Rollins, and K. A. Maasch, 1996 Geoarchaeological evidence from Peru for a 5000 B.P. onset of El Niño. Science 273:1531–1533.

Sandweiss, Daniel H., J. B. Richardson III, E. J. Reitz, James T. Hsu, and Robert A. Feldman, 1989 Early maritime adaptations in the Andes: Preliminary studies at the Ring Site, Peru. *In* Ecology, Settlement and History in the Osmore Basin. Donald S. Rice, Charles Stanish, and Peter Scarr, eds. pp. 35–84. Oxford: British Archaeological Reports, International Series, 545.

Santley, Robert S., and Kenneth G. Hirth, eds., 1993 Prehispanic Domestic Units in Western Mesoamerica: Studies of the Household, Compound, and Residence. Boca Raton: CRC Press.

Sapp, William D. III, 2002 The Impact of Imperial Conquest at the Palace of a Local Lord in the Jequetepeque Valley, Northern Peru. Ph.D. dissertation, Department of Anthropology, University of California, Los Angeles.

Sarmiento de Gamboa, Pedro, 1942[1572] Historia de los Incas, 2nd edition. Angel Rosenblat, ed. Buenos Aires: Emecé Editores, SA.

—— 1960[1572] Historia de los Incas. *In* Biblioteca de Autores Españoles (continuación), vol. 135, pp. 193–297. Madrid: Ediciones Atlas, Madrid.

Saunders, Nicholas J., ed., 1998 Icons of Power: Feline Symbolism in the Americas. London: Routledge.

Schaedel, Richard P., 1948 Stone sculpture in the Callejón de Huaylas. *In* A Reappraisal of Peruvian Archaeology. Wendell C. Bennett, ed. pp. 66–79. Memoirs, 4. Society for American Archaeology.

—— 1951 Major ceremonial and population centers in northern Peru. *In* The Civilizations of Ancient America: Selected Papers of the 29th International Congress of Americanists. Sol Tax, ed. pp. 232–243. Chicago: University of Chicago Press.

—— 1952 An Analysis of Central Andean Stone Sculpture. Ph.D. dissertation, Department of Anthropology, Yale University, New Haven.

—— 1966 Urban growth and ekistics on the Peruvian coast. Proceedings of the 36th International Congress of Americanists 2:531–539. Buenos Aires.

—— 1988 Andean world view: Hierarchy or reciprocity, regulation or control? Current Anthropology 29(5):768–775.

—— 1993 Congruence of horizon with polity: Huari and the Middle Horizon. *In* Latin American Horizons. Don Stephen Rice, ed. pp. 225–262. Washington, DC: Dumbarton Oaks.

Schiappacasse, Virgilio, and Hans Niemeyer, 1978 Descripción y análisis interpretativo de un sitio arcaico temprano en la Quebrada de Camarones. Publicación Ocasional, 41. Santiago: Museo Nacional de Historia Natural, Universidad de Tarapacá.

Schlesier, Karl L., 1959 Stilgeschichtliche Einordnung der Nazca-Vasenmalereien Beitrag zur Geschichte der Hochkulturen des Vorkolumbischen Peru. Annali Lateranensi 23:9–228.

Schreiber, Katharina, 1978 Planned Architecture of Middle Horizon Peru: Implications for Social and Political Organization. Ph.D. dissertation, Department of Anthropology, State University of New York, Binghamton.

—— 1984 Prehistoric roads in the Carahuarazo Valley, Peru. *In* Current Archaeological Projects in the Central Andes: Some Approaches and Results. Ann Kendall, ed. pp. 75–94. Oxford: BAR International Series, 210.

—— 1987a Conquest and consolidation: A comparison of the Wari and Inka occupations of a highland Peruvian valley. American Antiquity 52(2):266–284.

—— 1987b From state to empire: The expansion of Wari outside the Ayacucho Basin. *In* The Origins and Development of the Andean State. Jonathan Haas, Shelia Pozorski, and Thomas Pozorski, eds. pp. 91–97. New York: Cambridge University Press.

—— 1991a Jincamocco: A Huari administrative center in the south central highlands of Peru. *In* Huari Administrative Structure: Prehistoric Monumental Architecture and State Government. William H. Isbell and Gordon F. McEwan, eds. pp. 199–213. Washington, DC: Dumbarton Oaks.

—— 1991b The association between roads and polities: evidence for Wari roads in Peru. *In* Ancient Road Networks and Settlement Hierarchies in the New World. C. D. Trombold, ed. pp. 243–252. Cambridge: Cambridge University Press.

—— 1992 Wari Imperialism in Middle Horizon Peru. Anthropological Papers of the Museum of Anthropology, 87. Ann Arbor: University of Michigan.

—— 1993 The Inka occupation of the province of Lucanas. *In* Provincial Inka. Michael A. Malpass, ed. pp. 77–116. Iowa City: University of Iowa Press.

—— 1999 Regional approaches to the study of prehistoric empires: Examples from Ayacucho and Nasca, Peru. *In* Settlement Pattern Studies in the Americas: Fifty Years Since Virú. Brian R. Billman and Gary M. Feinman, eds. pp. 160–171. Washington, DC: Smithsonian Institution Press.

—— 2001 The Wari Empire of Middle Horizon Peru: The epistemological challenge of documenting an empire without documentary evidence. *In* Empires: Perspectives from Archaeology and History. Susan E. Alcock, Terence D'Altroy, Kathleen D. Morrison, and Carla M. Sinopoli, eds. pp. 70–92. Cambridge: Cambridge University Press.

—— In press. Imperial agendas and local agency. *In* The Archaeology of Colonies. Gil J. Stein, ed. Santa Fe, NM: School of American Research Press.

Schreiber, Katharina, and Josué Lancho Rojas, 1995 The puquios of Nasca. Latin American Antiquity 6(3):229–254.

Schroeder, Gert, 1958–59 Eine Postglaziale Abschlagkultur in der Peruanischen Kordillere. Quartär 10/11:283–286. Ludwig Röhrscheid, ed. Bonn.

Scott, James C., 1990 Domination and the Arts of Resistance: Hidden Transcripts. New Haven: Yale University Press.

Seddon, Matthew T., 1998 Ritual, Power, and the Development of a Complex Society. Ph.D. dissertation, Department of Anthropology, University of Chicago.

Seki, Yuji, 1998 El período formativo en el valle de Cajamarca. *In* Perspectivas Regionales del Período Formativo en el Perú. Peter Kaulicke, ed. pp. 147–160. Boletín de Arqueología PUCP, vol. 2. Lima: Departamento de Humanidades, Especialidad de Arqueología, Pontificia Universidad Católica del Perú.

Seler, Eduard, 1961[1923] Die buntbemalten Gefässe von Nasca im südlichen Peru und die Hauptelemente ihrer Verzierung. Gesammelte Abhanlungen zur amerikanischen Sprach- und Altertumskunde 4:171–338. Akademische Druck-U Verlagsanstalt Graz, Austria.

Sestieri, P. Claudio, 1971 Cajamarquilla, Peru: The necropolis on the Huaca Tello. Archaeology 24(2):101–106.

Shady Solís, Ruth, 1982 La cultura Nievería y la interacción social en el mundo andino en la época Huari. Arqueológicas 19:5–108.

—— 1997 La Ciudad Sagrada de Caral-Supe en los Albores de la Civilización en el Perú. Lima: Universidad Nacional Mayor de San Marcos.

—— 1999 El sustento económico del surgimiento de la civilización en el Perú. Boletín del Museo de Arqueología y Antropología 2(11):2–4.

—— ed., 1999 Cuadernos de Investigación del Archivo Tello 1: Arqueología del Valle de Lima. Lima: Museo de Arqueología y Antropología de la Universidad Nacional Mayor de San Marcos.

—— 2000 Los orígenes de la civilización y la formación del estado en el Perú: Las evidencias arqueológicas de Caral-Supe, segunda parte. Boletín del Museo de Arqueología y Antropología 3(2):2–7.

Shady Solís, Ruth, Jonathan Haas, and Winifred Creamer, 2001 Dating Caral, a Preceramic site in the Supe Valley on the central coast of Peru. Science 292:723–726.

Sherbondy, Jeanette, 1988 Mallki: Ancestros y cultivos de árboles en los Andes. *In* Sociedad Andina: Pasado y Presente. Ramiro Matos M., ed. pp. 101–136. Lima: Fomciencias.

——1992 Water ideology in Inca ethnogenesis. *In* Andean Cosmologies through Time. Robert V. H. Dover, Katharine E. Seibold, and John H. McDowell, eds. pp. 46–66. Bloomington: Indiana University Press.

Shimada, Izumi, 1976 Socioeconomic Organization at Moche V Pampa Grande, Peru: Prelude to a Major Transformation to Come. Ph.D. dissertation, Department of Anthropology, University of Arizona, Tucson.

——1978 Economy of a prehistoric urban context: Commodity and labor flow in Moche V Pampa Grande, Peru. American Antiquity 43:569–592.

——1981 The Batan Grande–La Leche Archaeological Project: The first two seasons. Journal of Field Archaeology 8:405–446.

——1987 Comment on the functions and husbandry of alpaca. American Antiquity 52(4):836–839.

——1990 Cultural continuities and discontinuities on the northern north coast, Middle-Late Horizons. *In* The Northern Dynasties: Kingship and Statecraft in Chimor. Michael E. Moseley and Alana Cordy-Collins, eds. pp. 297–392. Washington, DC: Dumbarton Oaks.

——1991 Pachacamac archaeology: Retrospect and prospect. *In* Pachacamac: A Reprint of the 1903 Edition by Max Uhle. Philadelphia: University Museum of Archaeology and Anthropology, University of Pennsylvania.

——1994 Pampa Grande and the Mochica Culture. Austin: University of Texas Press.

——1995 Cultura Sicán: Dios, Riqueza y Poder en la Costa Norte del Perú. Lima: Fundación del Banco Continental para el Fomento de la Educación y la Cultura.

——1997 Organizational significance of marked bricks and associated construction features on the north Peruvian coast. *In* Arquitectura y Civilización en los Andes Prehispánicos. Elisabeth Bonnier and Henning Bischof, eds. pp. 62–89. Archaeologica Peruana 2. Mannheim: Reiss-Museum.

——2000 The late prehispanic coastal states. *In* The Development of Pre-Columbian Peru, A.D. 1000–1534. Laura Laurencich Minelli, ed. pp. 49–110. Norman: University of Oklahoma Press.

——2001 Late Moche urban craft production: A first approximation. *In* Moche Art and Archaeology in Ancient Peru. Joanne Pillsbury, ed. pp. 177–205. Washington, DC and New Haven: National Gallery of Art and Yale University Press.

Shimada, Izumi, and Adriana Maguiña, 1994 Nueva visión sobre la cultura Gallinazo y su relación con la cultura Moche. *In* Moche: Propuestas y Perspectivas. Santiago Uceda and Elias Mujica, eds. pp. 31–58. Trujillo: Universidad Nacional de la Libertad.

Shimada, Izumi, and Melody Shimada, 1985 Prehistoric llama breeding and herding on the north coast of Peru. American Antiquity 50:3–26.

Sillar, Bill, 1992 The social life of the Andean dead. Archaeological Review from Cambridge 11(1):107–123.

——1996 The dead and the drying: Techniques for transforming people and things in the Andes. Journal of Material Culture 1(3):259–289.

Silva Sifuentes, Jorge E., 1996 Prehistoric Settlement Patterns in the Chillón River Valley, Peru. Ph.D. dissertation, Department of Anthropology, University of Michigan, Ann Arbor.

Silva Sifuentes, Jorge E., Daniel Morales C., Ruben García S., and Enrique Braygarac D., 1988 Cerro Culebra, un asentamiento de la época Lima en el valle de Chillón. Boletín de Lima 56:23–33. Lima.

Silverblatt, Irene, 1987 Moon, Sun, and Witches: Gender Ideologies and Class in Inca and Colonial Peru. Princeton: Princeton University Press.

Silverman, Gail, 1988 Weaving techniques and the registration of knowledge in the Cusco area of Peru. Journal of Latin American Lore 14(2):207–241.

—— 1998 El Tejido Andino. Un Libro de Sabiduria. Lima: Fondo de Cultura Económica.

—— 1999 Iconografia textíl de Cusco y su relación con los tocapu Inca / Textile iconography from Cusco and its relations to Inca tocapu. In Tejidos Milenarios del Perú / Ancient Peruvian Textiles. José Antonio de Lavalle and Rosario de Lavalle de Cárdenas, eds. pp. 803–836. Lima: Integra AFP.

Silverman, Helaine, 1988 Nasca 8: A reassessment of its chronological placement and cultural significance. In Multidisciplinary Studies in Andean Anthropology. Virginia J. Vitzhum, ed. pp. 23–32. Michigan Discussions in Anthropology 8. Ann Arbor: University of Michigan.

—— 1990 The early Nasca pilgrimage center of Cahuachi: Archaeological and anthropological perspectives. In The Lines of Nazca. Anthony F. Aveni, ed. pp. 209–244. Philadelphia: American Philosophical Society.

—— 1991 The Paracas problem: Archaeological perspectives. In Paracas Art and Architecture: Object and Context in South Coastal Peru. Anne Paul, ed. pp. 349–415. Iowa City: University of Iowa Press.

—— 1993 Cahuachi in the Ancient Nasca World. Iowa City: University of Iowa Press.

—— 1994 Paracas in Nazca: New data on the Early Horizon occupation of the Río Grande de Nazca Drainage, Peru. Latin American Antiquity 5(4):359–382.

—— 1996a The Formative Period on the south coast of Peru: A critical review. Journal of World Prehistory 10(2):95–146.

—— 1996b Contextualizando la muerte en los cementerios de Paracas. In Al Final del Camino. Luis Millones and Moisés Lemlij, eds. pp. 1–19. Lima: Sidea Fondo Editorial.

—— 1996c Musicians of the desert. In Birds on a Drum: Conservation of a Pre-Columbian Musical Instrument, pp. 8–12. Champaign: Krannert Art Museum and Kinkead Pavillion, University of Illinois at Urbana-Champaign.

—— 1997 The first field season of excavations at the Alto del Molino site, Pisco Valley, Peru. Journal of Field Archaeology 24(4):441–457.

—— 2002 Ancient Nasca Settlement and Society. Iowa City: University of Iowa Press.

Silverman, Helaine, and William H. Isbell, 2002 From art to material culture. In Andean Archaeology II: Art, Landscape, and Society. Helaine Silverman and William H. Isbell, eds. pp. 3–20. New York: Kluwer Academic/Plenum Publishers.

Silverman, Helaine, and Donald A. Proulx, 2002 The Nasca. Oxford: Blackwell.

Sinopoli, Carla M., 1996 The archaeology of empires. Annual Review of Anthropology 23:159–180.

Skar, Sarah, 1987 The role of urine in Andean notions of health and the cosmos. In Natives and Neighbors in South America: Anthropological Essays. H. Skar and Frank Salomon, eds. pp. 267–269. Göteborg: Göteborgs Etnografiska Museum.

Smith, John W., Jr., 1978 The Recuay Culture: A Reconstruction Based on Artistic Motifs. Ph.D. dissertation, Department of Anthropology, University of Texas, Austin.

Smith, Michael E., 1987 Household possessions and wealth in agrarian states: Implications for archaeology. Journal of Anthropological Archaeology 6:297–335.

—— 1992 Braudel's temporal rhythms and chronology theory in archaeology. In Archaeology, Annales, and Ethnohistory. A. B. Knapp, ed. pp. 23–34. New York: Cambridge University Press.

—— 1993 Houses and the settlement hierarchy in Late Postclassic Morelos: A comparison of archaeology and ethnohistory. *In* Prehispanic Domestic Units in Western Mesoamerica. Robert S. Santley and Kenneth G. Hirth, eds. pp. 191–206. Boca Raton: CRC Press.

Solis, S. Ruth, Jonathan Haas, and Winifred Creamer, 2001 Dating Caral, a Preceramic site in the Supe Valley on the central coast of Peru. Science 292:723–726.

Spence, Michael W., 1981 Obsidian production and the state in Teotihuacan. American Antiquity 46:769–788.

Spickard, Lynda, 1983 The development of Huari administrative architecture. *In* Investigations of the Andean Past. Daniel H. Sandweiss, ed. pp. 136–160. Ithaca: Cornell University Latin American Studies Program.

Soja, Edward W., 1989 Postmodern Geographies: The Reassertion of Space in Critical Social Theory. New York: Verso Press.

Stanish, Charles, 1985 Post-Tiwanaku Regional Economies in the Otora Valley, Southern Peru. Ph.D. dissertation, Department of Anthropology, University of Chicago.

—— 1989a An archaeological evaluation of an ethnohistorical model. *In* Ecology, Settlement, and History in the Osmore Drainage. Don S. Rice, Charles Stanish, and Peter Scarr, eds. pp. 303–320. Oxford: British Archaeological Reports, 545(i).

—— 1989b Household archaeology: Testing models of zonal complementarity in the south central Andes. American Anthropologist 91(1):7–24.

—— 2000 Negotiating rank in an imperial state: Lake Titicaca Basin elite under Inca and Spanish control. *In* Hierarchies in Action, Cui Bono? Michael W. Diehl, ed. pp. 317–339. Occasional Paper, 27. Carbondale: Center for Archaeological Investigations.

—— 2001 The origin of state societies in South America. Annual Review of Anthropology 30:41–64.

—— 2003 Ancient Titicaca: The Evolution of Complex Society in Southern Peru and Northern Bolivia. Berkeley: University of California Press.

Stein, Gil J., 2002 From passive periphery to active agents: Emerging perspectives in the archaeology of interregional interaction. American Anthropologist 104(3):903–916.

Steward, Julian H., ed., 1944 Handbook of South American Indians, vol. 2. The Central Andean Civilizations. Bulletin 143. Bureau of American Ethnology. Washington, DC: Smithsonian Institution.

Stone-Miller, Rebecca, 1986 Color patterning and the Huari artist: The Lima Tapestry revisited. *In* The Junius B. Bird Conference on Andean Textiles: April 7th and 8th, 1984. Ann Pollard Rowe, ed. pp. 137–149. Washington, DC: The Textile Museum.

—— 1995 Art of the Andes: From Chavín to Inca. London: Thames & Hudson.

Storey, Rebecca, 1992 Life and Death in the Ancient City of Teotihuacan: A Modern Paleodemographic Synthesis. Tuscaloosa: University of Alabama Press.

Stothert, Karen E., 1980 The Villa Salvador site and the beginning of the Early Intermediate Period in the Lurín Valley, Peru. Journal of Field Archaeology 7:279–295.

—— 1988 La Prehistoria Temprana de la Peninsula de Santa Elena, Ecuador: Cultura Las Vegas. Miscelánea Antropológica Ecuatoriana 10, Monografia. Guayaquil and Quito: Museo del Banco Central del Ecuador.

Strong, William D., 1957 Paracas, Nazca, and Tiahuanacoid Relationships in South Coastal Peru. Memoirs, 13. Society for American Archaeology.

Strong, William D., and John Corbett, 1943 A ceramic sequence at Pachacamac. *In* Archeological Studies in Peru, 1941–42. William Duncan Strong, Gordon R. Willey, and John M. Corbett, eds. pp. 27–122. Columbia Studies in Archeology and Ethnology, 1. New York: Columbia University Press.

Strong, William D., and Clifford Evans, 1952 Cultural Stratigraphy in the Virú Valley, Northern Peru. Columbia University Studies in Archaeology and Ethnology, 4. New York: Columbia University Press.

Strong, William D., Gordon R. Willey, and John M. Corbett, eds., 1943 Archeological Studies in Peru, 1941–1942. Columbia Studies in Archeology and Ethnology, 1. New York: Columbia University Press.

Stübel, Alfons, and Max Uhle, 1892 Die Ruinstaette von Tiahuanaco in Hochlande des Alten Peru: Eine Kulturgeschichtliche Studie. Leipzig: Verlag von Karl W. Heirsermann.

Stumer, Louis M., 1953 Playa Grande: Primitive elegance in pre-Tiahuanaco Peru. Archaeology 6(1):42–48.

—— 1954a The Chillón Valley of Peru: Excavation and reconnaissance, 1952–1953, pt. 1, Archaeology 7(3):171–178; pt. 2, 7(4):220–228.

—— 1954b Population centers of the Rimac Valley of Peru. American Antiquity 20:130–148.

—— 1957 Cerámica negra de estilo Maranga. Revista del Museo Nacional 26:272–290.

—— 1958 Contactos foráneos en la arquitectura de la costa central. Revista del Museo Nacional 27:11–30.

Sullivan, William, 1996 The Secret of the Incas. Myth, Astronomy, and the War Against Time. New York: Crown Publishers.

Tabío, Ernesto, 1965 Excavaciones en la Costa Central del Perú (1955–58). Havana: Academia de Ciencias de la República de Cuba.

Tate, Carolyn, and Gordon Berdersky, 1999 Olmec sculptures of the human fetus. Perspectives in Biology and Medicine 42(3):303–332.

Taylor, R. E., Austin Long, and Renee Kra, 1992 Radiocarbon after Four Decades: An Interdisciplinary Perspective. New York: Springer.

Tello, Julio C., 1917 Los antiguos cemeterios del valle de Nazca. Proceedings of the Second Pan-American Scientific Congress 1:283–291.

—— 1923 Wira Kocha. Inca 1(1):93–320; 1(3):583–606.

—— 1928 Los descubrimientos del Museo de Arqueología Peruana en la peninsula de Paracas. Proceedings of the 22nd International Congress of Americanists (Rome, 1926), pp. 679–690.

—— 1929 Antiguo Perú: Primera Época. Lima: Comisión Organizadora del Segundo Congreso de Turismo.

—— 1931 Un modelo de escenografía plástica en el arte antiguo peruano. Wira Kocha 1(1):87–112.

—— 1942 Orígen y desarrollo de las civilizaciones prehistóricas andinas. Actas y trabajos científicos del XXVII Congreso Internacional de Americanistas (Lima, 1939), vol. 1, pp. 589–720.

—— 1956 Arqueología del Valle de Casma. Culturas: Chavín, Santa o Huaylas Yunga y Sub-Chimú. Lima: Universidad Nacional de San Marcos.

—— 1959 Paracas. Primera Parte. Publicación del Proyecto 8b del Programa 1941–1942 de The Institute of Andean Research de New York. Lima: Empresa Gráfica T Scheuch, SA.

—— 1960 Chavín: Cultura Matriz de la Civilización Andina. Lima: Publicación Antropológica del Archivo "Julio C. Tello" de la Universidad Nacional Mayor de San Marcos II. Imprenta de la Universidad de San Marcos.

—— 1970 Las Ruinas de Wari. In Cien Años de Arqueología en el Perú: Fuentes y Investigaciónes para la Historia del Perú. Rogger Ravines, ed. Lima: Instituto de Estudios Peruanos.

Tello, Julio C., and Toribio Mejía Xesspe, 1979 Paracas. Segunda Parte: Cavernas y Necrópolis. Lima: Universidad Nacional Mayor de San Marcos and Andean Institute of New York.

Tello, Ricardo, José Armas, and Claude Chapdelaine, 2002 Prácticas funerarias Moche en el complejo arqueológico Huacas del Sol y de la Luna. *In* Moche: Hacia el Final del Milenio. Santiago Uceda and Elias Mujica, eds. pp. 163–204. Trujillo: Universidad Nacional de la Libertad.

Terada, Kazuo, 1979 Excavations at La Pampa in the North Highlands of Peru, 1975. Tokyo: University of Tokyo Press.

——1985 Early ceremonial architecture in the Cajamarca Valley. *In* Early Ceremonial Architecture in the Andes. Christopher B. Donnan, ed. pp. 191–208. Washington, DC: Dumbarton Oaks.

Terada, Kazuo, and Yoshio Onuki, 1982 Excavations at Huacaloma in the Cajamarca Valley, Peru, 1979. Tokyo: University of Tokyo Press.

Thomas, Julian, 1996 Time, Culture and Identity. London and New York: Routledge.

Thompson, Donald E., and Rogger Ravines, 1973 Tinyash: A prehispanic village in the Andean puna. Archaeology 26(2):94–100.

Tilley, Christopher, 1994 A Phenomenology of Landscape: Places, Paths and Monuments. Oxford and Providence: Berg.

——1999 Metaphor and Material Culture. Oxford: Blackwell.

Tomczak, Paula D., 2001 Prehistoric Soci-Economic Relations and Population Organization in the Lower Osmore Valley of Southern Peru. Ph.D. dissertation, Department of Anthropology, University of New Mexico, Albuquerque.

Topic, John R., 1982 Lower-class social and economic organization at Chan Chan. *In* Chan Chan: Andean Desert City. Michael E. Moseley and Kent C. Day, eds. pp. 145–175. Albuquerque: University of New Mexico Press.

——1990 Craft production in the Kingdom of Chimor. *In* The Northern Dynasties: Kingship and Statecraft in Chimor. Michael E. Moseley and Alana Cordy-Collins, eds. pp. 145–175. Washington, DC: Dumbarton Oaks.

——1991 Huari and Huamachuco. *In* Huari Administrative Structure: Prehistoric Monumental Architecture and State Government. William H. Isbell and Gordon F. McEwan, eds. pp. 141–164. Washington, DC: Dumbarton Oaks.

Topic, John R., and Michael E. Moseley, 1983 Chan Chan: A case study of urban change in Peru. Ñawpa Pacha 21:153–182.

Topic, John R., and Theresa L. Topic, 1983 Coast–highland relations in northern Peru: Some observations on routes, networks, and scales of interaction. *In* Civilization in the Ancient Americas: Essays in Honor of Gordon R. Willey. Richard M. Leventhal and Alan L. Kolata, eds. pp. 237–259. Albuquerque: University of New Mexico Press.

——1997 La guerra mochica. Revista Arqueológica "SIAN" 4:10–12.

——2000 Hacia la comprensión del Fenómeno Huari: Una perspectiva norteña. *In* Huari y Tiwanaku: Modelos vs. Evidencias. Peter Kaulicke and William H. Isbell, eds. pp. 181–217. Boletín de Arqueología PUCP, vol. 4. Lima: Departamento de Humanidades, Especialidad de Arqueología, Pontificia Universidad Católica del Perú.

Topic, Theresa L., 1977 Excavations at Moche. Ph.D. dissertation, Department of Anthropology, Harvard University, Cambridge.

——1982 The Early Intermediate Period and its legacy. *In* Chan Chan: Andean Desert City. Michael E. Moseley and Kent C. Day, eds. pp. 255–284. Albuquerque: University of New Mexico Press.

——1990 Territorial expansion and the kingdom of Chimor. *In* The Northern Dynasties: Kingship and Statecraft in Chimor. Michael E. Moseley and Alana Cordy-Collins, eds. pp. 177–194. Washington, DC: Dumbarton Oaks.

Topic, Theresa L., and John R. Topic, 1982 Prehistoric Fortifications of Northern Peru: Preliminary Report on the Final Season, January–December, 1980. Trent University Department of Anthropology, Peterborough, Ontario.

Toren, Christina, 1999 Mind, Materiality and History: Explorations in Fijian Ethnography. London: Routledge.

Tosi, Joseph A., 1960 Zonas de Vida Natural en el Perú. Memoria Explicativa Sobre el Mapa Ecológico del Perú. Instituto Interamericano de Ciencias Agrícolas, OEA. Zona Andina Proyecto 39. Programa de Cooperación Técnica. Boletín Técnico, 5. Lima.

Tourtellot, Gair, 1988 Developmental cycles of households and houses at Seibal. *In* Household and Community in the Mesoamerican Past. Richard R. Wilk and Wendy Ashmore, eds. pp. 97–120. Albuquerque: University of New Mexico Press.

Towle, Margaret A., 1961 The Ethnobotany of Precolumbian Peru. Viking Fund Publications in Anthropology, 30. New York: Wenner–Gren Foundation for Anthropological Research.

Townsend, Richard, 1985 Deciphering the Nazca world: Ceramic images from ancient Peru. Art Institute of Chicago Museum Studies 11(2):117–139.

Trawick, Paul, 2001 The moral economy of water: equity and antiquity in the Andean commons. American Anthropologist 103(2):361–379.

Tringham, Ruth, 1991 Household with faces: The challenge of gender in prehistoric architectural remains. *In* Engendering Archaeology: Women in Prehistory. Joan M. Gero and Margaret W. Conkey, eds. pp. 93–131. Oxford: Blackwell.

Tschauner, Hartmut, 2001 Socioeconomic and Political Organization in the Late Prehispanic Lambayeque Sphere, Northern North Coast of Peru. Ph.D. dissertation, Department of Anthropology, Harvard University, Cambridge.

Tschopik, Harry Jr., 1946 Some notes on rock shelter sites near Huancayo, Peru. American Antiquity 12(2):73–80.

Tsunoyama, Ykihiro, ed., 1979 Textiles of the Andes: Catalog of Amano Collection, Selected by Yoshitaro Amano. South San Francisco: HEIAN.

Tuan, Yi-Fu, 1977 Space and Place: The Perspective of Experience. Minneapolis: University of Minneapolis.

Tung, Tiffany A., 2003 The Health Impact of Wari Imperialism: A Bioarchaeological Assessment of Communities in the Core and Periphery. Ph.D. dissertation, Department of Anthropology, University of North Carolina, Chapel Hill.

Tung, Tiffany A., and Anita G. Cook, In press Intermediate elite agency in the Wari Empire: The bioarchaeological and mortuary evidence. *In* Intermediate Elite Agency in Precolumbian States and Empires. C. Elson and A. Covey, eds. Tucson: University of Arizona Press.

Turner, Robert J. W., Rosemary J. Knight, and John W. Rick, 1999 The geological landscape of the pre-Inca archaeological site at Chavín de Huántar, Perú. Current Research 1999-D; Geological Survey of Canada, pp. 47–56.

Turner, Victor, 1969 The Ritual Process: Structure and Anti-Structure. Chicago: Aldine.

Tykot, Robert H., and John Staller, 2002 The importance of early maize agriculture in coastal Ecuador: New data from La Emerenciana. Current Anthropology 43(4):666–677.

Ubbelohde-Doering, Hans, 1967 On the Royal Highways of the Inca. London: Thames & Hudson.

——1983 Vorspanische Graber von Pacatnamú, Nord Peru. Materialen zur Allegmeinen und Vergleichenden Archäologie, vol. 26. Berlin: C. H. Beck.

Uceda, Santiago, 1987 Los primeros pobladores del area andina central. Revisión crítica de los principales sitios (Parte I y II). Yunga 1(1):14–32. Trujillo.

—— 1995 Proyecto Huaca de la Luna: Evaluación y perspectivas. MASA: Revista Cultural del Indies, año 7, no. 9:35–40.

—— 1997 Esculturas en miniatura y una maqueta en madera. *In* Investigaciones en la Huaca de la Luna 1995. Santiago Uceda, Elias Mujica, and Ricardo Morales, eds. pp. 151–176. Trujillo: Universidad Nacional de La Libertad.

—— 2001 Investigations at Huaca de la Luna, Moche Valley: An example of Moche religious architecture. *In* Moche Art and Archaeology in Ancient Peru. Joanne Pillsbury, ed. pp. 47–68. Washington, DC and New Haven: National Gallery of Art and Yale University Press.

Uceda, Santiago, and Elias Mujica, eds., 1994 Moche, Propuestas y Perspectivas. Trujillo: Universidad Nacional de la Libertad.

—— —— eds., 2002 Moche: Hacia el Final del Milenio. 2 vols. Trujillo: Universidad Nacional de la Libertad.

Uhle, Max, 1903[1991 reprint] Pachacamac. A Reprint of the 1903 Edition by Max Uhle. Izumi Shimada, ed. pp. 15–66. University Museum of Archaeology and Anthropology, University of Pennsylvania, Philadelphia.

—— 1913 Die Ruinen von Moche. Journal de la Société des Américanistes de Paris, new series 10:95–117.

—— 1915 Las Ruinas de Moche. Boletín de la Sociedad Geográfica de Lima 30(3–4):57–71.

—— 1924a Explorations at Chincha. University of California Publications in American Archaeology and Ethnology 21(1):1–95.

—— 1924b Appendix A, Notes on Ica Valley. *In* The Uhle Pottery Collection from Ica by Alfred L. Kroeber and William Duncan Strong, pp. 121–123. University of California Publications in American Archaeology and Ethnology 21(3):95–133.

Uhle, Max, and C. Grosse 1903. Pachacamac: Report of the William Pepper, M.D., LL, Peruvian Expedition of 1896. Department of Archaeology, University of Pennsylvania, Philadelphia.

Urteaga, Horacio, 1931 El Imperio Incaico. Lima: Libreria e Imprenta Gil, SA.

Urton, Gary, 1990 The History of a Myth: Pacariqtambo and the Origin of the Inkas. Austin: University of Texas Press.

—— 1995 A new twist in an old yarn: Variation in knot directionality in the Inka khipus. Baessler-Archiv, new series 42:271–305.

—— 1997 The Social Life of Numbers. A Quechua Ontology of Numbers and Philosophy of Arithmetic. Austin: University of Texas Press.

—— 1999 Inca Myths. Austin: University of Texas.

Valdez, Lidio M., 2000 Aproximaciones al estudio del cuy en el antiguo Perú. Boletín del Museo de Arqueología y Antropología. Lima.

Valdez, Lidio M., et al., 1999 Excavaciones arqueológicos en el centro Wari de Marayniyoq, Ayacucho. Boletín del Museo de Arqueología y Antropología 2(9):16–19.

Valdez, Lidio M., et al., 2000 Marayniyoq, un establecimiento Wari en el valle de Ayacucho, Perú. *In* Huari y Tiwanaku: Modelos vs. Evidencias. Peter Kaulicke and William H. Isbell, eds. pp. 549–564. Boletín de Arqueología PUCP, vol. 4. Lima: Departamento de Humanidades, Especialidad de Arqueología, Pontificia Universidad Católica del Perú.

Vasquez, Guinaldo M., 1930 En derredor de las memorias historiales. *In* Memorias Antiguas Historiales y Politicas del Perú. Horacio H. Urteaga, ed. Lima: Libreria e Imprenta Gil, SA.

Vavilov, Nicolai I., 1926 Studies on the origin of cultivated plants. Institute of Applied Botany: Plant Breeding, 16. Leningrad.

Vega-Centeno, Rafael, L. F. Villacorta, L. E. Cáceres, and G. Marcone, 1998 Arquitectura monumental temprana en el valle medio de Fortaleza. Boletín Arqueológico 2:219–238.

Verano, John W., 1995 Where do they rest? The treatment of human offerings and trophies in ancient Peru. *In* Tombs for the Living: Andean Mortuary Practices. Tom D. Dillehay, ed. pp. 189–228. Washington, DC: Dumbarton Oaks.

——2001a War and death in the Moche world: Osteological evidence and visual discourse. *In* Moche Art and Archaeology in Ancient Peru. Joanne Pillsbury, ed. pp. 111–125. Washington, DC and New Haven: National Gallery of Art and Yale University Press.

——2001b The physical evidence of human sacrifice in ancient Peru. *In* Ritual Sacrifice in Ancient Peru: New Discoveries and Interpretations. Elizabeth P. Benson and Anita G. Cook, eds. pp. 165–184. Austin: University of Texas Press.

——2002 Avances en la bioanthropología de los Moche. *In* Moche: Hacia el Final del Milenio. Santiago Uceda and Elias Mujica, eds. pp. 517–534. Trujillo: Universidad Nacional de la Libertad.

Vescelius, Gary S., 1960 Rasgos naturales y culturales de la costa extremo sur. *In* Antiguo Peru. Espacio y Tiempo. Lima: Editorial Juan Mejía Baca.

——1965 Restos Precerámicos de la Región de Marcará. MS, Department of Anthropology, Cornell University, Ithaca.

Villar Córdoba, Pedro, 1935 Arqueología Peruana: Las Culturas Pre-hispánicas del Departamento de Lima. Lima.

von Hagen, Adriana, and Craig Morris, 1998 The Cities of the Ancient Andes. London: Thames & Hudson.

von Hagen, Victor W., 1959 Editor's introduction. *In* The Incas of Pedro de Cieza de Leon. Victor W. von Hagen, ed. pp. xxv–lxxx. Norman: University of Oklahoma Press.

Vranich, Alexei, 1999 Interpreting the Meaning of Ritual Spaces: The Temple Complex of Pumapuncu, Tiwanaku, Bolivia. Ph.D. dissertation, Department of Anthropology, University of Pennsylvania.

——2002 Visualizing the monumental: seeing what is not there. *In* Experimental Archaeology: Replicating Past Objects, Behaviors, and Processes. J. R. Mathieu, ed. pp. 83–94. Oxford: British Archaeological Reports, International Series 1035.

——In press. La Pirámide de Akapana: Reconsiderando el centro monumental de Tiwanaku. *In* Boletín de Arqueología PUCP, vol. 5. Lima: Departamento de Humanidades, Especialidad de Arqueología, Pontificia Universidad Católica del Perú.

Wachtel, Nathan, 1982 The mitimas of the Cochabamba Valley: The colonization policy of Huayna Capac. *In* The Inca and Aztec States, 1400–1800: Anthropology and History. George A. Collier, Renato I. Rosaldo, and John D. Wirth, eds. pp. 199–235. New York: Academic Press.

Wallace, Dwight T., 1959 Informe del reconocimiento del valle de Chincha. Revista del Museo Regional de Ica, año 10, no. 11:31–40.

——1960 Early Paracas textile techniques. American Antiquity 26(2):279–281.

——1962 Cerrillos, an early Paracas site in Ica, Peru. American Antiquity 27:303–314.

——1970a Trabajo de campo en la costa sur del Perú. Arqueología y Sociedad 2:17–27.

——1970b Informe del reconocimiento del valle de Chincha. Arqueología y Sociedad 2:7–16.

——1971 Sitios arqueológicas del Perú, valles de Chincha y Pisco. Arqueológicas 13:1–31.

——1980 Tiwanaku as a symbolic empire. Estudios Arqueológicos 5:133–144. Antofagasta.

——1991 The Chincha roads: Economics and symbolism. *In* Ancient Road Networks and Settlement Hierarchies in the New World. Charles D. Trombold, ed. pp. 253–263. Cambridge: Cambridge University Press.

Walter, Doris, 1997 Comment meurent les pumas: Du mythe au rite à Huaraz (Centre-Nord du Pérou). Bulletin de l'Institut Français d'Études Andines 26(3):447–471.

Weber, Max, 1947 The Theory of Social and Economic Organization. A. M. Henderson and Talcott Parsons, ed. and trans. New York: Free Press.

——1958 The city. In The City. Don Martingale and Gertrud Neuwirth, eds. pp. 65–230. New York: Free Press.

Wegner, Steven A., 1994 Cultura Recuay. Museo Arqueológico de Ancash. Huaraz: Ediciones Cordillera.

Wells, Lisa E., 1987 A fluvial record of El Niño events in northern coastal Peru. Journal of Geophysical Research 92:14463–14470.

Wheeler, Jane C., 1980 Faunal remains. In Guitarrero Cave: Early Man in the Andes. Thomas F. Lynch, ed. pp. 149–171. New York: Academic Press.

——1999 Patrones prehistóricos de utilización de los camélidos sudamericanos. In El Período Arcaico en el Perú: Hacia una Definición de los Orígenes. Peter Kaulicke, ed. pp. 297–305. Boletín de Arqueología PUCP, vol. 3. Lima: Departamento de Humanidades, Especialidad de Arqueología, Pontificia Universidad Católica del Perú.

Wheeler, Jane C., C. R. Cardoza, and D. Pozzi-Escot, 1979 Estudio provisional de la fauna de las Capas II y III de Telarmachay. Revista del Museo Nacional 43:97–109.

Whitley, James, 2002 Too many ancestors. Antiquity 76:119–126.

Whitten, Dorothea S., and Norman E. Whitten, Jr., 1988 From Myth to Creation. Urbana: University of Illinois Press.

Wiessner, Polly, 1984 Reconsidering the behavioral basis for style: A case study among the Kalahari San. Journal of Anthropological Archaeology 3(3):190–234.

Wilk, Richard R., 1991 The household in anthropology: Panacea or problem. Annual Review of Anthropology 20:1–12.

Wilk, Richard R., and Robert McC. Netting, 1984 Households: changing forms and functions. In Household: Comparative and Historical Studies of the Domestic Group. Robert McC. Netting, Richard R. Wilk, and E. J. Arnold, eds. pp. 1–28. Berkeley: University of California Press.

Wilk, Richard R., and William L. Rathje, 1982 Household archaeology. American Behavioral Scientist 25:617–639.

Willey, Gordon R., 1943 Excavations in the Chancay Valley. In Archeological Studies in Peru, 1941–42. William Duncan Strong, Gordon R. Willey, and John M. Corbett, eds. pp. 123–200. New York: Columbia Studies in Archeology and Ethnology, 1. New York: Columbia University Press.

——1953 Prehistoric Settlement Patterns in the Virú Valley, Peru. Bulletin 155, Bureau of American Ethnology. Washington, DC: Smithsonian Institution.

——1971 An Introduction to American Archaeology, vol. 2. South America. Englewood Cliffs: Prentice-Hall.

——1991 Horizonal integration and regional diversity: An alternating process in the rise of civilization. American Antiquity 56(2):197–215.

Willey, Gordon R., and John M. Corbett, 1954 Early Ancón and Early Supe Culture: Chavín Horizon Sites of the Central Peruvian Coast. Columbia Studies in Archeology and Ethnology, 3. New York: Columbia University Press.

Willey, Gordon R., and Philip Phillips, 1958 Method and Theory in American Archaeology. Chicago: University of Chicago Press.

Williams, Patrick Ryan, 2001 Cerro Baúl: A Wari center on the Tiwanaku frontier. Latin American Antiquity 12(1):67–83.

——2002 Rethinking disaster-induced collapse in the demise of the Andean highland states: Wari and Tiwanaku. World Archaeology 33(3):361–374.

Williams, Patrick Ryan, and Donna J. Nash, 2002 Imperial interaction in the Andes: Huari and Tiwanaku at Cerro Baúl. *In* Andean Archaeology I: Variations in Sociopolitical Organization. William H. Isbell and Helaine Silverman, eds. pp. 243–265. New York and London: Kluwer Academic/Plenum Publishers.

Williams León, Carlos, 1972 La difusión de los pozos ceremoniales en la costa peruana. Apuntes Arqueológicos 2:1–9. Lima.

——1980 Complejos de pirámides con planta en U: Patrón arquitectónico de la costa central. Revista del Museo Nacional 44:95–110.

——1985 A scheme for the early monumental architecture of the central coast of Peru. *In* Early Ceremonial Architecture in the Andes. Christopher B. Donnan, ed. pp. 227–240. Washington, DC: Dumbarton Oaks.

Williams León, Carlos, and Manuel Merino, 1979 Inventario, Catastro y Delimitación del Patrimonio Arqueológico del Valle de Supe. Report submitted to the Instituto Nacional de Cultura, Lima.

Williams León, Carlos, and José Pineda, 1985 Desde Ayacucho hasta Cajamarca: Formas arquitectónicas con filiación Wari, unidad del espacio andino. Boletín de Lima, 40:55–61.

Wilson, David J., 1981 Of maize and men: A critique of the maritime hypothesis of state origins on the coast of Peru. American Anthropologist 83:93–120.

——1988 Prehispanic Settlement Patterns in the Lower Santa Valley, Peru: A Regional Perspective on the Origins and Development of Complex North Coast Society. Washington, DC: Smithsonian Institution Press.

——1995 Prehispanic settlement patterns in the Casma Valley, north coast of Peru: Preliminary results to date. Journal of the Steward Anthropological Society 23(1 and 2):189–227.

Wing, Elizabeth, 1978 Animal domestication in the Andes. *In* Advances in Andean Archaeology. David L. Browman, ed. pp. 167–188. Chicago: Mouton.

Wissler, Clark, 1938 The American Indian. New York: Oxford University Press.

Wobst, H. Martin, 1977 Stylistic behavior and information exchange. *In* For the Director: Research Essays in Honor of James B. Griffin. E. Charles Cleland, ed. pp. 317–344. Ann Arbor: Museum of Anthropology, University of Michigan.

Wright, Melanie F., Christine A. Hastorf, and Heidi Lennstrom, 2003 Pre-Hispanic agriculture and plant use at Tiwanaku: Social and political implications. *In* Tiwanaku and its Hinterland: Archaeological and Paleoecological Investigations of an Andean Civilization, vol. 2. Alan L. Kolata, ed. Washington, DC: Smithsonian Institution Press.

Wright, Rita, ed., 1996 Gender and Archaeology. Philadelphia: University of Pennsylvania Press.

Yacovleff, Eugenio, and Jorge C. Muelle, 1932 Una exploración en Cerro Colorado: Informe y observaciones. Revista del Museo Nacional 1(2):31–59.

——1934 Un fardo funerario de Paracas. Revista del Museo Nacional 3(1/2):63–153.

Zárate, Agustin de, 1968[1556] The Discovery and Conquest of Peru. J. M. Cohen, ed. Baltimore: Penguin Books.

Zorn, Elayne, 1990 Modern traditions: The impact of the trade in traditional textiles on the Sakaka of northern Potosi, Bolivia. *In* Proceedings of the Textile Society of America Biennial Symposium, pp. 241–252. Washington, DC: Textile Society of America.

Zuidema, R. Tom, 1964 The Ceque System of Cuzco. Leiden: E. J. Brill.

——1972 Meaning in Nasca art. Artstryck 1971:35–54.

Index